POWER SHIFT IN GERMANY

MODERN GERMAN STUDIES
A Series of the German Studies Association

General Editor: Gerald R. Kleinfeld, Arizona State University

This series offers books on modern and contemporary Germany, concentrating on themes in history, political science, literature, and German culture.

POWER SHIFT IN GERMANY

The 1998 Election and the End of the Kohl Era

Edited by

David P. Conradt
Gerald R. Kleinfeld
Christian Søe

Berghahn Books

NEW YORK • OXFORD

Published in 2000 by

Berghahn Books

www.berghahnbooks.com

© 2000 by German Studies Review and Gerald R. Kleinfeld

Library of Congress Cataloging-in-Publication Data

Power shift in Germany : the 1998 election and the end of the Kohl era /
editors, David P. Conradt, Gerald R. Kleinfeld, Christian Søe.
    p.   cm.
Includes bibliographical references and index.
ISBN 1-57181-199-0 — ISBN 1-57181-200-8
    1. Germany. Bundestag—Elections, 1998. 2. Political parties—Germany.
3. Germany—Politics and government—1990– I. Conradt, David P.
II. Kleinfeld, Gerald R., 1936– III. Søe, Christian.
JN3971.A95 P65 2000
324.943'0879—dc21   99-087840

British Library Cataloguing in Publication Data

A catalogue record for this book is available from the British Library.

Printed in the United States on acid-free paper.

CONTENTS

LIST OF FIGURES AND TABLES

Figures

Tables

ACKNOWLEDGMENTS

Many people helped make this election study possible. The individual chapter authors have enriched the study by bringing their special expertise to the project. As deputy director of the Federal Press and Information Office, Wolfgang Gibowski invited several of the authors to be included in a study tour of the 1998 election. We are also grateful to Inter-Nationes, who arranged the election tour, to the many German colleagues who shared their political insights with us, and to the German Information Office in New York for its interest in, and support of, our undertaking. Dieter Roth and the Forschungsgruppe Wahlen in Mannheim have, as always, been generous in making available to many of the authors both data and analysis useful for their individual chapters. Wolfgang-Uwe Friedrich has provided several of us with an opportunity to stay abreast of German political developments through the annual summer meetings of the Deutsch-Amerikanischer Arbeitsgruppe. As publisher, Marion Berghahn has been strongly supportive of this study from beginning to end.

INTRODUCTION

D uring the past half-century, few electorates in Western democracies have been more stable or predictable than that of the Federal Republic. Allied occupiers' fears that West Germans in 1949—only four years after the collapse of the Third Reich—would undermine their new democracy by using the ballot to support radical, extremist parties were quickly dispelled as the great majority of voters backed parties and candidates firmly committed to the principles and policies of liberal democracy.

Indeed, Germans wanted their parties and candidates to be somewhere in the broad center. By the early 1950s it was already clear that a successful party needed only to promise a continuation of the moderate social-market economic policies begun in 1948 under Allied tutelage, coupled with support for the Federal Republic's integration into the Western Alliance as embodied by the European Community and later NATO membership.

This was a formula that brought the Christian Democratic Union (CDU) and its allies a string of victories unprecedented in Germany's democratic history. Led by Konrad Adenauer and later Ludwig Erhard, the CDU managed to remain in power for twenty years.

After a decade in the programmatic wilderness, the Social Democrats in 1959 finally conceded that the only royal road to political power was offering voters peace, prosperity, security, and above all, "no experiments." Most of its Marxist baggage was dropped after 1959 as the party assured voters that it would not do anything differently from the CDU, but would do many things better. Younger leadership provided an attractive package for this well-known message, and by 1966 the Social Democrats (SPD) were sharing power with the CDU. Three years later the SPD became the major governing party, and in 1972 it overtook the CDU as the largest party. By 1976 the Social Democrats had elevated their variant of the basic formula into a model to be envied and emulated at home and abroad.

The three elections of the 1980s saw major changes in this stable, if not tranquil, electoral landscape. The two major parties began to lose support. Turnout declined, while ticket splitting increased. The influence of class and religion—the two most important demographic factors structuring the party vote—declined; "new politics" issues such as the environment, disarmament, and civil liberties became salient to increasing numbers of voters; and in 1983 a new party, the Greens, broke the twenty-year monopoly of the three established parties—Christian Democrats (CDU/CSU), Social Democrats (SPD), and Free Democrats (FDP)—on parliamentary representation. At the January 1987 election, for the first time in postwar electoral history, both of the major parties—CDU and SPD—lost support at the same election. Partisan politics and electoral behavior became more complex and less predictable. Long-term electoral trends, such as the steady gains of the Social Democrats from 1957 to 1972, were replaced by short-term oscillations from election to election.

Elections in Unified Germany

The 1990s have brought even more volatility and complexity to national elections. To the trends identified with the 1980s came the unification of a country divided for over forty years and the addition of sixteen million new citizens with little experience in democratic electoral politics. The first unification election, in 1990, was contested under special conditions, including a one-time-only change in the electoral law. The elections were the culmination of a unification process begun with the opening of the Berlin Wall and the subsequent collapse of the East German regime. The workers in this former "workers' and peasants' state" did not vote for the Social Democrats as many observers expected, but instead eagerly embraced Helmut Kohl's Christian Democrats, with their promise of quick and painless Western-style prosperity. The ability of the former communists, renamed the Party of Democratic Socialism (PDS), to gain parliamentary representation was due to the special provision of the electoral law, which set a 5 percent minimum in *either* the "old" or the "new" regions of the Federal Republic. The Social Democrats' lukewarm support of unification, as enunciated by their chancellor candidate, Oskar Lafontaine, hurt the party in both East and West and doomed the SPD to a third consecutive defeat.

To the surprise of many analysts, the former communists did not go away at the next national election in 1994. Thanks to yet another little-known and seldom relevant provision of the electoral law, the PDS returned to parliament in increased numbers. More importantly, blue-collar workers in the East continued to show little regard for the classic laws of voting behavior. They largely remained with Kohl and the CDU; the SPD continued to do badly in the eastern states. After 1994 some observers were contending that Germany had two separate and distinct electorates in East and West.[1]

The German electoral landscape in 1998 thus bore little resemblance to the stable and predictable patterns of the "old" Federal Republic. The classic cleavages of class and religion continued their slow decline, but generational and regional influences became more significant. Issues, candidates, and the media became critical short-run factors. And there were now at least five parties with solid prospects for parliamentary representation.

The 1998 election could well turn out to be a milestone in the political development of Germany's Federal Republic. It produced the first complete ouster of an incumbent government in Bonn since the formation of the new German state in 1949. As a result of this power shift, the restoration of Berlin as the seat of national government took place under a wholly new political leadership. It was based on a left coalition of Social Democrats (SPD) and Greens, who also constituted the first postwar generation of Germans in power. From the beginning, it was clear that the new government had inherited some challenging problems whose resolution was not helped by the coalition's internal divisions.

This book gives a descriptive account and analytical assessment of the 1998 election and its immediate outcome. It follows the basic format of our previous volume, *Germany's New Politics*, which was devoted to an analysis of the election of 1994. The two books have many of the same contributors, but there are several new ones who have come to this publication as well. Since the books also examine the political development that led up to the Bundestag contest covered in each volume, they provide a record of German politics since reunification from an electoral perspective.

Following a brief overview of the campaign and election, the roles of the five parties that returned to the Bundestag are explored in separate chapters. A detailed analysis of the results is provided in four chapters focusing on voting behavior, the role of the media, the gender factor, and the election's meaning for the ongoing unification process. The book concludes with chapters that explore the domestic and foreign policy implications of the 1998 vote and its relationship to recent elections and voting patterns in other Western democracies.

The Parties

After four straight losing campaigns with five unsuccessful chancellor candidates, the SPD and Gerhard Schröder in 1998 finally reached the promised land. But as Gerard Braunthal's chapter on the SPD skillfully demonstrates, there was little time for celebration. The successful campaign was in large part the result of the extraordinary cooperation between the two key leaders in the party, Oskar Lafontaine and Schröder. But while it took two to win, events shortly after the election showed that only one could govern.

The 1998 campaign represented only a temporary truce in the ongoing struggle between traditionalists and modernizers. German voters, of course, do not like their parties to be internally divided (*zerstritten*), and in state elections since 1998, Schröder and the SPD have suffered heavy losses. As Braunthal points out, the SPD now hopes that Schröder's budget and tax cuts will "stimulate investment and produce a noticeable increase in employment by the time of the next round of state elections. Without any substantial improvement in this area, Germany's first red-green government will have a difficult time at the next federal election in 2002."

Clay Clemens' incisive analysis of the CDU focuses on four major factors in the 1998 debacle: the general climate of opinion that strongly supported change; the low level of competence attributed to the Union by the electorate, especially when dealing with the issue of unemployment; the choice of Kohl as chancellor candidate; and the CDU's confused and lackluster campaign. The party's defeat now gives it the chance in opposition for leadership and policy renewal. The defeat also enables the Union's Bavarian affiliate, the Christian Social Union (CSU), and especially its leader, Edmund Stoiber, to explore the possibility of leading the national Union at the next election. The scandal involving the former chancellor and the party's finances, which emerged in late 1999, is also briefly discussed in Clemens' contribution.

The Christian Democrats and Helmut Kohl were not the only losers at the 1998 election. After a remarkable twenty-nine consecutive years of national political responsibility as a junior coalition partner of the SPD (1969–82) and then the CDU, the FDP in 1998 finally went into opposition. Their defeat, as Christian Søe convincingly demonstrates, was foreshadowed by an unprecedented series of losses at state and local elections between 1994 and 1998. Anticipating opposition, the party's leadership attempted, while still in the government, to reposition the FDP as the voice of neoliberal reform in unified Germany. Thus for the "new" FDP the 1998 election was only the first stage in a long march back to national office. This neoliberal shift, Søe argues, is also a response to the serious modernization challenges now facing the fabled *Modell Deutschland*. More than any of its rivals, the FDP sent "the uncomfortable message that individuals should exercise more responsibility and the state less influence in society." Alas, it was a message that the great majority of voters, and even many potential FDP supporters, did not want to hear.

Gene Frankland's careful analysis of the Greens and the 1998 election highlights their transformation from an anti-parliamentary social movement to a national governing party. This process of normalization took well over two decades and was the outcome of countless "everyday experiences of thousands of local councilors and hundreds of state and federal parliamentarians and staff assistants." The status of governing party has now brought new challenges to the party. They are losing support among their traditional key electorate—young voters. Green reform initiatives in the environmental area are "failing to connect with young people's core concerns: education, training, technology and jobs."

In spite of unification and the prediction of some observers, the former East German Communists have not slipped quietly away. Led by the colorful Gregor Gysi, the Party of Democratic Socialism has now "won" three straight federal elections in the unified nation. But as Gerald Kleinfeld's contribution shows, the former Communists are still the lost children of united Germany. Kleinfeld's contribution is especially important for his treatment of the so-called "liberated cadre," an indigenous eastern elite that will play an important future role regardless of the long-term future of the Party of Democratic Socialism.

The Results

Wolfgang Gibowski presents a detailed analysis of the classic questions of who won in 1998, and especially, why. With a rich database of monthly polls covering the 1994–98 period, he is able to delineate the influence of social structure, issues, candidates, and the campaign itself in the 1998 decision. Of particular importance is his account of Kohl's inability to convince voters that his proposed tax and social spending reform program was directly linked to increased investment and a reduction in unemployment: "the objective of making Germany a more competitive place for business investment seemed to the population like systematic measures aimed at giving to the rich and taking away from the poor." Kohl and the CDU clearly underestimated their capacity to wean the electorate from the welfare state. Gibowski also documents the increase in the "floating" segment of the electorate and the prospects for more voter volatility.

As in other modern democracies, the media played a critical role during the 1998 campaign in shaping popular perceptions of the candidates and parties. The contribution by Semetko and Schoenbach, which is part of their ongoing study of the German and American media, centers on the coverage of the candidates and campaign in the television news and in the daily newspaper with by far the largest circulation, the *Bild Zeitung*. During the 1990 campaign, the first unified election, they found a clear "visibility bonus" for the incumbent Kohl government. Their 1998 findings were quite different. The prospect of a power shift and the end of the Kohl era prompted more coverage than in 1990 and 1994, even though the election had to compete in the final weeks with the Clinton-Lewinsky story. More importantly, there was less of a visibility bonus for Kohl in 1998. The sound bites for Schröder were actually longer (30 seconds) than those for the chancellor (19 seconds). Their careful content analysis also found that the relatively new private television channels gave more coverage to the campaigns and opinion polls than the public channels, which in contrast focused more on the substantive issues over which the campaign was being fought. Overall, both private and public channels were more neutral and less evaluative than their American counterparts. In 1998 the number of female candidates elected to the Bundestag increased to about 31 percent, the highest level in German history. Since 1983 the proportion of females has tripled. Mary Hampton's important study contends that women have now reached a "critical mass" in the political system. But while they have been marching through the political institutions, women have continued to "march in place" on vital policy issues such as childcare, pensions and unemployment. In comparison to the Greens and the SPD, the CDU in 1998 remained "behind the reform curve" in terms of both female representation and support of women's issues. The Union paid a heavy price: the party lost most heavily among women of working and retirement age. The CDU was "not only perceived as representing the most traditional approaches to women and women's issues, but they were also seen as hindering progress in issue areas that needed reform." The new Schröder government now has promises to keep: pension entitlement for child-rearing; improved female access to higher education, especially technical schools; expanded child care programs; and stiffer laws to protect women against violence. But as Hampton points out, many of these measures will require additional spending that will be difficult to effect in the current budgetary environment.

The effects of forty years of national division were clearly in evidence at this third election in unified Germany. The contribution by Helga Welsh assesses electoral patterns emerging in the East and the significance of the 1998 vote for the larger unification process. She argues that fissures between East and West will be "normal" for the foreseeable future. Indeed, "normality in inner-German relations demands the recognition of western dominance and eastern assertion." Her incisive study shows, however, that an open discussion of these fissures is hindered, by media and academic analyses that highlight the problems more than the achievements of unification. The East-West cleavage will continue to be a critical component of elections in the Federal Republic.

The Aftermath: Policy Issues and a Comparative Perspective

Herbert Kitschelt relates the results of the election to the pressing economic problems that any new government would face. His core argument, developed before Lafontaine's departure from the government, is as prescient as it is provocative: "competitive alignments in German party politics are quite inhospitable to social and economic reforms that would address the structural problems of the German economy, unless Social Democratic leaders headed by the new chancellor Gerhard Schröder and his Green coalition partners can liberate themselves from the grip of some of their own core constituencies that supported their bid to displace the liberal-conservative Kohl government." This is, of course, the core problem that the new government is now confronting. The sharp decline in SPD (and Green) support in the months following the national election is a direct result of Schröder's efforts to change the deeply rooted structural problems of the social market economy.

Wolfgang-Uwe Friedrich addresses the new government's definition of Germany's international role. He outlines the remarkable transformation of both parties and especially their respective leaders, Chancellor Schröder and Foreign Minister Fischer, from their traditional opposition to NATO and the deployment of German military forces "out of area" to their advocacy in government of NATO intervention in the Balkans, including the 1999 bombing campaign against Serbia. In explaining this change he assigns a critical role to leadership. Observers who focused on Schröder's past positions, which also included an effort to exploit popular resentments about European integration and the euro, overlooked his realism and above all pragmatism. His excellent account of the "mainstreaming" of the Greens was also largely the work of their leader, Joschka Fischer, who, "once the hero of the Greens on the barricades," made his transition from radicalism to pragmatism. The result is a remarkable continuity in German foreign policy.

In the final chapter David Patton examines the election outcome from a comparative European perspective and finds substantial convergence between the German results and those in other Western democracies: a shift to a center-left government; the failure of anti-communism as a campaign issue; the establishment of an alternative, the PDS, to the left of the Social Democrats; an increase in regional differences; and, finally, major generational change. He also cites one area of divergence: the far right in Germany, in contrast to other European democracies such as France, Italy, and Austria, remains weak and divided. Overall, however, there was no "special German path" in 1998.

Note

1. Russell J. Dalton and Wilhelm Bürklin, "The Two German Electorates," in Russell J. Dalton, ed., *Germans Divided* (Oxford: Berg Publishers, 1996), 183–208.

Chapter 1

THE 1998 CAMPAIGN AND ELECTION
An Overview

David P. Conradt

On 27 September 1998 Germans elected a new national parliament for the fourteenth time since the 1949 founding of the Federal Republic. For the first time in the Republic's history, their ballots removed an entire incumbent coalition and chancellor. This was not the first power shift, or *Machtwechsel*. After the 1969 election the Christian Democrats found themselves in opposition after twenty years in office, but they were replaced by the Social Democrats, who had been governing with the Christian Democrats in a grand coalition since 1966. In 1982 the Social Democrats suffered the same fate. Their coalition partner at the time, the Free Democrats, did not.

In 1998, unlike 1969 and 1982–83, the electorate made a clean sweep, removing Chancellor Kohl, his Christian Democrats, and their Free Democrat allies, and replacing them with Gerhard Schröder, the Social Democrats—a party out of power since 1982—and the Greens, a party never before in power at the national level.[1] In this book we will describe and analyze this election, which many observers consider a landmark in the history of the Federal Republic and German democracy.

This chapter will first briefly examine the institutional framework of elections in Germany, giving particular attention to the complex electoral law, which strongly influences the calculations and strategic considerations of the parties and candidates. Second, the major political developments since the 1994 election will be reviewed. The role of state elections in national politics, including their influence on party strategy and candidate selection, is essential to understanding the context of the national electoral struggle. Third, the strategy and tactics of the parties and the major campaign themes will be discussed. We conclude with a brief analysis of the results and the aftermath of this election.

Electoral Mechanics: That Strange Electoral Law

Germany's complicated electoral system is always a factor influencing the strategy and tactics of the parties. It is usually termed a "mixed" system, since the voter elects a district candidate by a plurality with his or her first ballot, and votes for a party with the second ballot. Half of the parliamentary seats are determined by the district vote (first ballot), and the remaining half by the party vote (second ballot). However, the second ballot percentage usually determines a party's final parliamentary representation since the first ballot district victories are subtracted from the total due a party based on the second ballot percentage.

In essence, then, this is a proportional system with three important exceptions to "pure" proportionality: (1) to participate in the proportional payout, a party usually must secure at least 5 percent of the second ballot vote; (2) this 5 percent requirement, however, is waived if the party secures at least three district seats (i.e., direct election of three candidates by a plurality in at least three of the 328 districts); if it succeeds, it can then also participate in the proportional distribution regardless of its second ballot percentage; (3) if a party wins more district seats than it is entitled to under its second ballot percentage, it is allowed to keep these excess seats (*Überhangmandate*) and the parliament is simply enlarged by the number of these excess seats.[2]

The 5 percent requirement has been by far the most important of these three exceptions from pure proportionality. It is almost always a factor for all parties except the two large parties, the Christian Democratic Union (CDU—in Bavaria, the Christian Social Union [CSU]), and the Social Democratic party (SPD). However, since unification in 1990 the three-district and excess mandate provisions have become more important. At the 1994 election the Party of Democratic Socialism (PDS), the former ruling communist party of the former German Democratic Republic, failed to clear the 5 percent mark, but did win a plurality in four districts. Hence, the PDS participated in the proportional distribution and received an additional twenty-six seats. At the same election, Chancellor Kohl's Christian Democrats were the beneficiaries of twelve excess seats in 1994, which expanded the government's majority from only two seats to ten (the SPD also received four excess seats).

In 1998 these quirks in the electoral law were less important than in 1994. The small size of many eastern districts and the presence of three-cornered races between SPD, PDS and CDU, also mainly in the East, did generate most of the twelve excess mandates that expanded the SPD-Green majority from eight to twenty seats. But the three-district victory provision did not go into effect, since the PDS surmounted the 5 percent barrier. None of the splinter parties, especially the far right parties, came close to the 5 percent mark, or to winning any district seats (see Appendix).

The two-ballot system, however, is a constant at elections and encourages ticket splitting, or the "loaning" of votes, usually from supporters of the CDU/CSU and SPD, to their smaller partners or possible partners. As the smaller parties, with the exception of the PDS, have little chance of winning a district plurality, their voters frequently support one of the candidates of the larger parties with their first ballot. The smaller parties then hope that some CDU/CSU and SPD voters will return the favor and support them with their second ballot, thus enabling them to pass the 5 percent mark. At recent elections, about one voter in six has split his or her ballot. Without splitting, neither the Free Democrats (FDP), with only 3 percent of the first ballot vote but 6.2 percent on the second ballot, nor the Greens—4.97 percent on the first ballot, 6.7 percent on the second—would have made it into the parliament.

Thus both FDP and Green party organizations make appeals, usually in the latter stages of the campaign, for second ballot support from voters of their potential coalition partners. The two large parties officially reject any "loaning" of votes, but a significant proportion of their clientele are sufficiently informed and realize the importance of strategic voting.[3] The 1998 election was no exception.

The Inter-election Period, 1994–98

In 1994 Kohl's coalition of CDU/CSU and FDP won reelection by a narrow margin. On election night 1994, the government had an advantage of only two seats; however, only the excess mandate provision of the electoral law increased this majority to ten when all the votes were counted early the next morning.[4] There was widespread speculation that a government with such a small majority would not remain in office for the full four years. The Social Democrats, while still in opposition in the Bundestag, controlled the second parliamentary body, the Bundesrat, and would be able to veto many of the Kohl government's plans to reduce spending on social programs and cut taxes. Also, the position of the Free Democrats, Kohl's junior partner, steadily worsened both before and after the 1994 election.

But in the aftermath of the 1994 election, the Kohl government in fact had little to fear from the Social Democrats. After 1994 the SPD became self-absorbed with its own leadership and policy struggles. Rudolf Scharping, the 1994 chancellor candidate and national chairman, spent a good part of 1995 publicly sparring with his fellow Social Democrats, especially Gerhard Schröder. Schröder was critical of the party bureaucracy and its parliamentary delegation for being unable to give up their attachment to big government and move toward a more modern economic policy of support and cooperation with business. Oskar Lafontaine, the SPD's 1990 chancellor candidate, who wanted another chance at Kohl, was also increasingly critical of the Scharping regime.

For months the internal wrangling paralyzed the party. It was unable to take advantage of a weak and aging Kohl government. While the national opposition party usually gains at state elections held between the national elections, the Social Democrats managed to decline at six of the eight state elections held between the 1994 national election and the end of 1995. In national opinion polls in mid-1995, the SPD had dropped to about 30 percent, an all-time low for the party. The October 1995 election in Berlin was the last straw. The SPD suffered the worst defeat in its post-war history in Berlin, a long-time stronghold.

Table 1.1 State Elections: Party Gains (or Losses), 1994–98

State	Date	CDU	SPD	FPD	Green	PDS	Other
Hesse	2–19–95	(1.0)	(2.8)	0.0	2.4	—	1.5
North Rhine-Westphalia	5–14–95	1.0	(4.0)	(1.8)	5.0	—	(0.2)
Bremen	5–14–95	1.9	(5.4)	(6.1)	1.7	—	5.5
Berlin	10–22–95	(3.0)	(6.8)	(4.6)	3.9	5.4	5.1
Baden-Württemberg	3–24–96	1.7 (	4.3)	3.7	2.6	—	(3.8)
Rhineland-Pfalz	3–24–96	0.0	(5.0)	2.0	0.4	—	2.6
Schleswig-Holstein	3–24–96	3.4	(6.4)	0.1	3.1	—	(0.3)
Hamburg	9–21–97	5.6	(4.2)	(0.7)	0.4	—	(1.7)
Lower Saxony	3–1–98	(0.5)	3.6	0.5	(0.4)	—	(3.1)
Saxony-Anhalt	4–26–98	(12.4)	1.9	0.6	(1.9)	(0.3)	11.9
Bavaria	9–13–98	0.1	(1.3)	(1.1)	(0.4)	—	2.9

Source: Official Statistics

Something had to be done, and Rudolf Scharping was the most visible target. At the November 1995 SPD convention, the so-called *Putsch Parteitag*, several SPD leaders, led by Oskar Lafontaine, pushed through a change in the party's rules, dumped Scharping, although he had been elected by a vote of the party's members in 1993, and replaced him with Lafontaine. For adherents of intra-party democracy, it was a step backward. The SPD had regressed in its commitment to a broad-based democratic leadership selection process. But the question of who would be the party's chancellor candidate in 1998 was left open.

Following this 1995 convention, the party's standing in public opinion polls improved. Support for the Kohl government continued to decline as unemployment increased and economic growth remained sluggish. The SPD went on the offensive and focused its criticism on Kohl. Lafontaine had unified the party, but the SPD still needed a candidate to challenge Kohl in 1998. Lafontaine yearned for another chance at Kohl, and Schröder was convinced that he was the only Social Democrat who could defeat Kohl. Lafontaine enjoyed the support of the party's rank-and-file activists, but Schröder's poll numbers were much better. The candidate question was postponed. In the meantime the Social Democrats focused their attention on unifying the party, modernizing their campaign organization, and mounting a strong opposition in parliament.

The candidate issue was not resolved until March 1998, six months before the national election, when Schröder was reelected decisively at the state election in Lower Saxony. Prior to the Lower Saxony election, the SPD vote had declined in eight consecutive state elections. The case for Schröder was compelling, even to his strongest opponents in the SPD. If the party was to defeat Kohl, it must be led by Schröder.

There was also a remarkable consensus within the SPD on the necessity of avoiding the type of intra-party conflict over its program that had hindered it in the past. In 1998 the party was focused above all on winning the election. Ideological and programmatic differences were set aside, or postponed until after the election.

Schröder's landslide victory in the March 1998 state parliamentary election in Lower Saxony gave the SPD's national campaign an enormous lift. The perception that the SPD would win the September federal election jumped from 48 percent before the state election to 67 percent in polls conducted just after Schröder's triumph in his home state. The Social Democrats then held this advantage throughout the campaign.[5]

Schröder's "New Middle" program ended the SPD's preoccupation with regaining the party's version of the prodigal son, the Greens. Ever since the 1980s, the SPD establishment, and especially the party's activists, have in fact been more concerned about the 5 to 8 percent of the electorate that voted Green than with the 50 to 60 percent in the center of the electorate that did not vote for the Social Democrats. After fifteen years in the wilderness, the party returned to its Godesberg strategy of embracing the center (*Umarmung der Mitte*): white-collar workers, civil servants, small businessmen, and skilled manual workers were the target groups. The SPD had discovered issues of security and law and order. Growth and jobs replaced environmental protection. But this new pragmatism would also become a provocation for the SPD's traditional left.

With Schröder's candidacy and an electoral program tailored to his specifications, the SPD also bade at least a temporary farewell to the hopes that the new politics of postmaterialism alone could return it to power. Gone is the 1980s vision of a postmaterialist majority, or *"links von der Union"* (to the left of the Union), to use Willy Brandt's 1983 phrase. The environment, women's issues, and peace concerns could not, in the view of the Schröder campaign team, displace the core problem of a stagnant economy and society. Anti-market sentiments, environmental *Belehrungen* (preaching), or universal visions of a peaceful, integrated society were out in Schröder's new middle. In their place was the theme of getting Germany moving again.[6]

Searching for a Partner

Following Schröder's selection as chancellor candidate, the SPD's strategy moved directly toward a coalition with the Greens. At the state level, the SPD had accumulated a substantial amount of experience in coalitions with the Greens since the mid-1980s. While these alliances were not without problems, they generally were stable and lasted for the entire parliamentary period.

The pragmatic or realist faction of the Greens, led by Joschka Fischer, also made little secret of its desire to finally achieve national political responsibility, albeit as a junior partner of the Social Democrats.

These plans were dealt a severe blow when, at the March 1998 Green Convention in Magdeburg, held just two weeks after Schröder's triumph in Lower Saxony, the more radical or fundamentalist wing of the Greens passed a series of resolutions—chief among them the proposal to raise gasoline taxes to DM 5.00 per liter—that were clearly unpopular with the great majority of the electorate, including, of course, the center, which the Social Democrats and Schröder were determined to capture. Schröder quickly distanced himself from the Greens and their proposals.

Schröder and Lafontaine campaigned as a team. At the standard SPD rally, Lafontaine spoke first and delivered a sharp attack on Kohl, blaming him for high unemployment and unjust cuts in social programs. Three measures of the Kohl government that drew the strongest response from the party faithful were the 1996 pension cuts, the reintroduction of a waiting period before blue-collar workers could receive sick pay, and weakened protection against dismissal and layoffs (*Kündigungsschutz*). Lafontaine was serving up traditional SPD fare. Schröder's standard speech emphasized the bright future of his new middle.

A Bump in the Road: The April 1998 State Election in Saxony-Anhalt

As in 1994, the results of the election in the eastern state of Saxony-Anhalt gave the SPD's national leadership cause for concern. Since 1994 the state had been governed by a minority SPD-Alliance'90/Green government that was tolerated by the former Communists, the PDS. In 1994 the CDU/CSU strongly attacked this arrangement as an example of the fundamental affinity between some Social Democrats and Communists.

The Saxony-Anhalt SPD had high hopes for an absolute majority at the April election and were disappointed when the results left them twelve seats short. The Greens had failed to surmount the 5 percent mark and were no longer available as a partner. The clear message from Schröder and the national SPD was that the Saxony-Anhalt SPD should seek a grand coalition with the CDU and avoid any further cooperation with the PDS. The regional party balked at Bonn's suggestion. First, they insisted that the CDU, which declined by a whopping 12.4 percent at the election, was the prime loser and should be grateful that it was being considered as a partner. Second, SPD Minister-President Reinhard Höppner and his local SPD demanded that the SPD, CDU, and PDS issue a joint statement condemning the presence in the parliament of the radical right Deutsche Volks Union (DVU), which had won over 12 percent of the vote. This demand was totally unacceptable to the CDU, which refused to elevate the former Communists to the status of a normal democratic party. Indeed, to the CDU the PDS was just as radical and threatening to the democratic order as the right-wing DVU. Clearly, in spite of the signal from Schröder, the Saxony-Anhalt SPD did not want to govern with the CDU, but saw no problem with a continuation of their arrangement with the PDS, in which the former Communists would once again tolerate the now single-party SPD government.

This incident reflects not only the influence of federalism on the national party system, but also the difference in political style between the western region and the new states in the East. Höppner was pressured by local party officials via petitions, telephone calls, and resolutions to maintain East German "consciousness and identity" against the pressure from the national leadership. Complete strangers, according to Höppner, appeared at his door with flowers and tears in their eyes, imploring him not to form a coalition with the CDU.[7]

The Grand Coalition Gambit

As the campaign progressed, the SPD discovered that, in the absence of any clear programmatic statements from Schröder, its most effective campaign weapon was the "Kohl must go" theme. Its other campaign issues, such as a new version of Kohl's Alliance for Jobs, increased child allowance support, and the restoration of the 1997 pension cuts, paled in comparison to the Kohl issue. Since Schröder had in fact no concrete plans beyond the "Alliance" for dealing with unemployment—the number one problem for over 80 percent of voters—the SPD focused on Kohl.

With about six weeks left in the campaign and the SPD's lead over the CDU quickly narrowing, Schröder, given the growing unreliability and sinking support of the Greens, the success of the Kohl issue, and the electorate's apparent disinterest in any major policy changes, took the next step and began to discreetly advocate a grand coalition. This was a first in German electoral politics. None of the major parties had ever before publicly advocated a grand coalition. In 1965 some leaders such as the Federal President Lübke or SPD parliamentary leader Herbert Wehner privately supported such an alignment, but it was never a campaign theme.

The advocacy of a grand coalition by the SPD was the result of three factors: the unreliability of the Greens, the success of the "Kohl must go" theme, and Schröder's unwillingness to give his campaign any specific programmatic content. The grand coalition theme would also resonate among many in the CDU—and even the CSU—who also wanted Kohl to step down, yet desired to stay in power, albeit in partnership with the SPD.

Since Kohl had repeatedly and emphatically stated that he would never serve as chancellor of a grand coalition, the SPD's advocacy of such an alignment was also designed to divide the Union. Both Kohl and his CSU finance minister, Theo Waigel, rejected the grand coalition, but others in the Union, such as Volker Rühe and Lothar Späth (Kohl's intra-party opponent in 1989, who was a late addition to his campaign team) saw absolutely no problem with a grand coalition.[8]

The grand coalition appeal would also diffuse the Union's "red-green chaos" argument. In his standard campaign speech Kohl linked the two parties and added the PDS for good measure. The election was a choice between "security and risk," "renewal and decline." In the important fundamental existential issues of the country, the SPD and Greens consistently made the wrong decision. They were against the 1980s NATO two-track decision, which precipitated the collapse of the Soviet bloc, and they never really wanted German unity. Whoever has failed so often in the past, Kohl argued, cannot be entrusted with the future.

Surveys consistently found that while voters were tired of the Kohl government and wanted some new faces, they were not interested in any fundamental policy changes that would require higher taxes and/or cuts in social programs and subsidies. Thus, as a painless way to change, the SPD shifted in mid-campaign, going from a new coalition with the erratic and unreliable Greens to a grand coalition with the CDU as its junior partner. There was a new face at the top, but not much more.

The Christian Democrats on the Ropes

The campaign problems of Schröder's SPD paled in comparison to those of Kohl's Christian Democrats. In spite of their 1994 victory, the Christian Democrats showed the effects of their long tenure in office. Chancellor Kohl's dominance of the national organization left little room for new leaders to emerge. At the state level the party continued to decline. By 1997 they were the major governing party in only four of the sixteen states. Younger party leaders wanted Kohl to step down before the 1998 election in favor of Wolfgang Schäuble, the leader of the CDU's parliamentary group, but Kohl, perhaps with the condition of the SPD in mind, insisted on running again. It was by all accounts the single biggest mistake the CDU made in a mistake-ridden campaign.

The CDU campaign was, in the words of one insider, characterized by "unparalleled confusion." Campaign strategists in Bonn designed appeals in the East without any consultation with CDU campaigners in the region. A "red hands" campaign, which reproduced the 1946 Communist symbol of SPD and KPD unification into the Socialist Unity Party (SED), the ruling Communist party in the GDR from 1949 to 1989, was largely ignored by CDU activists in the East. The campaign, which attempted to link the Social Democrats with the former GDR communists via a remake of the 1946 poster, was given a quick burial. The poster was never displayed in the East.

A perceived upturn in the economy was a major factor in the Union's narrow 1994 victory. The upturn came just in time and was just enough to reelect the Kohl government. In 1998, the Union tried again to play the economy card, pointing to some positive employment and economic growth numbers in the second quarter. The party also was not above trying to prime the economic pump. Between February and July 1998, the Kohl government released funds (about DM 1.6 billion) to create an additional 100,000 public works (ABM) jobs in the former East Germany. This "ABM Quickie," as *Der Spiegel* put it, had one condition: the money had to be spent in the current fiscal (election) year. But in 1998 it was too little, too late. Kohl's promise to cut unemployment in half by 2000 was simply not credible.

Two weeks before the national election the Union received a much-needed late campaign pick-me-up when the Bavarian CSU, contrary to the national trend, retained its dominant position at the state parliamentary election. This victory seemed to confirm the CDU and Kohl's assurances that there would be a last-minute swing to the government.

The Bavarian victory, however, was above all a triumph for the CSU and its leader, Minister-President Stoiber, and was not the result of any national factors. On the contrary, the CSU was rewarded for Bavaria's strong economy and relatively low unemployment. Stoiber was very popular not only among CSU voters (a 94 percent approval rating), but also among SPD (75 percent) and Green (70 percent) supporters. This strong record made it difficult for the SPD to make much headway with its theme of change. The SPD is also chronically weak in this heavily Catholic and conservative state. At the local level, the Free or Independent Voters Group, a collection of non-partisan candidates, actually has 500 more mayors and local council members than the Social Democrats.[9] While Schröder was more popular than Kohl in Bavaria, this did the SPD little good.

The CDU's longtime junior coalition partner was also in trouble. Between July 1990 and December 1997, FDP membership in the "new" states of the former East Germany dropped from 136,000 to less than 17,000, or by almost 90 percent. At thirty-five state elections between 1990 and 1998, the party failed to clear the 5 percent mark fifteen times (43 percent). Its failure rate in the five eastern states was even higher, at 55 percent. By 1998 the FDP was represented in only four of sixteen state legislatures, none of them in the East.

The Eastern Opposition: The Party of Democratic Socialism (PDS)

At the elections of 1990 and 1994, the PDS showed the West German political class that it could survive in a unified Germany. In 1998 the PDS was intent on demonstrating to its opponents that it could also thrive, at least in its part of unified Germany. The party had two main goals: to clear the 5 percent hurdle and thus become a full-fledged parliamentary party (i.e., with full Fraktion status), and to enter the state government of Mecklenburg-Vorpommern as a coalition partner with the Social Democrats. The election for the Mecklenburg state parliament was held on the same date as the national poll.

The PDS had good reason to be optimistic. Frustrations about the pace of economic development in the eastern regions had not declined. The party had positioned itself as the undisputed voice of the discontented, a role it played with great effectiveness. The absence of any significant eastern representation in the elites of the major national parties practically guaranteed that their campaigns would be unable to stop the PDS from returning to the Bundestag.

Public Opinion and Issues

The general climate of opinion throughout 1998 strongly favored a change. From January to June 1998, over 70 percent of voters in monthly surveys consistently stated that it was time for a new government. As the election approached, this proportion declined somewhat, but even in the final week before the vote 63 percent still wanted a change. When asked in pre-election polls which parties they expected to win the election, solid majorities named the SPD-Green combination as the likely new government. Only in the last week of the campaign did the governing parties narrow the gap from 33 percent (58 percent for change vs. 25 percent against) to 9 percent (46 percent vs. 37 percent). This was too little, too late.

German voters in 1998 had little confidence in the ability of either of the major parties to create new jobs, but in contrast to 1994, the SPD in 1998 had an advantage over the Christian Democrats. By the time of the October 1994 election, 37 percent of voters felt that the Christian Democrats had more competence to create new jobs than the Social Democrats (23 percent). Four years later the Social Democrats held a 28 percent to 22 percent advantage over the CDU. Public confidence in the job creating ability of the Christian Democrats had declined by 15 percent, but confidence in the SPD in 1998 had increased by only 5 percent.

Unemployment was by far the major campaign issue and the area where the Kohl government was most vulnerable to opposition criticism. Most polls found that unemployment was cited by about 90 percent of the electorate as the most important problem facing the country. No other issue was even close. Law and order, foreigners, and the security of the pension system were only mentioned by about 10 percent of the electorate as the "most important" problem.

By early 1998 over 4.8 million Germans—about 11.5 percent of the workforce—were officially unemployed. This represented an increase of almost 100 percent over the 1990 level. Since the 1990 unification over 3 million jobs have been lost; 2.5 million of them in the East. High unemployment also meant increases in poverty and welfare (*Sozialhilfe*) recipients. Between 1994 and 1998, the number of Germans below the poverty level set by the European Union jumped from 6 to 7 million. The welfare rolls increased from 1 million in 1983, the first year of the Kohl government, to 3 million in 1998.

Yet during the Kohl era, as the SPD, Greens, and PDS ceaselessly reminded voters, the number of millionaires grew from 230,000 in 1982 to over 1 million in 1998. During this same period, the capital resources —savings accounts, stocks, bonds, real estate—of private households grew from DM 1 trillion to DM 5 trillion.

The issue that by 1998 had declined the most in the public's consciousness was the environment. In the elections from 1987 to 1995, environmental protection was mentioned by about 40 percent of voters as the most important issue. In 1998, however, only a minuscule 5 percent of voters considered it the most important problem. This change, as Gene Frankland points out (see Chapter 5) had a major impact on the Greens' 1998 campaign.

The Results

When all the votes were counted, Schröder, Lafontaine, and their SPD campaign team had led the party to its greatest triumph since Willy Brandt's 1972 victory. For only the second time in the history of the Federal Republic, the Social Democrats had outpolled the CDU/CSU to become the largest party. The 5.7 percent difference between the SPD and CDU/CSU in 1998 was in fact much larger than the modest 0.9 percent advantage Brandt had achieved in his 1972 victory. The SPD had indeed moved back into the center of the electorate; it gained over 3 million new voters, largely at the expense of the Christian Democrats. Thanks to the electoral law, which this time worked in their favor, the Social Democrats also picked up all twelve excess mandates, and their 40.9 percent of the party vote yielded 44.5 percent of the parliamentary seats. Alongside the Christian Democrats, the Free Democrats and the Greens saw their vote decline. Thus the SPD was the only "West" party to make gains at this election.

The continued East-West cleavage in German politics was underscored by the substantial gains of the PDS, which increased its total by almost a half-million votes. With 5.1 percent of the second ballot vote, the PDS became a full-fledged parliamentary party with all the benefits associated with Fraktion status, i.e., the right to chair parliamentary committees, name one vice-president of the Bundestag, and have their own party foundation (the Rosa-Luxemburg Foundation).

The East Giveth and the East Taketh Away

East German voters continued to be different. The classic Western demographic moorings of religion and class are much weaker in the East. With little history of democratic voting, Eastern electors thus far have responded to short-run factors such as issues and candidates rather than long-term forces of party identification and socialization. The result has been greater voter volatility. At the first three "national" elections—the *Volkskammerwahl* of March 1990 and the *Bundestagswahlen* of 1990 and

1994—Kohl and the CDU were strongly supported by eastern voters. This support, which made the CDU the strongest party in the region, ran across the demographic spectrum. Easterners did not respect the classic laws of voting behavior: blue-collar workers and those in lower income groups were about as likely to vote for the CDU as were middle and upper-middle class East Germans. This support was strongly related to Kohl's promises of the deutsche mark, prosperity, and "flowering landscapes." Easterners got the deutsche mark, but they continue to wait for the prosperity. In 1998 their patience expired, and the Union's vote plummeted from 38.5 percent in 1994 to only 27.3 percent.

The election also marked the first time that the former East Germans had participated in a democratic shift of power, a *Machtwechsel* in which, as the analyses in this volume show, they played a significant role. There is some evidence that this experience of a peaceful change of government had a positive impact on the rather ambivalent attitudes that easterners have shown to political democracy. In surveys following the election, East German attitudes toward democracy became more supportive as two-thirds of the adult population, as compared to about half before the election, thought that the democratic political process had performed well. East German support for more authoritarian forms of government also declined in post-election surveys.[10]

The Christian Democrats were, of course, the clear losers of the election. With only 35.2 percent of the party vote, the Union dropped to its lowest level since the first national election in 1949. Post-election analyses focused on three major factors for the Union's defeat. First and foremost was the Kohl candidacy. For almost a year before the election, surveys found that a solid majority of Germans simply wanted a change in leadership. But as the undisputed leader of the party, Kohl refused to listen to any suggestion that he step down. Even in the last week of the campaign, as the gap between the two major parties narrowed, Schröder maintained a 53:39 advantage over the incumbent chancellor. This was the largest advantage for a challenging chancellor candidate ever recorded in German electoral surveys.[11] The Kohl candidacy had a particularly negative impact on the mobile segment of the electorate, i.e., those voters largely in the center who were undecided. Second, the Social Democrats were considered more competent than the CDU to deal with the most important issue of the campaign—unemployment. Only 24 percent of the electorate believed that the Christian Democrats could deal effectively with unemployment, as compared to 42 percent for the Social Democrats. Finally, the Union was clearly hurt by the general climate of public opinion, which favored a change of government. Even 22 percent of Christian Democratic voters, according to one study, wanted a change of governing parties.[12]

These negatives for the CDU were intensified in the East. The results for the CDU in the five eastern German states were even worse than their dismal showing in the "old" Federal Republic. In the East, the Union's proportion of the vote dropped from 38.5 percent to 27.3 percent. While most analysts attribute this poor showing to the anti-Kohl vote, poor economy, and slow pace of unification, others now argue that the 1998 results in the East, as compared to the 1990 and 1994 votes, indicate that easterners are now voting "normally," that is, consistently with their political beliefs and attitudes. The 1990 and 1994 votes were aberrations, exceptional votes caused by the exceptional circumstances of unification.

The Free Democrats also went down with Kohl. For the first time in almost thirty years the Free Democrats went into opposition. While the party was able to surmount the 5 percent barrier, it ran a lackluster campaign devoid of popular leaders or an attractive program. Many in the FDP saw the defeat as an opportunity to rejuvenate the party. Freed from its ties to Kohl and the Christian Democrats, the FDP can now strike out on its own.

In its new role as the junior opposition party the FDP faces three major challenges. First, it must rebuild its organization at the state and local level. The party is now represented in only five of sixteen state legislatures. At the local level the situation is equally bleak. In many cities the party is no longer represented in city councils. Second, it must develop policy alternatives that will distinguish it from the other parties. The party's leadership believes that there is an electoral market for a program that emphasizes lower taxes, less bureaucracy, less governmental regulation, and more freedom for business. In short, the party wants to return to its free-market roots. Finally, the FDP must learn to compete with the Greens, who in many non-environmental areas advocate policies similar to the FDP's.

The decline in the electorate's concern with environmental issues clearly hurt the Greens. While Germany remains one of the most environmentally conscious societies in Europe, the support levels for environmental projects have retreated from their highs of the early and mid-1990s. Between 1996 and 1998, the proportion of adults who were willing to reduce their standard of living for the sake of the environment dropped from 54 percent to 44 percent.[13] Popular fear of an environmental catastrophe has also declined in recent years. Among younger voters this decline is even more apparent; the environment is an "uncool" topic among young people. Strong majorities of voters also expressed opposition to the Green proposals to protect the environment by introducing speed limits on the Autobahn and sharply increasing gasoline taxes to about $10 per gallon.

The Greens also suffered from defections to the SPD because of the Schröder candidacy. If removing Kohl was the number one priority at this election—as Joschka Fischer tirelessly reminded the Green faithful—why not support the Social Democrats? After Schröder won his Lower Saxony victory and took a large lead over Kohl, a substantial number of Green voters decided that the best way to remove Kohl was to vote for the Social Democrats.

With their entrance into the government, the Greens have completed their long march. They are now "established." Can classic Green demands such as the elimination of atomic energy and drastic cuts in defense spending be achieved, or has the party been co-opted by the very consensual structures they once vowed to change?

Aftermath: What Did the Voters Want?

In the aftermath of the election, most commentators speculated on possible conflicts between the SPD and the Greens, particularly over the issues of closing down the country's nineteen nuclear power plants and the deployment of German military forces in NATO "out of area" operations. Also, Schröder's previous experience with the Greens as a coalition partner in Lower Saxony had not been entirely harmonious. Schröder publicly stated that he hoped eventually to govern without the Greens as he did in Lower Saxony after his 1998 reelection. But the Greens have thus far been remarkably compliant.

Schröder's biggest problem has been his own party, especially its "old" left wing led by Oskar Lafontaine. The 1998 victory did not end the conflict between the two men. Their differences had been put aside for the sake of the election campaign, but soon after the victory they resumed their struggle, this time within the new government. Lafontaine was appointed finance minister, and, as chairman of the party, he was the strongest single member of the Schröder cabinet. Many within the party actually considered Lafontaine more powerful than Schröder.

Disagreements between the two leaders were most apparent in economic and tax policy. Lafontaine, with the support of the party's traditional left and the trade unions, advocated an unabashed demand-side approach to economic growth: higher wages, increases in social welfare payments, lower interest rates. While advocating tax cuts for lower and middle-income groups, he did little to relieve high labor costs for business and actually planned to increase taxes on large business firms. Schröder's policies were aimed at making German business more competitive in the global economy: lower taxes, more investment incentives, and fewer government regulations. At times, Lafontaine appeared to be leading his own separate government as he criticized the slow pace of decision making under Schröder.

The conflict finally came to a head in March 1999, when Schröder, in a statement apparently directed at Lafontaine, announced at a cabinet meeting that he would not support any new legislation directed against business. He was referring to Lafontaine's proposal to tax the cash reserves of energy and insurance companies. The next day Lafontaine abruptly announced his resignation from the government and the leadership of the party. An emergency meeting of the SPD presidium then nominated Schröder as the new party chairman. In April 1999 a special party congress elected him to the post, albeit with the lowest majority (about 75 percent) in the postwar history of the party.

Lafontaine's departure has given the Schröder government a second chance after its fitful and ineffective start. Its much-heralded tax reform package was strongly opposed by business interests and had to be changed. The proposed citizenship law, which would have allowed children born in Germany of foreign parents to hold dual citizenship, also had to be changed. The planned dismantling of Germany's remaining nuclear power plants, a key issue for the Greens, is still in the discussion stage. Lafontaine's departure has given Schröder a freer hand in governing. It has also put the responsibility for success or failure squarely on his shoulders.

Notes

1. The 1982 power shift was essentially ratified by the electorate at the March 1983 federal election.
2. Until unification *Überhangmandate* were relatively rare. The highest number at any federal election between 1949 and 1987 was five, in 1961. At the four elections between 1965 and 1976 there were no excess mandates. For the next federal election, which is scheduled for 2002 (unless the government loses its majority in the meantime), the number of districts has been reduced from 328 to 299 and the total number of seats from the current 672 (plus 13 *Überhangmandate*) to 598. All district boundaries will be redrawn, which should reduce the number of underpopulated districts and hence *Überhangmandate*.
3. Lancaster presents evidence that ballot splitting may also relate to the characteristics of district-level candidates. Thomas D. Lancaster, "Candidate Characteristics and Electoral Performance: A Long-Term Analysis of the German Bundestag," in Christopher J. Anderson and Carsten Zelle, eds., *Stability and Change in German Elections* (Westport and London: Praeger, 1998), 281–300.
4. David P. Conradt , Gerald R. Kleinfeld, George K. Romoser, and Christian Søe, eds., *Germany's New Politics* (Providence and London: Berghahn Books, 1995).
5. Monthly Politbarometer polls of the Forschungsgruppe Wahlen.
6. Günter Bannas, "Ein Programm wie Schröder," *Süddeutsche Zeitung*, 17 March 1998 (Internet edition).

7. Stefan Dietrich, "Die CDU auf den Stand der PDS drücken," *Frankfurter Allgemeine Zeitung*, 9 May 1998, 8.
8. *Süddeutsche Zeitung*, 24 August 1998.
9. Forschungsgruppe Wahlen data cited in "Auch SPD und Grünen Wähler fanden Stoiber gut," *Süddeutsche Zeitung*, 15 September 1998 (Internet edition).
10. Forschungsgruppe Wahlen, Politbarometer.
11. Forschungsgruppe Wahlen, "Bundestagswahl 1998," Mannheim, 30 September 1998, 75.
12. See the data reported by Elisabeth Noelle-Neumann, "Rückkehr in das Leben, das wirklich zählt," *Frankfurter Allgemeine Zeitung*, 17 March 1999, 5. See also David P. Conradt, "Political Culture in Unified Germany: Will the Bonn Republic Survive and Thrive in Berlin?," *German Studies Review* 21, no. 1:83–104.
13. Forschungsgruppe Wahlen, "Bundestagswahl 1998," 74.

Chapter 2

THE SPD

From Opposition to Governing Party

Gerard Braunthal

The venerable Social Democratic Party of Germany (SPD) recaptured political power in the 1998 national election. It had reason to celebrate. Despite its status as a major party, it has governed Germany for only a sparse number of years since its inception in 1875. It was in perpetual opposition and was prohibited for twelve years during the pre-1918 Empire period, governed Weimar Germany for only brief periods, was crushed during the Nazi era, and since the founding of the Federal Republic of Germany in 1949 has occupied the opposition benches in the Bundestag for far more years than it has governed. From 1949 to 1966 it lost one national election after another to the Christian Democratic Union/Christian Social Union (CDU/CSU). It had a chance to govern in Bonn only after moderating its neo-Marxist program in 1959. Thus in 1966, when CDU Chancellor Ludwig Erhard resigned, it joined a CDU/CSU-led government as the junior partner. Finally from 1969 to 1982, the SPD, first under Willy Brandt and then Helmut Schmidt, was the senior governing party in coalition with the small neoliberal Free Democratic Party (FDP). In 1982, however, the coalition broke apart over discords in economic policy and the SPD once again became the major opposition party—until 1998.

This chapter, by focusing on the 1998 election, seeks to assess the causes of the difficulties the SPD has had in its quest for power at the national level. Are the causes internal or external to the party? Do the intra-party leadership struggles, the factional divisions, the ideological battles, and the corruption scandals sap the energy of the SPD? Are the problems external to the party, such as a politically conservative climate, changing milieus and social groups, postunification issues, voters' perceptions that the CDU/CSU is more able to solve economic problems, and hostile media? Or are the causes a mixture of internal and external factors? Finally, do the renewed difficulties the SPD has experienced since its 1998 victory indicate that even when it governs the nation in coalition with the Greens, it cannot expect to automatically fulfill its party program and campaign promises?

Policy and Leadership Issues: 1994 to 1998

To answer these questions, we must first give an overview of the SPD's record during the four-year period between the last two Bundestag elections, 1994 and 1998. In 1994, the SPD leaders had hoped that the tide for the party was finally turning. They expected the electorate to give them a mandate to govern, after having lost the 1983, 1987, and 1990 elections. Polls in early 1994 indicated that the SPD would outscore the CDU/CSU if an election were held then. The SPD's euphoric mood increased in March 1994, when in the Lower Saxony Land election the party received an unprecedented majority of seats in the legislature. As a consequence, the then minister-president Gerhard Schröder no longer had to share power with the Greens. SPD leaders also were optimistic because since 1991 the SPD has had a majority in the Bundesrat (the second legislative chamber representing the states). This gave the party a chance to block or change laws affecting the Länder, thereby giving it more political clout in the legislative process. In 1994, the SPD was a member of eleven out of sixteen Länder coalition governments and held the minister-presidency in nine of them.

But the optimism was premature. By spring 1994, the economy began to improve, to the political benefit of the Kohl government. Rudolf Scharping, SPD minister-president of Rhineland-Palatinate and the party's candidate for the post of chancellor, led a lackluster campaign, which the conservative media exploited. Even though the SPD gained a higher percentage of votes—36.4 percent—than four years earlier, it trailed the CDU/CSU, which received 41.5 percent. Once again, Helmut Kohl formed a coalition government with the FDP. Although the conservative governing parties lost votes in the 1994 election, a shift toward the SPD and other left-of-center parties was not sufficient to bring about a change in government.[1]

In 1995 the SPD was beset by continuing divisions between its ideological blocs and by a fratricidal struggle among its leaders. SPD chairman Scharping, a conservative pragmatist, had tried to dampen the feuds between the party's left and right wings. The left wing consisted of a small group of old left working-class members, a minority of SPD deputies, and a large group of new left members clustered in the Young Socialists (Jusos). The latter especially supported the "new politics" themes of the quality of life, participatory democracy, and other postmaterialist values. The right wing consisted of pragmatic and conservative leaders, deputies, and unionists who were still strongly anti-communist and anti-leftist. They espoused the materialist values linked to the "old politics" themes of job security and adequate income. A loosely knit center bloc sought to narrow, without much success, the differences between the two wings.

Scharping had as little luck in producing harmony among the party's wings as in preventing a leadership struggle. He fired Schröder as the SPD's economic policy spokesperson after Schröder accused Scharping of not consulting him and other top party leaders during and after the 1994 election campaign. Other SPD leaders criticized Scharping for his conservative and pragmatic positions, which reflected the "no experiment" national political climate, and his lethargic leadership style. As a consequence of this infighting, the party slid lower in national public opinion polls. In the Berlin election of 1995, the SPD, which had governed with the CDU in the city government, suffered its worst showing since the end of World War II, partly as a result of this intra-party strife.

In an episode unprecedented in the SPD's history, a majority of delegates at the November 1995 convention in Mannheim, many of them blaming Scharping for the low national standing of the SPD, refrained from supporting his renewed candidacy as chairman, even though he had been in office for only twenty-eight months. Oskar Lafontaine, minister-president of the Saar, after making a rousing speech to energize the delegates, received 321 votes to Scharping's 190 for the post. Scharping remained head of the SPD Fraktion in the Bundestag and became a party deputy chairman. Whether voter confidence in the party's stability and trustworthiness was enhanced by this dramatic turnover in the top leadership position—the fourth chairman in the eight years since Brandt had resigned from the post—remained to be seen.

Lafontaine promptly attempted to heal the party's divisions. As a member of the select group of Brandt's "grandson" generation and of the 1968 generation that was challenging the establishment, the new chairman had loose links with the party's left wing and with the trade unions. His fast climb to the top started when, at the age of 32, he was elected Saarbrücken's lord mayor. He became Saar minister-president in 1985, deputy chairman of the party in 1987, and the unsuccessful SPD candidate for the chancellor post in 1990. From 1995 on, Lafontaine, as the new chairman, defused the internal struggles but took positions on intra-party and inter-party issues, as well as national domestic and foreign policy issues, that were bound to alienate many in the party.

On intra-party issues, Lafontaine pushed for a reform of the bureau-cratic structure. He supported the project group "SPD 2000: A Modern Reform Party," whose members sought to make the SPD more responsive to the rapidly changing social milieus and to the declining popular inter-est in parties. The group proposed that nonmembers could attend, but not vote in, party meetings; that members should have a greater voice in choosing the party's officials; and that local branches sponsor more forums, seminars, street theater, and summer performances to stop mem-bership losses. In short, the group called on the SPD officials and mem-bers to present a modern and youthful image to potential members.

In spite of attempts to change the party's image, SPD leaders could not staunch the continuing dip in membership from a peak of over one million in 1976 (West Germany) to 780,000 by late 1997 (united Germany). The decline, not restricted to the SPD, affected all parties. Citizens, especially youth, had become disillusioned with them for not meeting their needs. In a changing political culture, youth retreated to the private sphere. The SPD also had to adjust to a change in the occupational profile of its members, which corresponded to a parallel shift in the German labor force. The per-centage of blue-collar workers among its members, who had made up the traditional core of the party, declined by half from 45 percent in 1952 to 23 percent in 1996. Conversely, the number of salaried employees rose from 17 percent in 1952 to 28 percent in 1996, and civil servants at a slower rate to 11 percent in 1996.[2] As a consequence the party had to address the needs not only of blue-collar workers but of other social groups as well, which in turn sparked internal controversies on tactics and goals.

In the former German Democratic Republic, the SPD has had difficulty attracting a mass membership. Founded in 1989, the party has had less than 30,000 members in the new Länder, even though its strength was in Saxony and Thuringia in pre-1933 Germany. For instance, in post-1989 Dresden there were only 500 members as compared to the 55,000 at the end of the Weimar Republic. After more than half a century of the party's forcible extinction, workers, lacking the Weimar traditions, have not streamed into the party, despite strenuous recruitment efforts in factories and shops. Many potential members have resented the dominance of the western German SPD, which has supplied funds, organizers, staff, and equipment to its fledgling eastern German counterpart. Although the east German SPD has a weak organization and low membership, in several Länder, such as Brandenburg, Saxony-Anhalt, and Mecklenburg-Pomera-nia, it has been able to attract enough voters to form governments.[3]

In the 1990s the Jusos in western and eastern Germany sought to recruit more young people into the party, but with little success given their apolit-ical stance. The problem was compounded by the Jusos' lack of unity, which had plagued the organization since its founding. Warring leftist factions could only agree on a common program with difficulty. Despite the Jusos' problems, Lafontaine cultivated links to them, especially to their popular 25-year-old chairwoman Andrea Nahles. Lafontaine, aware that only 13.5 percent of SPD members were under 35 years old in 1996 compared with 31 percent in 1974, did not want to see the party's "collective march into the old-age home," as one SPD functionary put it.[4]

In response to Jusos' complaints that they had little chance to advance within the party, Lafontaine and other chiefs allocated a few positions in the party's executive committee (*Vorstand*) to them. However, the 30- and 40-year-old activist members could not get selected to the highest SPD posts; these were occupied by the 1968 generation of leaders currently in power. In the 1994–98 Bundestag, only 5 of 252 SPD deputies were under 35. In 1998, the SPD top command decided that the Länder organizations must put fifteen young leaders high on the party's electoral slates in the Länder in order to rejuvenate the Bundestag SPD Fraktion. But when some incumbent deputies did not yield their top slots to their younger colleagues, the Bavarian SPD chairwoman exclaimed in exasperation, "Whom should I kill?"[5]

Although these internal power struggles made media headlines, in 1996 the SPD spent DM 1 million ($600,000) with little publicity on youth conferences, forums, and a membership campaign, but with few appreciable results.

Lafontaine also had to deal with relations to the other left-of-center parties. He said on more than one occasion that the SPD could win the 1998 election only if it and the Greens stood together. Should the Party of Democratic Socialism (PDS, successor to the GDR's Socialist Unity Party) support such a coalition, he had no objections because it was crucial to allow it to participate in the democratic process. Conservative members in the SPD disagreed with their party chairman. Lafontaine also took positions on some of the nation's key domestic and foreign policies, which in turn sparked discussion within the party. When he called for an international harmonization of taxes and customs, Schröder said that such a proposal was not realizable. The two leaders also clashed on German defense policy, such as Lafontaine's opposition to the building of the Eurofighter, a German army project, and Schröder's support of it.

State Elections

Such well-publicized SPD disputes on policy, coupled with an increasing public dissatisfaction with parties and politicians, were bound to have an effect on the SPD's fortunes in the Länder elections held between 1994 and 1998. In May 1995 the SPD suffered a double setback in North

Rhine-Westphalia and Bremen, two traditional strongholds of the party. In populous North Rhine-Westphalia, the Social Democrats lost the absolute majority that they had held in the Landtag since 1980. The SPD had to form a coalition with the Greens, with whom a compromise had to be reached on the planned expansion of an important surface coal mine (the SPD favored it to protect the jobs of miners; the Greens opposed it to protect the residents of adjoining towns). In Bremen, the SPD gained more votes than the CDU, but, lacking an absolute majority, was forced to enter into a grand coalition with its archrival.

In March 1996, Schleswig-Holstein, Baden-Württemberg, and the Rhineland-Palatinate held elections. The SPD suffered losses in all three states as a result of continuing policy differences among its leaders, which weakened the party's image. In this instance, they quarreled publicly over the issues of ecological tax reform (raising taxes on energy and lowering taxes on business and incomes), the European currency union, and the structural crisis caused by the globalization of the economy. In the CDU/CSU, no such quarrels took place. Chancellor Kohl assured voters that he would provide for the country's stability and security. In Schleswig-Holstein, the SPD lost its absolute majority in the legislature and allied with the Greens. In Baden-Württemberg, a stronghold of the CDU, the SPD mustered only 25.1 percent of the vote, compared to 29.4 percent four years earlier. In Rhineland-Palatinate, the SPD, which had governed with the FDP since 1992, slipped from 44.8 percent of the vote in 1991 to 39.8 percent. It barely gained more votes than the CDU. Political observers characterized the SPD as lacking profile and new ideas.[6]

In September 1997, one year before the national election, the SPD suffered another setback in the Hamburg election, although it remained the governing party. Voters blamed the SPD for the continuing high unemployment and crime in the city. The SPD mayor, Henning Voscherau, promptly announced his resignation.

Although the SPD suffered electoral losses in Länder elections during the 1994–98 Bundestag period, in 1997 it still held a majority of forty-two votes to the CDU/CSU's twenty-seven votes in the Bundesrat. This dominance provided the SPD an opportunity, if all SPD-dominated Länder presented a united front on a bill (which was not always the case), to block CDU/CSU-FDP proposals that it could not support. In such instances, a conference committee convened to seek an agreement between the two chambers.

To influence the content of CDU/CSU-FDP bills, some SPD Länder chiefs met with national government ministers before the drafts of bills proceeded from the ministries to the cabinet. The ministers hoped that by making early minor concessions to the SPD, the party in turn would support the ministry's bill in the Bundesrat. To achieve further inter-party consensus, federal-Länder bipartisan working groups on economic, finance, and social issues were set up. Most SPD chiefs hoped that the party would wring some concessions from the government on CDU/ CSU-FDP-generated bills in the working groups. Bavarian SPD chairwoman Renate Schmidt, however, urged the SPD, without success, to renounce membership in the working groups for fear that the party's profile would become blurred if it had to make concessions to the governing parties.[7]

Schröder versus Lafontaine

Several years before the 1998 national election, the SPD attempted to settle the burning issue of who its candidate for the chancellor post would be and what kind of program it would present to the voters. The right-leaning Schröder and the left-leaning Lafontaine were both in the running. Schröder, like Lafontaine, was a member of the generation of Brandt's "grandchildren." He was born of poor parents in 1944, studied law at the University of Göttingen, and became a member of the SPD in 1963. He was Juso chairman from 1978 to 1980, Bundestag deputy from 1980 to 1986, a member of the SPD presidium (the top policymaking body), deputy and chairman of the SPD Fraktion of the Lower Saxony parliament, and minister-president of Lower Saxony from 1990 to 1998. His career was marked by an ideological shift from left to right within the party's political spectrum. He had been on the left as Juso chairperson, shifted to the center as he rose in the party, and allied himself with party rightists in Lower Saxony. Many SPD leaders in Bonn viewed his shifts as signs of unreliability. They recalled 1993, when the party's rightists supported Scharping over Schröder as party chairman. At the time, Schröder had vowed to gain their support in his ambition to become party chairman and chancellor.

Lafontaine, party chairman since 1995, also wanted to become the chancellor candidate again (he had been the standard bearer in 1990). Polls in 1997 and early 1998 indicated, however, that the ambitious Schröder was more popular than Lafontaine (and Kohl) among German voters. Respondents viewed Schröder as the efficient modernizer of the economy in his state. The polls also showed that if Schröder were the party's candidate for chancellor, the SPD would muster more votes than the CDU/CSU in the national election scheduled for 27 September 1998. When the SPD gained nearly 48 percent of the vote in the 1 March 1998 election in Lower Saxony, Schröder's home base, Lafontaine and other senior party chiefs immediately chose Schröder as the nominee for the chancellorship. At a subsequent April convention in Leipzig, SPD delegates endorsed their leaders' choice, even though many of the delegates characterized Schröder as being too opportunistic, cold, conservative, and pragmatic. They would have preferred Lafontaine, who was emotionally closer to them and whose political views matched theirs. Nonetheless, they cast their votes, many reluctantly, for Schröder, aware that he was more popular among the electorate; the party's heart was with Lafontaine, but its brain recommended Schröder.

Schröder's appeal rested on his pragmatic, rather than ideological, approach to politics. He espoused a New Middle position, which borrowed heavily from British Prime Minister Tony Blair and U.S. President Bill Clinton's Third Way philosophy. The British and American model emphasizes personal responsibility, technological innovation, competitive enterprise and entrepreneurship, improvements in education, and cutbacks in the welfare state to cope with the challenges of a rapidly changing global order. It rejects the leftist redistribution of wealth or the rightist unfettered capitalist economy. It also calls for a limit on strong government and for the expansion of civic institutions that will respond to citizens' needs in their localities.[8] According to the writer Jane Kramer, Schröder "sees himself as a fixer, a mediator, a something-for-everyone, consensual sort of person."[9]

This pragmatic approach to problems, devoid of hostility to a social market economy, facilitated Schröder's friendship with the business community, especially when he had to consider the interests of the giant Volkswagen firm located in his home state. Wearing expensive Italian-tailored suits and smoking big Havana cigars, Schröder feels at ease with business people, whom he assures that the SPD is no longer the party of blue-collar workers. But when he speaks to workers, he projects a different image. Then he tells them of the hardships his widowed mother endured when raising five children, and of his close ties to trade unions.

Programmatic Pledges

In planning the 1998 election campaign, Schröder and Lafontaine were bound to clash on the contents of the party's electoral program, which would become the basis for the government program should the SPD win the election. Before the party convention on April 17, Schröder urged Lafontaine and other left-wing traditionalists, with only moderate success, to exclude radical proposals in order to win over New Middle voting groups, such as middle-management personnel, scientists, engineers, academics, and craftspeople. Lafontaine was more interested in retaining the support of the party's traditional clientele of skilled workers and salaried employees, and in differentiating the SPD's program from that of its conservative rivals. Thus he insisted that a SPD-led government must put a priority on creating new jobs, for instance, by expanding the youth apprenticeship program, which the Jusos had demanded as a priority. Schröder accepted this proposal. Less enthusiastically, he accepted a call for a 9 pfennig price increase on gasoline and other energy sources to limit environmental damages and raise taxes. He was worried that the burden on consumers and business would be too great.

To placate the business community and spur an economic revival in the nation, Schröder proposed a cut in the top income tax rate from 53 to 45 percent, but other party leaders accepted only a modest drop to 49 percent. Schröder, again to help the economy, proposed that a low-wage sector be permitted, but the party's left wing managed to strike it from the draft of the program. Schröder assented to Lafontaine's proposal that a new SPD government scrap the Kohl government's welfare cutbacks in pensions and in wage payments to workers on sick leave or construction workers during seasonal poor weather. As to integrating foreigners into German society, Schröder, who at one time had espoused the conservative view that criminal foreigners must be swiftly expelled from Germany, concurred with the platform's provision that the government had an obligation to deal with the social causes of criminality.

At the April convention, Schröder, in his maiden speech as the SPD's chancellor candidate, emphasized that once an SPD-led government was in power, its priority would be to cut back on the more than four million unemployed (10 percent of the labor force, 20 percent in eastern Germany). He asked business and unions to join the government in a reconstituted neocorporatist Alliance for Jobs (a previous one disbanded in 1996). He requested unions to consider more flexible organizations of work and urged businesses to invest and innovate more. He promised that the new government would cut back on the federal bureaucracy, increase spending on research, support the new euro currency, and harmonize national employment policies, taxes, and commercial duties in Europe. In short, the party's chancellor candidate sought to gain the support of both the party's traditionalists and modernizers (he himself fits into the latter category). Lafontaine requested party members to fully support Schröder, which they did.[10]

The Electoral Campaign

As in previous elections, the SPD and other parties launched massive, slick, and costly American-style campaigns in which the candidates become more important than the issues. In October 1997, seven months before the SPD chose Schröder as its standard-bearer, the party's secretary, Franz

Müntefering, assembled a large staff in a separate "Kampa '98" head-quarters in Bonn to map out the expensive (DM 77 million; $45 million) advertising campaign. Müntefering traveled to Britain, Sweden, the Netherlands, and the United States to study how left-centrist parties could beat their conservative rivals. Kampa '98 staff commissioned several public opinion institutes to measure the saliency of issues and the popularity of the candidates, contracted with public relations and advertising firms to prepare the propaganda (posters, slogans, advertisements, media spots, etc.) that emphasized the New Middle and youthful image, and established instant communication via computers with SPD branches in all of Germany.

The senior SPD candidates made numerous speeches at televised rallies and appeared on television talk shows. To placate the SPD traditionalists, Schröder claimed that he agreed with the party's platform and promised that a SPD government would maintain social justice and preserve the welfare state. But to woo the New Middle voters, who ranged in the middle of the political spectrum, who were disillusioned with the parties and the political system, and who in the past had not supported the SPD or had abstained from voting, Schröder made it clear that as chancellor he would not necessarily execute the party's wishes in all respects. More telling, he called for a modernization of the state, the economy, and the society, but hardly mentioned the party's earlier espousal of "democratic socialism." His party critics took such statements to mean that he planned to cut back on the welfare state's benefits, pensions, and health care. They were mistrustful of Schröder's ideas because he was strongly influenced in his New Middle thinking by Bodo Hombach, the former minister of economics in North Rhine-Westphalia, and Wolfgang Clement, the Land's new minister-president. Hombach urged Schröder to support the market economy model of former CDU chancellor Ludwig Erhard, which rejected a controlled economy and a nostalgic socialism.

The SPD's leftists criticized Schröder's personalized and depoliticized campaign. Schröder—correctly, in hindsight—did not heed their advice. Calculating that the voters were tired of the lackluster CDU/CSU-FDP government, the 54-year-old telegenic SPD leader projected a youthful image in his competition with the 68-year-old elder statesman Kohl. To win over the New Middle voters, Schröder appointed three men to his "shadow cabinet" who could be expected to follow a moderate line once the SPD formed a coalition cabinet. The first appointee was Just Stollmann, a wealthy computer entrepreneur and not a SPD member, to become minister of economics and technology. Stollmann's critical statements on unions, however, profoundly alienated them. Schröder backed Stollmann for the post until after the election, when Stollmann withdrew his candidacy because Lafontaine, as the new "super" finance minister, planned to transfer some of the Ministry of Economics departments into Finance. The second appointment of a moderate to the shadow cabinet was Walter Riester, deputy chairperson of the Metal Workers Union, to become minister of Labor. Schröder expected him to cultivate the good relations he had with the business community. The third appointment was the publisher Michael Naumann, who had headed a United States publishing house and was slated to become the chief cultural official in an SPD-led cabinet. Schröder intended to strengthen the national government's involvement in cultural policies, but Naumann's remarks on a range of cultural topics often became controversial.

While wooing the New Middle voters, Schröder could not neglect the SPD's traditional blue-collar core. At campaign rallies where they were present, he denounced the 100 tax-evading millionaires who sent their wealth out of Germany, praised the nation's welfare system, and vowed to narrow the widening economic gap between the poor and the rich. More specifically, he promised to reverse some social welfare cuts that the Kohl government had made. Schröder had to support some leftist positions, not only to attract the party's faithful but dwindling core voters, but also to win over potential Greens and PDS voters. He studiously avoided taking any position on the kind of coalition government—red (SPD)-green or an SPD grand coalition with the CDU/CSU—that might emerge if the SPD triumphed at the polls, although it was known that he favored a grand coalition. For tactical electoral reasons, he distanced himself from the more radical proposals of individual Greens leaders who had called for a steep increase in energy taxes, a speed limit on the *Autobahnen* to minimize environmental damage, and a ban on German participation in international military peacekeeping missions and in NATO forces. Leading Greens officials convinced those who had made these proposals to withdraw them in order to facilitate a possible red-green coalition.

Despite the SPD's and Greens' moderate electoral programs, Kohl, determined that the CDU/CSU and FDP should be the sole occupants of the New Middle terrain, pulled out the "red scare" card, as he had done four years earlier. He warned voters that should a red-green coalition not have an absolute number of seats in the Bundestag to govern, it would need the PDS deputies' votes. Kohl's message had little effect on voters because SPD and Greens leaders had said on numerous occasions that under no circumstances would they form a coalition if it depended on PDS support.

This SPD commitment did not apply to Länder governments. Schröder reluctantly advised SPD chiefs in the eastern Länder, where the PDS has considerable support, that if they formed minority governments and needed the support of PDS votes in their parliaments to pass legislation (policy of toleration) they could accept such support. In case the SPD preferred to form a coalition government with the PDS in order to have a clear governing majority, it could proceed. In 1998, two elections produced such alternative models. In Saxony-Anhalt, the new SPD government once again was tolerated in the legislature by the PDS, and in Mecklenburg-Pomerania an unprecedented SPD-PDS coalition government was formed.

The hot phase of the election campaign for all parties began on 17 August 1998. Top SPD politicians shuttled from one rally to another and appeared frequently on television, posters appeared in the smallest hamlets and the largest cities, party kiosks were set up in market squares, and the media was saturated with party propaganda. As in earlier election campaigns, the SPD presidium approved the draft of the 100-day program, entitled "The Start for a Modern and Just Germany," which an SPD-led government would attempt to carry out in the initial months subject to negotiations with its coalition partner. The 100-day program hardly differed from the party program that had been approved at the SPD convention in April. It called for a tripartite business, union, and government alliance for jobs; wage protection for discharged workers and employees; and more jobs, apprenticeships, and financial support to eastern Germany. It promised a tax reduction of DM 2,500 ($1,470) for families with two children, the cancellation of the planned CDU/CSU-FDP cut of pension benefits from 70 to 64 percent of pre-retirement income, talks with the nuclear industry about a timetable for dismantling nuclear energy plants, and tax reform to lower the tax rate by stages from 25.9 to 15 percent for low income wage earners and 53 to 48.5 percent for high income earners (the CDU/CSU had proposed a sharper drop from 53 to 39 percent). Not surprisingly, the CDU/CSU assailed the program for making promises that could not be fulfilled; the Greens faulted it for not setting a swift time frame to dismantle the nuclear power plants. Should the SPD win the election, as the senior coalition partner it would make minimum programmatic concessions to its coalition partner, whether the partner was the CDU/CSU or the Greens.[11]

The Election: SPD Victorious

On the evening of September 27 the SPD—and the Greens—had reason to celebrate. Projections from exit polls, shown on the parties' headquarters' television screens, indicated that for the first time since the 1972 election the SPD had gained more votes than the CDU/CSU. The SPD won 40.9 percent of the vote, gaining 4.5 percent over 1994. The CDU/CSU won 35.2 percent, the Greens 6.7 percent, the FDP 6.2 percent, and the PDS 5.1 percent. The SPD and the Greens' total vote translated into an absolute majority of seats (345 out of 669) in the Bundestag. They did not need the support of the PDS, which they would have rejected. Thus an unprecedented SPD-Greens coalition was in the offing, although an SPD grand coalition with the CDU/CSU would have been an alternative favored by many SPD centrist voters. The CDU/CSU declined to enter into such a coalition.

The SPD, in a euphoric mood, had succeeded in its campaign efforts to gain the support of voters in various occupational categories. A plurality of workers in eastern and western Germany, 56 percent of unionized workers and salaried employees, and a majority of the unemployed voted for it. Thus, for the first time since Germany's unification in 1990, the CDU lost the support of a majority of workers in eastern Germany, who shifted their support to the SPD and PDS. Clearly, these voters were protesting the Kohl government's perceived neglect of eastern German interests. The SPD's ability to gain the support of the largest occupational group, the salaried employees, who were also the largest pool of floating voters, was remarkable.[12]

Among age groups, the SPD was the most popular among those over 45, gaining support especially from women over 60 years old, a group known to favor the CDU. There were no significant differences between the number of men and women voting for the SPD, although the party was the least popular among the 18- to 24-year-olds. As in earlier national elections, the civil servants, the self-employed, farmers, and agricultural workers gave greater support to the CDU/CSU than to the SPD.[13]

In western Germany, the SPD maintained or regained its strength in urban, densely populated areas, but the opposite was true in eastern Germany. The SPD's ability to win over voters from other parties and those without party affiliation was crucial to its victory. It received the support of 1.4 million former CDU voters and numerous FDP and Greens voters, in addition to 1,350,000 first-time voters.[14]

The party gained from a destabilized party system in which traditional constituencies fragmented, although the social and economic upheaval that has plagued Germany since the early 1990s makes for an unsteady and unpredictable political landscape where political dominance is lost as quickly as it is won. In this instance Schröder's appeal to the New Middle groups paid off, even though for him to develop a mixture of policies that all supporters would find acceptable has proved exceedingly difficult. To make changes in such fields as tax reform and flexibility in the labor market, Schröder must have the support of the constituents benefiting from the present system—the same constituents, such as workers, on whom the SPD relies so heavily for votes.[15]

SPD-Green Coalition Bargaining

The victorious SPD and Greens, on the verge of constituting an unprece-dented coalition of two "leftist" parties, faced two tough weeks of coali-tion talks on the new government program and the composition of the cabinet. Four SPD and four Greens leaders met repeatedly to gain an accord on the government's basic policies and legislative priorities. As the stronger party, the SPD forced the Greens to make concessions, such as dropping their demand for a steep increase on energy taxes and for a swift phasing out of nuclear energy plants. To lower unemployment, the government intended to create the Alliance for Jobs and to support expansion of the private sector's apprenticeship programs by 100,000 young people. It planned to review the pension scheme, to overhaul the tax system by making cuts in the highest and lowest income tax rates, and to lower the non-wage costs of social security payments made by employ-ers and employees in order to lower the price of German products on the world markets. Such a policy was expected to increase demand and thereby employment. It reached agreement on reforming the country's antiquated naturalization laws.

In foreign and defense policies, the party leaders did not foresee mak-ing major changes. They pledged the country's continued support of the United Nations, the European Union, and NATO. The latter became a pressing issue months later when NATO members, Germany included, concurred on an aerial bombardment of Yugoslavia during the Kosovo crisis. German planes took part in the bombardment and the govern-ment provided troops for the international peacekeeping forces.

In addition to agreeing on a government program, the negotiating teams also reached agreement on the composition of the new cabinet. On 27 October, the newly installed Bundestag formally elected Schröder as the new chancellor. Federal President Roman Herzog administered the oath of office to Schröder and the fifteen cabinet ministers, most of whom were SPD leaders. They included Oskar Lafontaine (Finance), Otto Schily (Interior), Rudolf Scharping (Defense), and Herta Däubler-Gmelin (Justice). Werner Müller, without party affiliation, became min-ister of Economics and Technology. Three Greens leaders, Joschka Fischer (Foreign Ministry), Andrea Fischer (Health), and Jürgen Trittin (Envi-ronment, Conservation, and Reactor Safety), received posts. Schröder appointed Bodo Hombach, his close political advisor, as head of the Chancellery. Most of the appointees were baby boomers and veterans of the 1968 generation who had then been leftists but who had gradually become more mainstream.

The First Hundred Days: A Mixed Record

Schröder initiated a series of domestic reforms, such as tax reductions for the lowest-income individuals, that he had promised to make during the campaign. But soon the new government ran into problems. Ministers, who lacked experience and professional work, publicly disagreed with one another's proposals, which often were prepared too hastily and then corrected too hastily. The Chancellery had coordination problems with the legislative proposals. The new government's image was marred. Minister of Finance Lafontaine's plan to swiftly eliminate tax loopholes in order to raise more revenue, and his plan to impose a higher electricity tax on all industries and consumers, produced a storm of protest from the business community. Lafontaine, pressured by the chancellor, had to retreat. He disclosed that some tax loopholes would not be closed until 2000. Energy-intensive industries would be fully exempt from the new electricity tax, while most industrial firms would have to pay only one-fourth of the proposed new tax. Three SPD minister-presidents, hewing to the New Middle line, did not support Lafontaine's tax plans either. They insisted that the projected energy taxes would not raise enough revenue and opted instead for deeper cuts in individual and corporate taxes than planned in order to promote economic growth. The intra-party schism was unlikely to be healed.

Lafontaine, who was called "Little Napoleon" or "Red Oskar" by his detractors, repeatedly urged the Bundesbank, an independent agency, to cut interest rates to spur the economy and reduce the persistent high unemployment. The bankers told him that they made their decisions independently of any government pressures. He proffered similar advice to the European Central Bank and received the same answer. Yet on 3 December 1998, the ECB cut interest rates. Lafontaine urged the other European Union governments, of whom thirteen out of fifteen (Spain and Ireland excepted) were governed by social democrats and socialists, to eliminate unfair tax competition and coordinate wage policies between them in order to create more jobs for the nearly 17 million unemployed in the EU states. Lafontaine was ready to battle the globalized economy with supranational controls, but he received little support from the chancellor.

The much-publicized Alliance for Jobs met in December 1998 and on occasion thereafter to discuss ways of expanding employment and other pressing problems. To allay the business hostility to some government policies, Schröder announced that corporate taxes would be lowered in 2000 rather than 2002. In turn, business leaders promised to offer full, voluntary retirement benefits to workers at age 60 rather than the existing minimum age of 65 for men and 62 for women. Earlier retirements were expected to open up new jobs for younger workers. Schröder continued to block the swift phasing out of nuclear power plants, and in the following months rejected the recycling of junked cars, stronger summer smog controls, and other environmental proposals that Environment Minister Jürgen Trittin and other Green Party leaders had made. The Greens were discouraged that few of their proposals had been accepted by the chancellor.

Post-1998 Election Blues

In 1999, in a series of Land, European Parliament, and local elections, the SPD reeled from one defeat to another. Normally, the national governing parties suffer some setbacks in Land elections in the interval between federal elections because the Land contests often serve as a barometer of public attitudes on national issues. But in this instance, the SPD experienced unprecedented electoral reverses in the first year of its governance.

There were numerous reasons for these setbacks. The SPD-Green government in Bonn (and later in Berlin) was unable to avoid repeated dissension on intra-party and inter-party policy issues. The most dramatic one, the sudden resignation of Lafontaine as minister of finance, SPD chairperson, and Bundestag deputy on 11 March 1999, was the result of the ideological gulf between him and Schröder. The two leaders, who had portrayed themselves as a close team during the election campaign, differed sharply on economic policies. Lafontaine, backed by the unions, took exception to Schröder's kowtowing to the business community on taxation policies, but could not convince the chancellor to shift course. In a bitter parting shot at Schröder, Lafontaine complained of the "poor teamwork" that the government had provided in the first few months. His resignation signified a defeat for the left-wing traditionalists, who were in a minority in the SPD Fraktion, and a victory for the pro-business modernizers.[16]

The rank-and-file members, who had lost their leader, became demoralized. Many, especially those with low or modest incomes, felt betrayed by the Schröder government and stayed home rather than vote for the SPD in the Länder elections.

Their disappointment was heightened by the government's new austerity plan, approved by the cabinet in summer 1999. Schröder and Finance Minister Hans Eichel claimed that the SPD-Green government had inherited a debt of nearly DM 1.5 trillion ($900 billion) and an annual structural deficit of DM 30 billion ($18 billion) from the Kohl government, which was guilty of fiscal mismanagement. Eichel called for painful budget cuts of $16 billion, including a 7 percent average cut in all ministerial budgets. The plan called for reductions in social spending, a slower rate of increase in pensions, tax cuts for businesses, and an increase in fuel taxes. Designed to galvanize a slow economy, fight unemployment, and stabilize the Euro, it was strongly criticized by SPD traditionalists who suggested, unsuccessfully, a tax on wealth. In late 1999 the plan was passed by the Bundestag.

During summer 1999 there were other causes for voter disillusionment with Schröder, such as his cigar-smoking appearances in luxury suits and his month-long August vacation at the Italian resort of Positano at a time when the government was calling for austerity. Many voters did not like his style of governing and his zigzag course on some policy issues. SPD activists disliked his condescension toward the party. The voters' disappointment with the government came as early as February 1999, when Hesse held the first Land election after the September 1998 national election. The SPD and the Greens were confident that they would be able to form another coalition government in the former SPD stronghold. Although the SPD made slight electoral gains, the Greens suffered large losses. As a result, the CDU formed a new government, which caused the SPD to lose its slim majority in the Bundesrat. The Schröder government could no longer expect to carry out its legislative agenda without serious challenges from the Bundesrat on bills affecting the Länder. As long as the CDU/CSU can block bills in the Bundesrat, the government will have to make concessions to the CDU/CSU if it expects to enact important legislation.

One such bill was the government's plan, put forth by the Greens, to revise Germany's restrictive laws on citizenship and naturalization. Before the Hesse election, the CDU/CSU had waged a strong initiative campaign, which gathered five million signatures nationwide, against the bill's projected dual citizenship provision for naturalized citizens. After the Hesse election, the national government accepted a watered-down FDP proposal that children born in Germany, of whom at least one parent was born in Germany or had legally come to the country before the age of fourteen, would no longer have permanent dual citizenship. Such children would have to opt for German or foreign citizenship at the age of 23.[17] The Schröder government could have strengthened its case on the citizenship issue if it had waged a campaign to win over the public, but it never took such an initiative.

In May 1999, the SPD, as anticipated, received enough support from the Greens and other members at a federal convention to elect Johannes Rau, former SPD minister-president of North Rhine-Westphalia, as the new federal president, succeeding Roman Herzog (CDU). But this victory could not staunch further reverses for the SPD in the June national election to the European Parliament. The party had difficulty mobilizing both its traditional voters and its New Middle voters who had cast their ballots for the party for the first time in the 1998 national election. Although most of these voters supported the government's unprecedented military involvement in NATO military actions against Serbia in the Kosovo conflict, the economic problems at home were of greater importance to them.

In September, the SPD suffered further reverses in Land elections. In the Saar, the CDU, which won by a 2 percent margin over the SPD, replaced the fourteen-year-old SPD government, led for many years by Lafontaine. In Brandenburg, the SPD's share of the vote tumbled from 54 percent in 1994 to 39 percent, despite the popularity of Minister-President Manfred Stolpe, forcing it into a coalition with the CDU. In Thuringia the CDU captured a majority of votes and no longer had to govern with the SPD. In Saxony, the SPD slumped to a bare 10 percent of the vote, the lowest it had received in any Land election since 1949. The CDU again won a majority of the vote, partly because its minister-president is highly popular and partly because it is viewed once more as the party most competent to deal with economic policies. The PDS gained more votes than the SPD because voters see it as the party able to achieve social justice and to cope with the specific problems of east Germans. Finally, in local elections in North Rhine-Westphalian cities, the traditional strongholds of the party, where the SPD had held twenty of twenty-three lord mayor positions, it lost half to the CDU candidates. SPD scandals in several cities contributed to the party's disaster. In summing up all the defeats, an Italian newspaper said that for Schröder, "governing must be as much fun as a convention of undertakers."[18]

Conclusion

After the fall of the SPD-FDP cabinet in 1982, the SPD had difficulty regaining power at the national level, despite its functioning in a multiparty democratic system where the political pendulum swings from left to right and back again. Internal and external causes weakened the party's chance to recapture control of the government. The intra-party leadership struggles, the factional divisions, the ideological battles, and the corruption scandals in SPD-controlled cities marred its image. Its problems were compounded by external factors, such as a politically conservative climate, changing milieus and social groups, postunification economic and psychological issues, frequent voters' perceptions that the CDU/CSU was more able than the SPD to solve pressing economic problems, and, with exceptions, unsympathetic media.

Thus the SPD, which had spent sixteen years in opposition and could hardly overcome these internal and external obstacles, had cause to celebrate its victory in the 1998 national election. The Greens had equal cause to celebrate their unprecedented entrance into a national coalition cabinet. Schröder's insistence that the SPD had to widen its net and attract the votes of middle-of-the-road citizens if it ever was going to win a national election proved correct. But in the process of forming a coalition with the Greens and agreeing on a common government program, the new chancellor insisted that it reflect New Middle goals. When such a policy meant that an austerity program, which was not going to affect the wealthy as much as the poor, would have to be pursued, the SPD's traditionalist voters expressed their displeasure by staying home in the 1999 Land and local elections.

The SPD will need to draw conclusions from the dramatic reverses it suffered in these elections. Whether it can reverse the downward trend by hewing faithfully to Schröder's vague New Middle line is problematic. In June 1999 Schröder issued a joint manifesto with Prime Minister Blair that summarized their left-centrist philosophies.[19] The neoliberal manifesto, replete with such concepts as "modern," "innovative," "performance," and "individual responsibility," further alienated the SPD traditionalist voters. Yet the chancellor made it clear that he viewed the Third Way/New Middle document as the basis for a discussion within the SPD on a new basic program to supplant the 1990 Berlin program. He calls for a redefinition of the concept of social justice, important to the traditionalists, in the face of cutbacks to the welfare state and changes in foreign and security policies. At the December 1999 convention, the delegates were expected to create a program commission, headed by Schröder and Scharping, to work on a basic program that might reconcile the clashing views of traditionalists and modernizers. The program is expected to be ready in time for the national election in 2002.[20]

The SPD can ill afford to wait until then. Schröder's government policies need to incorporate more of the party's traditional values of social justice and equality, such as imposing higher taxes on giant firms and wealthy individuals, in any fiscal austerity plan. Schröder's failure to show such flexibility may rob the party of victory in the crucial North Rhine-Westphalia election of May 2000. Should the party be defeated then, Schröder may draw the consequences and resign as chancellor and party chairperson or form a grand coalition with the CDU/CSU. Normally, a loss of one Land election will not produce such a shakeup, but in this instance it would be the culmination of a series of party losses in Land elections. The reverses show not only that Schröder was unable to hold on to many of the SPD's core voters, but also that he lost to the centrist voters who were disillusioned by the government's failure to make significant policy changes. The SPD cannot afford such losses. Schröder is hoping that budget and tax cuts will stimulate investment and produce a noticeable increase in employment by the time of the next round of state elections. Without any substantial improvement in this area, Germany's first red-green government will have a difficult time at the next federal election in 2002.

Notes

1. For details, see Stephen J. Silvia, "The Social Democratic Party of Germany," in David P. Conradt, Gerald R. Kleinfeld, George K. Romoser, and Christian Søe, eds., *Germany's New Politics: Parties and Issues in the 1990s* (Providence and Oxford, 1995), 149–170.

2. SPD Vorstand, "Mitgliederstruktur: Mitgliederstand per 31.12.96" (mimeo, n.d.).

3. Gerard Braunthal, *The German Social Democrats Since 1969: A Party in Power and Opposition* (Boulder, Colo.: Westview Press, 1994), 27–24.

4. *Der Spiegel*, no. 17, 22 April 1996.

5. *Süddeutsche Zeitung*, 3 July 1997.

6. Gerard Braunthal, "The SPD Leaders in Power and Opposition," in *The Federal Republic of Germany at Fifty: The End of a Century of Turmoil*, ed. Peter H. Merkl (Houndmills, Basingstoke, Hampshire, England, 1999), 118.

7. Gerard Braunthal, "Opposition in the Kohl Era: The SPD and the Left," *German Politics* 7, no. 7 (April 1998):158.

8. See, e.g., Anthony Giddens, *The Third Way: The Renewal of Social Democracy* (Cambridge: Cambridge University Press, 1998).

9. Jane Kramer, "The Once and Future Chancellor," *New Yorker* (14 September 1998): 64.

10. Gerard Braunthal, "The 1998 German Election: Gerhard Schröder and the Politics of the New Middle," *German Politics and Society* 17, no 1 (Spring 1999): 36–38.

11. Ibid., 38–43.

12. Simon Green, "The 1998 German Bundestag Election: The End of an Era," *Parliamentary Affairs* 52, no. 2 (1999): 307.

13. Forschungsgruppe Wahlen, "Bundestagswahl 1998: Eine Analyse der Wahl vom 27. September 1998" (Mannheim, 1998), 18, 22, 72–73; Ulrich von Alemann, "Der Wahlsieg der SPD von 1998: Politische Achsenverschiebung oder glücklicher Ausreisser?" in *Die Parteien nach der Bundestagswahl 1998*, ed. Oskar Niedermayer (Opladen: Westdeutscher Verlag, 1999), 52.

14. Infratest institute, cited by dpa press release, 28 September 1998; Infas institute, cited by Reuters press release, 28 September 1998.

15. Andrew B. Denison, "The SPD: Between Political Drift and Direction," in *Between Bonn and Berlin: German Politics Adrift?*, ed. Mary N. Hampton and Christian Søe (Lanham, Md.: Rowman and Littlefield, 1999): 89.

16. *New York Times*, 14 March 1999.

17. GIC, *The Week in Germany*, 12 February 1999.

18. *La Reppublica*, 13 September 1999.

19. Tony Blair and Gerhard Schröder, Europe The Third Way (London, 1999); *Süddeutsche Zeitung*, 24 August 1999.

20. See SPD, Grundwertekommission, "Dritte Wege – Neue Mitte: Sozialdemokratische Markierungen für Reformpolitik im Zeitalter der Globalisierung" (Berlin, 1999); *Tageszeitung* (Berlin), 16 September 1999.

Chapter 3

THE LAST HURRAH

Helmut Kohl's CDU/CSU and the 1998 Election

Clay Clemens

On 27 September 1998, Christian Democratic Union leaders gathered for a last Bundestag election night vigil at their Bonn party headquarters, the Konrad Adenauer House. After sixteen years in office under Helmut Kohl, the CDU and its Bavarian Christian Social Union sister (CSU) hoped for a new lease on life. To be sure, having trailed in the polls all year, they had scant hope of retaining a majority with their Free Democratic (FDP) ally. Yet Kohl's Union did seem to be closing in on the rival Social Democrats as election day drew near: it still hoped to remain Germany's strongest force, and head any new government. Those in attendance expected at least a close race, and a long night.

But projections that popped up on monitors around the large press room sent most home early—or into the bar for solace: their Union would suffer its worst defeat in five decades and be relegated to opposition. Within an hour, Chancellor Kohl—the man most responsible for both their past success and 1998's debacle—came on to give his first concession speech in twenty-two years.

Why did the Union lose—and lose so badly? The blame lay mainly with problems of climate and competence: after sixteen years, most voters were just ready for change, and could see no reason to reward a party that seemed unable to solve their major concerns, like unemployment. Yet defeat on this scale also called into question the party's choice of candidates: Germans lauded Kohl's past record, but wanted a new face. Then there was the chancellor's campaign itself: having learned history's lessons *too* well, he and top aides had trusted in an old formula that even many allies openly discounted, turning his last hurrah into a lost cause.

To some, the Union defeat also seemed to reflect and portend deeper or broader trends: generational change, even a whole new era in German politics, and a decline of center-right parties throughout the industrialized world. Yet much would depend on what lessons the CDU/CSU drew from this setback, and whether it sank into bitter disarray or handled opposition successfully.

A Long-Running Show: Kohl's CDU/CSU in the 1990s

The CDU/CSU was accustomed to power. During West Germany's first two decades (1949–69), it led governments in Bonn: first in an alliance with the smaller FDP, later in a brief grand coalition with the SPD. Feeling betrayed when those two parties cast it into opposition in 1969, the CDU recovered under its new, young reformist federal chair, Helmut Kohl. Though long underrated by rivals, he became the Union chancellor candidate and nearly helped it regain power in 1976. Thereafter, with a second title—head of the joint CDU/CSU Bundestag caucus—Kohl kept working to woo back the FDP as a partner, albeit cautiously: his CSU ally, accustomed to winning power on its own in conservative Bavaria, resisted "appeasing" the Liberals. In 1982 he was finally elected chancellor of a new middle-right governing alliance.[1]

Despite economic and diplomatic success, his government often seemed beset by feuds among CDU progressives, representing urban blue-collar Catholics or liberal Protestants, and conservatives from its middle-class, business, professional or farm base, as well as from the more cohesive, semiautonomous CSU. Anxious to stay above the 5 percent level needed for Bundestag seats, the centrist, market-oriented FDP also pressed its own agenda. Kohl's tolerance of quarrels undercut the coalition's image, and his own. Still, they came from behind in the polls to win in 1987.

After another slump, party foes planned a putsch against him in 1989. But his network of elite-level allies, moderating role among CDU factions, and contact with ordinary functionaries gave him a strong hand as chair, which also shielded his claim to remain chancellor: the party had long agreed that linking the two jobs made for effective leadership. And unlike voters in general, CDU supporters—as always—rated him above any colleague. The CSU and FDP also saw it as in their own interests for him to remain. Soon thereafter, he shrewdly seized upon the collapse of the Communist German Democratic Republic (GDR) to help reunite his nation's eastern and western halves. After this bold diplomatic triumph, his coalition crushed the SPD under Oskar Lafontaine in 1990.

But rebuilding the East's ruined economy took longer and cost more than Kohl had pledged, deepening a recession and forcing him to break a no-tax pledge. Strife wracked CDU branches in the "new Länder," which also charged Union allies in the richer West with neglecting their region. Passing bills in Bonn's two legislative chambers sparked more wrangling. Amid Land election setbacks and sagging popularity, his team again appeared at risk. Yet he benefited from his record in pushing German (and now European) unity; a modest but timely economic recovery; and the SPD's controversial decision to cooperate with eastern Germany's Party of Democratic Socialism (PDS), heir to GDR Communism. Besting a lackluster foe, Kohl helped the coalition eke out a narrow win in 1994.

Contrary to previous postelection letdowns, his government's fourth full term began auspiciously amid pledges of domestic policy reforms. As the CDU held a gala celebration of its fiftieth birthday, his Union hit an unusually high 52 percent support level, while a hopelessly torn SPD sank to 27 percent. Given his stature as Europe's premier statesman, and a moderation that compared favorably with the partisanship of rival opposition leaders, Kohl saw his popularity surge further to levels not seen since 1990. Rather than having to justify another run, he now faced calls from CDU, CSU, and business leaders to stand yet again.[2] In late 1996 he would break Adenauer's record of thirteen years in office.

Yet events were already eroding his position. After the 1994 upturn, the economy again slowed, and joblessness hit a postwar record of four million. Kohl's idea of a labor-industry "Alliance for Jobs" soon foundered, and his pledge to cut unemployment by two million by the year 2000 was shelved. While he could cite signs of growth, the East's economy in particular stagnated and joblessness remained at 20 percent. Anger grew there at FDP demands to cut a "solidarity" tax that funded western subsidies, CDU plans for allowing pre-1949 landholders to reclaim property in the ex-GDR, and talk by prosperous Union-governed western Länder about no longer sharing revenue with poorer regions, above all the East.

Kohl's team had pledged to spur investment by cutting outlays and labor costs through tax and entitlement reforms. But his sharp policy-oriented protégé, Caucus Chief Wolfgang Schäuble—wheelchair-bound since a 1990 attempt on his life—was blocked. CDU Labor Minister Norbert Blüm, the last member of Kohl's 1982 cabinet and a key ally, led fellow progressives (and easterners) in seeking to shield benefits for workers, senior citizens, or families, while taxing the wealthy. They clashed with their own party's business wing, and with Finance Minister Theo Waigel, who as CSU chair played a pivotal role in the coalition. Deriding the Union as a "second Social Democratic party," FDP leaders like Guido Westerwelle pressed it to agree to deep tax cuts and other investment relief. Thus coalition reform plans—except one to cap pensions—were mired in bitter debate even before making it to parliament. By early 1997, Waigel was coming under bitter CDU attack, Blüm was threatening to quit, Schäuble faced fire from all sides, and Union-FDP tensions were mounting. Given his penchant for consensus, Kohl hoped to satisfy everyone, but he lacked the expertise to hammer out compromise on such complex issues and was reluctant to help press his caucus chief's case for strong reforms for fear of damaging the coalition. Worse, opposition chief Lafontaine demanded a price for letting bills pass the SPD-dominated Bundesrat: Schäuble could not lure enough opposition leaders into defecting on key votes, and Kohl would not prod his Union or the FDP into major concessions, counting instead on voters to blame Lafontaine for "blockading" reform. Polls did show concern that such strife would hurt the economy, but since the coalition's own proposals were often seen as favoring the rich, the SPD suffered no backlash.[3]

Nor did foreign policy, Kohl's forte, help him politically. Amid debate, his government had sent peacekeeping troops to Bosnia, but it became a forgotten victory. His friendship with the erratic Boris Yeltsin undergirded Bonn's key eastern relationship, yet Russia remained a question mark. Above all, Kohl's lobbying helped to propel European monetary union (EMU). However, though Germans were pro-integration, they worried that losing their strong deutsche mark might mean inflation: EMU's political value remained unclear.[4]

By early 1997, 58 percent of voters rated the government negatively, and Kohl's appeal had slumped from +1.0 on a ±5 scale a year earlier to -0.1: a 56 percent majority now disapproved of his performance as chancellor.[5] Infighting, stalemate, and grim polls led to hints that molding a durable consensus might require in Bonn what existed in many Länder: a grand coalition. CDU progressives did not disagree, nor did easterners (FDP free market ideas had scant appeal in their region). The results-oriented Schäuble declared that a grand coalition would be no "national disaster": many thought that he would gladly ditch the Liberals, and indeed had even pushed economic reform partly in order to make them superfluous. But CSU leaders resisted sharply, uneasy that a pact with the SPD would hurt them in Bavaria and reduce their influence nationally. Though irked with FDP tax cut demands and Bavarian pressures, Kohl avoided even hinting at a grand coalition for fear of further rattling his allies: he would be unlikely to remain chancellor in any government with the SPD, and thus counted on his battered team to muddle through.

Yet Kohl's party was facing problems too, and he had bound it so closely to his coalition that they now seemed to be dragging each other down. Despite his talk of fostering CDU identity with a new program, it remained indistinguishable from government policy. His quest for consensus in the coalition kept straining relations among party factions. Partly for these reasons, membership continued sinking, from the record of 735,000 in his earlier days to 674,000 in 1994. By 1997, only 636,000 remained. Their average age was 53, despite his hope to woo younger Germans with, for example, a new youth ministry. CDU members, candidates, and officials remained three-quarters male even after the congress passed a loose quota for nominating women in 1996 (a stronger version had been rebuffed in 1995). Federal decision-making bodies he had once talked of empowering remained inert. Whereas past general-secretaries like prominent progressives Kurt Biedenkopf or Heiner Geissler had been top CDU strategists, loyal Peter Hintze rarely questioned the chancellor. His Bonn party headquarters dealt mainly with campaign logistics and publicity.

CDU party branches in each Land had more autonomy to chart their own course, yet even they could not escape Kohl's effort to promote candidates for chair or minister-president (such as the unsuccessful Johannes Gerster in Rhineland-Palatinate), or the effect of his federal government's image problems. To be sure, after February 1995—when Hesse's CDU fell from 40.2 percent to 39.2 percent, failing to kill a red-green government there—the party gained in most Land elections through 1997. Yet in all but two, it was already in opposition, near a twenty-year low in voter support, and still did not retake power. In May 1995, the CDU under Blüm helped end an absolute SPD majority in North Rhine-Westphalia, but did not become a real factor in Germany's largest Land. Bremen's chronically weak CDU made a tiny gain, rising to 32.6 percent and forcing the SPD to form a grand coalition. Such a government existed in Berlin before that city's autumn 1995 election, and after: mayor Eberhard Diepgen's party fell from 40.7 percent to 37.4 percent.

In two old bastions where the CDU had been waning, opposition missteps helped it to regain lost ground in 1996, though not enough to retake power. In Kohl's own Rhineland-Palatinate, the party rose one point to 39.7 percent, too little to oust an SPD-FDP coalition. Schleswig-Holstein's troubled CDU gained 3.4 percent, but its 37.2 percent did not jeopardize the red-green government. An anti-EU campaign by SPD leaders in Baden-Württemberg helped the CDU there gain 1.7 percent, ending a grand coalition. But 41.3 percent was its second-worst result since 1964 in this bastion, and the right-wing Republikaner won a dismaying 9 percent. Finally, at Hamburg in 1997, the CDU's weakest Western Land branch would gain 5 percent, though that just nudged it over 30 percent.

As of 1997, Kohl's CDU in the West thus governed with the FDP in only one Land, Baden-Württemberg, while serving in grand coalitions in Bremen and Berlin. Everywhere else it was in opposition. Voters were drifting to the SPD or smaller right-wing rivals. New generation leaders, the CDU's "young wild ones"—like Christian Wulff in Lower-Saxony and Roland Koch in Hesse—griped that the Bonn coalition's image could also hurt their future prospects.

Badly divided party branches in the new Länder were fortunate not to face elections in 1994–97. Veterans of the 134,000-member, Communist-era, pro-regime East-CDU—which Kohl had absorbed into his Union—remained a majority. But these old-guard leaders faced calls to account for their past from anti-GDR newcomers to the party, "reformists" like Environment Minister Angela Merkel. In 1996, Hintze swelled the latter ranks by luring top Communist-era democratic dissidents away from the SPD and Greens, a brief public relations success that did not ease frictions. Moreover, all native eastern CDU leaders were still just learning partisan democratic politics. Many either cut a poor image, or could not yet effectively preserve discipline. Brandenburg's CDU gained and lost five chairs in the 1990s. Only in Thuringia and Saxony was the CDU stable, thanks to western imports: Kohl's ally Bernhard Vogel, and his former general-secretary Biedenkopf, now a critic.

Worse, as 1994's brief recovery faded, joblessness, perceived domination by the West, and a related GDR nostalgia in eastern Germany sparked voter anger at Kohl's coalition. Many CDU leaders there saw the party in Bonn as indifferent to their region. They also warned that harsh western attacks on the ex-Communist PDS would only boost its image as an advocate of eastern interests. In 1996, two spokesman cautioned that their CDU would become a permanent minority in the new Länder unless its branches became more autonomous, like the CSU, and outbid the PDS by more freely voicing the East's unique concern for subsidies or taxes on rich westerners. Others opposed such separatism, yet also warned Bonn colleagues to treat the new Länder more delicately. Losing members and reliant on western funds, the eastern CDU crumbled.[6]

While more cohesive than its northern sister, the CSU also faced discord in the mid-1990s. Finance Minister Waigel played a key role in coalition efforts at economic reform, yet as party chair he faced pressure from back home. His rival, popular Minister-President Edmund Stoiber, pressed for a more conservative line and robust defense of Bavarian interests in order to shield the CSU's absolute majority from inroads by small right-wing parties. Each man rallied his supporters amid mounting factional tension.

As Kohl's divided coalition and Union limped toward another election, they faced a surprisingly united SPD under Lafontaine. A once-wide gap in the polls had eroded, and by early 1997 the latter enjoyed a widening lead.[7] Ever more voters viewed Kohl as ineffective and used up: he could still match Lafontaine in the polls, but slipped against another potential SPD rival: Lower Saxony's popular, moderate minister-president, Gerhard Schröder.

Not surprisingly, speculation about Kohl's future mounted. On two occasions since 1990 he had alluded to retiring of his own volition, something no chancellor had ever done. He had also hinted at an heir: Schäuble, whose mastery of policy detail and firm rhetoric won respect in the caucus, along with broader voter and media appeal than his boss (Defense Minister Volker Rühe's solid performance in a tough job gave him the next-best odds). Detecting alleged signs of Kohl's weariness or dejection, and noting the polls, many wondered if he might now pass the torch. Yet the chancellor wanted to leave on his own terms, from a position of strength and in a way that left his coalition intact. Thus he had never clearly named a date for a handover, and even chided his protégé not to push or overrate good press.[8] Kohl also longed to be in office for EMU's completion and the German government's 1999 relocation to Berlin. In any case, his self-confidence had weathered many such trials: if anything, the polls and skepticism steeled his resolve to stay on. Moreover, Kohl knew that some colleagues still resented Schäuble's taskmaster style, CDU progressives like Blüm resisted his zeal for economic reform, the CSU suspected him of wanting a deal with the SPD, and many still quietly doubted that he could campaign or govern from a wheelchair. Kohl did not share these reservations, but sensed that they might make a transition now risky for the government.

Thus, as 1997 slipped by and his ratings fell, Kohl let the window of opportunity for a handover slide shut. Old CDU critics like Biedenkopf and some "young wild ones" became more vocal in arguing that the party needed a fresh leader for the 1998 campaign: Schäuble fared better in the polls against Schröder, whose moderation on economics and crime not only won ever more public support, but threatened to steal Union issues. Some talked of urging Kohl to go, but knew that a coup against so entrenched a leader would be suicidally divisive, especially since his own loyalists were urging him to work his magic one more time.

In late 1997 Kohl at last formalized his plans to run again. An October CDU congress in Leipzig cheered his announcement. Yet delegates applauded Schäuble's fiery speech more vigorously.[9] As a concession, Kohl then openly endorsed his protégé as Germany's future leader—*after* another full term (he could not ask voters to reelect him in 1998 for just two years, the chancellor said). This move left many curious, and some furious. Schäuble's fans grumbled that he was being strung out longer, while the CSU—still wary of his hints at a grand coalition, and angry at not being consulted—resisted any anointment of a crown prince. Perhaps by design, Kohl had sparked a debate that showed how hard it would be for the Union to agree on replacing him just yet.

One Act Too Many: Kohl and the CDU/CSU's 1998 Campaign

Despite being well down in the polls as 1998 began, Kohl felt confident of bringing his team back yet again. The Union's voter base was larger than its SPD rival's, and his FDP ally had always defied skeptics by making 5 percent: this core support just needed to be mobilized. As in 1994, he and his aides counted on a recovery to help restore the coalition's image for economic competence; they also still hoped that voters would penalize SPD hardliners for blockading reform, and reward his push to unify Europe. A "Kohl curve" would then recur, as his opinion poll ratings overtook those of the SPD, allowing him to overtake any challenger.

Experience assured him that it would be Lafontaine, who had a strong base as party chair, would campaign on themes popular with its left wing, and could lead a red-green alliance. By contrast, while the telegenic moderate Schröder's talk of a "new middle" had broader support among voters and business leaders, Kohl saw him as a maverick without SPD roots who favored a grand coalition over a pact with the Greens. In any case, if Lafontaine sought to be nominated, the chancellor felt—again, based on his own past—that the SPD could not balk for fear of undercutting its own chair. And having beaten this rival in 1990 added to his confidence.

Kohl planned a traditional *Lagerwahlkampf*—a campaign that polarized opinion, mobilizing mainstream center-right voters by citing the risky alternative: an SPD led by ideologues who had blocked reform, would govern with the radical Greens, and even accepted PDS support (in the East). Though defined mainly by what it asked voters to oppose, this approach also upheld the chancellor himself as a guarantor of moderation, consensus, and stability at home, as well as continuity and credibility abroad.

CDU/CSU conservatives and many moderates agreed. Though irked with the FDP, they favored Kohl's government to the "collective political suicide" of a grand coalition. Though often critical of the chancellor for neglecting domestic policy and failing to consult them or exert discipline, the CSU in particular still saw him as a barrier to any experiments, such as a deal with the SPD. And most conservatives also preferred a *Lagerwahlkampf* against the left, which—bolstered by Kohl's record as statesman—they felt could still ultimately rally traditional Union supporters.

But surveys convinced many others that old formulas could not save Kohl's Union-FDP majority this time. Already seeing a grand coalition as the only hope for retaining a share of power, some in the CDU favored this broad alliance as a way to end stalemate on reform, provided that their Union still held more seats than the SPD (no one could imagine serving under a Social Democratic chancellor: the CSU would leave the caucus before doing so). And even those who still believed in Kohl's coalition doubted that he could bring it victory: his was just too familiar a face. Many young or progressive CDU members felt that they had to offer voters someone new, especially if facing Schröder. If Kohl insisted on running again, most agreed that he should at least share the limelight with Schäuble in a form of dual campaign leadership—and finally name a date for his own departure from office.

These skeptics all agreed that his *Lagerwahlkampf* offered voters nothing new and could not work, especially if the SPD went with Schröder's "ideology-free" campaign (CDU Easterners worried that it would simply mean more ritual condemnation of the PDS). They thus preferred Schäuble's proposal for a "discussion-oriented strategy": a point-by-point case for the best policies on taxes, pensions, and health care, which could turn the election into a referendum between his caucus's plans and opposition alternatives (or lack thereof). Union victory, this strategy implied, might compel the SPD Bundesrat majority—which would last beyond 1998—to abandon any "blockades" and accept real reforms. Moreover, by hinting at a consensus on ends, if not means, this option also had a bipartisan aura: unlike Kohl's *Lagerwahlkampf*, it did not require casting the SPD as riskily left-wing, and thus tacitly left more latitude for a grand coalition should the FDP not survive.

Who would run the campaign was as contentious an issue as its content. General-Secretary Hintze set up a select election commission at CDU headquarters, yet was increasingly confined to logistics and publicity. With greater policy expertise, Schäuble's caucus would dominate the body drafting a CDU "future program," the basis for a joint Union election platform. Though he defended Hintze from frequent public attack, Kohl too accorded him a minor role, and in any case preferred to see his caucus chief handling divisive policy details. And as in 1994, Kohl planned to make all key decisions with an inner circle of chancellory aides led by Friedrich Bohl, who would play a discreet but key role.

A Cold Shock

Union hopes took a blow early in 1998 when SPD leaders agreed to treat Lower Saxony's Landtag election as a chancellor primary: if Schröder's party made gains there, he would be crowned chancellor candidate, with Lafontaine conceding. Counting on and needing the latter's camp to prevail, Kohl threw himself even more vigorously than usual into this Land election. He appeared often in Lower Saxony with the CDU's young candidate, urging voters to "Reject Schröder [and] elect Christian Wulff." Without mentioning the minister-president's national ambitions, Kohl stressed this contest's federal implications. He hoped that Wulff could at least take votes from the SPD, end its absolute majority, and burden

Schröder with a Green coalition partner, reinforcing Union claims that this risk faced all of Germany.[10]

But Schröder's party made gains on March 1, and Lafontaine did concede. Suddenly the CDU/CSU faced a united SPD led not by its left-wing chair, but by a popular moderate with vague populist views insulated from easy attack. The chancellor tried to rally his Union against this "media phenomenon," demanding "Herr Schröder, what do you stand for?"[11] Yet CDU critics charged that Kohl had stumbled by campaigning so hard as to build his rival up into an equal and helping turn this regional race into a test of national support. CSU leaders also faulted his tactical error.[12]

Usually rallying by this stage of an election, Kohl soon trailed Schröder by three to one, and his party slumped as well. Critics compared him to George Bush, who—despite foreign policy success—had fallen to a pragmatic young outsider, or drew grim parallels with the collapse of Britain's Tories against Blair's new Labour.[13] Days later, adding insult to injury, his coalition split badly in Bundestag balloting on a key law enforcement bill.

Panicky CDU politicians began urging Kohl's aides to prod him into making way for Schäuble, who was not as far behind Schröder: polls showed that a switch would lift the Union by four points.[14] Critics openly urged Kohl to at least name a retirement date, or accept a dual leadership.[15] While stressing that he "naturally" stood by the chancellor of unity, Schäuble also cautioned the Union against a U.S.-style campaign built around one candidate.[16] Yet Kohl would not budge voluntarily, and regicide so close to elections risked bloody civil war. While reaffirming a wish to see Schäuble—"an excellent man"—succeed him, he still insisted "There is no reason to change the campaign strategy."[17] Supporters argued that only his stature could match Schröder's media skill, and a *Lagerwahlkampf* could still exploit red-green differences. Schäuble's critics began implying that the cerebral caucus chief lacked an emotional bond with Union activists, or even quietly fed doubts about a wheelchair-bound candidate. Though wary that Kohl's unpopularity might drag the CSU down in Bavaria's own fall Land election, Stoiber and his Bonn colleagues like Waigel—in rare accord—reaffirmed their support for the chancellor. Union voters split evenly on whom their party should nominate.[18] Insiders spoke of factions emerging around two men long seen as friends, even father and son. Their public praise for each other did not dispel such rumors, or a perceived need for mediation by mutual allies like Transport Minister Matthias Wissmann.

Seeking unity, Hintze suggested a CDU "campaign of direction" that would attack its foes on both ideological and policy grounds.[19] Such a tactic seemed promising, for the SPD's likely Green ally unveiled some controversial plans in March. Pouncing eagerly, the Union charged that withdrawing German peacekeepers from Bosnia or opposing NATO enlargement would hurt Bonn's image as an ally. The Greens' proposed big "ecological gas tax" hike was an even easier target: Hintze's headquarters launched a "fuel pump" flier to mobilize consumer anger. Green approval plummeted, eroding the center-left's lead. The CDU gained at Schleswig-Holstein's local elections.

But in April, Schäuble unveiled his draft "future program," labeling it more honest than Schröder's vague promises. One plank called for an energy tax: as he told caucus members, the Union had raised this idea before, and should not shelve it now just because of the Greens' much more extreme variant.[20] Though he did stipulate that such a tax be EU-wide, it still undercut Hintze's attack on the left. Schäuble's critics—above all the CSU—blasted him for undermining the campaign. Grumbling that his anointment as heir had proven a headache, he fended them off.[21] Caucus and Land allies praised his consistency. Also reluctant to see his successor savaged, Kohl defended him too—albeit without rebuking the CSU—and asked Wissmann to work out a compromise tax policy statement. Yet just as the SPD nominated Schröder in a glitzy show of unity (Schäuble acidly noted, "Without music and lights, it's all a bit thin"), a late April Union caucus meeting erupted into shouting among Schäuble, Waigel and others. Dismayed deputies looked on as Kohl sat glumly silent, neither halting the combat nor even offering a customary plea for unity. Some said that it seemed as if party leaders no longer wanted to win. While the CDU and CSU did agree to forge a joint election platform, the chancellor and a divided Union slid further behind in the polls; even most business leaders began to write off his coalition.[22]

Such strife weakened the CDU before an April 26 Land election in the depressed eastern Land of Saxony-Anhalt. Though braced for losses, it still hoped to weaken the SPD, which governed there with PDS support. But Kohl's eight speeches showed little grasp of eastern concerns; he even stumbled over the name of his own party's candidate, an error unlikely in the West. The CDU fell by a whopping 12 percent, losing its status as the single largest party, while the German Peoples' Union (DVU) won 13 percent, a postwar high for any extreme right-wing group. This grim omen for the Bundestag election in eastern Germany revived bitter debate back in Bonn. Schäuble voiced open criticism in the executive committee. Some leaders in the CDU—and now FDP as well—again urged Kohl to set a departure date.

Yet he still hoped to rally party support at a last pre-election congress in May. The Saxony-Anhalt SPD's decision to spurn a lukewarm grand coalition offer and govern again with PDS help offered an issue: Kohl assailed it as proof that Schröder's "new middle" was a front for Lafontaine's "old left." Delegates cheered and, as always, chanted "Hel-mut." Hintze attacked

Schröder's past leftist sympathies and "lack of character"; a few delegates even ridiculed his multiple divorces.[23] This time, Schäuble gave a low-key policy speech that did not overshadow Kohl, who patted him demonstratively on the shoulder. The caucus chief and Hintze also presented a scaled-down "future program," with what they called "hard truths" about the choices Germany faced, still trying to draw a contrast with Schröder's "soft sell" on reforms. Hoping to bury another old hatchet, Kohl even made time for Biedenkopf to speak.

A week later, Hintze's headquarters unveiled a poster meant to whip up anger at Schröder's party for dealing with the PDS: it featured the red-tinged handshake from an old GDR banner marking the forced 1946 SPD-Communist merger. As in 1994, uneasy CDU easterners voiced concern that this tact might just alienate their region's voters, and urged the party to focus on a refutation of PDS arguments rather than simplistic, polemical condemnation.[24]

The Hot Phase

The last phase of a CDU/CSU campaign had never begun amid more pessimism. Strategists worried that, unlike in 1994, Germans would not feel the dawning recovery's effect until *after* voting. Moreover, though EMU was approved in May and enjoyed more acceptance among Germans, the public still remained wary of losing their deutsche mark. Late spring's Politbarometer showed that a record 71 percent of Germans expected a red-green victory. Half of Liberal voters and even a third of Union supporters agreed that it was time for a new government. Ever more CDU leaders felt that their only hope lay in a grand coalition. Worried that Kohl might drag them down, too, wary FDP leaders like Westerwelle also began urging him to name a departure date.

Despite unflattering comparisons to its SPD rivals, Kohl's chancellory campaign team under Bohl assumed even more control. It hired Hans-Hermann Tiedje, a journalist and advertising expert from the tabloid *Bild*. Such a move further marginalized party headquarters, where—at Kohl's behest—the campaign commission was bloated into an oversized sounding board and met less often. Hintze's CDU staff now focused exclusively on merely publicizing posters or television spots (produced as usual by the public relations firm von Mannstein) and managing public rallies.

Kohl's team still hoped to woo back disenchanted supporters by arguing that any votes for small right-wing parties would be wasted, and that staying home would only help the left. Yet now it also attempted more positive or subtle tactics. With polls giving his CDU only 22 percent in the East, Kohl met with allies from that region in June. He also agreed to drop the red handshake pitch. Catering to sensitivities in the new Länder, Tiedje instead designed newsletters that looked like a popular GDR-era journal. Far from disavowing Kohl's oft-mocked 1990 pledge that the East would blossom, the campaign highlighted signs of growth. One new television spot showed nothing but pictures of new buildings. The popular Biedenkopf was asked to campaign more actively. Kohl stressed signs of a recovery and derided Schröder's clumsy effort to claim credit for it. The CDU echoed many views voiced by the SPD candidate's own shadow economics minister, a business leader, and thereby played up his own differences with Lafontaine and the Greens. Trying to de-accentuate the negative, Kohl's party also resisted CSU efforts to put a sharp anti-immigrant plank in their joint platform, though he otherwise continued placating the Bavarians.

Otherwise, the chancellor's team mainly relied on his image for reliability. In mid-July, the CDU put out a whimsical poster of an elephant bathing at his summer hideaway; it read "Keep Kohl" in English. In a more serious vein, billboards depicted him gazing out, statesmanlike, under the title "World Class for Germany." As in 1994, television spots highlighted his diplomacy: they risked underscoring that he was more at home on the world stage than in tackling unemployment, but sought to exploit his prestige, point up Schröder's own lack of experience, and reinforce concern about SPD (let alone Green) influence on German foreign policy.

And ultimately, CDU/CSU strategy also counted on the desire of German voters (especially older ones) for stability, arguing that any change should come through reform, not red-green radicalism. A CDU poster that appeared throughout Germany in the campaign's final weeks promised "Security Instead of Risk for Germany." It called to mind Adenauer's famous 1957 pledge, "No Experiments." In contrast to previous campaigns, the Union even attacked Kohl's SPD rival, calling Schröder a candidate "without character."

Always seemingly energized by a campaign, the chancellor would make some fifty public speeches, mostly out of doors. It meant a risk of small crowds or jeering, but aides counted on loyalists to show up—and on loudspeakers to drown out hecklers. Kohl boasted that he alone could still "fill the market squares" (and indeed, his rallies would draw a total of 600,000 people). He also made his patented tour of north German summer resorts, skipping by helicopter from beach to beach for seaside rallies.

Kohl's team sought maximum television exposure for him, especially on SAT-1, the sympathetic private network of his friend, press magnate Leo Kirch—a tactic that had worked well in 1994. Through interviews and talk shows, as well as print journalists, he gave the press (even newspapers once spurned as hostile) more direct contact than in 1994. Yet, though he was trailing, Kohl did not grant Schröder a one-on-one televised debate. Aides claimed that it might elevate the challenger, and such sparring sessions had backfired on him in past elections. Instead, Kohl's team built up September's Bundestag budget debate as a duel between Germany's two chancellor candidates. He began working closely on drafts of the text with his top speechwriters.

Schäuble and bullish Defense Minister Rühe hit the stump too, yet played clearly lower-profile roles. Biedenkopf also did his duty for the CDU, albeit without exerting himself for its chief. Surprisingly, Kohl asked the head of 1989's failed party putsch, whom he had all but purged, to be his economics spokesman: now the respected head of an eastern firm, Baden-Württemberg's Lothar Späth campaigned, but his remarks often undercut the chancellor.

After long wrangling, in August the Union began releasing its joint election platform, a condensed version of Schäuble's future program and CSU statements. It gave priority to economic growth, especially in eastern Germany, while endorsing curbs on crime and the inflow of foreigners. Yet this program offered few specific proposals and injected little new substance into the campaign.[25]

August polls showing a tighter race sparked some fresh hope. Some analysts said that the SPD had peaked in terms of potential voter support, and would keep sliding. Yet the Union still could not avoid self-inflicted wounds. An unusual interview by Schäuble's wife hinted at his anger by implying that he had lost interest in being chancellor. CDU leaders hastily reaffirmed his key future role, but that only evoked CSU anger at premature talk of a transition. When Kohl then reiterated his own intention to run for a full term, Schäuble noted that these words did not exclude leaving a bit early, a comment that angered chancellory aides.[26]

SPD and Green slippage in the polls also exacerbated tensions by seeming to increase odds of a grand coalition. Reluctant to stir the CSU and FDP, Kohl tried to rule that option out. But, more antsy about him now dragging them down, even moderate Liberals joined in calls for him to name a final departure date. An angry Kohl responded by hinting at a Union pact with the Greens. Though he stressed that it could only be conceivable in a distant future, after the latter had changed their policies, this comment seemed to undercut his own *Lagerwahlkampf* and fanned confusion.

Though the race kept narrowing slowly as September began, the chancellor still needed more momentum. It would not come from his foreign policy. Schröder had endorsed EMU, and even Kohl shrugged it off as a done deal now, no longer a topic for debate. Amid Russia's financial collapse, Hintze claimed that the campaign had found its theme—Bonn's chancellor as a global stabilizing force—but Kohl's aides feared charges of playing politics with this volatile situation, and again disavowed the general-secretary. The recovery offered more hope: for the first time in 1998, most voters credited his Union with more economic competence. And the chancellor held his own in a September 4 Bundestag debate with Schröder.

He stressed his diplomatic record, sparred with hecklers, reminded the SPD of its hesitance to embrace German unity, sardonically praised Lafontaine's fiery speech for having stolen the show from his party's candidate, and snidely reassured other opposition leaders that they might each aspire to run against him in more four years: "Why should I deny you hope?" Pleading for "clear policies," he concluded that "experiments bring nothing." His eighty-minute show drew stormy applause from Union deputies.[27]

Another event also held out some hope of late momentum. Stoiber had avoided scheduling Bavaria's Land election along with the Bundestag vote in order to avoid being dragged down by Kohl. Many now thought that a strong CSU showing on September 13 could even give the CDU a boost. Given his popularity, Stoiber's party did gain on Bavaria's weak SPD, winning 53 percent. Kohl praised his frequent critic in Munich, while aides insisted that this result exposed a shift in momentum and reflected Schröder's own lack of coattails.

Polls did indeed show the SPD lead sliding further. Hoping to score off this Bavarian "setup pass," Kohl campaigned with vigor, visiting sentimental spots like Dresden's Frauenkirche, where he had first addressed East Germans in 1989. Hintze also had him talk with voters on a computer chatline, despite his evident unfamiliarity with such technology. Yet in the race's last days, as if to remind them of all that had hitherto gone wrong, Schäuble openly chastised Kohl in a *Playboy* interview, even rejecting his use of a word like "friendship" to describe their "collegial" relations.[28] And then, when Family Minister Claudia Nolte clumsily hinted at a post-election coalition plan to raise sales taxes Kohl grumbled, "I wouldn't dream of talking about taxes ... before an election."[29]

Last-minute internal polls showed that Bavaria's shot in the arm would not suffice to preserve a Union-FDP majority. An ever more nostalgic tone in his final speeches suggested that Kohl was reconciling himself to being out of power. With two days to go, he even finally called a grand coalition "possible in principle," like any alliance among democrats. Since he also warned that the Union had no votes to spare, Kohl's main purpose now seemed to be somehow ensuring that the Union would end up with more seats than the SPD in any such government, denying Schröder and at last paving the way for another CDU chancellor—Schäuble.[30]

Final Curtain, No Encore:
The CDU/CSU's Defeat and Beyond

On September 27, Kohl's Union fell by 6.3 percent to its worst nationwide showing since 1949, just 35.2 percent of the second votes.[31] The CDU lost ground in every western Land, hitting a record low of 39.1 percent in Kohl's own Rhineland-Palatinate and finishing behind the SPD there for the first time in any federal election. Worse, the party won just 27.6 percent in eastern Germany, where turnout rose 10 percent. It finished first only in Saxony (even there falling from over 48 percent to 32.7 percent), and barely beat the PDS in Brandenburg. With 32.2 percent of the first vote, Kohl's CDU held just 74 direct mandates (compared to 212 for the SPD), and in the East clung to only three outside of Saxony. Cabinet members like Nolte and Interior Minister Manfred Kanther lost their own districts, as did the chancellor himself in working-class Ludwigshafen (a seat he had held since 1990). Waigel's CSU suffered only slightly less: just two weeks after Stoiber had earned 53 percent in Land elections, the party settled for a dismal 47.7 percent in Bavaria, less than in any Bundestag race since 1949. Its 38 direct mandates marked a loss of 6 from 1994. Although the FDP clung to life with 6.2 percent, its own worst national showing in years, Kohl's government was dead. So too was any talk of a grand coalition: with a 40.9 percent plurality, his SPD's best result since 1980, Schröder could now easily form a majority with the Greens, who had won 6.7 percent.

At a quarter after six, Hintze arrived to concede defeat; Kohl did so within the hour, assuming responsibility for this debacle, graciously wishing Schröder well, and announcing his resignation as CDU chair after a quarter century. He then had to discuss this worst setback of his career on television in an "elephant round" with the other party chairs, including a triumphant Lafontaine. Schäuble and Rühe circulated through the Konrad Adenauer House, visiting each press stand for an interview, looking almost like relieved survivors who could now focus on a recovery.

Analysis made clear what happened to Union support: 1.6 million voters had bolted directly to the SPD, giving it 109 former CDU/CSU direct mandates. An equally notable 275,000 easterners had defected to the PDS. A half-million other voters nationwide had stayed home. Analysis also revealed losses across the board in sociodemographic terms. Only among voters over 60 did the CDU/CSU beat its SPD rival, and even there by a wafer-thin margin. Whereas in 1994, the Union had led by almost 10 percent in the 45- to 59-year-old age bracket, it now finished second among those middle-aged voters. Germans aged 25–34 all but abandoned the party: in that group it won only 30 percent of men and 27 percent of women. Just as dismaying, the CDU/CSU placed behind its main rival among salaried employees (winning just 31 percent, down from 38 percent in 1994), the vital "new middle classes." Finally, whereas the CDU had been able to call itself the party of eastern workers since 1990, and had still won 40 percent of that vote in 1994, it could now claim only a quarter: the SPD had recaptured this "natural constituency."

Problems of climate, competence, candidate, and campaign had all cost the Union. Some analysts argued that the mood for change after sixteen years had simply proven insurmountable: almost independently of issues, Germans—especially swing voters—were just ready for something new. Others stressed the economy. To be sure, voters sensed improvement, and most (albeit less than in 1994) credited Kohl's government with more overall competence. But over 80 percent ranked unemployment as their major concern—with the next item, foreigners/asylum seekers, getting just 14 percent—and most rated a red-green alliance as more capable of creating jobs. Among parties, the edge was even clearer: the Union got 24 percent, the SPD 42 percent. CDU/CSU efforts at reform had not gone far enough to spur employment, but far enough (in trimming pensions, for example) to suggest lack of social compassion: those voters who took the party's talk of hard measures seriously did not reward it for telling them. Some analysts argued that joblessness outweighed, or generated, the "time for a change" mood; others disagreed—but plainly, the two together made for a damaging synergy.

A third factor helped explain the defeat's dimension. Despite his record and talents, Kohl was a flawed candidate. Even many backers conceded, "I just can't look at him any more." His miscalculation about the SPD challenger had left him in a hole, and confusion over Schäuble's future—to which both contributed—undercut his fabled skills at rallying the party in a campaign. Many of those at his last rallies were not demanding an encore, but merely watching the curtain call of a legend. Although he did narrow Schröder's huge lead of forty points, Kohl faced election day trailing a rival for the first time ever, by a margin of 10 percent. Though usually ranked first in approval among Union supporters, he ended in a tie with Schäuble among them as well. And given the caucus chief's greater appeal to independent voters, 41 percent in a Politbarometer poll felt that he would have helped the Union to a better overall result. Having hoped to be the first chancellor who chose the time of his own exit, Kohl had instead ended up as the first ousted by German voters.

Finally, some felt that the Union threw away any last hope by focusing on the chancellor and old themes like security or anti-Communism rather than a more argumentative strategy. They blamed the campaign for lacking coordination and substance, for conveying mixed messages, and for underestimating the opposition. Despite having recognized Lafontaine's control of his SPD, Kohl's team never really grasped that this very discipline could also keep the party in line behind Schröder's glitzy, populist, centrist strategy.

What was this defeat's larger meaning? Analysts talked of a historical watershed: the final election of the century, as well as the last one with Bonn as seat of government, a leader who recalled the war, and traces of Cold War ideology. Some hinted that it also marked the death of Kohl's old-style party politics in a time of policy wonks and media magnates.

Moreover, many saw this defeat as part of a crisis for the center-right in all industrialized nations (it now held power in just one EU member state, Spain). In this view, with the Cold War over and such left-wing rivals as Schröder's SPD less vulnerable to charges of being hostile toward business, parties like Kohl's were losing issues that had long helped bind their diverse constituencies: they were now exposed to forces of fragmentation new or old—economic insecurity, regionalism, multiculturalism.

Yet the Union by no means faced collapse. The party had never depended on government patronage power to survive, unlike Italy's old Christian Democrats or Japan's Liberal Democrats. Nor did it confront a deep regional rift like Canada's Conservatives, or the personal factions and far-right rival that so fragmented France's center-right. As opposed to its Austrian or Dutch counterparts, the Union faced no robust, right wing Liberal challenger.

Indeed, burned out after sixteen years and unable to complain of having been ousted illegitimately as in 1969—the 1998 results left no room for such bitter self-pity—many in the party generally welcomed a chance for renewal in opposition. As a start, even critics endorsed Caucus Chief Schäuble as CDU chair, leaving both top jobs in one man's hands. Rather than seek a new post as his sole deputy, Rühe settled for being one of four.[32]

Epilogue: The 1999–2000 Finance Scandal

In early November 1999, few CDU leaders paid attention to a news item about tax evasion charges against former Treasurer Walther Leisler Kiep. Most were too busy sniping at government fiscal policies and readying for spring Land elections: polls offered hope of taking power not only in Schleswig-Holstein, but even in the SPD stronghold of North Rhine-Westphalia. And on November 9, a Bundestag ceremony marked the tenth anniversary of German unity, seeming to cement Helmut Kohl's place in history.

But then Kiep confessed that cash from an arms dealer seeking approval of a 1991 weapons sale had reached the CDU through a secret account. Kohl denied knowing of the donation, and fumed "I am not bribable." But he soon conceded having kept "separate accounts" to prop up party branches in eastern Germany. Suddenly the CDU faced parliamentary hearings and possibly devastating financial penalties for not disclosing donations. Early December then brought new charges of money from a French firm bidding to buy the privatized eastern refinery at Leuna.

This stream of revelations began to erode party unity. Schäuble pledged a thorough investigation, without disavowing his old mentor, but grew angry when Kohl worked behind his back and, on television just before

Christmas, conceded taking millions in illegal donations—while refusing to break his "word of honor" by disclosing the sources of this cash. With their former patron facing breach of trust charges, Merkel, Rühe, and Wulff began urging the party to distance itself from him. Others retorted that loyalty and credibility forbade it from deserting Kohl. Moreover, auditors revealed that Union Bundestag caucus funds had inappropriately gone into party coffers, while new reports showed that branches in some Länder had set up their own secret accounts, suggesting that the former chancellor was not alone.

Still, in early January 2000 Schäuble finally insisted that Kohl identify his benefactors, leading to an angry meeting—and break—between them. But just days later, despite earlier denials, Schäuble too admitted having taken a donation from the same arms dealer. His insistence that he had sought to have it recorded could barely be heard above criticism from foes—and many colleagues. Rumor had it that Schäuble would give up both his posts, or be challenged by one of the ex-chancellor's defenders. Yet after another shouting match, he got colleagues to demand that Kohl disclose the source of secret donations or give up as honorary CDU chair. Angrily, the old man resigned, but clung to his Bundestag seat—downplaying the charges, portraying himself as someone who had put his party's interest and word of honor first, while insisting that he had never been bought or enriched himself.

Efforts to change the topic by talking about tax or pension policy drew scant attention and could not prevent the party from sliding behind Schröder's revived SPD in the polls. Schleswig-Holstein's CDU saw hopes of victory fade. But beyond electoral decline loomed a grimmer specter—schism. Though some of Kohl's old friends like Blüm defected, loyalists depicted him as a victim of panicky, cowardly colleagues. Any hint of legal action against the former chancellor seemed sure to divide the party. Though many younger CDU allies and the CSU still backed Schäuble, many wondered how long he could last—or keep the party together.

For some, this crisis stirred even deeper concern. Breaking with the nostalgic authoritarianism of many Weimar-era parties, the CDU had helped stabilize Germany's postwar democracy by integrating middle-class voters behind a broad, moderate, pragmatic conservatism, defusing any real right-wing radical threat. But especially without the Cold War anti-communism that had so long helped in that process, the party could not afford to be seen as a mere front for cliques of self-interested elites who placed their group loyalty and quest for power above the rule of law. Though there had been no apparent organized crime connection or massive patronage in Bonn, pessimists worried that the CDU might collapse like its Italian counterpart. Despite some talk of possibly exploiting their old partner's implosion, CSU and FDP leaders—and even many in the

SPD—worried that it could destabilize Germany's party system and feed radical right-wing populism. Abroad, this crisis stirred some uneasiness about the newly enlarged republic's ability to lead Europe, even about the strength of its democracy—fears that Kohl had striven to allay. With the now disclosed darker side of his long tenure putting his achievements at risk, it was becoming ever harder to tell which half of this dual legacy would ultimately prove more durable.

Notes

1. For a good recent introduction to German parties, see Gerard Braunthal, *Parties and Politics in Modern Germany* (Boulder, Colorado: Westview, 1998). For the early decades of the CDU (pre-1982) see Geoffrey Pridham, *Christian Democracy in Western Germany* (New York: St. Martin's, 1977), and Hans-Otto Kleinmann, *Geschichte der CDU* (Stuttgart: Deutsche Verlags-Anstalt, 1993).

2. In an Allensbach survey, 63 percent of German leaders favored Kohl standing again. *Die Welt*, 25 July 1996.

3. According to Emnid surveys, 61 percent of Germans opposed the coalition's tax reform plan; four in five felt that the system already favored the wealthy. *Die Welt*, 1 February 1997.

4. According to an Emnid survey, 49 percent of Germans were ready to vote against EMU if given a chance. *Die Welt*, 18 January 1997.

5. Kohl's Politbarometer rating during 1994–96 was as high as at any point in his career except at the time of German unification. *Die Welt*, 22 February 1997.

6. Eckhardt Rehberg and Paul Krüger, cited in *Frankfurter Allgemeine Zeitung*, 15 February 1995. From some 134,000 members in 1990, the CDU's eastern branches had only 79,000 left by 1994, and that number had dropped by another 15,000 to 20,000 by 1998.

7. Data cited from Politbarometer reports.

8. Ulrich Reitz, *Wolfgang Schäuble* (Bergisch Gladbach: Gustav Lübbe Verlag, 1996), 11–26.

9. CDU Bundesgeschäftsstelle, *Protokoll: 9. Parteitag der CDU Deutschlands*, 13–15 October 1997, Leipzig.

10. Kohl cited in *Die Welt*, 26 January 1998.

11. Cited in *Die Welt*, 3 March 1998.

12. Cited in *Süddeutsche Zeitung*, 6 March 1998.

13. The March Politbarometer, for example, found that 62 percent of all respondents wanted the SPD candidate, and only 28 percent backed Kohl.

14. On March 13, some young CDU leaders closer to Schäuble urged Rudolf Seiters to talk to the chancellor about stepping down (*Die Welt*, 24 April 1998). Kohl trailed the SPD candidate by 25 percent; Schäuble trailed by 15 percent (Politbarometer data from 13 March 1998, and a Basis survey for *Focus* cited in *Die Welt*, 23 March 1998).

15. Geissler cited in *Süddeutsche Zeitung*, 17 March 1998.

16. Cited in *Die Welt*, 12 March 1998; 16 March 1998.

17. Cited in *Die Welt*, 18 March 1998.

18. Politbarometer data from 13 March 1998.

19. Cited in *Die Welt*, 14 March 1998.

20. "Klare Inhalt gegen SPD-Beliebigkeitsspektakel," 7 April 1998, http://www.cducsu. bundestag.de/texte/schae56i.htm.

21. "With the CSU there will be no ecological tax." Waigel cited in *Süddeutsche Zeitung*, 6 April 1998. "Honestly," Schäuble told an interviewer, "[I] don't think much of such monarchical jobs." Interview in *Spiegel*, 19 April 1998.

22. Only one in four business and interest group elites now felt that Kohl would win (Emnid survey in *Die Welt*, 16 April 1998).

23. Some wore T-shirts that read "Schröder is the wrong man—three wives can't all have been wrong."

24. Kohl's new government spokesman then only fueled tensions by hinting that Bonn might cut aid to the East if it backed the PDS.

25. CDU Bundesgeschäftsstelle, *Wahlplattform 1998–2002*, No. 5488.

26. "Kohl said he is running for a four-year term, but in the end left it a bit open as to what can happen in those four years." Interview in *Die Woche* cited in *Die Welt*, 27 August 1998.

27. Cited in *Focus*, 7 September 1998.

28. Cited in *Tagesspiegel*, 19 September 1998.

29. Cited in *Der Spiegel*, 21 September 1998.

30. Cited in *Bonner Stadtanzeiger*, 24 September 1998.

31. Unless otherwise noted, all election results come from the data compiled for special editions of *Der Spiegel* and *Frankfurter Allgemeine Zeitung*, 29 September 1998, while all survey data are drawn from the Forschungsgruppe Wahlen's Politbarometer.

32. In early 1999, he would offer himself to stand as minister-president designate for Schleswig-Holstein's battered CDU at the 2000 Land election.

Chapter 4

NEOLIBERAL STIRRINGS
The "New" FDP and Some Old Habits

Christian Søe

Nine months before the Bundestag election of September 1998, Hans-Dietrich Genscher warned his Free Democratic Party (FDP) that it faced the most difficult electoral contest of its fifty-year history.[1]

The former party leader and foreign minister had issued similar alerts on other occasions when the FDP had faced existential threats. But this wakeup call seemed unusually urgent. In the most recent cycle of Land-tag elections, the small liberal party had failed to win representation in three quarters of the sixteen state parliaments. Its national poll standings hovered near 5 percent, the minimum support required for representation in the Bundestag.

As the campaign began to pick up, there were no indications of a substantial advance for the FDP. Right up until voting day, informed observers agreed that it would be touch and go for this inveterate establishment party. Its plight gave political humorists a field day. One typical cartoon portrayed Free Democrats as the hapless deck band aboard the Titanic, stoically playing on while the ship was sinking.[2]

And there was an inevitable revival of the old joke that the initials "F.D.P." really stand for *fast drei Prozent* or "almost 3 percent." Indeed, this meager percentage was held to be the approximate size of the FDP's remaining core of loyal voters, or *Stammwähler*—if it even made sense to speak of such an entity. The party's parliamentary survival depended once again on its ability to attract additional support among tactically oriented voters.

Between an "Old" and a "New" FDP

Given the FDP's perennial role as a strategically placed balancer in federal party politics, the small party's fate was arguably of more than parochial interest. A complete parliamentary shutout would presumably reshuffle the German party system and alter its coalition arithmetic. Even a more limited setback for the FDP, in the form of an ouster from the cabinet and relegation to the parliamentary opposition, seemed likely to have an impact on both style and direction of national governance. In that sense, at least, there was some plausibility in the maxim dear to Free Democrats: "Without the Liberals, Germany would be a different republic!"[3]

Their proposition would be only half tested by the result of the 1998 election. As widely expected, the FDP finally lost its cabinet tenure, after twenty-nine consecutive years of co-governing in Bonn. Yet it managed to hang on in the unfamiliar role of junior opposition party. The next few years will therefore provide some answer to the question of whether the Liberals still matter—in particular, whether their absence as a centripetal element in the cabinet really will affect the vaunted stability and continuity of governance in the Federal Republic.

But the election and its aftermath can also be read as a test of a new and different role claimed by the FDP: that of an agent of major societal reform. The small party has often presented itself as a motor of moderate innovation in Germany's system of coalition politics, but the last time it adopted a sharp reform image was in the late 1960s. At that time the FDP, operating as solo opposition party in the Bundestag, installed a new "social liberal" leadership and called for major changes in domestic and foreign policy. This new orientation brought the FDP to the brink of electoral oblivion in 1969, but it was a precondition for its pivotal role in the formation of Willy Brandt's reform coalition that year. During the decades that followed, the Liberals lost much of their reform image. Instead, they became identified with their role or "function" as pragmatic majority-makers in Germany's centrist system of coalition government. As junior partners first of the Social Democrats (SPD) and then, after 1982, of the Christian Democrats (CDU/CSU), the Free Democrats came to operate as a moderate co-governing party, with some special concern for the interests of its clientele of businesspeople and professionals.

That began to change in the mid-1990s, when a new generation of leaders responded to electoral adversity by once again seeking to redefine the FDP as a reform party (*Reformpartei*). There were some striking differences from the earlier reorientation. This time the political shift was initiated while the party was still a member of government and thus restricted by coalition discipline. Moreover, the new course now took a decidedly neoliberal, market-oriented direction that set the Free Democrats off from two small left-of-center rivals in the Bundestag, the postmaterialist Greens and the post-communist Democratic Socialists (PDS). Finally, the change was initially accompanied by a more confrontational style of rhetoric and imagery than had been typical of the FDP since the 1950s.

The FDP reformers resembled many other market-oriented politicians in western Europe with their demands for a "slimmer" state, substantially lower taxes, far-reaching privatization, and extensive deregulation. In effect, they called for a thoroughgoing liberalization of the vaunted socioeconomic model of postwar Germany. Not surprisingly, some of their more market-skeptical critics saw the FDP as engaged in an ideological attack on what they considered to be the country's social contract. The reformers tried to counter this delegitimizing charge by going beyond arguments drawn from supply-side economics. They dipped selectively into the revived liberal discourse on the role of individualism within civil society. And they usually avoided the "neoliberal" designation, which adversaries have loaded with the connotation of social uncern (*soziale Kälte*).[4]

Initially, the reformers liked to present their party as the "new" FDP. In rhetorical high gear, they would claim that it offered the only realistic alternative to the kind of hegemonic "social democratic" inertia or "structural conservatism" represented by all the other Bundestag parties. Their push for a reorientation of the FDP was rooted in ideological convictions. But it also reflected a strategic concern to find a distinctive niche on the increasingly crowded parliamentary stage, where the Greens had moved into some positions earlier identified with the more "social liberal" wing of the FDP.

The innovators received considerable backing within their small party, but they also ran into some resistance and considerable inertia. Moreover, it soon became clear that the "new" FDP was failing to generate much support or even interest among German voters. In other words, the reformers were unable to fully dismantle the ingrained habits or fix the structural problems associated with the more familiar "old" party. As a result, the FDP in 1998 combined some long established "functional" traits of the centrist majority-maker with the alternative trappings of a neoliberal *Reformpartei*.

A Lopsided Party Development

There could be no doubt that the FDP needed to "reinvent" itself if it were to survive. In the Bundestag contest of October 1994, the FDP had won only 6.9 percent of the vote, until then its second lowest result since 1949.

This meager score had been just enough for the Liberals to continue as majority-makers in Helmut Kohl's coalition government. It constituted a huge setback from their high mark of 11 percent in 1990, the *annus mirabilis* of national unification. As a result, the FDP lost its traditional position as third largest force in federal politics to the upstart Greens. Worst of all, the reversal was preceded, accompanied, and followed by a devastating series of defeats in Landtag elections. Already by late 1995 these losses had left the party absent from twelve of the sixteen state parliaments, where only two years earlier it had been present in every one. And Liberals were now members of only one, later two, state governments in their traditional role of junior coalition partners.

The FDP had been in downward electoral cycles before, but never one so severe. In past years, periodic strings of setbacks had always been followed by partial recoveries, even though there had been no fundamental repair of the structural problems that dated back three decades.[5]

In the 1990s, the FDP faced the prospect of being reduced to an almost purely federal presence. That in turn raised the question of how long it could eke out such an atrophied political existence.

The party's lopsided development had an additional, regional dimension. Even more than the Greens, the FDP had become a party with an almost exclusively western base. This was a sharp reversal of the electoral pattern in Germany at the time of unification. In 1990, the FDP had performed unusually well in the new eastern states by racking up electoral results that outranked any ever achieved in the "old" western Länder. It had also inherited a huge membership from two of the former "bloc parties," so that for a while there were twice as many party members in the thinly populated East as in the West, where about 80 percent of Germans now live. In advance of the "super election year" (*Superwahljahr*) of 1994, a massive defection of members and a collapse in poll standings indicated that the FDP's initial political windfall in the East had been dissipated. This was confirmed when that year's elections wiped out the FDP in every eastern Landtag. In the Bundestag election, its share of the eastern vote plummeted from 12.9 percent in 1990 to 3.5 percent in 1994. There had been a smaller drop from 10.6 to 7.7 percent in the West, resulting in the overall national total of 6.9 percent.

Membership losses underscored the basic message. By the end of 1998, the FDP's eastern membership had dropped to one-seventh of its original size eight years earlier, from over 110,000 to less than 16,000. There had also been some slippage in the West, but here the total remained at more than three-quarters, having declined from about 67,000 to 52,000 in the same period from 1990 to 1998.[6]

FDP leaders were keenly aware of the East-West divide affecting their party, but they came up with no adequate strategic response. Their various efforts to recover lost political terrain all seemed to run aground on the basic stylistic, political, and, ultimately, ideological differences that separated potential supporters in the two parts of Germany.[7]

The FDP's gaffe of briefly referring to itself in 1994 as "party of the higher income earners" (*Partei der Besserverdienenden*) clung to the party everywhere, but nowhere had it backfired so much as in the East. Here the party's strong market-orientation and emphasis on self-achievement found little positive response, given that region's prevailing state-oriented outlook and its staggering problems of socioeconomic dislocation. The neoliberal shift did not help matters.

In the long run, the FDP could perhaps hope to rebuild its shattered position in the new states. For the present, however, low electoral returns there had to be compensated for by higher margins in the West, if the 5 percent hurdle were to be passed nationwide. Not surprisingly, the FDP concentrated its federal campaign efforts of 1998 in areas where it was strongest, and that inevitably meant some unacknowledged neglect of the less responsive East.

Political Vicissitudes: 1995 to 1998

The FDP's reorientation in the mid-1990s resulted in large part from a new leadership's attempt to break the adverse electoral cycle. In February 1995, Free Democrats were briefly encouraged when they managed to retain their share of the Landtag vote in Hesse (7.4 percent), but only three months later the pattern of electoral misfortune resumed. In May 1995, the FDP went down to severe defeats in North Rhine-Westphalia (4.0 percent) and Bremen (3.4 percent). In October, Berlin would underscore the disastrous trend when the Liberals polled just 2.5 percent of that city's vote.

There followed an important political shakeup triggered by Klaus Kinkel's resignation as party leader in June 1995. Only four years earlier, he had brought with him a distinguished administrative record when he first joined the party and began to serve as one of its cabinet ministers. Almost by default, the political newcomer became party leader as soon as 1993, but from the beginning Kinkel seemed uncomfortable in this new role. Inevitably, if somewhat unfairly, he was blamed for the electoral setbacks that started soon after he took over the leadership. When he abruptly quit, it was in the wake of eleven routs in Landtag elections, offset only by the single victory in Hesse. Kinkel stayed on as foreign minister, however, and in this role he gained more visibility and even became a public relations asset to his party.

Wolfgang Gerhardt, the new party leader, came from Hesse, where he had presided over the FDP's lone electoral success. In contrast to his predecessor, Gerhardt knew his small party from years of active political involvement. Given the remarkably thin ranks of the FDP's successor generation, he could have been a strong contender for the leadership in 1993, if he had decided to run. By 1995 he appeared to be the only broadly acceptable candidate, although a spirited attempt was made by Jürgen Möllemann, one of the FDP's most talented, ambitious and controversial politicians. Gerhardt cut a somewhat lackluster figure, and he has never managed to become well known to the electorate at large. But he immediately made what turned out to be a crucial decision by keeping Guido Westerwelle as secretary-general and giving him considerable strategic freedom to revitalize the seemingly moribund party.

Westerwelle had been among the student founders of the Young Liberals, who in 1982 replaced the more left-leaning Young Democrats as the FDP's youth organization. He had gained recognition in the party as a politically energetic, outspoken, and somewhat flamboyant young man. Soon after the Bundestag election of 1994, Westerwelle had replaced a hapless Werner Hoyer as FDP secretary-general. He immediately began to make a mark as a determined party reformer who openly declared his goal of moving the FDP beyond its largely functional identity as pliant majority-maker into a more distinctive and "autonomous" programmatic position. Another important member of the reform team was the new federal manager, Hans-Jürgen Beerfeltz. The innovators had high hopes of capturing some of the "liberal potential" among the increasing number of German voters who show no strong party identification. So far, there had been little evidence of the FDP's ability to attract such support, but the modernizers believed a new party image would change that.

The debacle in Berlin in October 1995 could not damage the new leadership. Indeed, an electoral fiasco had been expected, in view of the internecine rivalry between left and right factions in the western part of the city, and the near disappearance of the Liberals as a political force in the eastern part. Instead of concentrating on this lost cause, the FDP made an all-out effort in three western Landtag elections on 24 March 1996. Under Westerwelle's strategic guidance, the FDP took advantage of this unusual electoral concurrence to promote a sharper image of itself as a party dedicated to reform. Its campaign focused on lower taxes and a thorough deregulation of the economy.

This gambit of presenting the FDP as the "tax reduction party" (*Steuersenkungspartei*) seemed to be vindicated by the outcome. The German media had largely written off the Liberals in advance, and it therefore became headline news when the election results instead suggested a political revival. In Baden-Württemberg, one of its old strongholds, the FDP won 9.6 percent of the vote, an advance of 3.7 points. Here it immediately moved into a new governing coalition with the CDU. On the same day in the Rhineland-Palatinate, the FDP won 8.9 percent, or 2 percent more than in 1992, enabling it to remain in that Land's government in coalition with the SPD. Even in the much more difficult political terrain of Schleswig-Holstein, the FDP surprised observers by advancing slightly to 5.7 percent of the vote.

The triple victory gave the Liberals an enormous uplift. For a while, the party overcame its "loser" image, and the new leadership gained crucial momentum. Although special regional factors had played a role in each election, the reformers chose to read the results as a vindication of their efforts. For them, the triumph could not possibly have been more timely. It came only two months before the 1996 party conference, where Gerhardt and Westerwelle presented the draft of a major new program prepared by a commission under the leadership of the secretary-general. After a year of discussion, an amended version was overwhelmingly approved by a Wiesbaden party conference in May 1997. It will be discussed further below.

The next state election came in Hamburg, a year and a half after the triple victory but only a few months after the adoption of the Wiesbaden program. Inevitably regarded as a first consumer test of the "new" FDP, it dashed early hopes of having reversed the electoral tide. In this, the only Landtag contest held during 1997, the FDP received only 3.5 percent of the vote. That was an ominous drop of 0.7 percent from the 1993 setback in this city-state, which had triggered the series of electoral routs in twelve Länder.

With the Bundestag election of 1998 approaching, the FDP now concentrated its efforts on the two Landtag elections in the spring of that year. Both were held in states where the party was thought to have a realistic chance of passing the 5 percent hurdle. In Gerhard Schröder's home state of Lower Saxony, the FDP did come extremely close. Here it was able to advance 0.5 percent with an attractive new top candidate, Michael Goldmann, and its now familiar emphasis on tax-cutting and a "slimmer state." But it managed to garner only 4.9 percent of the vote and thus failed by a very slim margin.

In April 1998 there followed another fairly close electoral defeat in Genscher's home state of Saxony-Anhalt, an eastern Land where the FDP had won impressive victories in the year of unification. Here, too, it presented an attractive top candidate, Cornelia Pieper, accompanied by enormous campaign support that included many "favorite son" appearances by Genscher. The Liberals did manage to advance 0.6 percent over their low 1994 score. Yet this lone electoral improvement in the East still gave them just 4.2 percent of the vote. The disappointment among Liberals was great, for Saxony-Anhalt had been regarded as the best, and perhaps only, opportunity to restore their parliamentary presence in one of the new Länder.

Shortly before the election, the FDP had held a special party conference in Berlin that endorsed more free market recipes for Germany's ailing economy, along with a full abolition of the special "solidarity" tax surcharge. This show of neoliberal consistency gained publicity for the party, but it can hardly have been attractive to eastern voters who identified the *Soli* with the public financing of their region's reconstruction.

It was fortunate for the FDP that there were no other elections in the East before the federal contest. But the mid-September race in Bavaria could hardly have come at a worse time, just two weeks in advance of the Bundestag election. As widely expected, the FDP put in a disastrous performance. It slipped from 2.8 percent to a mere 1.7 percent of the vote, placing seventh among all the contesting groups. This represented the party's lowest point in the 147 Landtag elections that had taken place in the Federal Republic up to that point.[8]

In sum, the FDP had been unable to reverse its overall negative trend in electoral politics. During the entire four-year period before the 1998 Bundestag election, the FDP had passed the 5 percent mark in only four state contests. So far, its programmatic renewal had failed to live up to the high expectations of the reformers.

"To Market, to Market": The Neoliberal Shift

The FDP's neoliberal shift can be read as a response to a major modernization challenge that confronts the hitherto largely consensual *Modell Deutschland* in a reunited Germany. It lies in the daunting task of simultaneously revamping the economy of the East and meeting the competitive demands facing all of Germany in an increasingly global market.[9]

The immediate origins of the FDP's new course, however, lay in the small party's desperate electoral condition and its leadership change in 1995. The reformers also had ambitious plans to streamline the party organization, but here they failed to accomplish most of their goals.[10]

The only organizational innovation of significance turned out to be the adoption in 1995 of a plebiscitary device for making binding policy decisions for the party through a vote by rank-and-file members. It was used almost immediately to bring the FDP to a new law-and-order position on a controversy that had long divided the party and caused tension with the more conservative CDU/CSU partner. At issue was a proposed measure that would permit a greater use of secret electronic surveillance by law enforcement agencies. Under judicially guarded limits, such eavesdropping would be made possible inside private quarters where residents were suspected of criminal activities. Supporters defended the measure as a way to fight organized crime more effectively, but civil libertarians in the party read their defeat on this "hot button" privacy issue as a sign of a neoconservative trend in the FDP. In a dramatic protest, Justice Minister Sabine Leutheusser-Schnarrenberger resigned from her cabinet post. Her successor, legal expert and fellow Liberal Edzard Schmidt-Jortzig, cut a far less distinctive public figure.

With this divisive issue apparently out of the way,[11] the new FDP leaders concentrated fully on their neoliberal agenda. The new basic program adopted at Wiesbaden in 1997 begins by lauding the achievements of liberal democratic politics and market economics in Germany. It then turns to a central theme: the country's failure to reform, remain competitive, and prepare for the future.[12]

The program condemns what it repeatedly castigates as a "politics of indulgence" (*Gefälligkeitspolitik*), or "giving-them-what-they-want." In place of this unsustainable practice, it calls for a "politics of responsibility" to cut back the web of entitlements, subsidies and regulations. Germany, the program argues, needs to replace its structural inertia with more open, competitive, creative forms of interaction. There is a passing admission that Free Democrats have contributed to the problem. Now, however, they are called upon to oppose the "social conservatives" and the "conservative socialists" of all parties by promoting a society that emphasizes individual responsibility and reduces the role of the state.

Taken in its entirety, the program strives for balance.[13] It includes an extended tribute to the value of individual freedom, which it links to such traits as responsibility, diversity, and tolerance, as well as progress and a special concern for future generations—all celebrated as constitutive elements of a "liberal civil society" (*liberale Bürgergesellschaft*). Yet the main emphasis in terms of policy implications is clearly on neoliberal socioeconomic reforms.

The Wiesbaden program received considerable publicity, but it has so far failed to give the FDP a distinctive and attractive profile among German voters. One major part of the problem probably lies in the inability of the small party to prove itself by delivering on its reform agenda. Very little of its program for deregulation and broad tax reform (including substantial tax reductions) came to see the light of day as legislation. When the CDU/CSU did not drag its feet, the SPD used its controlling majority in the upper chamber (Bundesrat) to block the enactment of a diluted tax reform advanced by the conservative-liberal government. In its campaign of 1998, the FDP took credit for a relatively small tax reduction, which scaled back the so-called "solidarity surcharge," as well as a modest liberalization of the laws regulating store closing hours in Germany. It also identified itself with a few fairly modest cutbacks in social benefits that had not required Bundesrat approval. But for the most part, the FDP had been unable to bring about the kind of changes it advocated.

There seems to be an additional problem with the message itself. The Liberals are not alone in urging socioeconomic reforms for Germany, and the introduction of more market-oriented approaches finds support among some important elements in the CDU/CSU, the SPD and, not least, the Greens. But the neoliberal message in its undiluted form, FDP *pur* as Westerwelle refers to it, has turned out to be a hard sell, both to potential coalition partners and to the German electorate, where it ultimately counts. Reservations can also be heard within the FDP itself. Many Liberals resent what they see as its transformation into a kind of single-note party. Such criticism comes primarily from the Freiburg Circle, where former minister Leutheusser-Schnarrenberger plays a leading role. The active members of this informal center-left discussion group number perhaps a couple hundred people, but it has a much larger mailing list and gets considerable press coverage. As Liberals, they are strong supporters of free market ideas, but they insist that the party not forget its civil libertarian heritage or social commitments. Similar views are expressed by some Free Democrats who are usually not identified with the party's left wing.[14]

A very different position is intermittently advanced by some members on the party's far right, who until recently were loosely organized as the *liberale Offensive*. They advocate a more national, law-and-order course for the FDP, and espouse political views similar to those of Jörg Haider's Freedom Party in Austria. The press has given them considerable attention, but they seem to represent a relatively weak undercurrent in the party. So far, at least, all predictions that electoral or ideological considerations might drive the FDP to embrace a right-wing populist position have come to naught.

The Campaign

The flippant self-designation as "party of higher income earners" may have permanently branded the FDP, but it stands in sharp contrast to the party's chronic financial problems. These are directly related to its steep electoral losses and its relatively low income from membership dues, insofar as both help determine the party's share of public financing. Private donations also play a role, but they provide no dependable supply of additional revenue. In the "Super election year" of 1994 and later, the party has drawn on its net worth to meet expenses, even as it implements cutback measures.[15]

The 1998 federal election campaign had to operate within a budget of only 6 million marks, and the need for austerity was a constant concern among the planners.[16] They urged the FDP to make unusual efforts to attract free publicity through special events or happenings that sparked the interest of the media. One such device was the party's sponsorship of a big "Internet truck" that toured the Federal Republic with a load of visitor-accessible computers, demonstrating the party's claim to show special concern for the needs of modern information technology. Like the other parties, the FDP also attempted to draw attention with its posters. Most of them carried the party's yellow and blue colors along with the slogan "It is your choice" (*Es ist Ihre Wahl*), but they seemed less distinctive or clever than some rival political advertisements.

As always, Liberals were urged to become active participants, even though the membership was far too small and passive to allow for a vigorous "grassroots" campaign. Leading party politicians made speaking appearances throughout Federal Republic, often joined by local or regional representatives of the party. The monthly party paper and other communications, including a relatively busy FDP web site (www.fdp.de), gave upbeat reports on the campaign.[17]

As in the past, the party also tried to work closely with a "liberal network" of several hundred volunteer backers.[18] They attracted support from a handful of diverse personalities, but here too the rival parties seemed more fully endowed with well-known names. One sympathetic manufacturer, Reinhold Würth, spent several hundred thousand marks to publish his personal ads backing the FDP, but that amount could not rival the eight million marks reportedly available to the trade unions in their SPD-oriented campaign for a change of government.[19]

The work of devising a federal campaign plan for the FDP resembled previous efforts of this kind. A small core group of planners, headed by the federal manager, met weekly at the party headquarters in Bonn starting in January 1997.[20] It included the department heads and a liaison from the parliamentary party, as well as a few outside consultants in advertising, logistics and polling. Overall strategic direction lay in the hands of the general secretary, while the party presidium and executive committee took responsibility for the final review and approval of major proposals with political implications.

The general plan had some distinctive features. It set up a four-stage campaign that sought to maximize the reach of the party's financially strapped promotion efforts.[21] Without explicitly saying so, the plan capitalized on both the "new" programmatic and the "old" functional attributes of the party, with a shift of emphasis toward the latter as the voting day approached.

During the first four months of 1998, the campaign would focus on the neoliberal message, now given symbolic expression by including the label *Reformpartei* with the party's official logo, *F.D.P. Die Liberalen*. This initial campaign stage overlapped with the important Landtag races in Lower Saxony and Saxony-Anhalt.

The planners designed the second campaign stage to span the weeks leading up to the regular party conference in late June. Here the FDP would give more attention to some specific reform items, including its familiar emphasis on tax simplification and tax reduction, economic deregulation, and other market-oriented innovations. The party would also herald such non-economic topics as its commitment to educational modernization and its "demand" for a liberalization of the country's antiquated naturalization laws.[22] These and other reform items, many already mentioned in the Wiesbaden program, constituted the major planks in the draft of the party's bulky election platform. With its neoliberal theme of "Less government—more freedom and responsibility," this document was intended to generate publicity during the three-day party conference.[23]

The plan's third campaign stage covered the summer months of July and August. Here the party's self-promotion was scheduled to adopt a more moderate pace, suitable to the hallowed vacation period. The FDP would emphasize its traditional claim to be a guarantor of political stability and continuity, with special attention to its foreign policy contributions. Finally, the last four weeks that constituted the "hot phase" of the campaign were to take off with a special one-day party conference in late August. Here the FDP would seek publicity for its "functional" contributions to coalition governance in Germany and issue its perennial appeal for the crucial "second vote."

The FDP's federal campaign basically followed this four-stage scenario, but contingencies left the execution less neat and orderly than planned. After the two Landtag election defeats in the spring, there followed some early adjustments that seemed primarily designed to reach CDU-oriented voters. In an early signal move, the FDP made a formal commitment to continue the coalition in Bonn. The decision itself came as no surprise, but it was moved up to the June party conference, two months sooner than planned.

The most basic adjustment in the Liberal campaign lay in this general move toward an earlier and stronger focus on the functional attributes of the FDP as majority-making coalition party. This went beyond the planned shift in emphasis. It toned down Westerwelle's original preference for a more "autonomous" and programmatic campaign designed to expand electoral identification with a neoliberal party. The change led to a decline in references to a "new" FDP and, even more striking, to the virtual abandonment of its logo designation as *Reformpartei*. Campaign planners later acknowledged that this label had failed to catch on with the voters: people simply associated it with "too much" change.[24]

There were other adjustments. One stemmed from the recognition that the FDP suffered from a weak personality profile, despite its ritual claim to be the home of some outstanding public figures. The decision to make greater use of Klaus Kinkel in the party's advertising was a remarkable admission of the problem, for he could hardly be called a commanding figure in German politics. Still, after six years as foreign minister, he ranked well ahead of any other FDP politician in poll ratings. The new emphasis given to Kinkel often took the form of presenting him as an experienced statesman in juxtaposition to his untested and unpredictable rivals from the Greens. It contrasted with the continued promotional neglect of his fellow Liberals in the government, Economics Minister Günter Rexrodt and Justice Minister Schmidt-Jortzig. Neither had been able to make a strong public impression, and it was widely speculated that they would be replaced in any new CDU/CSU-FDP cabinet. Gerhardt also suffered from low public recognition, but he was displayed as party leader on billboards throughout Germany. In a remarkable contrast to previous campaigns, the FDP's commercials made widespread use of its lively secretary-general. The political ads invariably showed Westerwelle in youthful poses. They were often directed at younger voters and included his personal web site address. Some veterans criticized what they regarded as an excessive display of the 36-year-old political manager.[25]

The FDP did not fully live up to its claim of conducting the "most argumentative" campaign of all the Bundestag parties, but it did try to position itself as antipode to the postmaterialist Greens in the West and the postcommunist PDS in the East. Both of these small rivals were targeted as representing a form of political nostalgia that was essentially reactionary, despite their own progressive claims. While the competition with the Greens in the populous West was far more serious for the FDP's campaign, the confrontation with the PDS was used to underscore the liberal reliance on markets rather than state intervention to address Germany's economic problems. It also gave the FDP a chance to present itself as a bulwark against both "red-green" and "red-green-red" experiments, which were portrayed as political specters in what became an us-or-them campaign.

But the Free Democrats also set themselves apart, if more softly, from the coalition partner—once again by emphasizing their own singular commitment to a more market-driven economics, including the use of supply-side incentives to combat the unemployment problem. They described the FDP as the *"Reformmotor"* of the coalition government, even as they reminded voters that it would be needed as majority-maker in any non-socialist government.[26] While the FDP officially avoided posing the chancellor question, some prominent Liberals, including Westerwelle, cautiously attempted to capitalize on the apparent "Kohl fatigue" by indicating a preference for an early post-election transition to Wolfgang Schäuble as head of government. Gerhardt limited himself to the functional reminder that there could be "no CDU chancellor without us."[27] The result was a strategy of limited confrontation with the CDU/CSU, in which the FDP appeared as an increasingly assertive junior coalition partner. No doubt was left about its maximum goal of continuing in a coalition under a CDU chancellor, be he Kohl or (later) Schäuble.

The many public opinion polls during the year gave little reason to believe that the incumbent coalition partners together would win a parliamentary majority. But this was a point the FDP could not afford to discuss openly, since it depended on winning the support of some CDU-oriented coalition supporters. In private, many Free Democrats were willing to speculate on the possibility of their party finally returning to the parliamentary opposition and facing either another grand coalition or an entirely new left-of-center government. Some optimists even saw such an exit from the cabinet as a possible blessing in disguise. In their view, a stint in the opposition would give the FDP a chance to win greater recognition for its distinctive ideas. The preferred outcome as an opposition party was to confront a grand coalition. It would presumably be far more difficult for the FDP to gain notice if it shared the opposition seats with the much larger Christian Democrats. Few Liberals were willing to discuss "the unthinkable," yet an electoral shutout could not be ruled out.

The Election Result

In the end, the FDP met only its minimum goal of parliamentary survival by winning 6.2 percent of the crucial second vote. The party's electoral strength declined 0.7 percent from its poor score in 1994, and the FDP remained in fourth place behind the Greens (6.7 percent). Only once had the Liberals recorded an even worse result—in the Bundestag election of 1969, when it received just 5.8 percent. Yet that distant low point, in a vagary of coalition politics, had been enough to provide the starting point for the FDP's record run of co-governing in Bonn, which now came to an end.

In terms of parliamentary arithmetic, the 1998 outcome would actually have sufficed for the formation of a new SPD-FDP majority coalition based on a narrow margin very similar to the one of 1969.[28] Politically, such a combination or its variant, a so-called "traffic light" coalition that included the Greens, was never considered seriously. It would clearly have lacked legitimacy right after the election, given not only the FDP's neoliberal campaign against "red-green" but also its greater policy affinity with the CDU/CSU, as well as its unambiguous coalition commitment in that direction. In any case, Gerhard Schröder's new SPD-Green government rested on a slightly wider parliamentary base, and it could plausibly claim an electoral mandate for a complete transfer of power.

The new party balance in the Bundestag also made irrelevant two other coalition scenarios, each of which would have made it easier for the FDP to distinguish itself as opposition party. Clearly there was not going to be any version of the "red-green-red" constellation in which the PDS would exercise leverage, possibly as a silent partner. And the election outcome also abruptly ended all speculation about a grand coalition. Instead, the power shift turned out to be more clear-cut and complete than any previous change of coalition governments at the national level.

The FDP was fortunate to have survived at all, for the party's modest vote greatly overstated its core of electoral strength. In a vindication of their return to a "second vote" campaign, the Liberals received crucial support from voters who favored the incumbent coalition government and the chancellor's party rather than the FDP per se. In fact, German electoral analysts concluded that such CDU/CSU-oriented "coalition voters" made up more than one-half (57 percent) of the potential FDP vote a week before the 1998 election. The figure had been very similar (61 percent) four years earlier, when the likelihood of a coalition victory had been much higher. As in all elections since 1957, the FDP benefited from vote-splitting. It received only 3 percent of all first votes, or slightly less than one-half its share of the second vote. The strong coalition-orientation of many FDP voters was also reflected in the fact that more than one-half of its second vote supporters cast their first vote for the CDU/CSU.[29]

The final tally showed that the FDP had won forty-three seats in the Bundestag, a loss of four. Its parliamentary group included nine new members, four of them women. Some veterans had retired, including the two former party leaders Hans-Dietrich Genscher and Otto von Lambsdorff. There were now only five Liberals elected from the eastern states (12 percent), whereas there had been seven (15 percent) in the previous legislative period and as many as seventeen (21.5 percent) after the successful 1990 Bundestag election. The new parliamentary group included a total of nine women (21 percent). This number is low by today's German standards, but it is at least a slight advance over the previous legislative period (17 percent). Cornelia Pieper was the only FDP woman elected from the East, but there had been none in the previous Bundestag.

A closer look at the votes cast for the FDP shows only a slight modification of the East-West divide that marked its performance four years earlier. In 1994 the FDP had received only 3.5 percent of the vote in the East, and it slipped further to 3.3 percent in 1998. In the "old" states of the West, the FDP had declined somewhat more, from 7.7 percent to 7.0 percent, but its losses had been within an overall support level that remained more than twice as high as in the East. Whereas the Free Democrats were unable to clear the 5 percent hurdle in any of the eastern states or Berlin, this was true only for the Saar in the more populous West. In the East, the

FDP has by now almost disappeared from view, at least above the local level of government.[30] This situation was poignantly emphasized in Mecklenburg West-Pomerania, where the FDP scored an all-time low statewide result for all Bundestag elections since 1949 (2.2 percent), and, in a separate contest held on the same day, managed to set another new low record for Landtag elections as well (1.6 percent).

Apart from this continuation of the sharp East-West divide established in 1994, the FDP's electoral result in 1998 showed relatively few noteworthy structural variations. The socioeconomic dimension revealed the strongest and most significant differences, for the FDP continues to be a party whose supporters come overwhelmingly from the German middle classes, both "old" and "new." As always, the FDP had a disproportional level of support among the self-employed (15 percent), where it received more than twice as many votes as in the population at large. It also continued to do fairly well in the small group of farmers (9 percent), as well as among non-unionized members of the salaried white-collar class of *Angestellten* (8 percent). In addition, administrators in highly placed positions appear to have given greater support to the FDP, as in past elections. The large group of civil servants also used to give it above-average backing. That was no longer the case in 1998, but it is likely that the FDP's support from the higher civil service continued to be somewhat stronger than its overall performance in this broad and very diverse occupational group (6 percent). As in the past, the FDP scored very poorly among the unemployed (4 percent) and among all blue-collar workers (3 percent), with the lowest support found among those who were union members (2 percent).

Compared to this general socioeconomic profile, the gender and age group variations among FDP voters were minimal and even less marked than in the recent past. The party enjoyed a slight overall advantage among male voters, especially those between 45 and 59 years old (8 percent). This was offset by a somewhat poorer showing among all voters in the 35 to 44 age group (5 percent). The party's call for pension reform had not set it back significantly among voters older than 60, where it received average support (6 percent). However, in comparison to recent elections, the FDP had recovered somewhat among the youngest voters, from 18 to 24 years of age, where it now stood at 6 percent as well. In this case also, the support came at a somewhat higher level among young men (7 percent) than among young women (5 percent).[31]

Conclusion

In 1998 the FDP finally lost its strategic position as balancer in federal coalition politics, four years after first it first fell behind the rival Greens in electoral strength. The small party's minimum goal will continue to be parliamentary survival, but its maximum goals include a restoration of the co-governing role in Germany's federal government as well as a more general recovery in local and state politics. That is a tall order—and one that is unlikely to be met any time soon, if ever.

Instead, it is entirely possible that the FDP will become even less significant in German politics, eventually disappearing from the Bundestag as it already has vanished from most elected bodies at the sub-federal levels of government. The first election results of 1999 do not bode well for the Liberals: in February, the party slid from slightly more than 7 to just over 5 percent in Hesse, and it fell into the 3 percent range in the June elections to the parliaments of both Bremen and the European Union. In the national poll standings, the party continues to hover near the 5 percent mark.

Yet the FDP *has* won a new lease on life in the Bundestag, at least for the first legislative term in Berlin. That means an extension of the chance to build a more secure niche in the multiparty system of post-unification Germany. The party must now make a convincing case that its continued presence in parliament and its return to the cabinet both matter. How to do that remains an open question. Party strategists continue to believe that the "liberal potential" is much higher than the FDP's modest share of the vote, reaching solid double-digit figures. So far, they have not found a successful way to tap into any such electoral reservoir.

The reformers proclaim that the party now has a golden opportunity to gain political recognition through a practice of "gleeful opposition" (*putzmuntere Opposition*). Westerwelle celebrates the chance to pursue what he calls an undiluted FDP program, FDP *pur*. This may be little more than whistling in the dark. On election eve in 1998, The Economist described the FDP as clearly having "the best ideas" of any German party,[32] but it also recognized that the neoliberal reform proposals met with little voter support or even interest in Germany's corporatist and risk-averse culture. That continues to be the case, although a much softer version of market-oriented reforms could well become part of the new government's policy agenda.

In response to the lukewarm public reception of its ideas, the FDP toned down its sharp reform image during the last half of the 1998 campaign. Since then, the party has tried to explain its "caring" positions more clearly, arguing that "being more liberal means being more social" (*liberaler ist sozialer*).[33] This new programmatic thrust is also a reply to the party's own critics of a one-dimensional economism, many of them linked to the Freiburg Circle.[34]

The Free Democratic campaign in 1998 ended with a renewed emphasis on the party's traditional role as moderate and pragmatic majority-maker in German coalition politics. This "functional" part of the FDP's dual identity came to outrank its programmatic neoliberalism in the final search for more tactical supporters. A credibly maintained balance between these "old" and "new" party attributes could possibly make the Free Democrats politically attractive again, if they should manage to remain players in future electoral and coalition politics in Berlin. And that will in part depend on factors beyond their control—above all, the comparative test performance of a governing coalition without the Liberals.[35]

Acknowledgments
I am grateful to many people in Germany, including a number of active Liberals, who have been willing to inform me about the FDP and other political parties. It is not possible to name them all, but Hans-Jürgen Beerfeltz, Hans-Jürgen Beyer, Martin Biesel, Carola von Braun, Rudolf Fischer, Wulf Oehme, Wilfried Paulus, Klaus Pfnorr, and several FDP Bundestag members were particularly helpful in responding to my requests for interviews and documentary information. None of them would agree with everything in this chapter. I bear responsibility for any errors of fact or interpretation. My research has benefited from participation in the annual meetings of the German-American Research Group, organized by Wolfgang-Uwe Friedrich. A research grant from California State University, Long Beach has supported my research.

Notes

1. "Die FDP bangt um ihr politisches Überleben," *Süddeutsche Zeitung*, 31 December 1997.
2. Dieter Zehentmayr's political cartoon in *Berliner Zeitung*, 29 June 1998.
3. The phrase was often used by Klaus Kinkel in 1994. Genscher picked it up during the 1998 campaign. See *Frankfurter Allgemeine Zeitung*, 18 September 1998.
4. For a representative collection of neoliberal views by FDP reformers, see Guido Westerwelle, ed., *Von der Gefälligkeitspolitik zur Verantwortungsgesellschaft* (Düsseldorf: Econ Verlag, 1997). The book includes the text of the Wiesbaden Principles of 1997. See also Westerwelle's arguments for a "change of politics" rather than a "change of government" in his election year book, *Neuland. Einstieg in einen Politikwechsel* (Düsseldorf: Econ Verlag, 1998).
5. For a fuller discussion, see Christian Søe, "The Free Democratic Party: A Struggle for Survival, Influence, and Identity," in David P. Conradt, Gerald R. Kleinfeld, George K. Romoser, and Christian Søe, eds., *Germany's New Politics* (Providence: Berghahn Books, 1995), 171–202, esp. 181–83.
6. These end-of-the-year data are based on figures provided by the FDP headquarters in Bonn, but I have differentiated between the higher membership in the western part of Berlin and the much lower membership in the eastern part of the city. This distinction should be kept in mind when examining reports that lump together members in both parts of the city and list the total under East. See *F.D.P. Geschäftbericht 1997–1998*

(Bonn: F.D.P. Die Liberalen, 1999), 50. For detailed earlier data along with a fuller explanation, see Søe, "The Free Democratic Party" (1995), 185, Table 9.2.

7. See the party's short internal reports, *Zur Situation der F.D.P. in den neuen Bundesländern* and *Netzwerk Ost* (updated versions of January 1997).

8. The FDP had once before scored 1.7 percent, in 1994 in the eastern state of Saxony. It would soon establish a new all-time low of 1.6 percent in the Landtag election of Mecklenburg-West Pomerania that coincided with the Bundestag election of 1998.

9. These challenges have been widely discussed. See, for example, the chapters by David Keithly and Irwin Collier in Mary N. Hampton and Christian Søe, eds., *Between Bonn and Berlin: German Politics Adrift?* (Lanham: Rowman and Littlefield, 1999).

10. See the proposals presented to the FDP by its party reform commission in *Reform. Für eine radikale Reform der Parteiarbeit* (Bonn: F.D.P. Die Liberalen, 1996), 1–136.

11. The issue returned in the spring of 1998, when several Free Democrats in the Bundestag voted with the opposition parties to significantly increase the number of occupational groups that were to be exempted from electronic surveillance measures.

12. See *Wiesbadener Grundsätze—Für die liberale Bürgergesellschaft* (Bonn: F.D.P. Die Liberalen, 1997), 1–34.

13. In a typical "catch-all" manner, the Wiesbaden program contains additional sections that express a liberal commitment to greater devolution, gender equality, toleration of minorities, and special attention to the need for continued immigration, including changes in the immigration and citizenship laws to encourage the integration of the legal newcomers. There are other pages dealing with the "social" side of the market economy, the importance of individual freedom and responsibility in the emerging information society, the danger of luddite reactions to scientific research and the new technologies, and a commitment to a liberal understanding and support of the constitutional order as well as culture, the arts, and education. After stating a commitment to the unification of Europe as a priority of the FDP's foreign policy and another to international human rights, the program returns to the theme of reducing the role of the state as an act of responsibility toward the next generation. Here it also expresses a preference for using market devices to advance environmental protection.

14. One example would be Genscher. See Günther Bannas, "Der Denkmalstürmer," *Süddeutsche Zeitung*, 26 May 1997.

15. For comparative reports on political donations and party finances, see *Frankfurter Rundschau*, 21 November and 4 December 1997, and *Die Woche*, 28 November 1997. See also F.D.P. *Geschäftbericht 1997–1998*, and the 1997 financial reports by the political parties in *Drucksache 13/8923* and *Drucksache 14/246* (Bonn: Deutscher Bundestag, 23 December 1998).

16. According to Gerhardt, the SPD and CDU had campaign budgets of 100 million and 70 million marks respectively. See *Neue Zürcher Zeitung*, 18 September 1998. Yet the Free Democrats could count themselves fortunate to have any cash reserves at all. Toward the end of 1997, the FDP had been faced with bankruptcy as the result of an unfavorable administrative court ruling. At issue was the FDP's contested eligibility for some 12 million marks in public funding, most of which already had been turned over to the party and spent by it. The problem stemmed from the discovery of a procedural error made by the party treasurer in his official application for the funds. The case was temporarily resolved early in the election year, when another administrative court suspended the previous ruling that would have required the FDP to repay some 10 million marks and forego some additional millions. A final judicial decision was postponed until after the 1998 election. Even if the dispute appeared to do no serious harm to the party's campaign efforts, it brought a surge of media attention to the financial plight of the FDP. Ironic commentaries pointed out that the original error had been

made by the very party that prided itself on a special competence in economic and financial matters. See *Süddeutsche Zeitung*, 21 February 1998.

17. In September 1998, the FDP home page recorded more than 350,000 hits per week. *F.D.P. Geschäftbericht 1997–1998* (Bonn: F.D.P., 1999), 4.

18. See "FDP. Laufkundschaft gesucht," *Focus*, 31 August 1998.

19. See the interview with Gerhardt, *Neue Zürcher Zeitung*, 18 September 1998.

20. Based on the author's interviews with FDP campaign planners in Bonn, in June and September 1998. See also the campaign reports in the monthly membership paper, *Die liberale Depesche*, and the campaign special, *Wahl liberal 98* (Bonn: F.D.P., 1998), 2.

21. See the outline presented by Hans-Jürgen Beerfeltz in the manuscript of his speech at the FDP strategy conference, 8 February 1998, 1–7. See also his later summary reports in the party's monthly paper, *Die liberale Depesche*, where the four campaign stages reappear. The federal party manager's strong preference for a more programmatic, reform-oriented campaign by the "new" FDP is well argued in his article, "Wir sind der Ruck durch Deutschland. Überlegungen zur Strategie und Wahlkampfplanung der F.D.P. für die Bundestagswahl 1998," in *Liberal*, August 1997, 5–12.

22. The FDP plan, which became known as the "option model"(*Optionsmodell*), reflects the party's traditional interest in civil rights. It would grant German citizenship to children born of foreign parents residing in Germany. One crucial provision allows a relatively long, but not indefinite, period of double citizenship for such children. Sometime between the ages of 18 and 25, they must eventually opt for one or the other citizenship. See the election program of the FDP, *Es ist Ihre Wahl* (Sankt Augustin: Liberal-Verlag, 1998), 57. It became the blueprint for new legislation in 1999 after the SPD-Green government withdrew its original, more far-reaching and controversial proposal for dual citizenship in such cases.

23. *Es ist Ihre Wahl. Das Wahlprogramm der FDP zur Bundestagswahl 1998.* (Sankt Augustin: Liberal Verlag, 1998).

24. This view was expressed in each of the author's post-election interviews with FDP campaign planners in Bonn, September 1998 and June 1999.

25. The press reported extensively on this subject. See, for example, Claus Gennrich, "Es gärt und brodelt in der FDP," *Frankfurter Allgemeine Zeitung*, 11 July 1998, and Daniel Goffart, "Nervenprobe mit ungewissem Ausgang," *Handelsblatt*, 14 July 1998.

26. See *Die liberale Depesche*, May-June 1998, for short articles that contrast the party's drafted election program with those of its rivals, including the CDU/CSU.

27. See the interview, "Ohne uns kein CDU-Kanzler," in *Die Woche*, 4 September 1998.

28. In 1969, the SPD-FDP coalition had 12 more Bundestag members than the CDU/CSU opposition. In 1998, a social-liberal coalition would have had 13 more members than the combined opposition of CDU/CSU, Greens, and PDS. The "red-green" coalition that formed the new government in 1998 had a broader parliamentary majority of 21.

29. *Bundestagswahl 1998* (Mannheim: Forschungsgruppe Wahlen, 1998), 16–18 and 93.

30. Free Democrats like to point out that there are several hundred directly elected FDP mayors in the East. The reason for this relative success seems to lie in the personal recognition of many local FDP candidates rather than their liberal party affiliation.

31. The data in these two paragraphs come from *Bundestagswahl 1998*, 18–33 and 82–84.

32. "Germany's Choice," *The Economist*, 26 September 1998, 18.

33. See the party executive's proposal for a new policy position, *Liberaler ist sozialer. Der liberale Weg in einen modernen Sozialstaat*, 1–9, prepared for discussion at the 1999 party conference in Bremen.

34. Members of the Freiburg Circle have become more outspoken. See the group's newsletter of 5 July 1999, 1–4, which criticizes "market radicalism," warns against

right-wing populism, and cautiously suggests the need for eventual leadership changes in the party.

35. For an early discussion of some strategic challenges facing the FDP as a small opposition party in the Bundestag, see *Leitsätze zur Oppositionsarbeit* (Bonn: Freie Demokratische Korrespondenz, 12 (October 1998), presented by Wolfgang Gerhardt and Guido Westerwelle. There followed an early strategic discussion paper, which was prepared by federal party planners and reviewed by the secretary-general, *F.D.P. 2002. Strategische Überlegungen zur Zukunft der F.D.P.* (Bonn: FDP, 2 December, 1998). See also Hans-Jürgen Beerfeltz's suggestions for an expanded organizational reform of the party, *ReformPartei-ParteiReform* (Bonn: FDP, 8 December 1999).

Chapter 5

BÜNDNIS '90/DIE GRÜNEN

From Opposition to Power

E. Gene Frankland

"Grün ist der Wechsel" (Green Is Change) was the 1998 campaign slogan of Bündnis'90/Die Grünen (Alliance'90/The Greens). The party presented itself as the choice for voters wanting not just a change of government in Bonn, but also a change of politics. The Greens began the year with polls indicating support from 10 percent of the electorate. With speculations about Green ministerial assignments already making the rounds, Joschka Fischer warned his party about the danger of overconfidence. By mid-year, the Greens' national poll support had plummeted toward the 5 percent threshold. The federal campaign turned out to be harder than anyone could have anticipated. The emergence during the night of September 27–28 of a solid "red-green" majority in the Bundestag—despite Green losses and the return of the FDP and the PDS—was unanticipated by pundits and politicians alike. The Greens, born in 1980 as a party of anti-Bonn protest, were to become a party of government at the national level.

The Greens had won their first Bundestag seats in 1983; the breakthrough came after they had won seats in six Landtag. In 1985, the Greens, who had entered the Hesse Landtag as the "fundamental opposition," found themselves sharing power with the SPD in Wiesbaden. Although this development provoked furious intra-party strife, before the end of the decade the leftist affiliate of the Greens, the Alternative List, had joined a coalition with the Berlin SPD. In the 1990s, the Greens' participation in Land government was accepted as routine by the major parties; in January 1998, the once "anti-party" party was sharing power with the SPD in five Länder.

The "normalization" of the Greens was the outcome of everyday experiences of thousands of local councilors and hundreds of state and federal parliamentarians and staff assistants. Yet crises have accelerated the learning process. Even the stunning defeat of the (West) Greens in the 1990 Bundestag election was to disappoint those who had been predicting the disintegration of the Greens' unruly alliance of activists since the early 1980s. The party responded to electoral "shock therapy" with structural reforms, a more pragmatic and professional style, and greater intraparty civility.

The 1998 campaign was to be another unanticipated occasion for rapid learning about media-democracy. Although a replay of their 1990 disaster was averted and at the last minute the red-green "happy ending" materialized, the Greens ended up weaker in relation to the SPD than they had anticipated in January 1998.

Sharing national power with the SPD Volkspartei during a period of socioeconomic insecurities promised to be a high risk course for a postmaterialist party with a small core electorate, a weak central organization, and a lingering *Streitkultur*. However, *Realos* (realists) and *Regierungslinken* (governmentally inclined leftists) quickly seized the opportunity, in hopes of entrenching themselves as the third force of the party system. The self-described "reform motor" of the red-green government will have to work very hard to bring about the change of politics promised Green voters in 1998.

This chapter begins by reviewing the Greens' development since 1994. Their electoral strategy, tactics, and program as formulated in early 1998 are then examined. The negative dynamics of the federal campaign after the Magdeburg conference, and the Greens' struggles to go back on the offensive are then discussed. The electoral results of 27 September 1998, subsequent coalition negotiations, and Green party conferences are considered next. Finally, in view of the early record of the red-green government, the implications for the Greens are analyzed.

The Greens' Development, 1994–97

Although the Greens failed to replace Kohl's coalition with a red-green one in the October 1994 election, they were returned to the Bundestag as its third strongest Fraktion. Journalists soon were referring to Joschka Fischer, the Greens' parliamentary co-speaker, as the "secret" opposition leader (as a favorable comparison with SPD parliamentary leader Rudolf Scharping). Polls were to indicate that Fischer enjoyed a more positive public image than several leaders of the major parties. In addition, a group of younger Green MPs was emerging with the savvy to tackle the complexities of taxes, budgets, and social insurance. While the major parties seemed programmatically adrift in the mid-1990s, the Greens were closing ranks to present themselves as the party of ecological and social reform. Forschungsgruppe Wahlen projected the national support of the Greens in the range of 9–12 percent from October 1994 to March 1998.[1] Rüdiger Schmitt-Beck determined that the party's electorate had grown nationally from 4 to 6 percent since 1992.[2] Thus, the Greens' concerns appeared to be coinciding with those of citizens beyond their loyal partisans, especially in the western Länder.[3]

In each of the Landtag elections of 1995, the Greens' share of the votes increased while the SPD's decreased. In February 1995, the Hesse Greens gained 11.2 percent of the votes (+2.4) and renewed their coalition with the SPD in Wiesbaden, obtaining for the first time a "core" ministry (Justice), as well as a super-ministry embracing environmental policy. Soon the Hessians were to earn the dubious distinction a red-green of being the first governing Green party to have its record marred by scandals: in October 1995 and in February 1998 Green ministers resigned due to charges of unprofessional behavior. In May 1995, the Greens won 13.1 percent of Bremen's votes (+1.7). Although mathematically a red-green majority existed, a divided SPD opted for a coalition with the CDU. However, in North Rhine-Westphalia, 10 percent of the votes (+5.0) for the Greens and SPD losses translated into a red-green coalition in Germany's most populous Land. Although crisis-ridden due to the SPD's pro-development agenda, the coalition with two Green ministers managed to survive. However, the minority of the Landtag Greens, and a number of local parties and citizen action groups, protested the majority's concessions. In October 1995, the Alternative List won 13.2 percent of Berlin's votes (+3.9), but there was no majority with the SPD, which renewed its coalition with the CDU.

In each of the March 1996 Land elections, the Greens' share of the votes increased and the SPD's share decreased. The biggest increase (+3.1) occurred in Schleswig-Holstein, where the Greens' 8.1 percent brought them for the first time not only into the Landtag, but also into the state government with two ministers. Subsequently, the Greens and Social Democrats in Kiel clashed over developmental issues, and the Greens faced grassroots protests about compromising environmental quality. In Baden-Württemberg, the Greens' share of the votes climbed (+2.6) to its highest ever there, 12.1 percent. Nevertheless, there was disappointment because of the gains enjoyed by the FDP, which joined a coalition with the CDU. Rhineland-Palatinate Greens won 6.9 percent of the votes (+0.4), but the FDP's share increased still more, allowing for the renewal of the SPD-FDP government in Mainz.

In the September 1997 Hamburg election, the Green-Alternative List joined a red-green coalition with three Green senators on the strength of

13.9 percent of the votes (and the SPD's losses). Although the GAL's electoral share represented the historic high point for Green state parties, polls had forecast a bigger gain than 0.4 percent. Survey analysis indicated that the GAL's support had declined by eight points among 18- to 24-year-olds and six points among 25- to 34-year-olds since 1993.[4] Similar results in other elections have led observers to conclude that the party of youth is becoming the party of a middle-aged generation.

During 1994–97, the national membership of the Greens grew from about 44,000 to 49,000.[5] This incremental growth is noteworthy because during this period the CDU, SPD, FDP, and PDS had seen their memberships decline. The Greens had grown despite the negativism of public opinion regarding parties in the mid-1990s. In August 1998, the Greens' recruitment drive was to surpass its goal of 50,000 members. The federal office reported that around a third of the new members were younger than thirty,[6] evidence that the party of graying '68ers could still recruit members from the younger generation.

Although the party's membership had grown, its organization had changed little between 1994 and 1997. The Greens remained a very decentralized party. Party co-speaker Jürgen Trittin saw in reality "no federal party, rather a confederation of strong Land associations."[7] In fact, there were few functionaries at either level. For example, in 1996 the federal party office had twenty-two full-time employees while the well-entrenched party of Baden-Württemberg had nine,[8] in comparison, the SPD's federal campaign unit alone employed thirty people.[9] The staffs of the Greens' state and federal parliamentary groups dwarfed those of their state and federal parties. The Greens had discarded most of the anti-elitist rules, but inspired by the new social movements, they retained quotas to represent factional, gender, and regional diversities in their collective party and parliamentary leaderships. In November 1994, Green delegates rejected a loosening of the federal rule against the simultaneous holding of a parliamentary seat and a party leadership office. However, in the following years, activists moved toward acceptance of the media role of personalities, such as Rezzo Schlauch, who won 39.3 percent of the votes in the 1996 Stuttgart mayoral election.

Since 1994, the Greens have been able to project a less fractious image, with the notable exception of quarrels over Bosnia and NATO. In late 1995, nearly half of the Bundestag Greens voted in favor of Bundeswehr participation in NATO-led forces in the former Yugoslavia, despite the party's rejection of such action at the Bremen conference. Intense intraparty debates followed, but factional leaders, fearing a negative impact on looming Land elections, sidetracked the issue at the Mainz conference in March 1996. NATO's eastern expansion reignited quarrels in 1997. *Super-Realo* Fischer maintained that since NATO expansion was inevitable, the best thing was to get into federal government, where the Greens could influence the process. Leftist Ludger Volmer rejected NATO expansion in favor of strengthening the Organization for Security and Cooperation in Europe. Although Fischer and his allies had long sought to convince the party that a realistic foreign and security policy was "the" prerequisite for any red-green coalition, there was little evidence of their efforts in the 1998 electoral draft program, which the federal executive board released in October 1997. It reflected the views of those who opposed any Green compromises in advance of coalition negotiations with the SPD. Sharp exchanges between *Promis* (party prominents) followed, prompting observers to ask if the Greens really had "matured."

The Pre-campaign: Kassel to Magdeburg

At the November conference in Kassel, Green leaders steered around intra-party disputes over NATO, Bosnia, and gasoline prices. Delegates overwhelmingly approved a number of resolutions, for example, embracing Andrea Fischer's basic social support program (*Grundsicherung*) and supporting the scheduled launching of the European common currency. With both wings realizing that there was a good chance of red-green victory, the conference provided the media with no evidence of a revived *Fundi-Realo* (fundamentalist-realist) cleavage. Joschka Fischer's rhetorical efforts to reach across generational and factional lines earned him a first ever standing ovation at a federal conference.

In contrast to the SPD, the Greens had only two strategic options: red-green or opposition. *Realos* and *Regierungslinken* had worked since 1996 to keep alive the red-green government in North Rhine-Westphalia. At the federal level, the Greens distanced themselves from the PDS. Everyone recognized that the SPD would choose a grand coalition with the CDU /CSU over a minority red-green government tolerated by the PDS. Of the two SPD chancellor aspirants, the Greens programmatically stood closer to Lafontaine; however, he appeared more likely to cut into the Greens' left-alternative electorate. Schröder's "*Stammtisch*" populism of 1996–97 had caused Promis to assert that they were not prepared to share power at any price. However, many Greens believed that Schröder's centrist candidacy would be tactically advantageous, since it would be more likely to draw votes from the CDU/CSU.

The Bundestag campaign of 1998 promised more evidence of "Americanization." The media had already forced the SPD into making up its mind on its chancellor candidate earlier than had been planned. The Greens' managers decided to produce individual portrait posters of Joschka Fischer, Kerstin Müller, Jürgen Trittin, and Gunda Röstel.[10]

In the aftermath of Schröder's emergence as the SPD's chancellor candidate in March, Fischer discouraged efforts to have the Greens designate him as their top candidate. Resulting intra-party conflict would have diverted media attention away from the party's comprehensive reform agenda.

Yet the problem was that, despite growing expertise of the *Bundestagsfraktion* (parliamentary group) in socioeconomic areas, the public only attributed high competence to the Greens in environmental protection. Polls indicated that in January 1998 only 6 percent of the electorate considered environmental protection one of Germany's top two problems. Unemployment ranked first (87 percent) and was followed by asylum-seekers/foreigners (13 percent). During the 1998 campaign, polls were to indicate that concern for environmental protection was registered by 5 to 9 percent (averaging 6.7) of the electorate, while the numbers for unemployment concern ranged from 83 to 91 percent.[11] Schmitt-Beck pointed out that in the mid-1990s, Green voters were not so different from others in their economic concerns;[12] therefore, the Greens could expect trouble if they were perceived as a one issue party, even by those who shared their environmentalism.

As in 1994, the federal executive hired a professional advertising agency to reshape the party's public image. The Michael Schirner Agency designed a new logo, a "Ü," to create a new colorful image for a federal campaign whose central theme would be that only by voting Green was there going to be a change of politics. The traditional sunflower logo was pushed into the background to show that the Greens were a party with competence in numerous areas, especially social and economic policies.[13]

The Greens went into the 1998 campaign short of resources. Only DM 5 million was available to the federal managers. State parties balked at allocating more funds to the national office; as a result, the budget for federal activities was 25 percent less than in 1994.[14] The game plan was to target women, voters with above-average education, and young and first-time voters in the large cities. The Greens' limited resources could also explain the amateurism of their draft program's first preamble. The federal executive lacked the personnel to cover all its normal responsibilities, let alone those involved in preparing for a competitive national campaign.

One way of interpreting the intra-party conflict over the drafts of the electoral program is that it arose because the Greens were overdue for a new *Grundsatzprogramm* (fundamental program). The Greens' 1980 *Bundesprogramm* (federal program) was obsolete, and the 1993 *Grundkonsens* (basic agreement) was only an outline of the principles shared by the Greens and Bündnis '90. Activists, therefore, tended to approach the electoral program as an internal document to redefine the party's identity as much as an external document to appeal to voters.[15] Except for agreeing with the *Realos* that there could be no unilateral exit from NATO, the Left gave little ground in the second draft. Despite the protests of East Greens, significantly higher gasoline prices stayed in the program. Only days before the Magdeburg conference, leading *Realos* and leftists crafted compromise wording that opposed Bundeswehr participation in international peacemaking forces, but left the door open so that Green MPs could vote their consciences in the case of Bosnia.

In the 1 March 1998 Lower Saxony election, which the SPD leadership had transformed into a de facto party primary for chancellor, the Greens won 7 percent of the votes while the SPD won 47.9 percent and preserved its absolute majority. Green spokespersons viewed their party's slight losses (-0.4) as not discouraging.[16] However, the results demonstrated that Schröder's appeal could cut into the potential electorate of the Greens more than had been anticipated.

At the Magdeburg conference, the delegates overwhelmingly passed an electoral program that identified the Greens as a party standing for "sustainability, social justice, democracy and equality."[17] The party's goals were: modernizing ecologically, attacking unemployment, renewing the *Sozialstaat* (social welfare state), extending democracy, and advancing development of southern and eastern countries. The 154-page program's centerpiece was ecological and social tax reform, bridging the problems of unemployment and environmental protection. Its most controversial provision, gradually raising the price of gasoline to DM 5 per liter by 2009, passed with a solid majority. The program included numerous other proposals: ending the Transrapid project, exiting from nuclear power, halving the size of the Bundeswehr by ending conscription, introducing a basic social support program, protecting asylum seekers, liberalizing the citizenship law, treating homosexual and heterosexual couples equally, dismantling the NATO alliance, and democratizing the European Union. The program called for "a new beginning" with red-green and urged second votes (*Zweitstimmen*) for the Greens to prevent the SPD from forming a grand coalition with the CDU/CSU.

The surprise of the conference came when the compromise Bosnia resolution, which was backed by the federal party and parliamentary leaderships, failed to pass by a one-vote majority. Fischer and his allies had underestimated the resistance on the floor of the conference; some delegates were ideologically opposed to military intervention, but others were upset by the vagueness of the resolution, and by the way it had been worked out over their heads. In contrast to the Kassel conference, the Magdeburg conference resurrected the old questions about whether the Greens were ready for federal government.

The Dynamics of the Greens' Federal Campaign

In Magdeburg's aftermath, Kohl labeled a red-green government as a "security risk," and Schröder reversed himself on the Greens' governmental competence. However, the Bundestag Greens of the 1990s were not bound by "imperative mandate," which had complicated life for the Bundestag Greens in the 1980s. When the vote came up on NATO's eastern expansion, Fischer and thirteen other Green MPs supported it, while most of their colleagues abstained. Later in June, 70 percent of the Bundestag Greens voted to continue Bundeswehr participation in the NATO-led forces in Bosnia.

The West Greens' greatest misjudgment at the Magdeburg conference was the negative impact of their proposal to raise the price of gasoline to DM 5 per liter by 2009. The Greens' 1994 electoral program had included a similar plan without triggering a media frenzy. Most research institutes, environmental groups, and energy experts of the major parties were already on record in support of significantly higher gasoline taxes. The Greens' plan would be phased in over ten years. It would use the revenues from higher gasoline taxes to lower social insurance payments by employees and employers. There would be relief provisions for drivers who lacked access to public transit and for other hardship cases. The rising cost of gasoline would be partially offset in the short run by lower auto taxes, and in the long run by the development of more fuel-efficient automobiles.

However, in a modern media campaign, such technicalities are likely to be overlooked. CDU campaign managers sprang into action with a *Tankstelle* (gas station) campaign exposing the costs for the average driver, as if a red-green government would immediately raise the price of gasoline to DM 5 per liter. SPD spokespersons distanced their party from the Greens. Leading Greens publicly quarreled about whether (and how) the policy should be changed. Political cartoonists rediscovered the irresponsible Green party obscured in recent years by the popular Fischer. An Allensbach poll indicated that about as many people associated the Greens with higher gasoline prices (65 percent) as with environmental protection (67 percent) or alternative energy (65 percent); relatively few people associated them with the socioeconomic themes high on the public agenda.[18]

The party leadership's efforts to ease public anxieties about the Greens' energy taxes were dealt a setback on March 22. A backbench Green MP remarked that the price of jet fuel should be significantly raised, and that Germans should take a vacation flight only once every five years. These were the headlines on the day of the Schleswig-Holstein local election. In the low-turnout election, the Greens' support fell from 10.3 percent to 6.8 percent, while the SPD's support jumped from 39.5 to 42.4 percent. Disenchanted by the contentious image of the federal party and its controversial policies, Green voters stayed home or cast their ballots for the SPD. The federal executive decided to move up the meeting of the Länderrat (the Council of State Leaders and highest party organ between federal conferences) to consider a short (or four-year) program.

Even before the March wave of negative media coverage, Saxony-Anhalt Greens' prospects for retaining their Landtag seats (and junior partnership in the state government) were not good. In 1994, the Greens had barely cleared the 5 percent threshold. Although the SPD-Green minority government (tolerated by the PDS) had been characterized by a lot of cooperation, this had not translated into a stronger base for the Green party organization. Economic issues overshadowed environmental and social concerns in a Land with Germany's highest unemployment and lowest economic growth. The federal party's call for higher gasoline taxes could only further handicap the chances of Saxony-Anhalt Greens. The state SPD favored a renewed coalition with the Greens, but declined to "loan" them second votes. Despite interventions by western Promis, Saxony-Anhalt Greens ended up with only 3.2 percent of the vote on April 26; the SPD gained slightly to 35.9 percent and went on to form a minority government (tolerated by the PDS).

In three months, the Greens had seen their national poll support slide from 10 to 8 percent,[19] and they had lost votes in three consecutive elections. A number of *Realos* held Trittin responsible for a significant portion of the negative trend; however, in the cause of party unity, they restrained the urge to work to deprive him of a secure list place in Lower Saxony. In May, the left-leaning North Rhine-Westphalia Greens gave majority support to new SPD Minister-President Wolfgang Clement, despite their conflicts with him in recent years. To have done otherwise would have greatly complicated their party's federal red-green strategy.

The Greens' short (13-page) program, "*Neue Mehrheiten nur mit uns*" (New Majorities Only with Us), was overwhelmingly endorsed by the Länderrat in early June. Focusing on what would be doable during 1998–2002, it put the struggle against unemployment up front, underlined the fact that ecology creates jobs, and called for social justice. Fischer and others maintained that DM 5-per-liter gasoline tax had been "the wrong symbol for the right thing." All the controversial numbers were removed, but ecological-social tax reform remained at the core of the short program. Significantly, the Greens pledged to maintain "continuity" in Germany's foreign policy.

Only once did the Greens' campaign receive a boost from media coverage of outside events. The May–June exposés of the safety problems posed by excessive radioactivity of the containers used to transport nuclear wastes put the Kohl government on the defensive. This enabled the Greens to enhance their profile as the only party favoring a quick exit from nuclear power. Röstel maintained that it could be done in eight years. Schröder spoke out in favor of ending nuclear energy within twenty-five years. However, in August he signaled possible support for closing the oldest nuclear plants in the near future. Fischer considered the beginning of the end of nuclear power as a precondition for a red-green coalition. This was the only "radical" demand of the Greens that enjoyed majority support in the polls, but clearly it was a secondary issue in the campaign.

While Fischer (who had raised private funds for his own campaign bus tour throughout the country) sought to make the party more credible to the "new middle" voters, Trittin attempted to appeal to voters on the left. In June, on the occasion of a Bundeswehr induction ceremony in Berlin, he made anti-militarist remarks suggesting parallels with Nazi times, which provoked outrage in the conservative press and calls within the party for his removal as co-speaker. After some clarifications, the informal "G-7" committee, which brought together the party and parliamentary leaderships for crisis management,[20] stood behind Trittin. With, in effect, two federal campaign centers, it was no surprise that the Greens were having trouble projecting a unified image to the electorate.

In contrast to the SPD, the Greens had no gatekeeping arrangement for clearing press interviews. Therefore, the remarks in July by a Green MP calling for Autobahn speed limits of 100 km/hr (Tempo 100) again put the party on the defensive. Such a provision had been omitted in the short program (although it could be found in the electoral program). Polls indicated that not even a majority of Green voters supported Tempo 100.[21] Schröder flatly rejected it. The CDU ran an ad campaign exposing the Greens' attack on auto drivers and the freedom of mobility. The FDP labeled the Greens the party of "sacrifice and restriction." Fischer's response was that Tempo 100 was needed, but it was not a central issue of the Greens' 1998 campaign.

After a summer of largely self-inflicted wounds, and with only the issue of nuclear power allowing them to go on the offensive, the Greens saw their poll support in August slip to 5.0–6.3 percent.[22] Furthermore, Schröder's modernization appeal, which lacked any specifics or calls for sacrifice, had left the Greens the more exposed target for CDU and FDP attacks. The Greens presented themselves as the corrective to Schröder's commitment to little more than personnel changes in Bonn. Kerstin Müller, from the Green Left, underlined the many policy commonalities with the SPD. At the end of August, the federal executive condensed the party's short program into a three-page action program for the first one hundred days of a red-green government. Its first priority was to fight unemployment with a new alliance for jobs; other priorities included phasing out nuclear energy and phasing in ecological taxes—no numbers and no dates.

Bavaria has never been a social-structural stronghold of the Greens. In 1998, red-green was not a prospect there due to the weakness of the SPD; however, coming two weeks before the federal election, the election in Bavaria took on extra importance regarding power in Bonn. With polls indicating that the Bavarian Greens' support was barely 5 percent, the Greens ran a survival campaign with posters warning: "*Ohne Grün sieht Bayern schwarz*" (Without the Greens, Bavaria will look black). On September 13, Greens everywhere were relieved when the party won 5.7 percent of the votes (-0.4), retaining their Landtag seats. The Bavarians' efforts to mobilize youthful support paid off as they became the only Green party in 1997–98 to increase its share of the 18–24 age group's votes.[23]

In the final weeks of the federal campaign, the Greens sought to avoid any fatal errors. Werner Schulz's call for a new national anthem provoked critical reactions from the other parties (and uneasiness among his colleagues), but did not seem to hurt his party. Mid-September polls indicated sufficient support for the Greens to reenter the Bundestag, but the coalition question was wide open. Prominent Greens maintained that red-green was viable with a one-seat majority, while some SPD leaders spoke of the need of a majority of 20–25 seats. Upsetting a number of East Greens, Trittin encouraged tactical voting for the SPD in those eastern districts where the PDS might win seats directly.[24] Fischer's last-hour remarks warned voters of the dangers of a grand coalition.

The Electoral Outcome and Its Aftermath

The Greens won 6.7 percent of the crucial second or "list" vote, which was 0.6 percent less than in 1994. Only in three states did the party's share of the list vote increase (1.1 points in Berlin was the most). The Greens won 4.97 percent of the first or district vote (1.5 less than in 1994). They failed again to win any district seats; their best performance was 29.6 percent in Berlin-Kreuzberg-Schönberg. In the western states, including Berlin, the party won 5.5 to 11.3 percent of the list votes; in the eastern states it won 2.9 to 4.4 percent. The Greens' list votes yielded forty-seven Bundestag seats, two less than in 1994, but still enough to rank as the third largest Fraktion, which would include forty-two westerners and five easterners.

The results in the Mecklenburg-West Pomerania Landtag elections, also held on September 27, underlined the party's weakness in the East. The Greens won 2.7 of the votes (-1.0 compared to 1994). Their Land speaker attributed this dismal outcome to the Greens' DM 5-per-liter gasoline tax proposal and to the "Schröder-Effekt."[25] In view of the negative trend, Brandenburg Greens found some encouragement in winning

3.6 percent of the Bundestag votes (+0.7 more than in 1994) and in holding on to 4.1 percent of the votes in the local elections on September 27.

The national demographics of the Green vote indicated disproportionate support from voters under 45, but also losses compared to 1994 in the same age groups, especially those 18–24 years (-4.2).[26] Only in the 45–59 age group did the party's support increase (+0.7). As in 1994, the Greens had more support from women than men, especially from women under 35. The Greens enjoyed their only noteworthy gain (+2.0) of support among the self-employed. Among the unemployed, it hardly increased at all (+0.2).[27] In twelve districts, the Greens' list support rose 1.0–5.6 points; these gains tended to be in large cities.

On the night of September 27–28, Schröder's "dream scenario" emerged: a workable red-green majority (twenty-one seats) stemming from a strong SPD performance and a weak Green performance.[28] At Magdeburg, the Greens had designed their negotiation commission (six men and six women). Its membership would be balanced between the Left and the *Realos*. Nine members were federal parliamentarians or party leaders; three were Promis from Berlin, Baden-Württemberg, and North Rhine-Westphalia. Coalition negotiations between the Greens and the SPD progressed more harmoniously than most observers had anticipated. The Greens made numerous compromises on policy details and timetables in exchange for framework commitments by the SPD, for example, beginning the exit from nuclear power and the process of ecological tax reform. The Greens would obtain three cabinet ministries—Foreign Affairs (Joschka Fischer), Environment (Jürgen Trittin), and Health (Andrea Fischer)—plus one state minister, four parliamentary state secretaries, and one parliamentary commissioner. This "governmental team" would include six women and three men from various currents within the party.[29]

The major point of controversy at the October 23–24 Bonn conference was whether Green federal ministers would be obligated to resign their parliamentary seats, as has been the practice at the Land level (so that others on the party list can move up). The delegates decided that the ministers would keep their seats, at least until implications could be fully considered in two years. About 95 percent of the delegates voted to support the SPD-Green coalition agreement and the personnel lineup. A Green coalition committee was formed to bring together the ministers and the parliamentary and party leaderships on a weekly basis.

Bundestag Greens choose Rezzo Schlauch to replace Fischer as the parliamentary co-speaker. In the *Realos*' caucus earlier in October, Schlauch had defeated Werner Schulz, who had served as the Bündnis '90/The Greens parliamentary manager since 1990. Schulz, complaining about how things had been worked out behind the curtains, resigned as manager.

Kerstin Müller was reelected as the parliamentary co-speaker from the Left. Although the 1998 election reproduced the Fraktion's *Realo* majority, it also reinforced its leftist minority with Hans-Christian Ströbele (veteran Alternative List politician), Claudia Roth (veteran European MP), and Jürgen Trittin.

In December 1997, a proposal had surfaced to downsize the federal executive board and create a presidium, which would include Green parliamentarians and ministers. This would mean loosening the party's rule against holding both a parliamentary (or ministerial) seat and a federal party office. There was no factional split on the need for structural reform. Röstel and Trittin argued that federal governmental participation by the Greens would necessitate quicker decision-making and closer coordination of activities. Fischer's remarks indicated a preference for even more "normalization": a party chair. Other *Realos* urged abolition of the separation of parliamentary seats and party offices.

At the 11–13 December 1998 Leipzig conference a two-thirds majority of the delegates voted to reduce the federal executive to five salaried members, and to create a party council (*Parteirat*) of an additional twenty-five members, which would meet monthly. No more than twelve of the council members may hold parliamentary or ministerial positions. Membership election is governed by quotas requiring women to be at least equally represented and easterners to be at least proportionally represented. Trittin and Andrea Fischer were elected; Joschka Fischer declined because of his time demands as foreign minister. To replace Trittin as federal party co-speaker, the conference elected leftist Antje Radcke, who has maintained that the Greens must not allow the coalition agreement to delimit their profile. The delegates asserted themselves by amending the federal executive's structural proposal and rejecting its symbolic proposal to rename speakers as "chairpersons." It was clear at Leipzig that Green delegates still relish standing up to their leaders.

Implications

As the arm of the eco-peace movement, the Greens were viewed by mainstream observers in 1983 as a threat to parliamentary democracy. In 1985, when the Greens entered the state government of Hesse, there were predictions of economic collapse. During the 1998 campaign, critics sought to stick the "chaos" label on the party. However, in August Kohl undercut this effort by praising Fischer's political skills and thinking aloud about CDU-Green alliances. During the campaign, polls indicated that voters favored a grand coalition; nevertheless, in October a plurality favored red-green and viewed the Greens as a dependable partner.[30] Not even the

CSU viewed the former eco-peace movement party's national governmental role as a regime crisis.

The new coalition, which brought together a party divided between modernizers and traditionalists who had been out of national power for sixteen years, and a party divided between realists and leftists who had never shared national power, was bound to get off to a bumpy start. Although polls indicated a public willingness to give the red-green government the benefit of the doubt, the Emnid survey of elite opinion indicated great disappointment with the coalition's early performance, especially among media executives.[31] Most of the scorn was focused on its financial and tax policies, which were seen as reflecting the outmoded views of Lafontaine. Except for Fischer's futile suggestion that NATO reconsider its first use of nuclear weapons doctrine, his foreign ministry communicated well its pursuit of continuity.

On the other hand, Trittin's confrontationist approach to nuclear energy policy provoked both German industrialists, and the French and British, whose firms reprocess German nuclear waste. After weeks of feuding, Schröder intervened to delay Trittin's new atomic law. Environmentalists protested the feebleness of the government's efforts. Despite the negative editorials, January polls indicated that Schröder enjoyed high marks with the public and that red-green had majority support. The parliamentary and party leaderships of the Greens put a positive spin on the government's first one hundred days as the beginning of reform in numerous areas, e.g., citizenship, ecological taxes, and nuclear energy.

The February defeat of the red-green government in Hesse was unexpected. The CDU's petition drive against the new citizenship law, which would permit dual passports for Turks and other minorities, produced a late hour surge (+4.2) of votes for the CDU, enabling it to form a coalition with the FDP. Although the SPD increased its electoral share (+1.4), the Greens won only 7.2 percent of the votes (-4.0), their worst Hesse showing since 1983. Their weak performance involved Land factors, such as the ministerial scandals and the lack of leadership in Wiesbaden. However, federal factors appeared to be more important. On September 27, Hesse Greens had won 8.2 percent of their state's list votes for the Bundestag; the Greens' pursuit of social and ecological reforms in the Schröder government had not brought back their voters. Survey analysis indicated that the party's support fell eight points among 18- to 24-year-olds and thirteen points among 25- to 34-year-olds.[32] Röstel's explanation was that the Greens' reform initiatives were failing to connect with young people's core concerns: education, training, technology, and jobs.[33]

In March, polls indicated that national support for the Greens had slipped to 5 percent.[34] Warning of an existential crisis, Fischer called for structural renewal, i.e., doing away with collective leadership and the separation of party office and parliamentary seat. Trittin saw the need for a stronger leadership structure in dealing with the SPD and the media. Feminists, however, saw a threat to the quota system, especially since the names advanced for "party chair" were those of males. Others saw programmatic renewal as a more pressing need, essential to adapting to a political environment that has become less favorable to postmaterialist themes.

Schröder managed to deflect disproportionate blame for his government's indecisiveness during the first one hundred days onto others. After Lafontaine's resignation as finance minister and party chair, Schröder could better set the "new middle" course for his government. There are areas, such as budget, administration, and social reform, in which the Greens are less leftist than most of the SPD. However, Schröder's tactical temptation may be to portray the Greens as new "Jusos" (irresponsible leftists). In spring 1999, there were already speculations about Schröder's opting for an SPD-FDP coalition, which many in the SPD would not relish, given the ascendancy of economic liberalism within the FDP.

Various strategists have considered the scenario in which the co-evolution of the Green and the CDU provides a black-green alternative. After the 1994 local elections in North Rhine-Westphalia, twenty-four CDU-Greens alliances were formed. Experimentation is already conceivable in a couple of states, even more so if the Greens' federal relationship with the SPD goes sour. Trittin, venting his frustrations from dealings with Schröder, signaled that the door could be open to the CDU in the future. However, if the CDU/CSU should continue its nationalist-conservative course, as exemplified by its opposition to citizenship reform, it is hard to see black-green as viable.

Treating Kosovo as an exceptional case, *Realos* and *Regierungslinken* supported NATO's air war against Serbia to stop its abuse of human rights. Foreign Minister Fischer saw military action as the only way to force a political solution on Belgrade. However, anti-war opposition grew at the grassroots level. The PDS positioned itself as the only party opposing NATO's attacks. Since 1994, the PDS has sought to penetrate the alternative-left milieu of the Greens; awkward compromises by the Greens to remain the SPD's junior partner could set the stage for its western breakthrough. In early 1999, a member of the Green parliamentary group in Lower Saxony and a former leader of the Berlin Greens/Alternative List switched to the PDS. The weak eastern parties of the Greens face higher chances of defections to the PDS and other parties, if they appear doomed to be fringe parties. The Landtag comeback of the Saxony Greens (who won 4.4 percent of the state's 1998 Bundestag votes) would provide a big boost for party morale.

In conclusion, the Greens have been accepted as a "normal" party in recent years by their own members, competing party elites, and the general public. At Magdeburg, Green activists sought to define their reform agenda for the next decade in specific (and candid) terms. In the following months they struggled, often against themselves, to stabilize the party's declining support. As a result of the September 27 election, the Greens were set to become a governing party in Bonn. Since October, they have had mixed experiences in sharing power with the SPD Volkspartei in a media-democracy. Along the way, they have recognized the nonpermissive political environment (socioeconomic insecurities, generational changes, and increased voter volatility) that they will be forced to cope within the foreseeable future. In short, the Greens (if they do not splinter over emotional issues such as Kosovo) can look forward to the "exciting" life of a single-digit (5–9 percent) party on the national stage, ever vulnerable to outside forces. But a small party capable of rapid learning and not beholden to powerful economic interests could have a big impact in the Berlin Republic.

Notes

1. Forschungsgruppe Wahlen, Mannheim, *Politbarometer* (Monatliche repräsentative Umfrage), October 1994–March 1998 Reports.
2. Rüdiger Schmitt-Beck, "Wählerpotential von Bündnis '90/Grünen im Ost-West-Vergleich: Umfang, Struktur, politische Orientierungen," *Journal für Sozialforschung* 34: 45–70, and Rüdiger Schmitt-Beck, "Vor dem Wahljahr 1998: Wählerpotentiale von Bündnis'90/Grünen und ihre Wahrnehmungen politischer Probleme" (unpublished paper, University of Mannheim, September 1997).
3. Schmitt-Beck's research (1997) indicated that during 1992–96 the Green party's western core electorate had grown from 4 to 7 percent, but its eastern core electorate had declined from 4 to 3 percent.
4. Forschungsgruppe Wahlen, *Wahl in Hamburg: Eine Analyse der Bürgerschaftswahl vom 21. September 1997*, Bericht Nr. 87 (Mannheim, 24 September 1997), 54.
5. These unpublished membership data were provided by Dr. Norbert Franck of the Greens' federal office, Bonn, in January 1998.
6. "Mitgliederwerbung," *Schrägstrich* 11–12/98 (Bonn: Bündnis '90/Die Grünen, 1998): 4.
7. Quoted by Bettina Gaus, "Neue grüne Strukturen," *die tageszeitung*, 5 February 1998, 6.
8. Data are from the author's interviews with Green party officials in Stuttgart and Bonn, February 1996.
9. Christiane Schlötzer-Scotland, "Arbeitsplatz vor Umwelt," *Süddeutsche Zeitung*, 25 September 1997.
10. Twenty-two thousand copies of the Fischer poster, 10,000 of the Röstel poster, 3,000 of the Müller poster, and 3,000 of the Trittin poster were ordered by Green local parties (*Der Stern*, Nr. 37 [3 September 1998], 18).

11. Forschungsgruppe Wahlen, *Politbarometer* (Monatliche repräsentative Umfrage), January-September 1998 Reports (Mannheim).

12. Schmitt-Beck, September 1997.

13. Interview of Michael Schirner, "Wahlkampfagentur: Zeichen des Wechsels, *Schrägstrich* 1–2/98 (Bonn: Bündnis'90/Die Grünen, 1998), 16–17.

14. Interview of Dietmar Strehl, Green party treasurer, "Bundestagswahl 1998: Programme and PR," *Schrägstrich* (Bonn: Bündnis 90/Die Grünen, 1998): 22. Following the end of the campaign, the federal party was to report spending DM 6.5 million.

15. See Hubert Kleinert, "Wahlprogramm: Doppelter Charakter," *Schrägstrich* 1–2/98 (Bonn: Bündnis'90/Die Grünen, 1998), 17–18.

16. Although Lower Saxony Greens won a smaller share of the second or list votes compared to 1994, they increased their relative share of the first or district votes by +0.3 to 7.2 percent. See Forschungsgruppe Wahlen, *Wahl in Niedersachsen: Eine Analyse der Landtagswahl vom 1. März 1998*, Bericht Nr. 88 (Mannheim, 4 March 1998), 7.

17. Bündnis'90/Die Grünen, *Grün ist der Wechsel: Programm zur Bundestagswahl 98* (Bonn, April 1998), 5.

18. Cited in Renate Köcher, "Kommen die Grünen aus der Mode?" *Frankfurter Allgemeine Zeitung*, 25 March 1998, 5.

19. Forschungsgruppe Wahlen, *Politbarometer* (Monatliche repräsentative Umfrage), February–April 1998 Reports (Mannheim).

20. The "G-7" campaign committee operated outside of the party charter and met (without staff) to manage crises. It included the parliamentary co-speakers (Fischer and Müller), the party co-speakers (Trittin and Röstel), the parliamentary manager (Werner Schulz), the federal party manager (Heide Rühle), and the federal party treasurer (Dietmar Strehl). See "Keine Eigentore mehr," *Süddeutsche Zeitung*, 26 June 1998.

21. According to the Infratest/dimap poll, 7 percent of the national electorate and 26 percent of Green voters favored Tempo 100 on the Autobahn. Cited in *Das Bild Archiv*, "Bonn-o-meter: Die Politikumfrage der Woche," 11 July 1998.

22. Forsa had the Greens at 5 percent (27 August); Emnid (28 August), Infratest/dimap (29 August), and Forschungsgruppe Wahlen (14 August), at 6 percent; Allensbach (26 August), at 6.3 percent. "Wahlumfrage," *Der Spiegel On line*(/wahl98/forschung/index.htm).

23. Forschungsgruppe Wahlen, *Wahl in Bayern: Eine Analyse der Landtagswahl vom 25. September 1994* Bericht Nr. 75 (28 September 1994), 11, and *Wahl in Bayern: Eine Analyse der Landtagswahl vom 13. September 1998* Bericht Nr. 90 (16 September 1998), 58–59 (Mannheim).

24. At the outset, the East SPD had declined to wage a red-green campaign of stand agreements and loaned votes. Prominent East Green Marianne Birthler, a Berlin district candidate, was notably upset by Trittin's late hour tactical appeal.

25. Klaus-Dieter Feige, "Mecklenburg-Vorpommern: Ein Dammbruch," *Schrägstrich* 10/98 (Bonn: Bündnis'90/Die Grünen, 1998), 23.

26. Forschungsgruppe Wahlen, *Bundestagswahl 1994: Eine Analyse der Wahl zum 13. Deutschen Bundestag am 16. Oktober 1994* Bericht Nr. 76, Second Edition (21 October 1994), 18, and Bundestagswahl 1998: Eine Analyse der Wahl vom 27. September 1998, *Bericht* Nr. 91 (30 September 1998), 18 (Mannheim).

27. Forschungsgruppe Wahlen, *Bericht* Nr. 76, 21, and *Bericht* Nr. 91, 22.

28. Ian Traylor, "Kohl's long reign comes to an end," *Manchester Guardian Weekly*, 4 October 1998.

29. The Greens' initial demand for four ministerial positions (so they could balance men and women) was rebuffed by Schröder. To attain gender parity at the ministerial

level, they planned to nominate a Green woman as Germany's second European commissioner. Also, as compensation, two women were to be selected as federal party co-speakers.

30. Forschungsgruppe Wahlen, *Politbarometer* (Monatliche Repräsentative Umfrage) 10/98, 4 (Mannheim).

31. Cited by Rainer Zitelmann, "Führungskräfte geben Rot-Grün schlechte Noten," *Die Welt* On-Line, 30 December 1998.

32. Forschungsgruppe Wahlen, *Wahl in Hessen: Eine Analyse der Landtagswahl vom 19. Februar 1995*, Bericht Nr. 80 (7 March 1995), 12, and *Landtagswahl in Hessen: Eine Analyse der Wahl vom 7. Februar 1999*, Bericht Nr. 93 (10 February 1999), 17 (Mannheim).

33. Gunda Röstel, "Für einen politischen Neubeginn von Bündnis 90/Die Grünen," Discussion Paper, Bonn, 20 February 1999 (www.gruene.de/vorstand/roestel/neubeginn.htm).

34. Forschungsgruppe Wahlen, *Politbarometer* (Monatliche repräsentative Umfrage), 3/99 Report, 1 (Mannheim).

Chapter 6

THE PARTY OF DEMOCRATIC SOCIALISM
Victory across the East and on to Berlin!

Gerald R. Kleinfeld

The election party was joyous. The leadership was delighted. Supporters danced in the streets. Gregor Gysi, head of the PDS caucus in the Bundestag, proclaimed, "We are the left Opposition."[i] Writing in the *Süddeutsche Zeitung*, Jakob Augstein concluded "Alongside social democracy in the Federal Republic, there is now a socially accepted socialist force."[2] The Party of Democratic Socialism (PDS) had breached the 5 percent mark in the Bundestag elections, and thereby achieved Fraktion (caucus) status. Barely, but clearly, the PDS had done it, with 5.1 percent of the vote. At the same time, the party garnered enough votes in Mecklenburg-West Pomerania to become a coalition partner there with the Social Democrats, whose local leader Harald Ringstorff had already indicated that he would form the first red-red Land (state) government in Germany. For a party whose aging membership continued to die off, troubled by this biological imperative that drove it to any effort to attract new members, the victory was heady, even intoxicating. News that Party Chair Professor Lothar Bisky had been defeated in his own effort to be directly elected was tempered by victories for Gregor Gysi, Petra Pau, Heinrich Müller, and Christa Luft. These alone would have enabled the party to be represented again in the Bundestag under the election law that required either three directly elected members or five percent of the total vote. However, only the magical 5 percent figure could bring coveted Fraktion status, with all of its parliamentary privileges. How had the PDS developed since the last elections in 1994? What does the PDS stand for? How had they fought their campaign? What had contributed to this victory? And what does it mean for them and for Germany?

The Red Phoenix

When the German Democratic Republic was in its death throes, the ruling Communists, the Socialist Unity Party (SED), decided not to dissolve, but to rename themselves as the Party of Democratic Socialism. Caught up in the general euphoria over unity, and the rosy economic horizon presented by West Germany, the PDS issued a first Party Program that spoke hopefully of a market economy but was characterized by a generally confused and confusing confession of loyalty to socialism. It survived the first elections after unification in 1990, relying on a special ruling that allowed it to dispense with the 5 percent national minimum. Many observers expected a gradual demise as economic well-being spread over the East. Neither the one nor the other took place. The PDS did not die, and the East was overtaken by severe unemployment and dissolution of rotten, backward businesses in unexpected numbers. Surviving businesses needed far fewer workers than the bloated numbers stuffed by communist featherbedding into outdated factories. Agriculture faced an entirely new world, and the service industry did not take up the slack. Though the eastern economy improved, and spectacular rebuilding occurred, many easterners experienced a distinct malaise and a feeling of being treated as second-class citizens. In the 1994 elections, the PDS was no longer permitted entry to the Bundestag under special conditions, but instead won four direct seats. These enabled additional members to be seated, up to the percentage the party actually won, but the PDS did not gain Fraktion status since it was still under 5 percent. Again, there were those who doubted that the PDS could hold on. Most of its members were holdovers from the SED, and they were getting older. Even most of the party's voters might come from the almost 2,000,000 former members of the SED. Four years later there could, therefore, be a different result. The western parties hoped that the PDS might gradually decline. But on 27 September 1998, the party achieved its greatest federal election success. Was this really a decrepit party under a leadership from bygone days, just counting on the votes of elderly members and those who had once been part of the GDR establishment? Yes, maybe, but also no.

Inside the PDS

By no means is the PDS a monolithic party. Nor is it a party led only by graying remnants of the GDR who seek to restore the past. Its honorary chairman, Hans Modrow, was the last Communist prime minister, and holds his present post primarily to appeal to the old members, acting as a respected guarantor that their interests would continue to be represented.

Many remember that among his last acts in office, he helped sanitize their files before they were released to other hands. Above all, the PDS will not desert its core, and will ensure that they are protected and provided for in the new Germany. This core is the party's basis in local politics, and is exceedingly important to its success. Many of the older members seek a justification of their past.[3] They are loyal voters, and will accept much, even the occasional watering down of their beliefs if the leadership thinks this advisable. They never protested in the GDR, and only occasionally do so now. But they and Modrow represent only one faction. The Communist Platform, led by the young Sahra Wagenknecht, is a small group of ideologists who have not deserted communism. Although not powerful in party circles, the CP cannot be expunged and has many defenders. A third group within the PDS consists of a variety of Marxist sub-factions espousing various forms of the ideology. Finally, there are the real heirs of the GDR, who have been called the "liberated cadre." It is from this group that the PDS leadership is drawn. All of these groups are more or less losers in the death of the communist state, though many have become quite successful financially and are better off than before. Older citizens may get excellent double pensions. Younger ones may have good managerial jobs, and the PDS scores highly in the East among managers. The second most prosperous district in Berlin is Hellersdorf, and the sixth is Marzahn.[4] Both districts are characterized by an extraordinarily high vote for the PDS.

The liberated cadre includes many relatively young people, under 50 years old, even under 40, who received education and training in the GDR and in the Soviet Union and were poised to take their expected positions in the state and party apparatus. Then the state disappeared. Their political philosophy was framed by the communist training they experienced, humbled by the collapse of the Soviet bloc, and reinforced by negative experiences of the German economy and society since unification. Trained in leadership and government, some with backgrounds in economics as it was then taught, they suddenly found themselves without a future. The PDS provided it. They are now ready to move into the new society in such positions as could become available. The result is a metamorphosed left socialism or, for some, a reinvented communism. Forced by circumstances to concentrate on the East, they recognize the importance of regional identity for the PDS. It is this liberated cadre that forms the heart of the leadership of the PDS.

In January 1999, a drama that unfolded in Mecklenburg-West Pomerania graphically illustrated the role of this liberated cadre and even its plight in the new Germany. Two members of the PDS Landtag group were revealed to have had *Stasi* (secret police) connections as "IM" (informers). Both under forty years of age, they had been in their twenties when they became involved with the secret police and the local SED party leadership. Although the coalition government in Schwerin had decided not to research the past of Landtag members, this had come out, and both were forced to resign leadership positions.[5] Here were younger members of the cadre, poised to enter the next rank in the German Democratic Republic when the communist state disappeared. They remained with the renamed PDS, climbed ahead as their training, education, and talents decreed, and then were discredited when their past work for the *Stasi* was discovered. Their past has isolated them from today's Germany, but so does their present. Neither they nor their party is comfortable in today's Germany. No graying remnants they, but survivors, and still lost.

Aside from Hans Modrow, the honorary chair, the leadership of the party is in the hands of younger people. Party chair is Lothar Bisky, an affable and able professor, who has hopes of making over the PDS into a left socialist party of the Scandinavian model and pulling votes from the SPD in the process.[6] Party manager is Dietmar Bartsch, also professional and capable. Election chief and theoretician during the 1998 campaign was André Brie (whose brother, Michael Brie, is also one of the party's theoreticians). André Brie resigned in January 1999, frustrated with continuing resistance to new ideas within the party. Chair of the Bundestag Fraktion is Gregor Gysi, who is more of an election star and parliamentary director than the main power within the leadership. All are good debaters, and acquit themselves very well on television. After the vote on September 27, Bisky appeared for the first time on the televised *Elefantenrunde* (the round table of party leaders) with the chairs of the other parties that had received more than 5 percent, and cut a modest, unprepossessing but clearly expert role. Helmut Kohl was not the only other chair who was uncomfortable with his presence. Other leaders are Petra Pau (age 36—Power Pau, as she is sometimes called), who heads the Berlin PDS; Petra Sitte in Saxony-Anhalt; Petra Bläss (35), now vice president of the Bundestag; and Helmut Holter (45), now deputy minister-president in Mecklenburg-West Pomerania. Holter, who studied in the Soviet Union, is fluent in Russian, presentable and well-spoken, and a perfect example of those members of the liberated cadre who now have achieved leadership and a government role in the new Germany.

The relationship between the leadership and the party membership is not entirely a comfortable one, as Brie's resignation shows. Bundestag Deputy Dr. Ruth Fuchs conceded ongoing discord in an interview with the press shortly before the party convention of January 1999, especially on the question of the Communist Platform.[7] The membership at large is aging and dying off. Nevertheless, it is still larger in the East than that of the CDU and the SPD combined. These members have been invaluable.

They have assisted other easterners in adjusting to the strange new state and system by helping with forms and procedures. They have provided expertise in local government, and have even had considerable success in influencing local government beyond their actual numbers in the population. Thus, the PDS has an active and expert group of ward politicians. The party has elected many mayors and local council members who regularly cooperate with both the SPD and CDU.

The Marxist heritage has not disappeared on this level, and the older members do not like or accept the new system, but prefer to justify their own past. As Markus Meckel, SPD Bundestag deputy and prominent easterner (foreign minister in the last GDR cabinet) describes them, they are "ideologically tied to the SED past, but socially conservative."[8] This contributes to friction with new, younger voters who can be both ideologically *and* socially left. The high unemployment in cities and towns and the agricultural readjustments are grist to their mill as they fail to see the new, united Germany as delivering on its promises. Instead, rather than returning to the past, which they realize is gone; they prefer a new future, socialist and government-directed. Thus they accept the vague left-socialism of the leadership, but not comfortably. They do not reject either the Communist Platform or the other Marxist groups, which they see as belonging in their spectrum. This is difficult. Brie, in particular, found it difficult to reconcile his own socialist views with a party that has not been able to break formally with its past. He resigned his post in early 1998, but withdrew his resignation and returned to direct the campaign and remain on the party's executive board (*Vorstand*). However, he resigned again in January 1999, effective after the European Parliament elections, claiming that the PDS could never become a normal party because of its troubled relationship with its past.

The leadership tries to remain above the irreconcilable elements in the party and seeks to broaden the PDS still further. In other words, it ignores the problems, or papers them over. There is no acceptable option that might disaffect the party faithful, who provide both the membership and the bulk of the votes. The future will have to take care of itself. Thus the PDS takes unpopular positions—even for the East—in support of former SED members, *Stasi* members, and even GDR spies. The PDS leader in Thuringia considers himself one of the modernizers in the party, but rejects any thought that the PDS will ever adopt a Godesberg Program like the SPD in 1959, which accepted the social market economy and gave up on revolutionary socialism. Instead, he describes anti-capitalism as a necessary element in the PDS program, and looks forward toward a socialist future with a society different from that which currently exists in Germany.[9] There must be no conflict between his description of himself as a modernizer and his hopes for a socialist Germany.

The party structure allows for platforms, working groups (AGs), and subgroups. It deliberately encourages this splintering as a device to include diverse and disagreeing groups, while being certain to retain power for itself. Thus there is a new group called "Christians in the PDS," and the PDS nominated a western Christian pacifist as its candidate in the German presidential elections of 1999. Although this pattern resembles that of the SED and other communist parties, the party has also adopted much of the structure of modern German parties. It has officials and procedures that are similar to those of other parties, including the regular party convention. In fact, the more or less democratic organization has presented problems for the leadership as the members have attempted to check the Party Executive's reformist drift. In the Berlin Convention of January 1999, the membership rebuffed Party Chair Bisky and elected Michael Benjamin of the Communist Platform to the Party Executive. His victory was a defeat for the efforts of the leadership to promote a new image for the party, after they had succeeded in keeping the CP off the Executive since removing Wagenknecht four years earlier.[10] Almost immediately after being elected, Benjamin gave an interview to the press in which he defended the construction of the Berlin Wall as being necessary at the time. At the same convention, however, the Executive had demonstrated its own ambivalence, welcoming visiting representatives of the Communist Parties of China and several other countries.[11]

This picture of the PDS reveals that there are no simple descriptions of its ideology and goals. The PDS is a complex party with various wings and groups that co-exist but lack overall allegiance to a single understanding of socialism. Jonathan Olsen claims that it "exhibits at least three sub-types of post-communist socialism, grouped under a thin umbrella of nationalism."[12] But there are also many more, and communism as well, under the PDS's red umbrella.

Not even the reformist leadership is clear in what it wants or wants to be. The PDS is lost in the new Germany. Even the regionalism of the party, its one true appeal across differing ideologies, is ambivalent. The requirement of getting five percent of the total vote in order to remain a significant factor in the German political scene drives it to secure western adherents. So, too, does the idea that it has to offer a consistent ideology or raison d'être. Thus, to the degree that it wishes to present itself as a socialist party with a socialist alternative, its appeal must be described as having something to offer voters in both East and West. Here, comparisons with the CSU in Bavaria break down. The CSU has its CDU for the rest of Germany, and remains a more conservative party, but its power is based in a more conservative state. The PDS, therefore, becomes a party with a regional base, but one that nevertheless seeks to broaden its appeal to the West, as well. As it straddles this problem nationally, it still needs to garner eastern voters who regard it as defending eastern interests. In January 1999, the PDS elected a western ex-SPD member, a reasonably prominent social democrat from Frankfurt, to be Bisky's deputy. This, and the welcome extended to new former Alliance '90/The Greens members from the West, was not entirely well received by eastern delegates. Tensions also exist between the party leadership and the often more radical western former Communists and alternative lifestyle groups. Therefore, the PDS can be described as a regional party with national ambitions that are not entirely compatible with its regionalism. As Bisky has said, "we are also the nationwide-oriented party from eastern Germany," which straddles the regionalism and nationwide issue quite elegantly.[13]

The ideological incompatibilities are equally evident. André Brie's stunning resignation for the second time in one year only served to make them more evident and embarrassing. The party has not come to terms with its past because the membership cannot, and partly also because Germany itself is unsure of how to deal with former SED members, officials, and people who served the GDR in various capacities. What is the SPD to do with Manfred Stolpe, Social Democratic Minister-President of Brandenburg and member of the Evangelical Church leadership, who stands accused of informing for the *Stasi*? Or what about others in the SPD, other parties, and also the PDS, who exhibited varying degrees of cooperation with the secret police? This is not something on which all Germans, or all east Germans, or even most of them, have reached a conclusion. If the CDU has only just accepted Wolfgang Schäuble's suggestion to admit former SED members, it is still not entirely united on the question of how to treat former East-CDU members who cooperated with the SED regime. Nor do easterners and westerners agree. And, if 20 percent of easterners generally vote for the PDS, 80 percent still vote against the party. There are 92,000 present members of the PDS, but there are also 2,000,000 former members of the SED who are not. Some vote PDS, and some do not. Markus Meckel, Bundestag deputy and a founder of the East-SPD, has just formed a new group in his party called the "New Middle," in which he and his colleagues oppose any red-red coalition and other such forms of cooperation with the PDS as being both wrong-headed and politically ill advised for his party. Stolpe angrily disagrees with him. Not only has the PDS membership had difficulty in coming to terms with the past, but also some easterners and most westerners have difficulty in accepting the PDS as a normal party. The same Party Convention that elected reformer Bisky confirmed the decision to offer employment to the former GDR spy "Topas" as an assistant to the parliamentary group. Christian von Ditfurth's description of the membership as being unable to forget the past, and unable to live completely in the present, is apt.

Ideological Questions

All of this explains the party's approach to ideology. Communism is like a bad penny: the PDS seems to throw it out, but it keeps coming back. Benjamin's election to the Executive is no confirmation of left-socialism or justification of the reformist leadership. The membership does not protest against the leadership, nor is it so docile that it will totally reject the past when it is represented by attractive, young ideologues. The various Marxist groups confirm the kaleidoscopic image as a constantly changing mix of various socialisms. Every effort of some leaders to confirm acceptance of the Federal Republic is paralleled by backsliding in one way or another within the hierarchy. The party chair has been on both sides of the issue. Bisky and his colleagues claim to want a left socialism, along the lines of the Scandinavian model. This would suit not only the political ambitions of the liberated cadre, but also fit some of their modernizing ideas about the nature of society in the new Europe. They reject liberalism, capitalism, and the social market economy. In a Germany in which more than 40 percent of the economy is state-controlled and discussions over allowing shops to remain open a few more hours on Saturday almost reach the stage of national crisis, arguing for an increase in the state's share and for further government controls over citizens and their economy represents either a misunderstanding of social market economy, or a challenge to the basic political and economic order. Yet for many members, the reformist leadership goes too far toward integrating into today's Germany.

The Party Program and the Party Election Program show consistent backsliding from the early tentative acceptance of social market economy born in the midst of popular eastern enthusiasm for unity in 1990. Instead, party adherents are generally satisfied with referring to themselves as socialists (just as the Free Democrats have called themselves liberals), and with leaving this reasonably vague to fit the varying concepts floating among the members and voters. But this is not necessarily calculation more than it is failure to reach a decision. Not even Helmut Holter in Mecklenburg-West Pomerania is clear about what he understands to be the difference between a general acceptance of the social market economy and socialism, except that he now advocates change from the present society to an undefined future that is "socialist." None of this prevents party and membership from advocating popular policies and opposing unpopular ones, while defending their own past all the while. On local issues, the PDS is often for direct democracy, and urges popular decisions on schools and jobs legislation. This, too, brings votes.

The PDS is lost in these contradictions. The leadership is desperate to undertake something Gysi calls "an effort to become a nationally accepted socialist mass party."[14] They are pragmatic on many levels—in school building, for instance, or roads—and on many different issues, often cooperating with the CDU and SPD in the East. On the larger questions of the economy, politics, and society, however, the search for some form of socialism or communism dominates their policies and demonstrates the victory of ideology over pragmatism. Their full employment policy speaks of three steps: first, advocating a public employment sector in ecological, social, and cultural services; second, dividing up the existing work among the prospective workers by reshuffling hours; and third, implementing a "social-ecological tax reform, regionalised economic activity and an active economic and structural policy of the government directed at creating new jobs."[15] Nor can they reconcile the conflict between the needs of eastern regionalism and the demands of a national left socialist party. They also reject NATO.[16] This has opened a major gulf between them and the new Federal Government. While the SPD-Green coalition supported NATO in the Kosovo intervention, the PDS was outspoken in opposition. Since many Greens and some SPD members were also opposed, the PDS has hoped to win adherents and bolster its role as a left socialist alternative. The dilemma posed by this is the risk of offending the SPD, and endangering red-red coalitions in the East.

The PDS is also opposed to participation in the Euro under the conditions negotiated by Bonn and now supported by the new Federal Government. In an appeal "For a New Route to European Integration," the PDS joined with the Belgian Communist Party, the French Communist Party, the Party of the Left and of Progress of Greece, the Party of Communist Renewal of Italy, the Communist Party of Austria, the Portuguese Communist Party, the Socialist Party of the Netherlands, the Left Party of Sweden, the Swiss Party of Labor, the Green Initiative of Catalonia, and the United Left of Spain.[17]

The Campaign

Leading a divided party into a national election is never easy, but the PDS has always managed to paper over these divisions and portray itself differently to its various constituencies. United in its goal of surviving in the new Germany, the PDS entered the election year of 1998 facing a tough problem. They could not count on receiving 5 percent of the popular vote, and needed to achieve at least three directly elected Bundestag seats. They were certain of Gysi's, and Christa Luft's, but not of Manfred Müller's. On the other hand, they thought that they had good prospects in Rostock, and a chance in Saxony, where they would run Gustav-Adolf Schnur, an old track star and sports hero from the days of the GDR and a member of the GDR Volkskammer from 1958 to 1990, now a sexagenarian but still robust, if not popular. In 1994, they had run Stefan Heym, the famous author, against Wolfgang Thierse of the SPD in the Prenzlauer Berg district of Berlin, and won. But Heym soon resigned, and was not going to run again. To snag his seat, they needed someone prominent. In a dramatic move, the PDS leadership settled on a westerner, Vice Admiral Elmar Schmähling, a critic of the military policy of the Federal Republic for years and something of a gadfly, if not a political oddity. He was forced to bow out by the outcry over the peculiarity of such a choice, and the leadership settled on Petra Pau to run in his place. She was given little chance. Nevertheless, the flap was not good for the electoral chances of the party in general. Almost simultaneously with the candidate squabble came the Land elections in Saxony-Anhalt, where the PDS had been a quasi-coalition partner of the minority SPD state government led by Reinhard Höppner since 1994. Officially, they "tolerated" Höppner's government, but unofficially they were actively involved. Höppner recognized that the "Magdeburg Model" would be used by the CDU in the national campaign against the SPD, just as had been done four years earlier, but wanted to preserve it anyway, and hoped that it would not hurt the SPD too much outside of his state. While stating that he might possibly be open to forming a grand coalition with the CDU, he ran the state election campaign for the SPD with the strong hint that the minority government would be continued.

Saxony-Anhalt is making very little headway in the economically troubled East. Unemployment is high, and the state is bordered on the south by the two more prosperous—though also sorely hurting—Länder of Saxony and Thuringia. On the west, it adjoins Lower Saxony, where then Minister-President Gerhard Schröder in March scored a stunning victory over the local CDU, supposedly bolstered by special campaign trips of Helmut Kohl. In the Saxony-Anhalt elections, Höppner won by achieving more votes than the CDU, while the PDS held on and the DVU (*Deutsche Volks-Union*), a radical right-wing party, unexpectedly came in with 14 percent. The DVU was so taken by surprise that its candidates did not even know what to say when the journalists arrived. Höppner then formally rejected a grand coalition, but the arrival of the DVU in the state legislature was discomforting to all. For the PDS, it was a shot across the bow. Young protesters had chosen not the PDS, but the DVU. Had the PDS been too representative of the "establishment"? There was no massive drift to or away from the PDS. It was both a good and a bad sign for the Bundestag elections. It was good in that they held their own and still could count on around 20 percent of the electorate. It was bad in that they did not improve their totals after four years of tolerating and working with/in the Höppner SPD minority government. Bisky's response was that these were "protest voters, and the PDS is not interested in protest voters."[18]

There are still two different German electorates, West and East. In the West, the smaller parties of the Alliance '90/The Greens and the FDP together shared about 10 to 15 percent of the vote and played a role in state governments. In the East, both were insignificant. There, where unemployment dominated the industrial and agricultural scenes, voters had little sympathy for an environmental party. Particularly in the East, the FDP still suffered from its association with social groups it had itself characterized as "those who earned more." Both of these smaller parties failed to gain election to the Landtag. Saxony-Anhalt had reinforced the fact that the only possible state governments in the East were either grand coalitions or some form of cooperation between the SPD and the PDS. Thus, the voters retained their "eastern model" of the three parties—CDU, SPD, and PDS—assuming that nobody would cooperate with the DVU or the Republikaner (Reps), or that the right-wing radicals' success in Magdeburg would not be repeated elsewhere.

The PDS Bundestag campaign had begun even before the Saxony-Anhalt election, and made much of the weakness of Chancellor Kohl and the continuing high unemployment in the East. The failure of Saxony-Anhalt to move dramatically forward since 1994 was attributed not to any inadequacy of the Land government that the party supported, but to the failure of the national government to provide the necessary lift to the German economy as a whole. The defection of young protest voters to the DVU was a troubling sign for the PDS, but they had still achieved their goal. If the PDS could remain at 20 percent for the Bundestag election and the state elections in Mecklenburg-West Pomerania, to be held on the same day, the party would have a major achievement. The main target of the PDS election campaign was the Kohl government, and the party sought to emphasize the economic difficulties of Germany, especially in the East. Its goal was not only three direct mandates and representation once again in the Bundestag, but Fraktion status, for which they needed 5 percent of the overall vote.

Instead of emphasizing "Gysi's motley crew" as they had in 1994, Brie and the PDS election managers hit hard at the economic distress facing Germany and, particularly, the East. The PDS had considerable company in decrying the state of the German economy. Both the SPD and the Alliance '90/The Greens were making the same charges. Although the SPD was a competitor, the PDS recognized that the two leading social democrats were not universally admired in the East. Oskar Lafontaine had alienated many easterners with statements in 1990 about the cost of unification, and Gerhard Schröder was regarded as too friendly to business interests. On the other hand, Lafontaine was considered to be generally in favor of red-red coalitions in the East.[19] Avoiding assaults on potential allies, Brie concentrated on attacking Kohl and the CDU. Gysi was in excellent form, appearing on television and in speeches across the country. A brilliant speaker with a genuine gift for finding the tone of his audience, the parliamentary chief galvanized the troops and was clearly attractive to younger voters. The PDS campaign used professionally scripted television spots, and sported a very modernist image. There was a special CD just for younger techies. There was nothing amateur about a smaller party. It is difficult to gauge how effective these devices were, but they seemed to emphasize how one might dare to be different by voting PDS. Voting left was to be acceptable. If the standard CDU recipe was to galvanize the party faithful, the PDS ads tended to search for the new, the undecided vote. The PDS faithful were already on board.

Gysi's speeches had the same quality. Image was important, and he switched guises to offer biting criticism of Kohl's Germany, which continually promised to reduce unemployment but failed to achieve it. Alternating between attacking the chancellor and raising fears of cutbacks in business, Gysi portrayed Germany as having taken the wrong path. Neoliberalism, what Margaret Thatcher had wrought in Britain and Tony Blair promoted as the "third way," was not for Germany. Privatization of state enterprises and competition in the marketplace, lean business, and individual responsibility were not the future as the PDS saw it. Bisky, campaigning for his own seat, was the laid-back, dressed-down man of the people. Socialism, not the current economic system, would control the big companies that manage the economy. The little man and the little woman would be protected.[20] It was the people's battle against big business. The PDS posters were less professionally perfect than those of 1994, partly revealing some dissatisfaction with their ad agency.[21] They emphasized again the party's commitment to socialism, but stressed dissatisfaction with the state of the economy.

Campaigning simultaneously in Mecklenburg-West Pomerania for legislative seats, the PDS also emphasized to easterners that it was an eastern-based party. Not only was the Magdeburg model fresh in people's minds, but also the CDU campaign orchestrated by Peter Hintze had replaced the red socks of 1994 with a new symbol attacking the PDS. Here, two red hands were depicted in a handshake. This obvious reference to the old SED symbol was meant to frighten voters away from a possible SPD-PDS coalition, something that was real in Schwerin but could also have been threatening in Bonn. Even many non-PDS supporters in the East were unhappy with this campaign. It was expected to help considerably in the West, where there were more voters, and not hurt too much in the East. Whatever good it did in the former West Germany, it continued to antagonize the East. And, where eastern voters were feeling disregarded too much by western politicians, this certainly did not help the CDU in that region and may have helped the PDS.

The Results: 5 Percent and Fraktion Status

The federal election results were dramatic. Early in the evening, it was clear that the PDS had breached the 5 percent mark, and later figures confirmed that the party had arrived. The party pulled votes in almost equal measure from both CDU and SPD, and even a few from the FDP and Alliance '90/ The Greens.

The final results for the five eastern states and Berlin are presented in Table 6.1. The PDS achieved about 20 percent on both ballots throughout the region. The party's total in Berlin is lower, because PDS strength in the eastern part of the capital is diluted by western districts, i.e., the former West Berlin. In Saxony and Saxony-Anhalt, where the party had previously been weaker, the PDS gained significantly, pulling toward the overall average. The heaviest PDS voting was in the former GDR district capitals, which also have the largest concentration of former SED members as well as party and state functionaries. Through exit polls, the opinion research firm Forschungsgruppe Wahlen found that the PDS had roughly equal strength among various age groups from 25 to 60. The party is not a blue-collar workers' party, although the percentage of factory workers voting PDS increased in 1998, but one in which civil servants and white-collar employees are heavily represented. A significant percentage of unemployed also voted PDS in 1998.[22] The CDU lost heavily in the East, dropping almost sixteen points in Saxony, while the SPD picked up votes. The news magazine *Der Spiegel* concluded that the CDU and SPD each have about 20 percent of the eastern German population as regular voters, and the PDS about 15 percent. The remainder, 45 percent, are probably swing voters.[23] However, neither the FDP nor the Alliance '90/The Greens cleared the 5 percent hurdle in the East, and they failed to enter the legislatures of Saxony-Anhalt and Mecklenburg-West Pomerania in 1998 as well. Thus, the PDS is the swing party. By helping to keep out the Alliance '90/The Greens and the FDP, the PDS preserves this status and prevents the CDU and the SPD from finding other alternatives.

The PDS voters in 1998 came from a broad cross-section. Some PDS officials happily proclaimed that their party was now a true *Volkspartei*, a mass party. All economic levels were represented; all age groups, with seniors not especially over-represented. In other words, the PDS also attracted younger voters. If workers did not especially favor the PDS, the unemployed did gravitate more heavily in their direction. Despite the loss of protest voters to the right wing in the legislative elections in

Table 6.1 PDS Vote in the Eastern States and Berlin, 1994–98

State	First Ballot		Second Ballot	
	%	1994	%	1994
Mecklenburg-West Pomerania	24.8	(+.04)	23.6	(0.0)
Brandenburg	21.1	(+0.8)	20.3	(+1.0)
Berlin	16.7	(-0.1)	13.4	(-1.4)
Saxony-Anhalt	20.1	(+2.5)	20.7	(+2.7)
Saxony	19.7	(+2.5)	20.0	(+3.3)
Thurginia	21.0	(+4.6)	21.2	(+4.1)

Saxony-Anhalt, the PDS did garner some of the protest vote. They were a party of opposition, the eastern party of the left-out, the ones who did not see today's Germany as their Germany. Some of them might be doing well economically, but that did not mean that they favored the economic system of the social market economy. Refusing to see this as a "third way," they resolutely stood for some form of socialism, whatever that might mean. Since 1990, polls have consistently shown that the typical eastern voter has a more favorable attitude toward socialism than the typical westerner, and reacts more unfavorably toward criticism of it.

Even more than Alliance '90/The Greens voters, the typical PDS voter is non-religious. Of those who are practicing Catholics, only 1 percent vote PDS. For Protestants, the sum is only 2 percent. About 16 percent of PDS voters admit to being without a religion. Although western Germans are considerably more secular than Americans, despite a high level of official membership in churches, organized religion is even weaker in the East. This, and widespread atheism, is one of the legacies of the German Democratic Republic. Among all eastern voters, 8 percent admit to being Catholic, 9 percent Protestant, and 26 percent without religion. Churches are even emptier than in the West. Nationally, the SPD garners more Protestants than Catholics, and the CDU/CSU more Catholics than Protestants. The SPD has more non-religious voters than the CDU nationwide, but eastern Germany is a different story. There, the remaining legacy is Protestant, and Protestants outnumber Catholics (which hurts the CDU), but more than half the population is openly without religious belief. Thus, all parties have voters among the non-religious or atheists. In this category, the CDU leads the SPD, but the PDS comes in second.[24]

Just as discord and indecision on what constitutes socialism have emerged more evidently in the ranks of the PDS, and the East-West dichotomy of the country has made regionalism and national politics even more complicated, the party has achieved a new status in Germany. The other parties and the country at large are attempting to discern what this will mean over the next years. Oskar Lafontaine, while still SPD Party Chair, was willing to comfortably accept SPD/PDS coalitions in the East, but much of the party rejected that at the national level. On the other hand, if the 1999 elections show continued PDS strength in eastern state legisla- tures, further coalitions might put the Bundesrat, the upper house that rep- resents the states (Länder), into a situation in which the PDS would hold the balance of power for a longer term. After the elections in Hesse in 1999, the SPD-Alliance '90/The Greens lost their majority in the Bundesrat, and the red-red coalition in Mecklenburg-West Pomerania seemed a threat of what could come. The PDS is clearly not passing from the scene, despite the aging membership. It has even more power and influence than after the last Bundestag election, and could play a role in the Bundesrat.

The new middle Social Democrats, such as Richard Schröder, Markus Meckel, and Stefan Hilsberg, are urging the party leadership to avoid future coalitions with the PDS. Others, such as Wolfgang Thierse, Harald Ringstorff, and Reinhard Höppner, see no immediate danger, but a tem- porary advantage for the SPD. The country itself is not ready for the PDS to share in national government, but PDS Party Manager Dietmar Bartsch says that his party should prepare itself to be ready for this by 2002.[25] However, André Brie, chief architect of the victorious 1998 campaign, has resigned from the party in frustration that it cannot be brought into the new world of ideas that he has urged. The reformist leadership is struggling with the membership, and the voters are divided between protest, holdovers, and regionalist adherents of vague and disparate forms of socialism and communism. An energetic and competent young leadership cadre faces grim faces of nostalgia and self-justification, joined by agile young socialist or communist ideologues, at every party conven- tion. This leadership is itself uncertain as to what is the best path. Success is there, but within bounds. The CDU lost many votes after its failure to paint a picture of victory and inability to alter the frustrating permanence of unemployment. If the SPD also fails to roll back unemployment, will the PDS gain further support among easterners? It is a legitimate ques- tion. What is the right policy for the SPD: to avoid coalitions, as Schröder's new middle urges, or to form coalitions but achieve a separate profile? Will the new CDU policy gain support in the East, where voters generally regard the PDS as a normal party like any other?

In the meantime, there are questions for the PDS as well. The problem of survival is still not answered, because the voting pool contains too many protesters and too many elderly SED veterans. Nor is it clear whether suf- ficient numbers of the German electorate would endorse the solution of the PDS leadership—a vague socialist alternative to the SPD, based in the East, and a foreign policy without NATO. The NATO factor is untested. In the aftermath of the Yugoslavian adventure, in a Europe with a very uncertain and unsteady east, will eastern Germans endorse a PDS policy on NATO? More easterners than westerners do so now.

The PDS is still a holdover party, given a new lease on life by the travails of the German economy and the loyalty of its traditional voters. It has many facets, and an able, young leadership. It has strong local organization that serves it in both elections and governing. Nonetheless, it lacks an overall definition, and it has failed to come to terms with unified Germany or even the Basic Law. It is still a socialist party, and a communist one as well, somewhat lost in the new Germany.

Notes

1. Quoted in *Der Spiegel*, September 29, 1998, Special Issue, 29.
2. On 29 September 1998, cited in *SZonNet*.
3. See especially Christian von Ditfurth, *Ostalgie oder Linke*, M Alternative, Meine Reise durch die PDS (Cologne: Kiepenhauer and Witsch, 1998)
4. *Der Tagesspiegel*, 22 January 1999.
5. Interview with Lothar Bisky, October 1998.
6. *Thüringer Allgemeine*, 15 January 1999, 2, and *Thüringische Landeszeitung*, 15 January 1999, 3.
7. *Ostthüringer Zeitung*, 16 January 16 1999, 2.
8. In "Koalitionen helfen nur der PDS," *Die Welt*, 16 January 1999.
9. "Antikapitalismus ist notwendig," in *Frankfurter Allgemeine Zeitung*, 14 January 1999.
10. *Die Welt*, 18 January 1999, 2.
11. Armin Fuhrer, "In der DPS wachsen die Spannungen," *Die Welt, 18 January 1999, 10.*
12. Jonathan Olson, "Germany's PDS and Varieties of 'Post-Communist Socialism,'" *Problems of Post-Communism*, 45, no. 6 (November–December 1998): 43.
13. Speech "Für einen Politikwechsel in Deutschland und Europa!" at the Election Conference of the PDS given on 23 August 1997, 3.
14. "Eine bundesweit akzeptierte, sozialistische Volkspartei," in Gregor Gysi, *Nicht nur freche Sprüche* (Berlin: Schwarzkopf und Schwarzkopf), 1998, 279.
15. *Eine neue Art der Vollbeschäftigung will die PDS?* PDS leaflet, Berlin, 1999.
16. Withdrawal from and dissolution of NATO and the WEU, in *Militarisierung der Politik–ohne uns!* PDS leaflet, Berlin, 1999.
17. Leaflet, *Für einen neuen Weg der europäischen Integration*, issued by the parties mentioned in Paris, 15 January 1999.
18. Interview with the author, Berlin, October 1998.
19. Interview with André Brie, June 1994.
20. Bisky campaign appearance in Berlin streets, September 1998.
21. Interview with Lothar Bisky, Karl Liebknecht House, Berlin, September 1998.
22. "Bundestagswahl 1998, Eine Analyse der Wahl vom 27. September 1998," *Berichte der Forschungsgruppe Wahlen e.V.*, Nr. 91, 1998, 22, 85.
23. *Der Spiegel*, 29 September 1998, 30.
24. *Bericht*, Forschungsgruppe Wahlen, 25–27, 86.
25. *Thüringer Allgemeine*, 16 January 1999, 2.

Chapter 7

WHO VOTED FOR WHOM—AND WHY

An Analysis of the 1998 German Federal Election

Wolfgang G. Gibowski

For the first time in the history of German elections, a change of federal government has been brought about as a direct consequence of a general election. The 1998 general election produced greater shifts in the percentage of votes received by the CDU/CSU and the SPD than in any previous national election. After the 1994 election the Christian Democrats were ahead of the Social Democrats by five percent. Now the situation is virtually reversed. The SPD overtook the CDU/CSU in both the western and eastern parts of Germany and replaced it as the governing party.

Table 7.1 Bundestag Election Results 1998 and Differences to the Results of 1994

Party	Total		West		East		Seats	
SPD	40.9	+4.5	42.3	+4.8	35.1	+3.6	298	+46
Greens	6.7	-0.6	7.3	-0.6	4.1	-0.2	47	-2
CDU/CSU	35.1	-6.3	37.0	-5.1	27.3	-11.2	245	-49
FDP	6.2	-0.7	7.0	-0.7	3.3	-0.2	44	-3
PDS	5.1	+0.7	1.2	+0.2	21.6	+1.8	35	+5
REP	1.8	-0.1	1.9	-0.1	1.5	+0.2		
DVU	1.2	+1.2	0.8	+0.8	2.8	+2.8		
Others	2.9	+1.2	2.5	+0.6	4.3	+3.2		
Total	100%		100%		100%		669	-3
% Voting	82.2	+3.2	82.8	+2.3	80.0	+7.4		

Note: The SPD seats include 13 *Überhangmandate*.

The East-West comparison of 1998 corresponds to the pattern from past general elections held in Germany. All western German parties (except for the radical right, Deutsche Volks Union [DVU]) do better in the western part of the country than they do in the East. The clearest East-West difference continues to be the results obtained by the PDS, which received more than 20 percent of the vote in eastern Germany while it continued to be at around 1 percent in the West. There are clear East-West differences with regard to the changes that have taken place in comparison with 1994. In the East the Christian Democrats lost a little more than twice as many votes as they did in the West.

While the SPD was able to win nearly as many votes as the CDU/CSU lost in western Germany, in the eastern part of the country the SPD did not even come close to achieving this. A large part of the CDU's landslide losses in the East went to the many smaller parties that showed considerably stronger gains in the East than they did in the West. This applies in particular to the right-wing extremist DVU (2.8 percent) that did not field any candidates in 1994.

East-West differences in voting behavior, so noticeable at the 1990 and 1994 elections, actually declined in 1998.[1] The results of the 1998 general election show that with the exception of the gains for the DVU, there was no further widening of differences between voting patterns in eastern and western Germany.[2] The well-known four-party system in western Germany continues to stand in contrast to the three-party system in eastern Germany. The changes noted in both regions point in the same direction for both parties, although, as in the case of the CDU, they were stronger in the East than they were in the West. The fact that voter turnout showed a considerably stronger increase in the East (6.9 percent) than in the West (2.2 percent) helped to even out the very sizeable differences noted in the past. There have been no indications of a further deepening of differences in voting patterns between east and west, or of any growth in factors separating the electorates. The SPD's cooperation with the PDS in Mecklenburg-West Pomerania and Saxony-Anhalt, although questionable when viewed from a different political perspective, is a definite exception.[3]

Who Voted for Whom

The analysis of voting behavior in various demographic and sociological groups is of particular interest in every election, since one hopes to gain information about the motives of floating voters on the basis of changes that occur. The very strong changes that occurred in this general election led to the question of whether there was a general trend that affected all groups in about the same way, or whether specific changes in individual groups made it possible to draw conclusions regarding the reasons for the changes.

This analysis is based on an exit poll carried out by the Forschungsgruppe Wahlen. On the day of the election, a total of 15,570 voters in western Germany and 5,424 in eastern Germany were interviewed as they were leaving their polling stations. The fact that these polls were taken right after the people in question had voted means that the responses are very reliable. The size of the sample makes it possible to deduce information about voting structures within groups, which would not be possible with traditional polling methods. On the other hand, this exit poll, like any other, has its limitations. Results obtained with regard to the smaller parties must be interpreted with a certain amount of caution.

Age and Gender
Being part of a group defined in terms of age and/or gender is normally not associated with interest-related policy positions. From the outset, the Greens have been particularly successful among younger and highly educated voters, something that was always explained by the special interest this group had in Green policies. However, the voters' level of education was not included in the exit poll. There has always been a tendency among the older members of the electorate to vote for the CDU or CSU. What is probably involved here is not a case of new cleavage, but rather a generational factor.

When voters are divided up into men and women, no particular differences to the general trend are evident for the West. In the East, on the other hand, the CDU showed somewhat greater losses among women, while the PDS showed gains.

In a comparison of age groups, there are clear differences between eastern and western Germany. In the West, the CDU/CSU had most of its losses in groups 35 and older, particularly among voters aged 45–59. The SPD had its greatest gains in the same age groups. The Greens had their highest percentages among voters up to the age of 44. In the two youngest groups, they failed to do as well as they did in 1994. The FDP had very similar results in all groups.

The CDU in eastern Germany suffered major losses in all age groups. These were above-average among voters over the age of 35. In the same groups, and among the youngest voters, the SPD was able to improve its results significantly. There was a noticeable increase in voters for the PDS among the oldest group of voters.

Even with an overall sample of this size, the combination of age and gender results in group sizes, particularly in eastern Germany, that rule out any all-too-bold interpretations. But despite this limitation, it can be

Table 7.2 Party Support by Gender and Age in East Germany—Results 1998 and Differences to 1994

	SDP		CDU/CSU		Greens		FDP		PDS	
Total	35.1	+3.6	27.3	-11.2	4.1	-0.2	3.3	-0.2	21.6	+1.8
Gender										
Men	37	+5	27	-10	3	0	4	0	19	0
Women	35	+3	27	-13	5	0	4	0	21	+4
Age Group										
18–24	31	+4	20	-9	8	-2	4	- 2	0	-1
25–34	31	-2	25	-6	8	+2	5	0	19	-2
35–44	35	+4	25	-11	7	+1	4	-2	20	+1
45–59	38	+6	28	-13	5	+1	3	–	22	+3
60 +	39	+6	35	-11	1	0	3	0	21	+6
Age and Gender										
18–24 Men	31	+9	22	-9	5	-4	4	-2	18	-2
18–24 Women	31	0	17	-8	11	0	4	0	23	0
25–34 Men	30	-2	27	-8	7	+2	5	-1	17	0
25–34 Women	32	-2	23	-5	10	0	5	0	21	-3
35–44 Men	38	+5	26	-10	6	+1	3	-2	18	0
35–44 Women	32	+2	24	-13	7	+2	4	-1	24	+3
45–59 Men	41	+10	26	-16	4	+1	4	-2	18	+1
45–59 Women	35	+3	28	-10	6	+1	3	-1	22	+4
60 + Men	38	0	34	-2	0	-1	2	0	22	+2
60 + Women	39	+9	35	-15	2	0	4	-1	17	+6

said that in the West CDU/CSU losses among women above the age of 35 were greater than among men, while the SPD did particularly well among women in these age groups. The CDU/CSU continued to be the majority party only among the oldest voters. The losses the Greens suffered among younger voters were of about the same amount in all groups and, as such, were relatively higher among younger men than they were among younger women.

In eastern Germany, the joint comparison of age and gender did not produce any new knowledge with regard to the results attained by the CDU and the SPD. The losses suffered by the Greens among the youngest voters were found among young men. The largest gains for the PDS among the oldest voters came from women.

The bulk of the changes that took place in both the west and the east involved voters over the age of 35. From this it can be assumed that what was involved were responses to reform legislation that these age groups feel more strongly affected by than younger age groups.

Table 7.3 Party Support by Gender and Age in West Germany—Results 1998 and Differences to 1994

	SDP		CDU/CSU		Greens		FDP		PDS	
Total	42.8	+4.8	37.0	-5.1	7.3	-0.6	7.0	-0.7	1.2	+0.2
Gender										
Men	42	+5	37	-3	7	-1	7	-1	1	0
Women	43	+6	37	-6	8	-1	7	-1	1	0
Age Group										
18–24	37	0	35	0	11	-4	7	- 1	2	0
25–34	45	+4	30	-3	11	-3	6	+1	1	0
35–44	45	+5	32	-5	12	0	6	-2	2	+1
45–59	44	+6	38	-8	6	+1	8	-1	1	0
60 +	40	+6	45	-5	3	0	7	-2	1	0
Age and Gender										
18–24 Men	36	+1	35	-1	9	-4	7	0	2	0
18–24 Women	38	0	34	+1	12	-4	6	-1	2	0
25–34 Men	45	+7	31	-5	9	-4	7	+1	1	-1
25–34 Women	45	0	28	-1	13	-2	6	+1	1	0
35–44 Men	45	+4	32	-3	10	0	6	-2	2	0
35–44 Women	45	+7	31	-7	14	0	6	-2	1	+1
45–59 Men	43	+5	39	-6	5	+1	9	-1	1	0
45–59 Women	45	+8	37	-10	6	+1	8	0	1	0
60 + Men	40	+6	45	-6	2	0	8	-3	1	+1
60 + Women	41	+8	45	-8	3	0	7	-1	0	0

Jobs and Union Membership

The stability of voter behavior in Germany can be explained by the fact that certain sociological groups see the two major parties, the SPD and the CDU/CSU, as representing their interests, and for this reason the majority of them vote for these parties. As explained in detail in another publication,[4] the SPD is seen as representing the interests of blue-collar workers, in which context it should be said that union membership greatly strengthens this tie. Established at the same time as the German party system, this affiliation has undergone considerable change in the course of the past few decades. On the one hand, social evolution has brought about a change in group sizes; on the other, interest-group-related factors are becoming more tenuous, since their foundations are gradually being lost. By way of example, after the war blue-collar workers were the largest single occupational group in West Germany, ahead of the self-employed (mostly farmers) and the white-collar workers.

Today, white-collar workers are the largest single occupational group, ahead of blue-collar workers and the self-employed, who are starting to grow in number once again, albeit from a low level. Unification has led to an increase in the number of blue-collar and white-collar workers at the expense of the number of civil servants and self-employed.[5] Analyses of the first free elections held in eastern Germany showed that blue-collar workers there did not feel their interests were represented by the SPD, as is traditionally felt in western Germany.[6] Interest-group-related factors have faded in the course of time. They have become weaker, since the reasons that led to their origin, such as the need for social protection and protection under labor law, no longer exist in the same way. Still, the effects of these traditional ties are found in the analysis of every election.

In his election campaign Gerhard Schröder stated, probably inspired by Tony Blair's "New Labour," that the SPD represented the interests of the "New Middle" and was aiming at attracting votes from the large group of white-collar workers. Strategically, this was the absolutely correct thing to do, since there has always been a particularly large number of floating voters in this occupational group.

Analysis of Tables 7.4, 7.5, and 7.6 shows that the SPD succeeded in increasing its already high percentage of voters among blue-collar workers, particularly in western Germany, and in making gains in all occupational groups. Their gains are particularly large among white-collar workers, i.e., the largest occupational group. The CDU and CSU lost in all groups except for western German farmers and eastern German civil servants. The decline of the CDU in eastern Germany was particularly noticeable among blue-collar workers and farmers, while in western Germany CDU/CSU losses were particularly noticeable among white-collar workers and the self-employed. As a result of these changes, the SPD

Table 7.4 Party Support by Occupation—Results 1998 and Differences to 1994

	SDP	CDU/CSU	Greens	FDP	PDS
Total	40.9 +4.5	35.1 -6.3	6.7 -0.6	6.2 -0.7	5.1 +0.7
Profession					
Blue-collar workers	48 +3	30 -7	3 -2	3 0	6 +1
White-collar workers	42 +6	32 -6	8 -1	3 0	6 0
Civil servants	36 +4	40 -3	11 0	7 -1	3 0
Self-employed	22 +4	44 -8	10 +2	15 0	4 0
Farmers	15 +1	69 +5	2 -2	9 0	3 0

Table 7.5 Party Support by Occupation in West Germany—Results 1998 and Differences to 1994

	SDP	CDU/CSU	Greens	FDP	PDS
Total	42.3 +4.8	37.0 -5.1	7.3 -0.6	7.0 -0.7	1.2 +0.2
Profession					
Blue-collar workers	53 +3	31 -4	4 -1	3 0	1 0
White-collar workers	43 +5	34 -6	9 -1	8 0	1 0
Civil servants	37 +4	41 -3	11 0	7 -1	2 +1
Self-employed	22 +5	46 -7	10 +2	17 +1	1 0
Farmers	10 -2	75 +10	2 -2	9 -1	1 0

Table 7.6 Party Support by Occupation in East Germany—Results 1998 and Differences to 1994

	SDP	CDU/CSU	Greens	FDP	PDS
Total	35.1 +3.6	27.3 -11.2	4.1 -0.2	3.3 -0.2	21.6 +1.8
Profession					
Blue-collar workers	39 +4	27 -14	2 +1	3 0	17 +2
White-collar workers	35 +4	24 -8	7 +1	4 0	25 -1
Civil servants	35 10	34 +4	10 +4	4 +2	15 -20
Self-employed	35 15	43 -5	3 0	8 2	8 -8
Farmers	35 15	43 -16	3 -4	8 +4	8 -1

became the majority party among blue-collar and white-collar workers in both western and eastern Germany. The Christian Democrats continue to be the majority party among the considerably smaller groups constituted by the self-employed and farmers, as well as among the civil servants in western Germany. The strong changes that have taken place in the voting behavior of civil servants in eastern Germany at the expense of the PDS and to the benefit of all the other parties can be attributed to the structural changes that have taken place in public administration there.

The inclusion of union membership confirmed theoretical expectations. The SPD achieved higher percentages among voters who are union members, but was able to make the same gains among voters who are not

Table 7.7 Party Support, Occupation, and Trade Union Membership in West Germany—Results 1998 and Differences to 1994

	SDP		CDU/CSU		Greens		FDP		PDS	
Total	42.3	+4.8	37.0	-5.1	7.3	-0.6	7.0	-0.7	1.2	+0.2
Union membership										
Yes	60	+6	23	-7	7	+1	3	0	2	0
No	39	+6	40	-5	8	-1	8	0	1	0
Blue-collar and union mem.										
Yes	66	+6	19	-8	3	-2	2	0	2	0
No	40	+3	36	-4	4	-2	4	-1	1	0
White-collar and union mem.										
Yes	58	+6	21	-7	11	+1	4	0	2	0
No	41	+6	37	-5	9	-1	9	0	1	0

union members. The CDU/CSU lost votes among union members. Despite having a small base of union members to begin with, it still lost more among them than among non-members. It was clear that the absence of union connections was advantageous for the FDP, and that it had virtually no effect for the Greens.

In summary, it can be said that the traditional ties between blue-collar workers and the SPD continue to apply with regard to western Germany. At the same time, the SPD has achieved its objective of improving its results among white-collar workers. Whether or not this is the new middle is more a political issue that a question relating to the sociology of elections. On aggregate, the SPD was able to improve its position in western Germany among civil servants and the self-employed, groups who tend to show a stronger preference for the Christian Democrats. This speaks for a general trend in favor of the SPD in this election.

Eastern Germany is a different story. Because the traditional connection between blue-collar workers and the SPD in the East was lost during the communist dictatorship in the GDR, the majority position of the SPD there is volatile, something that applies in principle to the election results of all the other parties as well. The fact that the SPD managed to maintain the level of its overall average in all occupational groups in eastern Germany speaks more for a general trend toward the SPD in this election than for the establishment of western German structures. In eastern Germany, no party can be sure of the voters who have cast their ballots for it in the past.

The only exception to this rule is the PDS, which, as the successor to the former East German Communist Party, is the only party in eastern Germany with a loyal voter base. PDS losses among civil servants and the self-employed were caused more by structural changes than by changes in voting behavior in these groups.

Religion and Church Affiliations

A relationship exists between Catholics and the CDU/CSU comparable to the one between blue-collar workers and the SPD. This relationship does not have a tradition that goes back as far as that of workers and the SPD. When these parties were formed after the war, they inherited voters from the former Center Party (*Zentrum*). The Center Party represented the political interests of the Catholic minority that lived in the predominantly Protestant, Prussian-dominated "Kaiserreich." The founding of the CDU as a party committed to Christian values but non-denominational was intended to overcome the one-sided focus on Catholics, something which has worked only to a certain degree. The stronger a voter's connection is to the Catholic Church, the stronger it is to the CDU and CSU as well. The same thing applies with regard to Protestants, but to a much lesser extent. In eastern Germany these relationships exist only in part. In 1994 the CDU attained results among the few Catholic voters (5 percent of the total) similar to the results attained among Catholics in the West. In 1998 that was no longer the case. Although in eastern Germany the CDU did better among Catholics living there as well as among Protestants (approximately 27 percent) than it did among voters without a religion, this relationship is weaker than in western Germany and, as such, is not comparable.

Social change has diminished the importance of religious affiliations for the CDU/CSU vote. One out of every five persons in western Germany no longer has religious ties; at the same time, the frequency of church attendance is diminishing strongly for both religions. In 1953 the number of Catholics who had strong ties to the church was 60 percent, in 1994 it was 29 percent, and in the exit poll of 1998 it was down to 20 percent.[7]

In this analysis there are once again nearly equal gains for the SPD, compared with similar losses for the CDU/CSU. It is only in the combination of religious and church ties that the changes are somewhat more differentiated. The CDU/CSU maintained their dominant position among Catholics who have strong or not-so-strong church ties, showing average losses; in the insignificantly small group of Protestants with strong church ties there was virtually no change. As such, no reasons for shifts in voting behavior were in evidence specific to the interests of these groups.

**Table 7.8 Party Support, Religion, and Church Attendance in West Germany—
Results 1998 and Differences to 1994**

	SDP		CDU/CSU		Greens		FDP		PDS	
Total	42.3	+4.8	37.0	-5.1	7.3	-0.6	7.0	-0.7	1.2	+0.2
Religion										
Catholic	36	+5	47	-5	6	0	6	-1	1	0
Protestant	48	+4	37	-5	7	-1	8	0	1	0
No religion	47	+7	22	-6	13	-1	7	-1	4	+1
Church attend.										
Often	21	+4	66	-3	4	+1	6	0	0	0
Sometimes	40	+5	43	-5	5	0	8	0	0	0
Never	47	+3	31	-3	8	-1	7	0	1	0
Religion and church attend.										
Catholic										
Often	20	+6	70	-4	3	+1	5	-1	0	0
Sometimes	36	+7	50	-4	4	-2	6	-1	0	0
Never	43	+2	35	-2	8	-1	7	0	1	0
Protestant										
Often	28	-2	48	+1	9	+1	9	0	1	0
Sometimes	45	+5	36	-6	6	+1	9	0	1	0
Never	50	+3	29	-3	8	+1	7	0	1	0

The Political Climate between Elections

The changes that occurred in the 1998 general election, which in the German context were dramatic, can be explained in terms of the developments that took place in the political climate in the course of the past legislative term: by no means did they come like a "bolt out of the blue."

The incumbent CDU/CSU and FDP government won the election in 1994 because after a phase of economic stagnation, a long-predicted period of economic recovery set in early in the election year.[8] The particular importance of a good economic situation, and corresponding public perceptions, for satisfaction with a given government was analyzed in great detail in connection with past general elections.[9] In 1994 Chancellor Helmut Kohl succeeded in linking public perceptions of economic recovery with his leadership and thus with the economic competence of his government. As a consequence, the German public linked the Kohl government with its expectations for at least a gradual improvement in the employment situation.

The most urgent problem people living in the eastern German states have faced since reunification has been unemployment. The same has

Figure 7.1 Preferred Chancellor, 1997–98

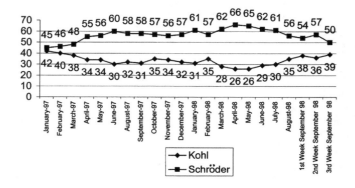

applied in western Germany since 1993. The upward trend seen on the employment market in 1994 and 1995 went into decline again as of 1996. Detailed media coverage and debate made it increasingly clear to the public that, at the very most, a good economic situation was able to mitigate the biggest problem faced by German society to a certain degree, but that it was in no way able to resolve the problem on a long-term basis. It may seem contradictory and unjust to make a government solely responsible for the situation on the employment market. On the other hand, the legislative branch of government has responsibility for the timely correction of undesirable structural trends.

It can be seriously doubted that voters would have attributed these structural problems to the incumbent government to such an extent that it would have been decisive for the election, if the image of the SPD had remained as it was in the first year after the general election. The SPD played a subordinate role as the strongest opposition party. Weakened by constant debates about the leadership qualities of Rudolf Scharping, the party chairman at the time, the image the SPD projected of itself was desolate.

This situation is, of course, reflected in representative polls. As of mid-1995 the SPD was seen as playing an increasingly marginal role in its work as an opposition party. Accordingly, the CDU/CSU occasionally led by a considerable margin in the approval ratings at the time (Figure 7.3). This changed only after what came to be called a "historical" SPD party conference held in Mannheim in November 1995, at which the premier of Saarland, Oskar Lafontaine, surprised the country by winning the party chairmanship from Rudolf Scharping in a challenge vote. From then on

Figure 7.2 Popularity Rating: Schröder, Schäuble, Kohl, January–September 1998 (mean score ±5)

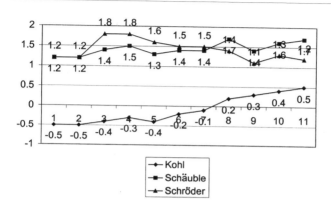

the SPD's opposition work improved, facilitated by a weakening situation on the employment market. The economic situation in Germany was not perceived by the general public as being all that bad. However, people had learned by then that a good economic situation would not necessarily lead to an improvement in the employment situation.

The rest of the legislative term was characterized by debate on various reforms, the necessity of which had been largely accepted by the politically interested public but were nonetheless a subject of party-political controversy. Under Lafontaine's leadership, the Social Democrats made systematic use of the red-green majority in the Bundesrat to stop government bills or to amend them to read the way they liked. This applied in particular to a tax reform strongly called for by many economists. However, to pass it the Kohl government needed to compromise with the red-green majority in the Bundesrat. The planned tax reform was an example of a project that suffered the effects of being initiated too late. It lay too close to the election campaign, which got underway much earlier than usual, making it difficult to arrive at what would otherwise have been obvious compromises in the Bundesrat. But even if it had been possible to pass a tax reform, the hoped-for positive effects on the economic situation would have come too late to have any effect on the general election.

The Kohl government's criticism that the SPD had refused to permit the passage of necessary reforms, failed to convince the electorate. On the contrary, the dispute over tax reform, played out against the governing parties, which the public perceived as not being able to get the job done. Even those reforms the governing parties were able to pass without Bundesrat approval did not work in their favor. The Kohl government was

Figure 7.3 Party Preference, 1997–98

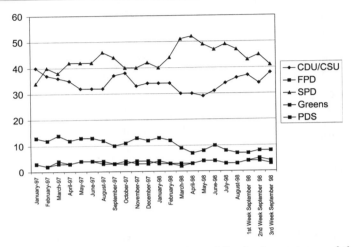

simply not able to communicate to the public the importance of these reforms in improving Germany's attractiveness as a place for business investment. The Alliance for Jobs broke apart because of the government's decision to impose cuts in sick pay. Plans to restrict pension increases in the future were misunderstood by pensioners as plans to cut pensions. Cuts in statutory insurance coverage of dental prostheses for young people were seen as discriminatory. The reforms with which the governing parties pursued the objective of making Germany a more competitive place for business investment seemed to the population like systematic measures aimed at giving to the rich and taking away from the poor. The government was unable to communicate to the public the objectives the reforms were intended to achieve. Parallel to the improvement of its approval ratings (Figure 7.3), the SPD succeeded in overtaking the CDU/CSU in public perceptions of its competence for resolving major political problems.

In the case of the most pressing problem, unemployment, more competence was attributed to the SPD for dealing with it than to the CDU/CSU. The same applied to perceived competence to maintain the security of the pension system, to deal with problems of health care, and to handle general social welfare policy problems. Issues for which a larger measure of competence was attributed to the CDU/CSU, such as fighting crime, monetary and economic stability, or foreign and security policy, were either not "in the news" or were viewed as in the process of being resolved.[10] The fact that shortly before the election the CDU/CSU succeeded in moving ahead of the SPD in perceived economic competence failed to have any significant influence. In 1998 the question of economic competence came nowhere near having the importance it had had four years earlier. And in any case, the German public showed a much larger measure of confidence in Gerhard Schröder in this matter than it did in Helmut Kohl.[11]

The CDU/CSU's low level of perceived competence with regard to key issues doubtless contributed to the party's weak position in public approval ratings after mid-1996. However, this is not a sufficient explanation for the enormous lead the SPD enjoyed at times. The second coalition partner, the FDP (the Liberals), had relatively modest approval ratings throughout the legislative term. In the monthly polls, the Liberals, like the PDS, were usually just under the 5 percent mark. For a party without ties to specific sociological groups, the visibility of its leaders in the media is one of the most important prerequisites for good results. Wolfgang Gerhardt's replacement of Klaus Kinkel as party chairman resulted in an improvement of media presence, but did not attain the intensity that is both necessary and possible for a party like the FDP. The polls taken in the run up to the general election raised doubts as to whether the FDP would make it over the 5 percent barrier.

These doubts were based on the fact that the polls were showing clearly that the coalition partners of many years were not going to win this time around. The FDP had always been able to count on receiving "second votes" from the ranks of CDU and CSU voters to ensure their common success. Despite the justified doubts with regard to the coalition winning the 1998 general election, the FDP, as in the situation in 1994,[12] received 60 percent of its votes from persons who indicated, in a poll held shortly before the election by Forschungsgruppe Wahlen, that the CDU or CSU were their actual parties of preference.

The Greens made their best gains when SPD ratings were low (Figure 7.3). They had good results in the state elections held during that period of time. As approval ratings rose for the SPD, they declined for the Greens. However, the strong dip experienced in the early part of the election year was not a result of the growth in public approval for the SPD, but of a clumsy presentation of energy-policy plans they had made for their possible involvement in a future government. For this, the Greens came under fire from their own clientele, which further favored the upward trend in approval ratings for the SPD.

The Role and Importance of the Major Candidates

Future analyses of this election will certainly focus on the influence of the chancellor candidates for the CDU/CSU and SPD: Helmut Kohl and Gerhard Schröder. The question most often debated in this context is whether Helmut Kohl's candidacy damaged the CDU/CSU and, if this was indeed the case, whether the Christian Democrats would have achieved better results with Wolfgang Schäuble. The night of the election, Helmut Kohl accepted political responsibility for his party's election defeat, and in so doing largely prevented the occurrence of a public debate over the question as to who was at fault. Needless to say, the question as to whether a different set of candidates would have produced different results is of particular interest for purposes of scholarly analysis. However, it is not a very easy question to answer.

Election researchers operate, for the most part, on the assumption that the results of individual elections are determined not by any one single factor, but by a combination of factors. Identification with a party, the assumptions made with regard to the ability of a given party to resolve important problems, and public perceptions of the leading candidate of a party are considered crucial determining factors in American research on elections.[13] These factors work together in combination, without a voter having to be aware of the importance of any one individual factor. In the analysis of voting behavior in Germany, it is often argued that orientation toward a given party predominates in individual voting decisions, since in German general elections it is parties that are voted for, not chancellor candidates.[14] This is doubtless true for voters loyal to the two major parties as well as for most PDS voters, but not for floating voters, whose reactions can have a decisive influence on the outcome of an election. In the age of electronic media, most voters get their information about an election campaign from television coverage.[15] However, the willingness of the population to follow complicated discussions of politics on television is quite limited. Since the viewing public is strongly oriented toward entertainment, long and complex analyses of political issues are not a viable option. This situation is not much different in most other countries.

A charismatic and attractive-looking politician will be particularly successful in getting his message across. Positive feelings for a politician are always connected with an assumption of competence. A politician will use public approval to gain support for his policies without this mechanism having to be understood in detail. There can be no doubt that the leading candidates of the parties, and the candidates for the chancellorship in particular, are of major importance for the election results of their parties, given that floating voters can be effectively reached through the media. However, as we know from past elections, approval ratings for a politician cannot simply be translated into votes and percentages.[16]

For a political system such as Germany's, whose institutional and social structures make it necessary in almost every instance to have coalition governments, tactical voting behavior must also be taken into account.[17] Tactical voting behavior is present when voters divide their first and second votes between two different parties in such a way that the optimum result is achieved for both parties. This is why, in this and in

Figure 7.4 Satisfaction with the Government and SPD Opposition, 1997–98 (mean score ±5 scale)

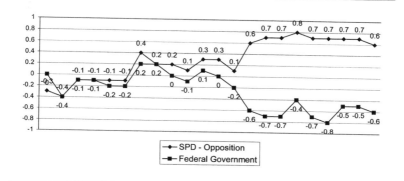

Figure 7.5 Most Important Problems in Germany

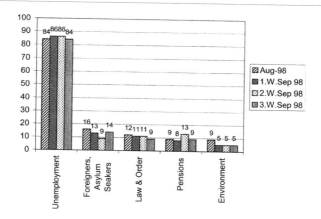

past general elections, so many CDU/CSU supporters cast their second votes for the FDP, i.e., to help to ensure that it got into the Bundestag. The same applies to first votes given to the PDS in their most successful eastern constituencies by persons who are actually SPD voters.

The leading candidates for the two major parties were not chosen until fairly late in the game. Prior to the general election in 1994, Helmut Kohl had said on a number of occasions that this was going to be his last election campaign. On a television program in April 1997, he declared his candidacy for the office of chancellor once again. In assessing this event, which took the general public and large sections of the party rank and file by surprise, it is often forgotten that there were many in the CDU and the CSU who had urged Kohl to run again.

At the same time, the situation in the SPD was characterized by the dualism of Oskar Lafontaine and Gerhard Schröder, then the premier of Lower Saxony. The Social Democrats had decided to wait until after the March 1998 state election in Lower Saxony to determine who the challenger would be. To everyone's surprise, both politicians stuck to this agreement and resisted public pressure to make the choice at an earlier point in time. Based on public opinion polls taken at the time, the situation was quite clear. In a comparison between Kohl and Lafontaine, Kohl came out ahead. In a comparison between Kohl and Schröder, Schröder came out ahead by quite a large margin.

After his victory in the state election and his immediate nomination as his party's candidate for the chancellorship, Schröder's lead continued to grow in the approval ratings and in response to the question of whom voters would like to have as their chancellor. As expected, this advantage diminished in the course of the election campaign, but at no time did Kohl come close to catching Schröder. In 1994 Kohl trailed behind his challenger, Rudolf Scharping, until May and June. After that he moved to the front and remained there. At the time, there were a number of events that had a positive effect for Helmut Kohl and the CDU/CSU. The German presidential election was won by the CDU/CSU candidate. The European Parliament election went favorably for the CDU/CSU. Finally, Kohl's early prognosis of a forthcoming improvement in the economic situation was confirmed.

There were no events of this kind in 1998. The final determination of currency values with regard to the euro in May 1998 was not an event that brought about a fundamental change of mood, but it did put an end to all speculation regarding this controversial issue.

What was the importance of the two leading candidates for the election results of their parties? Was public opinion with regard to Helmut Kohl and Gerhard Schröder a causal factor for the strong change in the results attained by their parties? Or was the desire for a change of government the primary determining factor, with public opinion toward the candidate a secondary factor?

In their analysis of the importance of the candidates for this election, Gabriel and Brettschneider came to the conclusion that candidate effects were very strong among floating voters, and that a larger percentage of these voters were in favor of Schröder. The authors contended "… that Helmut Kohl helped to bring about one of the worst election defeats suffered by the CDU/CSU since 1949."[18]

In making its reform plans, the CDU/CSU government had not reckoned with the possibility that a population conditioned by welfare state attitude and expectations might not (or not yet) be able to understand the objectives of this reform policy. For floating voters the objective was to correct the policy trends of the recent past by changing the faces in the government. In contrast to the situation in 1969, when Willy Brandt stood for a different policy toward Eastern Europe and a different style of government, and in contrast to 1982 and 1983, when Helmut Kohl wanted to bring about a change in policy direction, this third change of government involved not new departures but rather restoration. It goes without saying that loyal SPD voters had greater expectations with regard to SPD policies than did floating voters.

Schröder's election campaign appealed to the general feeling that it was time for a change. One SPD campaign slogan ("We're grateful, Helmut, but 16 years is enough") expressed what many people felt: Helmut Kohl has his merits, but now we need a younger and more modern head of government. Schröder's statement "We won't do anything differently, but we'll do a lot of things better" was aimed at those voters who felt there was a need to correct mistakes made by the incumbent government but did not want a radical policy change.

Whether a different chancellor candidate for the CDU/CSU would have led to a different election result may seem academic, but considerations of this kind are legitimate. Kohl's decision to run for office again was based on the assumption that he would be running against Oskar Lafontaine and not against Gerhard Schröder. When this assumption proved to be wrong, it was still possible to change leading candidates, even though this would have been difficult to explain to the public. If Wolfgang Schäuble had taken Kohl's place as the leading candidate, his approval ratings would doubtless not have continued to be as positive as they in fact turned out to be (Figure 7.2). The political debates in the election campaign would have exposed Schäuble to strong party-political polarization. As such, it would be naïve to argue only on the basis of his poll results that Schäuble would have been the better candidate. On the other hand, Schröder's election campaign arguments would not have worked well against Schäuble. At the same time, it is not very probable that Wolfgang Schäuble as a last-minute candidate could have brought about a majority for the governing coalition. Public dissatisfaction with the federal government was too great to have been able to save the situation on short notice by fielding another chancellor candidate. However, there is a lot that speaks in favor of the thesis that the losses suffered by the CDU/CSU would not have been as great if Schäuble had been the leading candidate, since the protests that were aimed at Helmut Kohl personally would not have applied in the same way to Schäuble.

One should be wary of believing that everything that can be deduced logically from polls can be implemented politically. The political process has its own mechanisms and its own laws. After Kohl had announced his willingness to run again and the party's top leadership bodies had approved this, a change in the leading candidate was not possible any longer when the assumption that his opponent was going to be Oskar Lafontaine turned out to be wrong. The confrontation with Kohl was very much up Schröder's alley when it came to campaigning style. On the other hand, Kohl would doubtless have looked better campaigning against Lafontaine than he did against Schröder. As such, there are two candidate-specific effects that influenced the observed changes in voting patterns and must be assessed in conjunction with one another: the positive effect generated by Gerhard Schröder for the SPD, and the negative effect generated by Helmut Kohl for the CDU and CSU. These two effects were mutually conditional. As such, it would be more correct to say that Gerhard Schröder won the general election as a result of an ably conducted election campaign and his approval ratings, than to conclude that the election was lost due only to Helmut Kohl. All in all it can be said that with regard to the issues focused on in the campaign and the situation of the two leading candidates, the SPD had a clear advantage. The expectation was expressed very early on that this time the opposition would win the election. The governing parties were able to narrow the gap in the course of the campaign, but there was never a feeling that they would be able to catch up with or pass the opposition.

Political Change or Structural Evolution

Even though the traditional social bases of the parties were preserved, changes within the various sociological groups were so significant that it should be asked whether they were caused only by short-term political influences, or by the effects of medium and long-term trends with regard to social change. The effects of social change on the structural composition of the (western) German electorate were discussed in our analysis of voter behavior in the various social groups. On the basis of the known relationships between specific sociological groups and voting for the major parties, effects on election results would seem probable, but have manifested themselves only to a limited degree. In western Germany, the two major parties have not done as well in general elections since 1987 as they did in the general elections held after 1961.

Careful analysts of voting behavior in Germany should have long since become aware that on the basis of the structural changes that have taken place in society, the potential has also been created for significant changes in voting behavior. Apparently, many floating voters had only been waiting for the right opportunity to demonstrate this potential.

The political mood in the 1998 general election was characterized by the strong influence exerted by the leading candidates and public expectations

Table 7.9 Final Predictions of Major Public Opinion Polling Organizations, 1998

	*IFD Allensbach	EMNID Bielefeld	**FGW Mannheim	Forsa Berlin	Infratest München	Actual Result
Date	25 Sept.	21 Sept.	18 Sept.	24 Sept.	25 Sept.	(2nd Ballot)
SPD	40.5	41.0	39.5	42.0	40.5	40.9
CDU/ CSU	36.0	39.0	37.5	38.0	38.5	35.1
Green	6.0	6.0	6.0	6.0	6.5	6.7
FDP	6.5	5.0	5.5	5.0	6.5	6.2
PDS	5.0	5.0	4.5	4.0	5.0	6.2
Other	6.0	4.0	7.0	5.0	5.0	5.1
						6.0

*Institut für Demoskopie
**Forschungsgruppe Wahlen

regarding rapid corrections of current policies. More than ever before, floating voters wanted to bring about a change of government and were certain that they would be able to do so. The polls taken in the last two to three weeks before the election left no doubt about this.

The major polling organizations predicted that the SPD would emerge ahead of the CDU/CSU as the strongest party, and almost all of them correctly indicated which party would come in third. Three of the five polling institutes in question thought the PDS would end up under 5 percent, but there was no doubt as to whether the PDS would be represented in the Bundestag, given that it was certain to win at least three direct mandates. Even though the governing majority that was eventually elected cannot be read out of every forecast, all of the institutes involved were successful in addressing the challenge of correctly predicting the first change of federal government ever to take place as a result of a general election.

The volatility of voter behavior that has grown steadily over several decades and then more rapidly since the 1990 unification, will make it difficult in the future for the major parties to be certain of receiving the same kind of electoral support they enjoyed in the past. Their sociological constituencies have become too small for this, as shown by the drastic losses sustained by the CDU/CSU. In the future, electoral gains and losses could be larger than what we have been accustomed to seeing. The changes that were evident in this election will not be an exception. For the smaller parties, this will increase the danger of not being able to surmount the 5 percent barrier.

In the future, the outcome of general elections will be more unpredictable than in the past, with corresponding uncertainties for the planning of coalitions. Election analysts and polling institutes will need to be more aware that their polls will not be able to predict the intentions of floating voters with reasonable accuracy until shortly before the election. Polls taken well in advance of election day, e.g., at the beginning of an election campaign, will only be able to describe the mood of public opinion at the time and will have little long-term predictive value. This is, of course, not new, but the stability of past voting behavior made it possible to make educated guesses quite early on with regard to the outcome of an election. In the future, speculation of this kind will be riskier, since the motives of floating voters who may well change their minds in the course of an election campaign cannot be identified in advance.

Relatively stable general election results are a thing of the past. Floating voters do not necessarily have to switch their preferences in every election, but they can. Party campaign strategists will need to adjust to this situation and base the presentation of their candidates more than they have in the past on the expectations of floating voters. The SPD's successful campaign in the 1998 election provided us with a foretaste of things to come.

Conclusions

The 1998 election was characterized in western Germany by a largely uniform trend in favor of the SPD, to the disadvantage of the CDU/CSU. This trend varied slightly in the various demographic and sociological groups, depending on the strength of the parties at the outset. In terms of the sociology of elections, prior relationships between social structure and voting behavior were generally maintained. The SPD did not manage to encroach on typical CDU/CSU structures. It was "only" able to achieve improvements that were on the order of its overall average gains. The most noticeable changes were those among voters 35 and older. In western Germany, this was the case particularly among women, a fact which bespeaks criticism of CDU/CSU reform legislation.

In eastern Germany volatility was stronger, since the relationship between social structure and voting is not as pronounced as in the West, i.e., all other things being equal, there will be more volatility in the East. As a result of this election, gains and losses for the various parties will continue to be stronger in eastern Germany than in the West.

The voters who brought about the change of government in 1998 did not want to achieve a fundamental change of policies, but rather sought a correction of the policies that had been pursued by allowing a new group to take over the reins of government. The desire to do this was very important among floating voters, which is why there was an increase in voter turnout, particularly in eastern Germany. It would seem probable that the ideas for policy change among the members of the red-green coalition might be more extensive than a mere correction of past policies. However, there is no legitimacy for this on the basis of the election results. The influence of the leading candidates on the electoral behavior of floating voters was quite considerable in this election.

The constellation of leading candidates was ideal for the SPD. It was able to present a pragmatic and non-ideological chancellor candidate, who also promised relatively painless reform. Schröder's youth and more dynamic image was merely icing on the cake. In this regard, Gerhard Schröder was very useful to the SPD. Helmut Kohl was unable to neutralize the "Schröder effect" or stop the CDU/CSU's decline. But we must not forget the contribution of Lafontaine. His Mannheim "coup" and subsequent opposition strategy enabled the SPD to mount an effective challenge during the inter-election period.

After this third national election in unified Germany, there are still clear differences in voting behavior between the eastern and western regions of the country. There continues to be a four-party system in western Germany. Eastern Germany continues to have a three-party system. When joined together, they produce a five-party system for Germany as a whole. Differences in voting behavior between East and West have not grown larger. However, with the exception of voter turnout, they have also not grown any smaller.

Notes

1. Russell J. Dalton "Unity and Division: The 1994 Bundestag Election," in Russell J. Dalton, ed., *Germans Divided: The 1994 Bundestag Elections and the Evolution of the German Party System* (Oxford, Washington, DC: Berg 1996), 15.
2. Kai Arzheimer and Jürgen W. Falter, "Annäherung durch Wandel? Das Wahlverhalten bei des Bundestagswahl 1998 in Ost-West-Perspektive," *Aus Politik und Zeitgeschichte*, B 52/1998, 18 December 1998, 42–43.
3. Dalton, "Unity and Division," 16–17.
4. Franz Urban-Pappi, "Sozialstruktur, gesellschaftliche Wertorientierungen und Wahlabsicht," in Max Kaase, ed., *Wahlsoziologie heute* (Opladen: Westdeutscher Verlag, 1994), 195–229. See also Wolfgang G. Gibowski, "Election Trends in Germany: An Analysis of the Second General Election in Reunited Germany," in Geoffrey K. Roberts, ed., *Superwahljahr: The German Elections in 1994* (London: Frank Cass, 1996), 36; also Thomas Emmert, Manfred Jung, and Dieter Roth, "Zwischen Konstanz und Wandel. Die Bundestagswahl vom 16. Oktober 1994," in Max Kaase and Hans-Dieter Klingemann,

eds., *Wahlen und Wähler. Analysen aus Anlaß der Bundestagswahl 1994* (Opladen: Westdeutscher Verlag, 1998), 79.

5. Gibowski, "Election Trends in Germany," 42, Table 4. See also Manfred Jung and Dieter Roth, "Wer zu spät geht, den bestraft der Wähler. Eine Analyse der Bundestagswahl 1998," *Aus Politik und Zeitgeschichte*, B 52/98, 18 December 1998,5.

6. Günther Eckstein and Franz-Urban Pappi, "Die politischen Wahrnehmungen und die Präferenzen der Wählerschaft in Ost und Westdeutschland: Ein Vergleich," in Hand-Dieter Klingemann, Max Kaase, eds., *Wahlen und Wähler. Analysen aus Anlaß der Bundestagswahl 1990* (Opladen: Westdeutscher Verlag, 1994), 397–421.

7. Emmert et al., "Zwischen Konstanz und Wandel," 8.

8. Gibowski, "Election Trends in Germany," 36–40.

9. Manfred Küchler, "Ökonomische Kompetenzurteile und individuelles politisches Verhalten: Empirische Ergebnisse am Beispiel der Bundestagswahl 1983," in Dieter Oberndörfer, Hans Rattinger, and Karl Schmitt, eds., *Wirtschaftlicher Wandel, religiöser Wandel und Wertewandel. Folgen für das politische Verhalten in der Bundesrepublik Deutschland* (Berlin: Duncker und Humbolt, 1985), 157–80.

10. Jung and Roth, "Wer zu spät geht," 8–9.

11. Oskar W. Gabriel and Frank Brettschneider, "Die Bundestagswahl 1998: Ein Plebiszit gegen Kanzler Kohl?" *Aus Politik und Zeitgeschichte*, B 52/98, 18 December 1998, 28.

12. Gibowski, "Election Trends in Germany," 8.

13. Angus Campbell et al., *The American Voter* (New York: Wiley, 1960).

14. Emmert et al., "Zwischen Konstanz und Wandel," 76.

15. Kenneth Berg and Manfred L. Kiefer, *Massenkommunikation V: Eine Langzeitstudie zur Mediennutzung und Medienbewertung 1964–1995* (Baden-Baden: Nomosverlag, 1996), 30.

16. Gibowski, "Election Trends in Germany," 30.

17. Ibid., 27.

18. Gabriel and Brettschneider, "Die Bundestagswahl 1998," 32.

Chapter 8

THE CAMPAIGN IN THE NEWS

Holli A. Semetko and Klaus Schoenbach

I n Germany today, television continues to be the medium able to reach the largest portion of the population.[1] In the mid-1990s, 83 percent of Germans were exposed to television each day, compared with 75 percent to radio, and 65 percent to newspapers. Overall in Germany in the mid-1990s, 60 percent were reached by political content on television, compared with 57 percent for radio and 46 percent for newspapers. The figures for East Germans' exposure to political content on television were even higher (75 percent) than West Germans' (65 percent). In this chapter, we discuss key characteristics of the German media system with respect to how the 1998 German campaign was presented in television news, and then present the results of a content analysis of election news on television and in the large circulation newspaper, the *Bild.*

We address the following questions: How important was the 1998 election campaign in the news? What were the main topics and issues in the news? How visible were the two chancellor candidates, and the incumbent parties of government in comparison with the opposition parties? Did the coverage of politics during the campaign result in a visibility bonus for the chancellor and the incumbent party as it had in previous elections? Were there any noteworthy similarities or differences between the main evening news programs and the *Bild* with respect to these questions?

German Media System Characteristics

The balance between public and commercial broadcasting has changed in Germany, as in most European countries, over the past decade.[2] In the late 1970s and up into the mid-1980s in the West, we could still speak of a broadcasting system that was entirely public. West Germany's public system was financed by a mixture of state funds and advertising revenue. In the West, private channels introduced in the late 1980s were financed entirely by advertising. As audiences shifted from public to private channels, advertisers put more revenue into the private channels and the competition between the public and private channels intensified.

The form of financing broadcasting systems has important implications for the range and quality of political programming.[3] On a continuum ranging from entirely state-owned at one end to entirely market-driven on the other, the U.S. is perhaps the most well known example of a market-driven system, with many European countries having moved recently from entirely state-owned to the center of the continuum. The more public service-dominant the system, the more likely it is that prime-time television will include a broad range of political news and current affairs programming; the more commercially driven the system, the more market pressure for ratings and hence the more reluctant prime-time television will be to replace popular entertainment programming with political information programming.[4] This predisposition for more or less political programming, stemming from the balance of public service vs. commercial in the broadcasting systems, is likely to also be reflected in the amount of election-related programming during campaigns.

Although in Germany there was an initial concern that the launch of private television in the mid-1980s would have a negative impact on news by bringing in American-style reporting, that in fact did not happen. The news on the private channels initially tried to be more entertaining and sensational, but soon resembled the German public channels far more than originally anticipated.[5]

The rules, traditions, and practices surrounding party access to broadcasting during election campaigns have changed along with the broadcasting system. An important, related characteristic is the political autonomy of broadcasting from government and political parties. As competition and the number of channels increased, in Germany and elsewhere, there was also a diversification of income sources and a corresponding lessening of control by political authorities. The more commercial the broadcasting system, the less opportunity for government or political parties to exert direct influence over broadcasting organizations. Public service channels in Germany are subject to oversight by state-level boards comprised of socially relevant groups including representatives of the political parties in each state-level parliament. The German private channels are licensed, and oversight is dealt with by independent commissions with responsibilities similar to that of Britain's Independent Television Commission, for example. German public broadcasters' concerns over possible repercussions in the advisory boards could have consequences for the quantity and quality of election-related programming.

One crucial difference between the German public and private channels is in the ways in which journalists advance in their careers. In the public channels, career advancement is related to a concept of political "balance" in the newsroom that requires journalists to affiliate with one or another of the two main parties.[6] Major positions in the newsroom are occupied by senior news executives who are not only exceptionally well-qualified professionally, but also appropriately qualified politically.[7] Political parties can nowadays purchase advertising time on private television, whereas that was previously forbidden, and they continue to receive an allocation of free time for advertising on the public channels. Political programs on the public channels are also expected to be balanced over the course of the campaign with respect to the visibility of political parties. Popular assumption has it that the First Public Network (ARD) and one of the major private networks, Radio-Television Luxemburg (RTL), are more sympathetic with the SPD, while the Second Public Network (ZDF) and another private network, SAT1, are generally considered pro-CDU/CSU/FDP stations.

Political debates among the top candidates, the so-called "Elephant Rounds," were key events from the 1972 to 1987 election campaigns. These were valuable and unique opportunites for parties to reach voters. Baker, Norpoth and Schoenbach, in comparing the 1972 and 1976 debates, found that politicians who displayed a more positive style of debate were more likely to be perceived as the "winner" of that debate.[8] Baker and Norpoth's study of the 1972 debate found that electors did learn more about the candidates and parties from this event, and that this had a particular impact on evaluations of the opposition party.[9] Schrott's analysis of the electoral impact of the 1972, 1976, 1980 and 1983 debates suggested that debates do make an important difference to electoral outcomes.[10] Controlling for party identification and other factors, citizens were significantly more likely to vote for the candidate they believed had won the debate. Thus, winning debates improved not only the candidates' images, but also their chance of getting elected. Because the German debates were usually held only a few days prior to the election, their short-term effects may have further enhanced their importance to the voting decision. Perhaps concerned about the possible negative impact of debates, especially since the former East German Communist Party, the PDS, would be present, chancellor Helmut Kohl refused to participate in any after 1987. There were thus no chancellor debates in the 1990, 1994 or 1998 Bundestag election campaigns.

Our study of the December 1990 Bundestag election campaign in the newly unified Germany drew on content analysis of fifteen high circulation newspapers across the country and main evening television news programs on public service and leading private channels, as well as a representative panel survey of voters in the western part of the country during the "hot phase" of the campaign—the final eight weeks when the parties' campaigning activities were in full swing.[11] Two key findings are important here. One concerns the effects of the campaign: significant changes in public opinion about the incumbent coalition were a consequence of the visibility of politicians in the news. Another concerns the content of the news: there was a significant difference between the chancellor candidates, and between the government and opposition parties, in terms of their visibility in the news.

The visibility bonus of the incumbent coalition in television news showed that the main opposition party could not expect the same amount of time or space in the news, whereas in other democracies the broadcast news media made special efforts to provide equal or balanced coverage of the leading parties and candidates at election time. There was no equal opportunity for the opposition parties to communicate to voters via the main evening news, and this was buttressed by a low level of attention paid to the 1990 campaign in the press. The imbalance between the government and opposition parties in the news was not due to biased or evaluative remarks by television reporters, however, for these comments were almost always neutral or simply descriptive. We concluded that this was not a problem of ideology or partisanship among news programs, or a reflection of the personal political preferences of television news executives. The visibility bonus existed on all television news channels, so if the parties of government were to change, it was potentially just as likely that such an advantage would begin for the new parties in power.

We argued that in the 1990 election it was television news reporters' professionalism—in reporting largely without evaluations and in selecting only those stories that satisfied certain news value criteria—that made mere visibility a bonus in 1990. A scandal or a running negative news story could have meant that the visibility bonus had negative consequences for perceptions of the parties in power, but there were none in 1990.

How visible was the 1998 election campaign, and the issues, in the news? How were the candidates and the parties reported? We content analyzed the main evening news programs on ARD, ZDF, RTL and SATl, which were broadcast between the hours of 7 p.m. and 8:30 p.m. each evening and are the German equivalents of U.S. network evening news or Britain's Independent Television News (ITN) at 6:30 p.m. We also content analyzed the first two pages of the largest circulation newspaper in the country, the *Bild Zeitung*. The newspaper customarily deals with the most important political information on those pages, and devotes the third page to local news. The content analysis focused on the hot phase of the campaign for the seven weeks before election day, from 20 August to election day, 27 September 1998. All stories that mentioned parties or politicians were selected for coding. This resulted in a total of 524 television news stories and 384 newspaper stories. Coding was conducted by a team of three trained graduate students. The intercoder reliability ranged from 0.92 to 0.96.

We focus on the main evening news programs because these have the highest audience ratings, these audiences are more representative of the public at large demographically and in terms of political interest, and they are a common basis for cross-national comparison. Audiences for the later evening current affairs news programs each evening on ARD and ZDF, such as *Tagesthemen* or *Heute Journal* (Germany's *Newsnight* equivalents), are quite different, in terms of size and demographic characteristics, and are already politically interested.

An Exciting Election

No observer of German politics will be able to recall an election in recent years that received more attention in the news than this one. The campaign itself was mentioned much more often in the news than the historic 1990 election, which was the first national election after reunification, when the vast majority of news stories about politics in the final six weeks before election day simply ignored the election campaign.[12]

One reason the campaign preceeding the December 1990 election was barely visible in the news was that the result was largely a foregone conclusion. At the start of the hot phase some six weeks before election day, more than 80 percent of the population believed the incumbent coalition would return to power. Another reason why the 1990 campaign was barely visible had to do with journalists' responses to the opposition chancellor candidate, Oskar Lafontaine, whose public support had lagged well behind Helmut Kohl's since May 1990, when the SPD was split by Lafontaine's insistence that the party seek to prevent the passage of the unification treaty in the Bundesrat. According to one ZDF TV news producer who was interviewed during the 1990 campaign, and who was not an SPD man himself, "even SPD journalists were not willing to fight for Lafontaine," and so there was less coverage of the 1990 SPD campaign in the news. Other journalists who were more sympathetic with the SPD in 1990, however, suggested that the likelihood of Helmut Kohl's victory provided a "chilling effect" that discouraged them from making a case for bringing more coverage of the campaign or the SPD's campaigning activities into television news.[13] As a consequence, the coverage of the 1990 election campaign in the news was extremely limited, while the coverage of day-to-day activities of the government and the chancellor continued as usual, even in the final two weeks preceding the vote. In 1998, it could not have been more different. First, it was a much more competitive election, with polls showing a change of government as the most likely outcome for many months leading up to election day. The victory of the SPD and its minister-president candidate Gerhard Schröder in the Lower Saxony elections in March 1998 signaled the beginning of an exciting and unusually long and interesting Bundestag election campaign. The official hot phase began in August, six weeks before election day, and the Bundestag campaign heated up further in the last two weeks when the CSU won and the SPD lost by an unexpectedly large margin in the state elections in Bavaria. The 1998 Bundestag election was thus far more competitive, and hence far more interesting, in terms of sheer news values. Gerhard Schröder was also an altogether different challenger than Oskar Lafontaine had been. Schröder kept the SPD united. At the same time, with his relative youth, vigor, and telegeneic qualities, he stood in stark contrast to Kohl. As a future potential chancellor, then, Schröder in 1998 also ranked high in news value terms.

Campaign Visibility

The 1998 Bundestag election campaign was mentioned in over half (53 percent) of the stories on television news in the final weeks before the vote. There was considerable variation among channels, however, and the private channels mentioned the campaign far more often than the public channels. A full 71 percent of stories on RTL mentioned the election campaign, compared with 58 percent on SAT1, 47 percent on ZDF, and 40 percent on ARD. Campaign-related stories were also, on average, longer than those that were not campaign related. The average length of a story that mentioned the election campaign was 96 seconds on RTL, 147 seconds on SAT1, 116 seconds on RTL, and 107 seconds on ARD, whereas the average length of a story that did not mention the campaign was 77 seconds on RTL, 88 seconds on SAT1, 70 on ZDF, and 67 on ARD.

In the *Bild*, a full 38 percent of stories on the first two pages mentioned the election campaign. A look at the headlines in the *Bild* and on television news shows how the emphasis was on the opinion polls, the closeness of the race, and the possible coalition outcomes. Table 1 gives the front page headlines in the *Bild*, a newspaper that traditionally supported the incumbent coalition and in particular the CDU and Helmut Kohl in the final weeks, along with election headlines from ZDF and RTL main evening news.

Table 8.1 *Bild*, ZDF and RTL Election-Related Headlines,
14–27 September 1998

14 September
BILD: Riesenschub für Kohl: Stoiber triumphiert in Bayern, SPD verliert,
Bundestagswahl wieder offen (Major push for Kohl: Stoiber triumphant
in Bavaria, SPD loses, Federal election campaign wide open)
ZDF: Nachlese: Bonn am Tag nach der Landtagswahl in Bayern (Second har-
vest: Bonn one day after the State Parliamentary election in Bavaria)
RTL: Endspurt in Bonn: Der CSU-Sieg in Bayern macht die Bundestagswahl
jetzt richtig spannend (Final push in Bonn: The CSU victory in Bavaria
makes the federal election really exciting)
15 September
BILD: Arbeitslosen- und Sozialhilfe zusammenlegen? -Pläne der CDU/CSU im
Falle eines Wahlsieges (Combine unemployment payments and social
benefits? The plans of the CDU/CSU if they win)
RTL: Volldampf im Osten: Im Endspurt vor der Wahl kämpfen die Parteien
um jede Stimme in den Neuen Ländern (Full steam ahead in the East: in
the final push before the election, the parties fight for every vote in the
new states)
16 September
RTL: Wahlkampf pur: In Bonn eskaliert der Streit um eine Erhöhung
der Mehrwertsteuer (Pure Campaigning: The row escalates over proposed increases to the value-added tax)
18 September
BILD: Wahl-Prügel: Der Kanzler, die SPD, die FDP: alle hauen auf Frau Nolte
(die Ministerin, die den neuen Steuer-Streit auslöste) (Election Thrash-
ing: The Chancellor, the SPD, the FDP: all beat up on Mrs. Nolte)
ZDF: Politbarometer: Der Abstand zwischen Opposition und Regierung wird
kleiner (Politbarometer: The gap between the opposition and government is narrowing)
19 September
BILD: Wahl: Es wird gaaaanz knapp
8 Tage bis zur Wahl: der Abstand schrumpft nach Angaben von
Meinungsforschungsinstituten (Election: It will be reeeeaaaaaallllly close
8 days before the election: The distance shrinks, according to public
opinion research institutes)
21 September
BILD: 6 Tage bis zur Wahl: dimap-Prognose, Doppelte Staatsbürgerschaft,
Grüner fordert neue Nationalhymne, Kohl gegen große Koalition, Stollmann läßt sich von L. Späth beraten, Lafontaine will bei illegaler
Beschäftigung hart durchgreifen (6 days before the election: dimap's [one
institute's] forecast, Dual citizenship, Greens want a new national
anthem, Kohl against grand coalition, Stollman advised by Lothar Späth
[SPD shadow cabinet minister for economics advised by former CDU

Table 8.1 *Bild,* **ZDF and RTL Election-Related Headlines,**
14–27 September 1998 *(cont.)*

minister-president of Baden-Württemburg], Lafontaine wants to take
strong measures against illegal employment)

ZDF: Wahlkampf: Im Endspurt setzen Regierung und Opposition auf die
Zweitstimme (Election Campaign: Government and opposition's final
push for the second ballot vote)

RTL: Solidarität aus Bonn: Mit Abscheu und Empörung reagieren deutsche
Politiker auf die Veröffentlichung des Clinton-Videos (Solidarity from
Bonn: German politicians react to the publication of the Clinton video
with disgust and indignation)

22 September

ZDF: ZDF-Interview: Herausforderer Schröder im Wahlkampfendspurt ZDF
(Interview: Challenger Schroder's final push in the election race)

23 September

ZDF: ZDF-Interview: Bundeskanzler Kohl zur Frage einer möglichen großen
Koalition (ZDF Interview: Chancellor Kohl addresses the question of a
possible grand coalition)

RTL: Hochspannung vor der Wahl: Kohl schließt eine große Koalition nicht
mehr kategorisch aus (High voltage before the election: Kohl does not
categorically rule out a grand coalition)

24 September

BILD: Kohl: "Große Koalition prinzipiell möglich" (Kohl: "Grand coalition
possible in principle")

ZDF: Wahlkampfbilanz: Die Parteien mobilisieren ihre letzten Reserven
(Election in the balance: Parties mobilize last reserves)

RTL: Wahlkampfbilanz in Bonn: 3 Tage vor der Wahl sehen sich alle Parteien
als Sieger (Election in the balance in Bonn: 3 days before the election,
each party considers itself the winner)

25 September

BILD: 2 Tage bis zur Wahl: Wählertäuschung durch Lafontaine? Wirtschaft-
prognose Kohls, FDP-Wahlkampf (2 days before the election: Voters
deceived by Lafontaine? Kohl's economic forecast, FDP campaign)

ZDF: 2 Tage vor der Wahl: Haushaltsstreit im Bundesrat (Two days before the
election: A row about the budget in the Second Chamber)

RTL: Noch 48 Stunden bis zur Entscheidung: Kohl und sein Herausforderer
treten ein letztes Mal vor die Wähler (Only 48 hours before the decision,
Kohl and his challenger meet the voters for the last time)

26 September

BILD: Jede Stimme zählt, auch Ihre. Letzte Umfragen: Kopf-an-Kopf Renne
(Every vote counts, yours too. Last polls: Head-to-head race)

ZDF: Wahlfieber: Wer hat morgen die Nase vorn? (Election fever: Who will
win tomorrow?)

RTL: Kopf-an-Kopf-Rennen: 1 Tag vor der Wahl wird der Abstand zwischen
Union und SPD geringer (Head to Head: One day before the election, the
gap between the Union and the SPD narrows)

The election-related headlines on ZDF and RTL were somewhat less sensational and evaluative than those in the *Bild*. The news on 14 September, for example, focused on the outcome of the Bavarian Landtag elections, in which the CSU, the Bavarian sister party of the CDU, performed better than expected and the SPD lost more votes than expected. As a result, this race was billed in the *Bild* as one that provided momentum to the CDU/CSU's race across the country, making the national election campaign "wide open," and Bavarian CSU Minister-President Stoiber was described as "triumphant." Television news headlines claimed that the Bavarian outcome made the federal election now "really exciting." But this apparent boost was short-lived. A controversial statement about value-added tax policy by CDU Minister Nolte caused a major embarrassment to the governing coalition, and this very problematic story was featured in all television news outlets and on page 1 of *Bild* only 10 days before the vote. From then on, many of the stories focused on the narrowing gap between the CDU and the SPD, and provided conflicting accounts of the coalition outcome possibilities. On 19 September, the day after the bad news on Minister Nolte, the front page of *Bild* reminded voters that the election result would be "gaaaanz knapp" (reaaaally close). The front page on 21 September announced that Kohl was against a grand coalition, but only a few days later on 23 September, after Kohl's interview aired on ZDF, it said that Kohl thought a grand coalition was possible. On the day before the vote, *Bild* urged voters to go to the polls and devoted its front page to the theme "every vote counts." Television news described the country as having "election fever" and claimed the race was "head-to-head."

The election made it into the headlines despite the news value of other events in the world, not least the developments in the story of U.S. President Clinton and former White House intern Monica Lewinsky. The Clinton-Lewinsky affair reached a high point in the news in the final weeks before election day, when the president testified on videotape before a grand jury, and this was subsequently leaked to the media. German electors, like most Europeans and Americans, were fed an almost daily dose of the Bill and Monica story in the seven weeks before election day. Here are examples of how this story surfaced in the headlines in the final two weeks of the campaign:

Bild 14 September
Die Clinton-Protokolle: Heute 3 Seiten Wortlaut in Bild
The Clinton protocols (testimony): Today 3 pages of transcripts in *Bild*

Bild 15 September
Oh Gott, Clinton! Noch 'ne Monica? Bild zeigt das neue Video aus dem Weißen Haus

Oh God, Clinton! Still another Monica? *Bild* shows the new video from the White House

ZDF 18 September
Lewinsky-Affaire: Prasident Clintons Videoaussage wird veröffentlicht
The Lewinsky Affair: President Clinton's video statement will be published

RTL 19 September
Warten auf das Video: Prasident Clinton bangt: Wie werden die Amerikaner auf seine Aussagen zur Sex-Affäire reagieren?
Waiting for the video: President Clinton fears: How will Americans react to his statements about the affair?

RTL 20 September
Die Stimmung kippt: Einen Tag vor der Veröffentlichung des Videos des Clinton-Verhörs sind immer mehr Amerikaner für einen Rücktritt des Präsidenten
The opinion shifts: One day before publication of the video of Clinton's grand jury testimony, the number of Americans who would like the President to resign is growing

RTL 21 September
Clintons schwerster Tag: Weltweit verfolgen Millionen Menschen das Video mit der Sex-Beichte des US-Präsidenten
Clinton's most difficult day: More than one million people worldwide follow the president's sex confession video

ZDF 21 September
Lewinsky-Affäire: Prasident Clintons Video-Aussage sorgt weltweit für Diskussionen
The Lewinsky Affair: President Clinton's video statement causes worldwide discussions

ZDF 22 September
Rückendeckung: Auch nach der Videoausstrahlung stehen die Amerikaner zu Präsident Clinton
Continuing support: Even after the video broadcast, Americans back their president

Bild 23 September
Clinton wieder erstärkt: Video-Ausstrahlung hat ihm eher genutzt als geschadet
Clinton recovers: Broadcast of the video helps rather than hurts him

This story continued to fascinate German news editors, and apparently therefore the public, throughout the final weeks of the campaign. It displaced the national election campaign as news on many occasions. There were many days in August and September, in fact, when this long-running story made the headlines and the election did not.

Table 8.2 Themes in Political TV News Stories, 10 August–27 September 1998 (percentages)

	ARD	ZDF	RTL	SAT.1	Total
Political system	4	3	3	3	3
Campaign	17	21	28	30	24
Polls	1	5	18	9	8
Manifestos/platforms	13	14	15	16	14
Social welfare	13	8	6	5	8
Environment	3	3	1	3	3
Economy	17	19	13	12	15
Infrastructure	2	1	1	3	2
Law and order	4	3	2	3	3
Education	7	2	–	1	3
Foreign affairs	14	15	7	12	12
State profiles	1	2	–	1	1
Ex-DDR	3	1	2	1	2
Other	3	4	3	2	3
Responses	237	249	209	209	904
N	154	145	111	114	524

Source: Klaus Schoenbach and Holli A. Semetko, media content analysis of the 1998 German Bundestag campaign.

The Election and Various Themes in the News

Each election news story was coded for up to six subjects or themes, in order of predominance. These give us an indication of the visibility of various issues in the news. It also shows the extent to which the election campaign was a focus in a story, which means that the story went beyond simply mentioning the campaign (as discussed above) to actually deal with the campaign in a major way. The election campaign in comparison with other themes in television news during the period under study is presented in Table 8.2.

As shown in Table 8.2, the campaign itself—in other words, the activities of the political parties and the chancellor candidates on the campaign trail, at evening rallies, and at press conferences—accounted for the largest portion of themes in the news on all the channels. The opinion polls were in a separate category. Overall, the campaign accounted for some 24 percent of themes in television news and opinion polls some 8 percent. The economy was the most important substantive issue, which accounted for 15 percent of themes in television news, and the party manifestos and records accounted for 14 percent of themes. These figures are displayed in the last column in Table 8.2. The economy was the single most important issue in the campaign on all channels, and on television this was followed by foreign affairs, and social welfare. Less attention was given to other issues—education, law and order, the environment, infrastructure. These seven substantive issues together accounted for about half (45 percent) of all themes in television news.

There were important differences between the public and private channels in reporting the election. Taking together the key seven substantive issues—economy, social welfare, environment, infrastructure, law and order, education, foreign affairs—there was a clear difference in emphasis on issues by the public and private channels. These substantive issues accounted for 59 percent of themes on ARD and 50 percent on ZDF, in comparison with 31 percent on RTL and 38 percent on SAT1. The editorial decisions taken at each channel thus had considerable influence over the presentation of the dynamics of the campaign and the issues. Campaign events were far more important on the private channels, with some 30 percent of themes on SAT1, 28 percent on RTL, 21 percent on ZDF, and only 17 percent on ARD. The private channels also chose to report the opinion polls more often. On RTL, for example, opinion polls accounted for 18 percent of themes in the news, compared with less than half that on SAT1, under 5 percent on ZDF, and under 1 percent on ARD.

In comparison with television, *Bild*, as Table 8.3 shows, paid less attention to the polls, the manifestos and platforms of the political parties, and more attention to the events on the campaign trail. The rank order of the other substantive issues in this newspaper was: economy, social welfare, foreign affairs, education, law and order, the environment, and infrastructure.

Political Parties and Leaders in the News

We were interested in the visibility of the chancellor candidates and the political parties, relative to one another, in the news. We coded up to ten actors in each political story. In the 524 television news stories, there were a total of 2,295 actors. In the 384 *Bild* stories, there were a total of 1,221 actors. We also measured the amount of time devoted to politicians' soundbites or quoted statements in television news.

Helmut Kohl was more visible than his challenger in all the news outlets here, but the visibility bonus was less than it had been in 1990. Overall, Kohl appeared in 37 percent of stories on television, in comparison with 26 percent for Gerhard Schröder, as can be seen in Table 8.3. Although this gap was still considerable, it was down 5 percentage points from what it had been in 1990, when Kohl appeared in 22 percent of stories and

Table 8.3 Themes in Front Page News in the *Bild*, 10 August–
27 September 1998 (percentages)

Political system	7
Campaign	29
Polls	3
Manifestos/platforms	8
Social welfare	9
Environment	2
Economy	15
Infrastructure	2
Law and order	5
Education	6
Foreign affairs	8
State profiles	2
Ex-DDR	2
Other	4
Responses	538
N	384

Source: Klaus Schoenbach and Holli A. Semetko, media content analysis of the 1998
German Bundestag campaign.

Note: Columns may not sum to 100 percent due to rounding.

Lafontaine in 6 percent. In the *Bild*, Kohl appeared in 25 percent of stories, and Schröder appeared in 15 percent, in comparison with 1990
when the comparable figures were 32 percent for Kohl and 17 percent
for Lafontaine.[14]

There was another aspect to visibility, however, in which Helmut Kohl
was actually less visible than Gerhard Schröder, and that was in terms of
the average time devoted to soundbites or quoted remarks. Soundbites
refer to the actualities in the news, when the candidate is seen and heard
speaking on the screen. Other quoted remarks (*indirekte Rede*) are statements by the candidates that are given by the news reader. Taken together,
these soundbites and quoted remarks represent the amount of time available to the two leaders to get their message across on television news, in
their own words. Although Schröder made fewer appearances in the news
than Kohl, the average length of a statement from Schröder was 30 seconds, compared to 19 seconds for Kohl. In 1990, by contrast, the situation
was reversed. The average length of a statement from Kohl was 30 seconds, compared to 19 seconds for Lafontaine.[15]

In 1998, the CDU/CSU and FDP party actors were also more visible
than the SDP and Green party actors in all news outlets studied here,

Table 8.4 Party Actors in Political News Stories on Television,*
10 August–27 September 1998 (percentages)

	ARD	ZDF	RTL	SAT.1	Total
Kohl	26	35	46	43	37
CDU/CSU	79	91	95	97	89
FDP	30	39	51	33	37
Government	21	15	14	17	17
Schröder	15	26	43	24	26
SPD	50	71	78	75	67
Green	30	26	47	36	34
SPD+Green	2	5	4	4	3
PDS	12	10	27	11	14
SPD+Green+PDS	4	1	–	1	2
Other parties	10	6	12	11	9
N	154	145	111	114	524

Source: Klaus Schoenbach and Holli A. Semetko, media content analysis of the 1998 German Bundestag campaign.

*Proportion of stories in which the actor was one of the first ten actors in the story.

Note: Columns are not additive because multiple responses were possible.

although the gap between the CDU/CSU and the SPD was less than it had been in 1990. In 1998, the CDU/CSU actors appeared in 89 percent of stories, the FDP in 37 percent, the SPD in 67 percent, the Greens in 34 percent, and the PDS in 14 percent, with some mixture of the three opposition parties in an additional 2 percent. Table 8.4 displays the actors in television news in 1998.[16]

There was considerable variation among media outlets, however, with respect to the presentation of parties and leaders in the news. Two points are especially noteworthy. First, RTL devoted a greater portion of news to the two chancellor candidates and the main parties than any other channel. Second, ARD devoted considerably less attention to the chancellor candidates and political actors from the main parties. In comparison with ARD, which gave the least attention to the candidates and parties in comparison with all the TV news programs, the political actors were even less visible in stories in *Bild*. The figures for the *Bild* are presented in Table 8.5.

These differences in the visibility of the political party actors did not translate into positive or negative news on television. There was little in the way of explicitly positive or negative evaluations of political actors in television news. For every political actor in television news, we coded any evaluation as neutral or straight/descriptive, positive, negative, or a mixture of

Table 8.5 **Actors in Front Page News in the** *Bild*,* **10 August–**
27 September 1998 (percentages)

Kohl	25
CDU/CSU	72
FDP	25
Government	14
Schröder	15
SPD	44
Green	19
SPD+Green	1
PDS	6
SPD+Green+PDS	1
Other parties	7
N	384

Source: Klaus Schoenbach and Holli A. Semetko, media content analysis of the 1998 German Bundestag campaign.

*Proportion of stories in which the actor was one of the first ten actors in the story.

Note: Columns are not additive because multiple responses were possible.

positive and negative. German television news was largely descriptive/ neutral. Taking all television news programs together across all channels, 84 percent of evaluations of political actors were descriptive or neutral, only 12 percent were negative, and 3 percent were positive, with less than one percent mixed. The only news program that varied considerably from this was ARD, which carried more negative news than the other programs. ARD's coverage of political actors included 81 percent of descriptive or neutral evaluations, 17 percent of negative evaluations, and 2 percent of positive evaluations.

Overall, television news in 1998 was more evaluative and less descriptive than it had been in 1990, when 96 percent of evaluations were descriptive, one percent were positive, and 2 percent were negative.[17] Interestingly, there was no real difference between the evaluations of the candidates and parties. The government was not criticized more heavily than the opposition, or visa versa.

Conclusion

The 1998 Bundestag election was the most highly reported federal election campaign in decades. With this emphasis on the campaign, German election news on television appeared to be moving in the direction of the U.K. or the U.S., with the associated hoopla and horse race elements. The 1998 campaign was more exciting in terms of news values, not only because the polls showed that the SPD's chances of winning were greater than in any previous campaign in recent decades, but also because its leader presented a formidable alternative to the incumbent chancellor. The SPD itself was also united throughout its campaign, and had learned a lot strategically from Tony Blair's leadership and the Labour Party's successful bid for power in the British 1997 general election.

There was a clear difference between the public and private channels in the emphasis on the campaign in the news. The private channels devoted far more attention to the campaign and the opinion polls than the public channels, and correspondingly less to the substantive issues over which the campaign was being fought. There was nevertheless still a strong similarity between German public and private television coverage in the predominantly neutral or descriptive coverage of politicians. In comparison with the U.S., where election news about presidential candidates was often negative, German television news was predominantly neutral or descriptive.[18] That said, the amount of negative coverage of German politicians increased over the past decade, but this trend was in fact not more evident on the private channels. In 1998, the highest percentage of negative evaluations of politicians appeared on the public service channel ARD.

Although the chancellor visibility bonus continued to exist in 1998 in terms of the number of stories in which the candidates appeared, it was not as great as in previous campaigns. It also disappeared entirely, and was actually reversed, in terms of the amount of time the candidates were seen speaking in television news.[19]

In conclusion, we observed major changes over the past decade in Germany's broadcast media system, which has become more commercial and more competitive than ever before. This may have had consequences for the reporting of the 1998 election, and we observed more attention to the events and the polls in comparison with the substantive issues on the private channels, whereas on the public channels this was reversed. But the 1998 national election campaign satisfied all possible news value criteria—with an outcome that was predicted to be quite close, a formidable challenger to the incumbent chancellor, and a campaign that followed years of negative news for the incumbent parties. The CDU's visibility bonus in the news was not as great as it had been in the past, and it was not really a bonus considering the negative news that was generated in the campaign. This negative news was not a consequence of television journalists' evaluations, however, it stemmed instead from the statements of political actors who appeared in the news. So journalists left it to the politicians to criticize one another and selected more of such news in

1998 than they had in 1990. But even in 1998, the vast majority of the news contained no explicit positive or negative evaluations, only neutral or descriptive accounts of events and issues. In comparison with the main evening news reporters in the U.S. who are quick to offer positive or negative judgements on the candidates each day, German television reporters largely refrained from explicit evaluations.

Acknowledgments

We would like to thank the Amsterdam School of Communications Research at the University of Amsterdam and the School for Music and Theater in Hanover for providing support for this study. We are grateful for the invaluable assistance of Marina Caspari, Andreas Genz, Melanie Schneider, and Edmund Lauf for their research assistance on the project. A major part of this chapter draws on our article entitled "Parties, Leaders and Issues in the News" published in *German Politics*, vol. 8, no. 2 (1999): 72–87.

Notes

1. Klaus Berg and Marie-Luise Kiefer, *Massenkommunikation V: Eine Langzeitstudie zur Mediennutzung und Medienbewertung 1964–1995* (Baden-Baden: Nomos Verlagsgesellschaft, 1996), 40, 183.
2. Kees Brants and Karen Siune, "Public Broadcasting in a State of Flux," in Karen Suine and Wolfgang Truetzschler, eds., *Dynamics of Medial Politics: Broadcasting and Electronic Media in Western Europe* (Beverly Hills and London: Sage, 1992), 101–15.
3. Jay G. Blumler and T. J. Nossiter, eds., *Broadcasting Finance in Transition* (Oxford: Oxford University Press, 1990).
4. Jay G. Blumler, Malcolm Brynin, and T. J. Nossiter, "Broadcasting Finance in Transition," *European Journal of Communication* 1/3 (1986): 343–64.
5. Barbara Pfetsch, "Convergence through Privatization? Changing Media Environments and Televised Politics in Germany," *European Journal of Communication* 11/4 (1996): 427–51.
6. Holli A. Semetko, "Journalistic Culture in Comparative Perspective: The Concept of 'Balance' in U.S., British and German TV News," *Harvard International Journal of Press/Politics* 1, 1 (1996): 51–71.
7. See Holli A. Semetko and Klaus Schoenbach, *Germany's "Unity Election" Voters and the Media* (Cresskill, NJ: Hampton Press, 1994).
8. Kenneth L. Baker, Helmut Norpoth, and Klaus Schoenbach, "Die Fernsehdebatten der Spitzenpolitiker vor den Bundestagswahlen 1972 und 1976" [The television debates of leading politicians in the Bundestag election campaigns, 1972 and 1976], *Publizistik* 26 (1981): 530–40. See also Klaus Schoenbach, "The Role of Mass Media in West German Election Campaigns," *Legislative Studies Quarterly* 12 (1987): 373–94.
9. Kendall L. Baker and Helmut Norpoth, "Candidates on Television: The 1972 Electoral Debates in West Germany," *Public Opinion Quarterly* 45 (1981): 329–45.

10. Peter R. Schrott, "The West German Television Debates, 1972–1983." Unpublished doctoral thesis, State University of New York, Stony Brook, 1986. Peter R. Schrott, "Electoral Consequences of 'Winning' Televised Campaign Debates," *Public Opinion Quarterly* 54 (1980): 567–85.

11. Holli A. Semetko and Klaus Schoenbach, "The Campaign in the Media," in Russell Dalton, ed., *The New Germany Votes: Unification and the Creation of the New German Party System* (Providence, RI, and Oxford: Berg, 1993), 187–208.

12. Semetko and Schoenbach, *Germany's "Unity Election" Voters*. See Chapter 5. Additional sources on media coverage in recent German elections include: Klaus Schoenbach, "Mass Media and Election Campaigns in Germany," in Frederick J. Fletcher, ed., *Media, Elections and Democracy* (Toronto and Oxford: Dundurn Press, 1992); Klaus Schoenbach and Holli A. Semetko, "Medienberichterstattung und Parteienwerbung im Bundestagswahlkampf 1990," *Media Perspektiven* (1994): 328-40; Barbara Pfetsch and Katrin Voltmer, "Geteilte Medienrealität? Zur Thematisierungsleistung der Massenmedien im Prozess der deutschen Vereinigung," in Hans-Dieter Klingemann and Max Kaase, eds., *Wahlen und Wähler: Analysen aus Anlaß der Bundestagswahl 1990* (Opladen: Westdeutscher Verlag, 1994); Rüdiger Schmitt-Beck and Peter Schrott, "Dealignment durch Massenmedien? Zur These der Abschwächung von Parteibindungen als Folge der Medienexpansion," in Klingemann and Kaase, *Wahlen und Wähler*.

13. Semetko and Schoenbach, *Germany's "Unity Election" Voters*. See Chapter 5.

14. Ibid., 51, Table 4.4. The period under study in 1990 was 1 October to 2 December, in comparison with 1 August to 27 September 1998, approximately eight weeks in each election. See also the findings from the 1998 election content analysis discussed in Melanie Schneider, Klaus Schoenbach, and Holli A. Semetko, "Kanzlerkandidaten in den Fernsehnachrichten und in der Wählermeinung: Befunde zum Bundestagswahlkampf 1998 und früheren Wahlkämpfen," *Media Perspektiven* 5 (1999): 262–69; Marina Caspari, Klaus Schoenbach, and Edmund Lauf, "Bewertung politscher Akteure in Fernsehnachrichten: Analyse der Berichterstattung in Bundestagswahlkämpfen der 90er Jahre," *Media Perspektiven* 5 (1999): 270–74.

15. Ibid., 52, Table 4.5.

16. Ibid., 53, for comparable figures for 1990.

17. Ibid., 53.

18. For trends in U.S. news, see Thomas Patterson, *Out of Order* (New York: Vintage, 1994).

19. To learn more about how German coverage of politics during election campaigns compares with the most recent general election in Britain, see Norris, Pippa, John Curtice, David Sanders, Margaret Scammell, and Holli A. Semetko, *On Message: Communicating the Campaign* (London: Sage, 1999); and Holli A. Semetko, Margaret Scammell, and T. J. Nossiter, "The Media's Coverage of the Campaign," in Anthony Heath, Roger Jowell, and John Curtice, eds., *Labour's Last Chance? The 1992 Election and Beyond* (Aldershot, U.K. and Brookfield, VT: Dartmouth, 1994), 25–42. Effects of the British press on voters is discussed in John Curtice and Holli A. Semetko, "Does It Matter What the Papers Say?" Anthony Heath, Roger Jowell, and John Curtice, eds., *Labour's Last Chance*, 43–64.; also Holli A. Semetko, Jay G. Blumler, Michael Gurevitch, and David H. Weaver, *The Formation of Campaign Agendas: A Comparative Analysis of Party and Media Roles in Recent American and British Elections* (Hillsdale, NJ: Lawrence Erlbaum, 1991). See also Jay G. Blumler, Michael Gurevitch, and T.J . Nossiter, "The Earnest versus the Determined: Election Newsmaking at the BBC, 1987," in Ivor Crewe and Martin Harrop, eds., *Political Communications: The General Election of 1987* (Cambridge: Cambridge University Press, 1989), 157–74.

Chapter 9

REACHING CRITICAL MASS?

German Women and the 1998 Election

Mary N. Hampton

M en are coming under pressure—women are reaching for power"
headlined the popular German tabloid newspaper, the *Bild*, within
a month after the 1998 election.[1] The election was a watershed in German
politics. Not only did the government change hands for the first time in
sixteen years, but the party Alliance '90/The Greens achieved political
maturity as it ascended to partner status in the coalition government led
by Chancellor Gerhard Schröder. Aside from this political power shift, the
status of women as a force in German politics indeed changed as well. The
number of women in parliament increased significantly as a result of the
election, reaching over 30 percent for the first time. In this sense, women
have reached "critical mass" in the political system.[2]

The profile of women in positions of political power should also be expected to rise under the new government. The left-of-center parties have
championed the cause of promoting women longer than the center-right
parties. For example, in 1983, the year the Greens entered parliament, the
proportion of women in the Bundestag was 9.8 percent. By 1987, it was
15.4 percent. The increase was due largely to greater numbers in the Green
faction.[3] As Eva Kolinsky notes, although the Greens won just over 8 percent of the vote that year, they claimed about one-third of female members.[4] While worldwide the overall proportion of women in parliaments
between 1988 and 1995 dropped from about 15 percent to 10 percent, the
proportion of women who were members of the Bundestag increased
from 20.7 percent to 26.6 percent in the October 1994 elections, or 177 of
the 672 members.[5] After the 1998 elections, the number of female members of parliament increased again to 30.9 percent. This figure placed

Germany at the number six position worldwide in the measure of numbers of women in parliaments, behind Finland (5), Netherlands (4), Norway (3), Denmark (2), and Sweden (1). In contrast, the U.S. lags far behind Germany in forty-first place.[6]

In a number of critical issue areas, however, progress for German women remains slow. Popular quips about women voting for the handsome Schröder notwithstanding, the woman's vote was in fact driven by serious political concerns. For example, with unemployment at around 11 percent, about 85 percent of the electorate considered it the foremost problem facing the country.[7] Women suffer the most from shrinking employment opportunities, and those in the eastern states are the worst off. According to a number of statistical measures, women from the eastern states remain the net losers of the ongoing unification process. Less-than-adequate childcare policies also continue to hamper the career progress of women in the East and West. The promise (or threat) of cuts in social programs would also affect women more than men, since women live longer and are more dependent on state benefits in their retirement years. Because of these and other substantive political issues, women in 1998 voted for change in large numbers.

In this chapter, I will discuss the dual track of women's progress in the political system: their march forward through the political institutions alongside their continued marching in place on vital policy issues. In analyzing the dual track phenomenon, I will examine the actual voting behavior of women in the election, and then relate that behavior to gains and losses for women in substantive policy areas.

How Women Voted: The Center-Right Parties

In discussing the statistical outcome of the 1998 election, I will first compare it to previous election results, then discuss women as a group, and finally examine the voting behavior of women in the West and the East. The most significant indicator of women's voting behavior in 1998 was the sharp drop in their support for the center-right parties. Helmut Kohl and the CDU/CSU took their largest hit among women, a slide that has been gaining momentum since the 1990 unity election. The center-right parties had their biggest losses among women in the East. However, they lost in the West as well. The wide gender gap of the 1950s, when West German women voted for the conservative parties in far greater numbers than did men, has been narrowing since the 1970s and is now gone.

In 1990, the CDU/CSU received 44.9 percent of the total female vote; in 1994, that figure shrunk to 42.2 percent.[8] In 1998, the CDU/CSU received only 35 percent of the female vote, exactly the same as among

Figure 9.1 Women's Voting Percentages in German National Elections

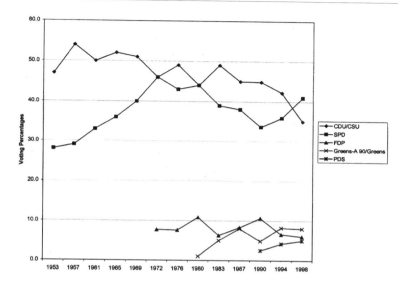

Figure 9.2 Men's Voting Percentages in German National Elections

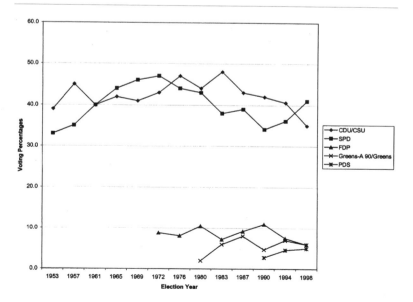

Figure 9.3 Women's Voting Percentages for Coalition Partners

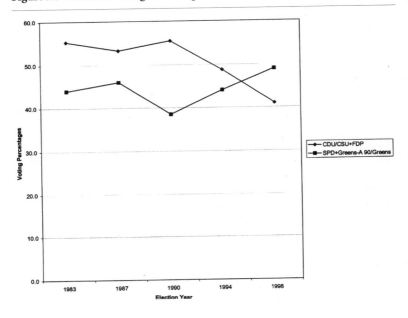

Figure 9.4 Men's Voting Percentages for Coalition Partners

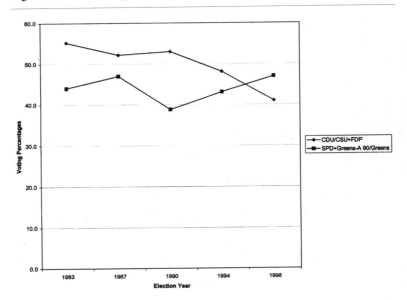

male voters. Figures 9.1 and 9.2 trace the steady decline of support for the CDU/CSU among men and women. The graphs also reveal that the rate of decline in support for the CDU/CSU is greater than the increase of support for the SPD, and that the decline in support is greater and more rapid among women than men.

It is clear that eroding support among women for the CDU/CSU made a real difference in the election's outcome. With a loss in support of approximately 10 percent among women in less than ten years, the outcome is dramatic and in need of further explanation. I will explore the ten-year downward trend later in the chapter and link it to some policy areas that help illuminate the increased dissatisfaction of women with the political status quo underwritten by the long-governing CDU/CSU/FDP. Figures 9.3 and 9.4 show clearly that the coalition parties led by Helmut Kohl lost above all to the new coalition of the SPD and Alliance '90/The Greens. Since the SPD-Greens' political nadir during the unification election of 1990, they have been steadily gaining on the CDU/CSU among women and men, but especially among women.

Losses for the CDU/CSU

The Christian Democrats' decline among females was strongly related to age, with the largest losses found among older age cohorts. Particularly damaging was the CDU/CSU's decline among women in the two oldest age groups: the 45–59 age bracket, and those over 60.[9] Figure 9.5 shows the dramatic impact that the decline in support had in these two groups. Viewed together, the CDU/CSU's support among these women has hemorrhaged since 1990. In the unification election, 47.7 percent of women from the 45- to 59-year-old age group voted for them; in 1994, the numbers fell to around 43 percent. In 1998, only 35 percent of these women voted for them.

Similarly, even though the CDU/CSU continued to be the party of choice for women over 60, the numbers have dwindled since 1990. This cohort was traditionally one of the CDU's bastions of support.[10] In 1990, 53.9 percent of this group voted for the center-right; in 1994, they had lost about a point in percentage. But by 1998, only 44 percent of women over sixty voted for them. Again, the loss here was about 10 percent. In the 35- to 44-year-old age group, the CDU/CSU vote again fell precipitously. In 1990, the two parties received 40.2 percent of the vote; in 1994, the figure fell to 37.6 percent. In 1998, the parties got a meager 29 percent from this age group. Mirroring the older groups, the support level fell by 10 percent in less than a decade.

The CDU/CSU lost the least ground between 1994 and 1998 in the youngest age groups of women, the 18- to 24-year-old and 25- to 34-year-old cohorts. In the 18- to 24-year-old group, the CDU/CSU essentially held even since 1994, at around 31 percent. Among the 25- to 34-year-olds,

Figure 9.5 Voting Percentages for Select Women's Age Groups

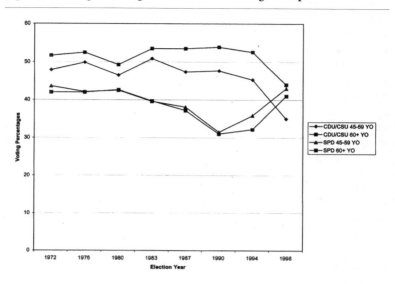

they lost about two points, down to 27 percent from about 29 percent in 1994. It should be noted, however, that these were rather low support levels to begin with.

The CDU/CSU: East and West

As Figure 9.6 shows, the CDU/CSU did worst among women in the eastern states. Overall, the Union lost 13 percent between the 1994 and 1998 elections, compared to a loss of 6 percent among women in the West. The biggest loss came again from the older age groups. From 1994 to 1998 the CDU/CSU lost fully 15 percent of its support among the over-60-year-old cohort. This is the second biggest drop in support for any party in this time frame. Only the 16 percent loss in support from 45- to 59-year-old men in the East tops this number.

Among 45- to 59-year-old women in the East, the CDU/CSU got only 28 percent of the vote, dropping 10 points since 1994. The Union fell even more among the 35- to 44-year-olds, going from 37 percent in 1994 to 24 percent in 1998. Finally, the party received 17 percent of the 18- to 24-year-old and 23 percent of the 25- to 34-year-old vote in 1998, compared to 25 percent and 28 percent in 1994.

Among female voters in the West, the CDU/CSU dropped 6 percent since 1994, receiving 37 percent in 1998. Again, the greatest erosion occurred in the two oldest age groups. Among the 45- to 59-year-olds, the CDU/CSU vote went from around 47 percent in 1994 to 37 percent in

Figure 9.6 Women's Voting Percentages

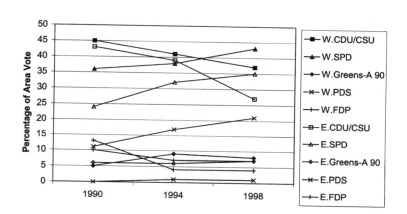

1998. In the over-60 cohort, the Union dropped from 53 percent in 1994 to 45 percent in 1998. Among the 35- to 44-year-old cohort, the party's vote dropped from 38 percent in 1994 to 31 percent in 1998. As was the case with women voters in the East, the Union gave up the least in the two youngest age groups, falling only 1 percent among 25- to 34-year-olds, and actually gaining a percent among 18- to 24-year-olds.

In sum, the CDU/CSU lost a large amount of support among women in 1998, especially in the East. As I will show in a discussion below, these losses can be explained by the inability of the parties to reform their organization, and by their failure to address critical problems that affect women's lives, above all the problem of jobs.

Losses for the FDP

The FDP suffered only marginal losses among women in 1998. In 1990, the party received 10.6 percent of the votes cast by women. By 1994, this figure had dropped to 6.6 percent. It fell again in 1998 to a flat 6 percent. While the party did fall overall, its losses were not as dramatic as those of the CDU/CSU.

Between 1994 and 1998, the party gained votes only among the 25- to 34-year-old cohort. Among these voters, the FDP received 9.6 percent of the vote in 1990, but dropped to 4.9 percent in 1994. A slight gain was made in 1998, when the party received 6 percent of the vote.

In all other groups, support for the party fell among women. The biggest losses occurred among 35- to 44-year-olds. This group gave 12.7

percent of its vote to the FDP in 1990. That support fell to 6.4 percent in 1994, and was down to 5 percent in 1998. Over a period of less than ten years, these figures reflect a substantial decline.

In the 18- to 24-year-old group, the FDP got 10.3 percent of the vote in 1990. In 1994, the numbers dropped to 6.2 percent, and were down to 5 percent in 1998. Among the 45- to 59-year-olds, support for the party dropped over the three election cycles as well. In 1990, the party received 12.3 percent of group's votes, but the level fell to 7.2 percent in 1994, and to 7 percent in 1998. Again, in the group over 60, support for the FDP dropped between 1990 and 1998. In 1990, the party got 8.8 percent of the vote. In 1994, support was at 7.2 percent, and fell to 6 percent in 1998.

The FDP: East and West

Like the CDU/CSU, the FDP in 1998 lost more female support in the East than in the West. Overall, the party lost 2 percent in the East, compared to a 1 percent loss in the West. The greatest decline came in the three oldest age groups. In the 35- to 44-year-old group, the party registered 4 percent support in 1998, down from 6 percent in 1994. Likewise, in the West the FDP dropped 2 percent, going from 8 percent to 6 percent. Among the 45- to 59-year-old cohort, the party lost 2 percent among women in the East, receiving 3 percent in 1998, but held even among women in the West, receiving 8 percent of the vote, or the highest level of any age group. Among women over 60 years old, the party lost 1 percent among women in the East and 1 percent from those in the West. Western women from this group gave the FDP 8 percent of their vote, while those in the eastern states voted for them at 4 percent.

Among the youngest age group, the 18- to 24-year-olds, the party held even at 4 percent in the East from 1994 to 1998. In the West, this age cohort gave the party 6 percent of the vote, down only a point since 1994. The FDP did the best among the 25- to 34-year-olds; it stayed even in the East at 5 percent, and actually increased its support a point in the West, going from 5 percent to 6 percent.

How Women Voted: The Left and Center-Left Parties

As Figures 9.3 and 9.4 show, the left-of-center coalition parties benefited the most from female voter dissatisfaction in 1998. When placed together, the SPD and the Alliance '90/The Greens have gained steadily among women voters since 1990, going from only 38.5 percent in 1990 to 49 percent in 1998. The left-of-center's gain among women was marginally greater than that among men.

Gains for the SPD

As shown in Figures 9.1, 9.3, and 9.5, the main beneficiary of the shift in female votes in 1998 was the SPD. The party went from 33.6 percent of the female vote in 1994, to 41 percent in 1998. While the percentage gains for the SPD among age groups are not as dramatic as the losses for the CDU/CSU, they are nonetheless significant. Mirroring the losses of the center-right, the SPD's largest gains came from the oldest age cohorts, especially in the 45–59 age group. Again, the least amount of change occurred in the two youngest groups, where support for the SPD was already substantially higher than for the CDU/CSU or FDP.

The most dramatic change was among the 45- to 59-year-old group, where the SPD gained about 12 percent between 1990 and 1998. As Figure 9.5 indicates, this shift came largely at the expense of the CDU/CSU. The increased support for the SPD between 1994 and 1998 was also substantial among the over-60 age group where support rose from 32 percent in 1994 to 41 percent in 1998.

Among females in the 35–44 age group, the SPD received 41 percent of the vote in 1998; a large gain from 34.7 percent in 1990 and 35.9 percent in 1994. Finally, in the two youngest age cohorts, the 18- to 24-year-olds and 25- to 34-year-olds, women supported the SPD more than in the last two national elections, but not by much. Essentially, the 18- to 24-year-olds increased their support over the nine years by about 1 percent, going from 36.2 percent in 1990 to 36.5 percent in 1994, and to 37 percent in 1998. SPD voters among the 25- to 44-year-old cohort increased from 39 percent in 1990 to about 42 percent in both the 1994 and 1998 elections.

The SPD: East and West

The SPD registered its biggest gains in east and west among the three oldest age groups. Its largest increase came from women in the East over 60 years old: the party went from 30 percent in 1994 to 39 percent in 1998. The party gained less from other age groups in the East, actually losing votes among the 25- to 34-year-old women. Here, the party went from 34 percent in 1994 down to 32 percent in 1998. Among the 18- to 25-year-olds, the SPD held even at 31 percent. These are particularly interesting figures when compared to the youngest male cohort. In this group, the SPD gained more than any other party (who all actually lost votes from this group since 1994), a full 9 percent since 1994, going to the same 31 percent registered by their female counterparts.

Among the 45- to 59-year-olds, the party went from 32 percent in 1994 to 35 percent in 1998. The 35- to 44-year-old women increased their level of support by 2 percent, going from 30 percent in 1994 to 32 percent in 1998.

Among women in the West, the party gained the most in the 45- to over-60-year-old age groups, gaining 8 percent from both since 1994:

from 37 percent to 45 percent among the 45- to 59-year-olds, and from 33 percent to 41 percent among the over-60-year-olds. The party held even in both of the youngest age groups, remaining at 38 percent among the 18- to 24-year-olds and at 45 percent among the 25- to 34-year-olds. In the 35- to 44-year-old cohort, the party gained 7 percent between 1994 and 1998, going from 38 percent to 45 percent.

Mixed Results for Alliance '90/The Greens

The SPD in 1998 did much better in adding to their female vote than did the Greens. Despite the fact that the Greens pursued much more ambitious party and programmatic reforms than the other parties in promoting women to positions of power, the party in fact lost female voters between 1994 and 1998. While the Greens gained women's support after their poor showing in 1990, when they received only 4.9 percent of the women's vote, their support has dropped since 1994. In that year, the Alliance '90/The Greens got 8.2 percent of the female vote but received only 8 percent in 1998.

The Alliance '90/The Greens increased their number of women voters in 1998 in only the 45- to 59-year-old age group. In that cohort, the party went from only 2.7 percent support in 1990 to 5 percent in 1994, and to 6 percent in 1998. The gain was not very significant, but it represents the only increase for the party.

In all other age groups, the party's support level among women decreased slightly. The biggest loss was in the 18- to 24-year-old cohort. In 1990, this group gave 11.4 percent to the Greens. That level rose to 15.8 percent in 1994, but fell back to 12 percent in 1998. The second-largest hit came in the 25- to 34-year-old group. Here the party went from 14.2 percent in 1994 to 12 percent in 1998.

In the 35- to 44-year-old group, the party held constant between 1994 and 1998 at 12 percent. The party almost doubled its support from 1990 to 1994, going from 6.3 percent to 12 percent. Among the over-60-year-olds, the party more than doubled its support between 1990 and 1994. In 1990, it had just 0.9 percent support from this group, while in 1998 this rose to 3 percent.

Alliance '90/The Greens: East and West

The regional results for the Greens among women voters reveal some diversity. The party gained most in the East, where it lost no votes among women. It actually gained in all but one category—the over-60-year-olds, where it held even at 2 percent. In all others, it increased its support since 1994. In the 18- to 25-year-old cohort, the party went from 10 percent to 11 percent. Among the 25- to 34-year-olds, it climbed 2 percent, from 8 percent to 10 percent. Its biggest increase came in the 35- to 44-year-old cohort, where it gained 3 percent, going from 4 percent in 1994 to 7 percent in 1998.

The Greens did not fare as well among western women, where it lost votes in two age groups, held even in two, and gained in only one, the 45- to 59-year-old group. In this group, the party went from 5 percent in 1994 to 6 percent in 1998. The party actually lost 4 percent among the 18- to 25-year-olds, going from 16 percent in 1994 to 12 percent in 1998. It lost 2 percent among the 25- to 34-year-olds, down to 13 percent in 1998 from 15 percent in 1994. The party held even in the 35- to 44-year-old cohort, at 14 percent, and in the over-60 group, at 3 percent.

Gains for the PDS

In 1998, the PDS finally "arrived" politically among women voters at the national level. In 1990 and 1994, despite the fact that this predominantly eastern protest party received well over the 5 percent threshold among women in the eastern states, it did not get more than 5 percent from all German women. In 1990, this party received only 2.5 percent of the vote from women nationally, but 10.9 percent from women in the East. Again in 1994, it took in 4.2 percent of the national female vote, while getting 17 percent in the East. However, in 1998, the party actually got 5 percent of the total female vote, exactly the same as for men. Moreover, its level of support rose among all female age groups.

The greatest gain for the PDS came from the 35- to 44-year-olds. In 1990, the party received a meager 2.7 percent from this cohort. That number increased to 5.1 percent in 1994, and rose to 7 percent in 1998. While the numbers may still be small, the level of support has more than doubled since the party's appearance on the national scene. The party's support among women rose slightly in the other age categories.

However small the gains by the PDS may be, the reasons are significant. The increased votes among women reveal rising frustration among many females with the mainstream parties. But compared to their male counterparts, very dissatisfied women were less likely to turn to the extreme right.[11]

The PDS: East and West

As in the elections of 1990 and 1994, the PDS continues to do much better with women in the East than in the West. In the East, the party got 21 percent of the vote, up from 17 percent in 1994; it got a miniscule 1 percent of the votes from women in the West, the same as in 1994. The statistic for women in the East is especially important in that their support level for the party was higher than among their male counterparts, who gave the PDS 19 percent of their votes. Eastern women are clearly more likely to support the PDS than their sisters in the West. In 1998 this

East-West difference in the PDS vote actually grew larger. Female voters in the East are apparently responding to PDS appeals that focus on their specific issue concerns such as unemployment and discrimination. Compared to those in the West, women in the East were as likely to turn from the CDU/CSU and to the PDS or the Greens in 1998 as to the SPD. The SPD gained 3 percent among eastern women since 1994; the PDS gained 4 percent.

The PDS lost votes among women in only one age category, held even in two, and gained in the rest. As with the left-of-center parties, the PDS made the most significant inroads with the oldest age groups. Its largest increase came from women over 60 years old in the East: the party gained 6 percent, going from 10 percent in 1994 to 16 percent in 1998. Among the 45- to 59-year-olds, it went from 18 percent in 1994 to 22 percent in 1998. The party increased its support among the 35- to 44-year-old women in the East by 3 percent, going from 21 percent in 1994 to 24 percent in 1998. The party fared the worst among the two youngest groups in the East. It lost 3 percent among the 25- to 34-year-olds, going from 24 percent in 1994 to 21 percent in 1998. The party held at 23 percent among the 18- to 24-year-olds. In the West, the party's support essentially remained constant among all age groups.

In sum, the PDS is a force to be reckoned with among women voters in the East. It has clearly taken support away from the CDU/CSU in this region.

The Parties and Structural Reforms

One way to gain female party members and attract women voters is to reform party organizations. Party membership statistics from 1996 are revealing of the parties' success, or lack thereof, in attracting women. The PDS had the highest female membership percentage at 42.6 percent (1994), followed by the Greens (37 percent), the SPD (28.4 percent), the FDP (25.3 percent), the CDU (24.9 percent), and the CSU (16.4 percent).[12] Not surprisingly, the left-of-center and leftist parties have proportionately the most women members: they have pursued the most aggressive policies concerning the full integration of women into their ranks and throughout the workforce. To date, the Greens, the PDS, and the SPD have formally adopted quota rules for party positions. The CDU has a "quorum" rule. Among the parties, the CDU/CSU and the FDP continue to lag behind in terms of implementing reforms that would enhance the role of women. The free fall of the CDU/CSU among women voters in 1998 reflects in part this relative neglect. However, some caution is in order since the Greens did not gain women voters in 1998, despite the fact that they have been the party that has spearheaded the progress of women since the 1980s, and that the FDP did not lose as much as the CDU/CSU, despite this party's lack of innovation in structural reform. In short, party policies regarding the promotion of women may have an effect on how women vote, but it is one issue among many others.

Alliance '90/The Greens and Reform: Leading the Way
The arrival of the Greens in national politics at the 1983 election guaranteed that women's concerns would be placed prominently on the national political agenda. From the beginning, the Greens promoted equality for women systematically and across the board. Whereas the SPD earlier represented the voice of women's progress, the Greens would now compete for that mantle under the rubric of feminism and environmentalism. From the mid-1980s onward, the Greens drove women's issues into the foreground of West German concerns. The Greens went far beyond any pro-women policies pursued by the SPD. They called for the "redistribution of work" in German society, addressing the gendered nature of work and homemaking that existed, or the dichotomized division of the public and private spheres. This was an issue that the SPD never quite mastered. As Andrei Markovits and Philip Gorsky observed, the Greens' objective "was no less than the end of patriarchy."[14]

The scope of reforms sought by the Greens was dramatic. Their 1985 anti-discrimination bill advocated revising West German law on issues like rape, and extended reform to a number of other areas of discriminatory practices. The most politically potent aspect of the bill was the call for quotas to be introduced throughout West Germany in order to correct the historical discrimination against female recruitment and hiring practices. The "quota law" goal of filling 50 percent of all posts with women applied to government and private sectors, to educational practices, and to the parties themselves.[15] To follow through on its convictions, in 1986 the party adopted the 50 percent quota policy rule that required half of all party organization and candidate positions to be filled by women.[16]

By the 1987 Bundestag election, all parties followed the Greens' lead in declaring themselves serious about improving women's representation in the Bundestag and in their respective party organizations.[17] The SPD was particularly compelled to follow suit since it was losing women voters to the Greens.[18]

The reforms of the Greens have given women a higher profile in the party. Their delegation in the Bundestag now stands at 27 women and 20 men. The quota rule also gave the party a female and a male spokesperson. However, both the Greens and the SPD came under criticism from their female members just after the 1998 election, when it was argued that promises concerning the allocation of government "power posts" to women were not materializing.[19] The Greens were supposed to divide government posts in such a way that half of these "power positions" went to women. Of the three ministries that the party received after the coalition was formed, only one went to a woman: Andrea Fischer, the new Minister of Health. Both the Foreign Ministry and the Environment Ministry went to men.

Despite the reform efforts of the Alliance '90/The Greens to give women more power and enhance their interests, the party did not gain female voters in the 1998 election. In particular, the Greens failed to attract younger female voters in the West; in fact, since 1994 they have lost 6 percent among 18- to 34-year-olds. The losses for the party among young people, male and female, were repeated again in the Hesse state elections in February 1999. Despite the party's pioneering efforts at integrating women into the party structure and society, the Greens are now seen increasingly as the "old guard" by younger people, and as irrelevant to many of the problems they face.[20]

Catching Up: The SPD and Reform

The SPD has in fact actively sought to win back its former mantle as the party representing women's progress. Following the lead of the Greens, the SPD decided in 1988 to increase the proportion of women who stood as party candidates by establishing a quota of 33 percent. The SPD increased their quota to 40 percent for party office posts in 1992. And in 1998, the party's quota for women candidates also went up to 40 percent.[21] To a large extent, the party has been successful. Today, more than a third of SPD members in the Bundestag are female.[22] Support among women clearly helped the SPD governmental power. Citing this success, SPD women in 1998 demanded that 40 percent of all "power posts" be given to them. The SPD is aware of its debt to women voters, and as one author states: "Jobs for women in the new government are a signal to women voters that their credit won't be gambled away."[23] Like the Alliance '90/The Greens, the SPD was moved by women's demands regarding the allocation of government posts, although women still do not occupy many SPD "power posts." Of the federal ministries controlled by the SPD, four of them now have women at the helm, and of those, only the appointments of Herta Däubler-Gmelin at the Justice Ministry and Heidemarie Wieczorek-Zeul at the Ministry for Economic Cooperation and Development might be considered non-traditional female posts. Further, SPD women demanded that the posts of parliamentary president and federal president should not both go to men.[24] This has not yet occurred, but the SPD's Präsidium is now about 40 percent female.

Gaining Ground: The PDS and Reform

The PDS today has proportionately the largest number of female members of parliament, 60 percent. The party also has proportionately the largest female membership. Part of the PDS's success with women comes from the party's role as the successor party to the former East German ruling communist party, the Socialist Unity Party of Germany (SED). This unique aspect of the PDS helps explain why some women join the party and why others vote for it. However, the PDS's success goes well beyond that factor. The party's platform since 1993 has appealed directly to women, especially eastern women, as the champion of their interests. In 1998, the party used the phrase "left and a woman" in their campaign.[25]

Like the Greens, the PDS promotes complete equality for women, including a quota system which requires that 50 percent of positions in the party be filled by women. Further, the party speaks directly to the economic, social and psychological dislocations felt by women in the East because of unification. The party has managed to position itself as a champion of reform in removing discrimination against women in employment, tax laws, pensions and retirement, and domestic violence.

Behind the Reform Curve: The CDU/CSU/FDP

The CDU has responded haltingly over the years to the political pressure for a more prominent role for women. In 1985, just a short time after the Greens appeared in parliament, the CDU's party congress finally focused on women's concerns. In an attempt to regain flagging female support, especially among young women, the CDU concluded that singing the "praise of the family, of home, hearth and children, without recognizing that the modern woman also wanted to work and be socially and financially independent" was counter-productive.[26]

After losing female votes to other parties in 1994, and with the continued lack of success in recruiting women members, Kohl tried to reform the CDU. In a bold move, he recommended after the 1994 elections that the CDU adopt a quota system, to be called "quorums," wherein women would receive 30 percent of all party posts and 30 percent of all candidacies. Despite prior hostility to the left's support of quotas, the CDU's executive committee approved such a resolution in September 1995.[27] However, in October 1995 at the party's Karlsruhe Conference, just days after the European Court of Justice banned quotas as justification for promoting female civil servants, the CDU rank and file, much to Kohl's chagrin, narrowly rejected the measure.[28] They adopted instead a somewhat weaker alternative.[29] Finally, at the party's annual meeting in 1996, the 30 percent "quorum" rule was approved.[30] The relatively late reform efforts of the CDU are reflected by the numbers of female CDU members in parliament: only 17 percent of the CDU delegation are female. In the CDU's last government, only two of seventeen ministry posts had been filled by women, and Kohl had dubbed Claudia Nolte, his Minister for Women's Affairs, "the little girl."[31]

For the CDU, 1998 marked a low point in their support among women. The former CDU parliamentary President, Rita Süssmuth, saw a clear relationship between the CDU's electoral defeat and their slow response to party reform in gender politics. She stated: "Those who do not move will be moved aside."[32] Noteworthy is the fact that though the party lost votes in every age group, it lost the most among women of working and retirement age in the West, who voted in larger numbers than before for the SPD, and in the East where votes went to the PDS and the SPD. Both CDU recruitment patterns and the slow pace of the innovation in policies most affecting women, such as unemployment, pensions, and childcare, contributed to the party's diminished appeal to women.

Women's Work and the 1998 Election

The current German political system still remains controlled by western Germans. This has significant repercussions for the lives of women and their relationship to work. East and West Germany had very different cultural attitudes toward working women. The West German system largely retained its traditional emphasis on the role of the woman as homemaker and mother, while in East Germany, state policy "promoted the equal importance of family and employment roles for women," reflected through the government's *Muttipolitik*, or "mommy politics."[33] Until 1977, for example, under West German law a woman could be employed only as long as her employment was "compatible with her duties within the marriage and the family."[34] East German women were given a clear message that it was their "duty" to work outside the home. Not surprisingly, women in East Germany contributed about 40 percent to the family's income, as compared to only 18 percent in West Germany.[35]

West Germany experienced its own version of *Muttipolitik* in the 1980s, as politicized West German women began debating women's representation. The Green Party was a catalyst for such debates. While obviously not reflecting the state-driven policy of the GDR's *Muttipolitik*, it became clear in the West German context that women's issues remained electorally contestable, and that there existed no consensus about the proper political approach to issues like motherhood and gender relations.[36] Yet many women, even feminists, continued to define women primarily as mothers, and to emphasize the traditional gender roles while seeking policies to address the special needs of mothers, thereby reinforcing the structural policies dividing woman and men in the workplace.[37]

Women in West Germany continued to leave the workplace for childbirth and rearing in far greater numbers than did East German women.[38] The "three-phase model" still largely held in the West, where women might work before marrying and having children, but would leave the workplace until their children reached school age and then return to work part-time.[39] Therefore, in West Germany it was frowned upon for women with small children to work full-time, while in East Germany it was expected and became part of the life experience for women.

These differing models regarding working women continued well after unification. Polls taken in 1992 still reflected divergences between women in the East and West regarding work and family. For example, one report in 1992 showed that around 25 percent of women in the West considered being a homemaker their "dream job," as compared to only 3 percent of women in the East. Also, almost 70 percent of western women preferred to work part-time, as compared to 45 percent of women in the East.[40] These competing perceptions continued to be found in polls taken in 1997. In one study, half of the women in the West, but only one quarter of those in the East, responded positively to the statement that it was better "if the man was fully involved with the career and the wife stayed home and attended to the house and children."[41]

This East-West cultural split was reflected by the expectation of westerners that after unification, large numbers of women in the East would choose to leave the marketplace and become homemakers. In commenting on the expected decline of working women in the East, the Federal Minister for Women stated in 1991 that such a trend was "natural, because the opportunity to be a housewife did not really exist in the GDR."[42] In fact, women in the East continue to seek work in the face of postunification employment obstacles, and this phenomenon has been accompanied by a decrease in marriage and childbearing.

Women and Employment Policy

These West German conceptions of the female role still affect the united country in important ways. First, employment policies have a distinct impact on women. At the 1998 election, concern about unemployment was the top issue. While the overall number of women entering the work force has increased over the last twenty years, the percentage of women working in 1995 was 60.4 percent, as compared to 78 percent for men.[43] In 1996, women comprised just over 40 percent of the work force.[44] However, these figures belie the reality of working women. First, women earn about 30 percent less than men for similar work. Second, the eastern regions have a higher level of part-time workers than the western states, and most of these part-timers are women. Women now comprise about 88 percent of all part-time workers, a higher percentage than that found in most other western countries. In the U.S., for example, about 70 percent of part-time workers are female; the corresponding figure for France is 79 percent.

Women are also more negatively affected by the country's high unemployment level than are men. In 1995, for example, unemployment among men was at 7 percent, as compared to about 8 percent for women.[45] The current unemployment rate is now around 11 percent, and the number of unemployed women has increased proportionately. Women also suffer more than men in terms of long-term unemployment. Again, using figures from 1995, 51 percent of women were unemployed long term, as compared to 46 percent for men.[46]

These circumstances are even more pronounced for women living in the East. Whereas nine out of ten East German women worked full time, fully 40 percent of West German women did not work, and about one quarter of working women had part-time jobs. Today, with the restructuring problems brought on by the unification process, women in the eastern states have lost their jobs at much higher rate than men in those states. While the percentage of working women is still higher in the East (65 percent) than in the West (45 percent), unemployment among women in the East has remained at around 20 percent, twice the rate of women and men in the West, and about 5 percent higher than among men in the East.[47] To put the matter in more dramatic terms, 1995 figures showed that 64 percent of all unemployed people in the eastern states, and 77 percent of the long-term unemployed, were women.[48] Compounding the problem is the greater likelihood since unification that women in the East would take early retirement. The voting behavior of women in the retirement years testifies to the high costs they bore. Finally, these statistics must be considered in the specific cultural context of the East, where work is generally more valued by women than in the West; the psychological costs of unemployment are therefore greater.[49]

Childcare Policies

Beyond the analysis of raw employment figures, it is also important to examine policies related to women and their employment opportunities. Important in the German case are state policies concerning childcare. Compared to countries like Denmark, France, and Belgium, Germany has very limited public care programs for children less than three years of age. Denmark, which accommodates 48 out of 100 children in this age group, far surpasses Germany, which serves only 3 out of 100. Opportunities for German children over three years of age then jump to 78 percent, but Germany still lags behind Denmark (85 percent), Italy (92 percent), Belgium (95 percent), and France (100 percent).[50] German women are further hindered in work potential by official school hours (the school day usually ends at 1:00 p.m.), and by restrictive shopping hours.

Obviously, the lack of childcare accommodation negatively affects the ability of women with young children to work full-time. Again, women in the eastern states have been particularly affected, since their experience of near full employment under the GDR was accompanied by the policy of *Muttipolitik*, where full childcare services were available. As one author puts it: "Early on in the transition, it was clear that the West German government considered the state services that benefited GDR women—most visibly childcare—too expensive to continue in united Germany."[51]

In short, since unification women in the East have lost much of their independence. Diminished employment possibilities and childcare programs have, not surprisingly, reduced childbearing. Childbirth rates for women in the eastern states have dropped since 1989 from about 1.6 children per female to 0.8.[52] Women in the East also are marrying at reduced rates compared to 1989.[53] As one East German male put it:

> Herr G. makes a distinction between the sexes. His son-in-law will have a bright future; his daughter, on the other hand, has just had a baby. If she had known how detrimental that would be for her job security and her chances in the labor market, she might not have had a baby at all.[54]

The Parties and Their Responses to Women's Work

Recently, the political parties—especially the SPD, Greens, and PDS—have been competing with one another to try to reform the German workplace model and promote women's employment prospects. But even the CDU/CSU and the FDP are now pushing for more flexibility in Germany's workplace so that women and men will begin to share more of the family and childrearing experiences. How successful the concern for women's employment will be as the economic pie continues to contract is open to question, but certainly it was pressure from the left-of-center and leftist parties that at least put these issues on the agenda, and arguably affected the way women voted in 1998.[55]

Too Little, Too Late? The CDU/CSU-FDP

Leading up to the 1998 election, the ruling CDU/CSU-FDP coalition was perceived as increasingly rudderless on many critical domestic reform issues. The *Reformstau* (reform backlog) that became so central to the domestic political debate was associated with Kohl's government and was seen as blocking progress in many policy areas, including many that directly affected women's lives: employment, tax reform, pension reform, and childcare reform.[56] Thus the ruling parties were not only perceived as representing the most traditional approaches to women and work issues, but they were also seen as hindering progress in many of the issue areas that needed reform.

The CDU/CSU-FDP government did, however, make some progress in pushing workplace-related reforms. In Article 31 of the Unification Treaty, for example, the obligation to further the cause of equality between men and women through legislation was articulated. Helmut Kohl declared in his 1991 government policy statement: "Women rightly demand their equal place in society—in the marketplace as well as in public life. With an equality bill, we will be able to better spell out the conditions."[57] After this, various laws and reforms were undertaken by the Kohl government to meet equality objectives. The pension law was changed to count three years of childrearing in pension payments. Pensions for farmers' wives were increased. In 1992, a pension law change allowed time spent as home care providers to be considered as part of the pension entitlement calculations. These and other reforms aside, however, the policies were not very bold, and the CDU/CSU-FDP became identified with *Reformstau*.

Promises to Keep: The SPD

Over several decades, the SPD has called for greater efforts to forge gender equality, both in the workplace and in the family. In its 1998 election program the party called for dramatic changes that would benefit women, such as the promotion of equal pay for equal work among men and women, and the advocacy of more equitable employment opportunities for women. The SPD's commitment to improving the lives of women was further elaborated in the SPD-Green coalition agreement. The determination to integrate and promote women throughout business and government sectors was emphasized, and represented a departure from the preceding government's policy.[58]

Since unemployment in Germany continues to affect women more negatively than men, it is not surprising that the party made some of its greatest gains in the election among working-age women, especially those in the 35–59 age group. Also, during the 1998 campaign, the working group of SPD women (ASF) offered "twenty good reasons for women to vote SPD."[59] Among the reasons was the SPD's determination to help women of all ages achieve more financial independence, and to help especially those of retirement age lead a more independent and secure existence through increased benefits. The election results showed an increase of support for the SPD among this age group as well.

The SPD promised to initiate a new "Women and Career" action program that would advance the attainment of equality for women. A short list of promised reforms that would help the condition of women included: assisting young women to achieve—in quotas where necessary—fairer admittance to education, including technical schools; helping all women achieve better access to, and pay in, the marketplace; reforming pension entitlement policies so that older women have more financial independence; improving the provisions for childcare; reforming tax laws that harm women; and passing stronger laws protecting women against violence. Obviously, the SPD has much on the table in the way of reform. Campaigning on promises to women and delivering the policies are different things. Given the pivotal role women played in the election, there will be tremendous pressure to deliver.

An Image Problem: Alliance '90/The Greens

At first glance, the weak showing of the Greens among women does not make much sense. The party spearheaded many of the equality policies now adopted by the SPD and PDS. The Greens were the first to call for the 50 percent quota rule to be applied throughout German society, in order to further women's ability to find work on a par with men. The party also demanded equal pay for equal work. The party has also been out front in advocating tax reform that would help both married and unmarried women; in short, they have sought the reform of tax laws in order to help women achieve greater financial independence. The party has also promoted government policies that would help sustain women in their retirement years.

Yet, given all these progressive stands, the Greens have faltered at the polls among women voters, and especially among younger voters. One explanation is that the party is increasingly perceived as part of the old guard, representing issues that have either been absorbed by the political center, like environmental concerns, or issues that are viewed as ever more irrelevant to the lives of today's "more careerist" young people, like nuclear energy and disarmament.[59] One might also speculate that by making policy proposals during the 1998 campaign, such as hiking gasoline prices $5 to $10 a gallon or restricting overseas vacations to once every five years, the Greens were seen as out of touch with the real problems facing the public, such as the severe unemployment situation.

Finally, a possible explanation for the weak showing of the Greens among women may well be that they have over time come to represent what is called "postmaterialism," where political issues of the postindustrial society come to the fore: environmentalism, feminism, and other "isms" that focus on a fundamental concern for quality of life and social issues. Postmaterialist politics work best during periods of prosperity in postindustrial societies. However, despite the glossy Americanized media campaign, the 1998 German election was, in a sense, a return to the politics of basics, or a return to the concerns of materialism: job security, retirement security, and other fundamental security issues were foremost on voters' minds. The top six problems listed by voters before the national election—unemployment, law and crime issues, pensions and retirement security, foreign residents, tax issues, and the economic situation—were the type of bread-and-butter issues that generally are not identified with the Greens.[60] Although the party presented many specific progressive policies that addressed most of these issues, their image as the party of the "1968 generation" likely led many female voters to other parties who also presented solutions: the SPD in the West, and the PDS and SPD in the East.[61]

"Left and a Woman": The PDS

The PDS clearly promoted policies aimed at dissatisfied women, especially in the East. In their 1998 campaign program, the party pushed for "real equality between men and women." The PDS supported a general quota law for the promotion of women to 50 percent of positions throughout German society. Like the SPD and the Greens, the PDS called for equal pay for equal work. The party also advocated the reform of tax laws that are seen as particularly harmful to women, such as separate taxation for husbands and wives. Similarly, the PDS called for the reform of pension policies in order to give women more security and independence, particularly in their old age. The PDS also promised to change childcare policies that keep women from fair access to the marketplace. Finally, like the other two parties, the PDS advocated tougher laws regarding violence against women.

The PDS declared in its program that it would not stand for policies that "force women out of the market place, or for the social and political discrimination against them." These words were clearly aimed at women in the East. The party's pledge to work toward "the economic independence of women from men" clearly spoke directly to women in the East, who did indeed lose much of their independence after unification.[62]

Like their counterparts in the West, young eastern German women in 1998 bucked the trend of their elders. These voters did not turn to the PDS in increased numbers. The only party that had gained votes since 1994 among the two youngest female east German age groups was the Alliance '90/The Greens. The PDS may be having the same problems in the East that the Alliance '90/The Greens have among young women in the West: it is an outmoded old guard.

Conclusions

Women have reached a critical mass as participants in German political institutions. This progress has enhanced their power to voice women's concerns and demand accommodation at the political center. However, women still have a long way to go in terms of benefiting equally from state policies and workplace politics. In order to achieve these kinds of objectives, much more is needed than multiplying their numbers in the parliament and state governments. Changes in the political culture must accompany changes in state benefits and entitlement policy if the objectives presented in 1998 by the left-of-center and leftist parties are to be realized. Finally, while the new coalition government has promised much to women, it is difficult to understand how the bold changes, many of which would place increased burdens on social spending policy, can be implemented in the current period of budget contraction and looming fiscal crisis.

Notes

1. Leon Mangasarian, "Frauen Power in Germany—Women Demand Top Political Posts," *Deutsche Presse-Agentur*, 7 October 1998.

2. The term "critical mass" regarding women in politics was used by Jane S. Jaquette in "Women in Power: From Tokenism to Critical Mass," *Foreign Policy* 108 (Fall 1997): 23–37. I thank Christian Søe for leading me to the reference, and for all of his kind assistance. I also thank Helga Welsh and Michael Huelshoff. For their much needed help with the graphs, I thank Eric Bulloch and Joe Roberts.

3. Christiane Lemke, "Old Troubles and New Uncertainties: Women and Politics in United Germany," in Michael G. Huelshoff et al., eds., *From Bundesrepublik to Deutschland: German Politics After Unification* (Ann Arbor: The University of Michigan Press, 1993), 147–66.

4. Eva Kolinsky, "The West German Greens: A Women's Party?" in *Parliamentary Affairs* 41, no. 1 (January 1988): 129–39; esp. 133.

5. The statistics come from a UN report cited in *The Week in Germany*, 28 October 1994, 2, and from "Women Were Big Winners in German Elections-More Female Deputies," *Deutsche Presse-Agentur*, 17 October 1994, LEXUS.

6. Forschungsgruppe Wahlen, *Bundestagswahl 1998: Eine Analyse der Wahl vom 27. September 1998.* Nr. 91 (Mannheim: Forschungsgruppe Wahlen, 1998): 64.

7. Mary N. Hampton, "Women and the 1994 German Elections: Dissatisfaction and Accommodation," in David P. Conradt, Gerald R. Kleinfeld, George K. Romoser, and Christian Søe, eds., *Germany's New Politics* (Providence and London: Berghahn Books, 1995), 69–89; 70.

8. The breakdown in age groups and region for women voters comes predominantly from three sources: Hampton, "Women and the 1994 German Elections," and from Forschungsgruppe Wahlen, *Bundestagswahl 1994: Eine Analyse der Wahl zum 13. Deutschen Bundestag* (Mannheim: Forschungsgruppe Wahlen, 1994), Forschungsgruppe Wahlen, *Wahlergebnisse in Deutschland 1946–1998* (Mannheim, December 1998), and Forschungsgruppe Wahlen, *Bundestagswahl 1998: Eine Analyse der Wahl.*

9. Forschungsgruppe Wahlen, *Bundestagswahl 1998*, 77.

10. See discussion in Forschungsgruppe Wahlen, *Bundestagswahl 1998*, 18

11. Beate Hoecker, "Zwischen Macht und Ohnmacht: Politische Partizipation von Frauen in Deutschland," in Beate Hoecker, ed., *Handbuch Politische Partizipation von Frauen in Europa* (Opladen: Leske and Budrich, 1998), 65–90; chart on 67.

12. See discussion of the Greens in Andrei Markovits and Philip S. Gorski, *The German Left: Red, Green and Beyond* (Cambridge: Polity Press, 1993), quotation on 165.

13. Markovits and Gorski, *The German Left: Red, Green and Beyond*, 165.

14. Ibid., 165–66, 178–79.

15. Ibid.

16. Kolinsky, "The West German Greens," 130.

17. Ibid., 129. See also Myra Marx Ferree, "Making Equality: The Women's Affairs Offices in the Federal Republic of Germany," in Dorothy McBride Stetson and Amy G. Mazur, eds., *Comparative State Feminism* (New York: Sage, 1995), 95–113, esp. 101.

18. Tina Hoffhaus, "Wahlsysteme und Frauenrepräsentation," *Aus Politik und Zeitgeschichte* 45/93 (5 November 1993), 29.

19. Christiane Schlötzer-Scotland, "Subtiles Spiel mit der Frauenquote," *Süddeutsche Zeitung*, 7 October 1998; see also Mangasarian, "Frauen Power in Germany."

20. See Gunda Röstel, "Für einen politischen Neubeginn von Bündnis '90/Die Grünen," speech delivered on 20 February 1999 in Bonn.

21. Hoecker, "Zwischen Macht und Ohnmacht," 82–85.

22. Christiane Schlötzer-Scotland, "Subtiles Spiel mit der Frauenquote," *Süddeutsche Zeitung*, 7 October 1998.
23. Schlötzer-Scotland, "Subtiles Spiel mit der Frauenquote," my translation; see also Mangasarian, "Frauen Power in Germany."
24. Mangasarian, "Frauen Power in Germany."
25. Schlötzer-Scotland, "Subtiles Spiel mit der Frauenquote."
26. Kolinsky, "The West German Greens," 146.
27. See Marjorie Miller, "Kohl's Party Sets Quota for Women," in the *Los Angeles Times*, 29 November 1994. See also "CDU Leadership Proposes Quota for Women in Party Positions," in *The Week in Germany,* 15 September 1994, 2. To avoid copying the left's approach, the CDU called the quota a quorum and determined that another third of the party's faction must be men.
28. *New York Times*, 18 October 1995, A3. See also Martin S. Lambeck, "Herbe Niederlage für die CDU-Parteireformer," *Die Welt*, 19 October 1995, 1.
29. Clay Clemens, "The CDU/CSU: Undercurrents in an Ebb Tide," in Mary N. Hampton and Christian Søe, eds., *Between Bonn and Berlin: German Politics Adrift?* (New York: Rowman and Littlefield, 1999), 51–72; esp. 58.
30. Hoecker, "Zwischen Macht und Ohnmacht," 84; Rita Süssmuth, "Ohne geht es eben doch nicht—Die Quotendebatte der CDU," in Inge Wettig-Danielmeier, *Greift die Quota?* (Cologne: Stadtwage-Verlag, 1997), 85–100; esp. 99.
31. Mangasarian, "Frauen power in Germany."
32. Schlötzer-Scotland, "Subtiles Spiel mit der Frauenquote."
33. Marina A. Adler and April Brayfield, "Women's Work Values in Unified Germany," in *Work and Occupations* 24, no. 2 (May 1997): 245–66; quotation on 246.
34. *The Economist*, 18 July 1998, 5.
35. Adler and Brayfield, "Women's Work Values in Unified Germany," 248, 251.
36. Kolinsky, "The West German Greens," esp. 145.
37. Ferree, "Making Equality: The Women's Affairs Offices in the Federal Republic of Germany," 96; Kolinsky, "The West German Greens," esp. 142–43.
38. See discussion in Friederike Maier, "The Labour Market for Women and Employment Perspectives in the Aftermath of German Unification," *Cambridge Journal of Economics* 17, no. 4 (December 1993): 267–80, esp. 268.
39. Marina A. Adler, "East-West Differences in Attitudes About Employment and Family in Germany," in *The Sociological Quarterly* 37, no. 2 (1996): 246–60; esp. 250.
40. Adler and Brayfield, "Women's Work Values in Unified Germany," 251.
41. Hildegard Maria Nickel, "Der Transformationsprozeß in Ost- und Westdeutschland und seine Folgen für das Geschlechterverhältnis," in *Aus Politik und Zeitgeschichte* 51/97: 20–29; quotation on 23. My translation.
42. Dinah Dodds, "Five Years After Unification: East German Women in Transition," in *Women's Studies International Forum* 21, no. 2 (1998): 175–82; quotation on 178–79.
43. Friederike Maier, "Entwicklung der Frauenerwerbstätigkeit in der Europäischen Union," in *Aus Politik und Zeitgeschichte* 52/97: 15–27; figures on 21.
44. *The Economist*, 18 July 1998, "Survey: Women and Work," 4.
45. Maier, "Entwicklung der Frauenerwerbstätigkeit in der Europäischen Union," 25.
46. Ibid.
47. Adler and Brayfield, "Women's Work Values in Unified Germany," 257; *The Economist*, "Survey: Women and Work," 5.
48. Adler and Brayfield, "Women's Work Values in Unified Germany," 246.
49. Adler and Brayfield, "Women's Work Values in Unified Germany." Especially, see their conclusions, 262–64.

50. Mechthild Veil, "Zwischen Wunsch und Wirklichkeit: Frauen im Sozialstaat," *Aus Politik und Zeitgeschichte* B52/97: 29–38, graph on 37.

51. Lynn Kamenitsa, "Post-Communist Obstacles to Mobilizing Women in Eastern Germany," in *Problems of Post-Communism* 45, no. 6 (November/December 1998): 3–12; quotation on 8.

52. *The Economist,* "Survey: Women and Work," 5.

53. Ursula Beer and Ursula Mueller, "Coping with a New Reality: Barriers and Possibilities," *Cambridge Journal of Economics* 17 (1993), 281–94; quotation on 289.

54. I thank John Francis for his helpful comments.

55. For discussions of *Reformstau*, see David M. Keithly, "The German Economy: Shocks to the System," and Irwin Collier, "Welfare State Reform: The Gridlock of Social Entitlements," both in Hampton and Søe, eds., *Between Bonn and Berlin.*

56. Kohl, cited in Süssmuth, "Ohne geht es eben doch nicht," 85. My translation.

57. See discussion in Irwin Collier, "Welfare State Reform: The Gridlock of Social Entitlements," in Hampton and Søe, eds. *Between Bonn and Berlin,* 201–16, esp. 212.

58. SPD, *25 ASFB Wir haben die richtigen Frauen* (Bonn: Vorstand der SPD, 1998), 84–85.

59. E. Gene Frankland, "Alliance '90/The Greens: Party of Ecological and Social Reform," in Hampton and Søe, eds. *Between Bonn and Berlin,* esp. 110–13; quotation on 113.

60. Forschungsgruppe Wahlen, *Bundestagswahl 1998,* 64.

61. Frankland, "Alliance '90/The Greens," 113.

62. Quotations from the PDS 1998 Election Program. My translations.

Chapter 10

EAST-WEST ELECTORAL ENCOUNTERS IN UNIFIED GERMANY

Helga A. Welsh

The outcome of the 1998 federal election was nothing short of re-markable.[1] Many observers have called it historic: for the first time, government changed as a result of the vote of the electorate and not through the maneuvering of the political parties. Another novelty concerns the Social Democratic Party of Germany (SPD) forming a red-green coalition government with Alliance '90/The Greens. But another term kept creeping up in descriptions of the election: normality. How can an election be a historic event and, at the same time, a sign of normality?

The Quest for Normality

It is at least open to question what being normal entails for a country but in the case of Germany, it stands for the desire to be a reliable, and thus predictable, democratic partner whose foreign and domestic policy actions reflect stability and contentment with the present nation state. In 1990, German unification was seen by many as a major step toward becoming a normal state (Markovits and Reich 1997: 137; Pulzer 1994: 1), but, in fact, unification has not put the issue to rest. Some assert that, due to its historical burden, the quest for normality will forever be elusive. There are those who believe that Germany has reached the status of a normal state but is unwilling to accept the implications. For example, Markovits and Reich emphasize that for Germany to become normal, it has to normalize its relations to power. In this view, "power ignored is not power dissolved; it is power used irresponsibly (xii)." Finally, there are those who think that Germany has promoted certain principles, such as its self-definition as a civilian power, that should become the norm for other countries as well.

One dimension of normality that was boosted by the 1998 election applies to the democratic nature of Germany. The relaxed response to the election outcome was much in contrast to 1969, when, for the first time in the history of the Federal Republic, the SPD was able to form and lead a coalition government. Then the power shift was seen as a momentous change that divided the Republic along policy and ideological issues. In 1998, the change to a red-green coalition, which even a decade ago might have evoked strong reactions, was merely a reason to ponder. From Eckhard Fuhr in the conservative newspaper *Frankfurter Allgemeine Zeitung* (28 October 1998), who asked whether the "unbearable lightness of democratic being" has finally dawned on Germany, to Heribert Prantl in the liberal *Süddeutsche Zeitung*, who spoke of the "magic of the new beginning," the election outcome was greeted with amazing repose. Indeed, as Prantl said, the "power shift was a historical event exactly because one did not know its historical significance. For the first time in the history of the Federal Republic, something that should be a matter of fact turned out as such" (28 October 1998).

That another litmus test of democracy had been passed is important in itself, but of particular significance when one recalls that just eight years ago the specter of unification had raised questions regarding the future of German democracy. On the one hand, unification and the accompanying international treaties were a step toward normalization of the German nation state. On the other, it opened new challenges. Could the social, economic, and political barriers of a forty-year separation be overcome and the constitutional consensus be maintained?

Emerging democracies are said to have successfully completed regime change when they progress from the transition to the consolidation phase. The transition phase is characterized by a flurry of decision-making activities whose outcome is often uncertain, whereas during the consolidation phase, the actors are habituated to the new circumstances, political trends become more stable, and democracy deepens (Welsh 1998). Seemingly without much ado, and with the assistance of western Germany, the former GDR moved with great speed to consolidation. But is swiftness a sign of efficiency? What does it tell us about the status of unification? Using the federal election of 1998 as the focal point, this chapter assesses electoral patterns emerging in the eastern part of Germany. The process of unification, with its achievements and problems, provides background and context. I argue that in electoral trends, as in other areas, divergence and convergence between eastern and western Germany will continue and fissures will remain: for the foreseeable future, this will be normality. To accept it as such, however, demands the acknowledgment and acceptance of differences between eastern and western Germans.

German Unity: What Now?

More than eight years after the formal completion of unification, many Germans are still at odds with the consequences of this momentous and unforeseen event. Immediately following unification, a comprehensive institutional and legal transfer from west to east took place. Privatization of the economy started and was concluded in an amazingly short four-year time frame, but the mental distance is carefully maintained by eastern and western Germans, and may in fact have widened. The one issue that initially received the least attention—cultural differences—has turned out to be one of the most enduring and difficult to address. The diversity in orientations, attitudes, and values between eastern and western Germany was soon framed as lack of progress in achieving "inner unity." The term "inner unity" refers to traditional elements of political culture, but also to differences in life styles, milieus, and mentalities (Kaase 1993). What constitutes progress toward inner unity is far from clear. Evidence exists that "the road to inner unity is a long and rocky one" (Bauer-Kaase and Kaase 1996: 1), or that "we are already living in a condition of inner unity and that means greater variety. More unity is not necessary for democracy" (Veen 1997: 28).

Just how different the two parts of Germany can be politically without jeopardizing the democratic consensus is relevant to the interpretation of the political landscape, including the elections. The national elections of 1990 and 1994 were substantially influenced by the popular posture toward, and the issues associated with, unification. By contrast, in 1998 they hardly created any waves, despite their persistence. Among them are the unresolved economic particulars of eastern Germany, the mental distance between eastern and western Germans, and the question of how to reconcile eastern interests with the majority position of westerners. With few exceptions, these problematics were relegated to the sidelines of the political debate. This is not to say that they have lost their significance in the political realm or that they are being ignored; rather, they exhibit themselves in more circumscribed ways. Nor is this circumscription new. The strategy of relegating unification issues to the back burner has been followed since the middle of the 1990s. For example, in the national media—which are in western hands—statistical information is now rarely broken down by region. This strategy conveys an important message: the commonality of unified Germany is being emphasized at the expense of acknowledging the differences. The sensitive issue of the cost of unification is to be avoided or at least downplayed if it is mentioned; this was particularly evident in the electoral campaigns of 1998. After all, between 1991 and 1998, the net transfer of funds to the new federal states amounted to more than 1,031 billion DM, with no end in sight.[2]

But there are also elements of saturation that contribute to the absence of open discussion. Saturation is partly the response to the widespread negative reporting on unification. Despite unquestionable achievements in the unification process, both the media and academic analyses consistently highlight its problematics (Bulmahn 1997; Von Beyme 1994).[3] But it is also the result of a natural progression: issues that affect both parts of Germany—for example, structural long-term unemployment, the consequences of the globalization of markets, the demands associated with European integration, the challenges of modernizing the welfare state— have become more important. Finally, the mental distance between eastern and western Germans adds to miscommunication. In particular, eastern Germans feel that their fellow citizens in the West have little knowledge and understanding of the lives–either in the old GDR or in the refashioned FRG.

A Retrospective Look: The 1990 and 1994 Federal Elections

When the first all-German election took place in December 1990, the important issues spelled out in the Unification Treaty of 1990 were waiting to be implemented. Not surprisingly, unification was the dominant issue in the election, and the posture toward it determined the outcome. Had it not been for unification, the electoral cycle of Helmut Kohl might well have ended earlier (Jung and Roth 1998: 4). For one time only, the electoral landscape was formally divided into East and West; that is, the distribution of seats in the national parliament was based on the separate electoral results in the two parts of Germany. This circumvented the five percent threshold level at the national level and gave the East's smaller parties a better chance of getting elected. But it became quite clear that the western German parties had successfully extended their tentacles into the East. The Christian Democratic Union (CDU) and the Free Democratic Party (FDP) absorbed existing bloc parties, the SPD merged with a new party, the Greens tried to counter the trend by not merging with Alliance '90 until 1993, and all were more or less united in condemning the continued existence of the former communist party's successor, the Party of Democratic Socialism (PDS). The electoral success of the PDS in the eastern part of the country, where it achieved 11.1 percent of the vote, disrupted the picture of thorough westernization, though at the time few thought that its success would last.

The 1990 election seemed to indicate the successful transplantation of the western political party system to the East, but the next federal election, in 1994, revealed that the political landscape in the East was far from settled. Four points stood out. First, the election results confirmed a seeming paradox. Electoral wisdom has it that blue-collar workers generally vote for parties of the left. In addition, the majority of Catholic voters in the West favors the CDU. But the low level of religious affiliation and attachments and the even lower number of Catholics in the East change the effects of the religious cleavage substantially.[4]

Just as in 1990, however, a plurality of working-class, secular voters in eastern Germany confirmed their preference for the conservative CDU. Based on the "anomalies in the social basis of voting choice in the West and East," Dalton and Bürklin spoke of "two electorates—and two party systems—existing within the Federal Republic" (1995: 80). Second, in former GDR territory both the Liberals (FDP) and Alliance '90/The Greens lost dramatically in the national and regional elections. Third, the eastern electorate's weak party identification not only encouraged electoral volatility but seemed to favor a vote based on personality rather than ideology. Fourth, thanks to a little known provision in the electoral law, the PDS regained representation in the federal parliament. Indeed, the number of votes (19.8 percent) indicated a substantial jump in support.

The vote for the PDS was not the only indicator that not everything was settled in eastern Germany. For example, the voter turnout of 72.6 percent remained substantially below the 80.5 percent level in western Germany, and was also lower than in 1990. Thus, while major elements of the western political system had been adopted, some specifics of the eastern electorate emerged that related both to voting behavior and to the development of the political parties.

Unification and the 1998 Electoral Campaign

Electoral campaigns serve mobilizing and integrative functions. Eastern and western electorates were united by one common campaign theme—unemployment—which has been seen as by far the most important issue in German politics for some time. In many ways, other campaign topics were spinoffs: Standort Deutschland, modernization and technology, tax reform, even the use of atomic energy. But the fact that four-fifths of the electorate live in the western part of Germany is not lost on the major parties. With the exception of the PDS, they continue to be thoroughly Western and, though united, are still separated by East-West divides (Birsl and Lösche: 1998). National campaigns are western campaigns and are mainly tailored to reach the western electorate, at times at the East's expense. For example, in 1998 the CDU attempted to once again play the anti-communist card. In 1994, the "Rote Socken" campaign aimed to discredit the PDS. In 1998, it tried the "Rote Hände" campaign to compromise evolving cooperation between SPD and PDS in the new federal states. These tactics were predominantly used to capture western votes; that they alienated many eastern voters was a calculated risk that backfired in the new federal states. Among others, almost 9 percent of previous CDU voters supported the PDS in 1998.[5]

All political parties started with similar campaign strategies in the East and West. However, the closer the date of the election, the more differentiated their strategies became in the two parts of Germany with regard to advertising and, to some extent, also content; that is, issues addressed. Since the national newspapers of the West have a low readership in the East, regional newspapers were employed to aim at eastern German voters. The use of campaign posters also differed. The CDU counted on personality to play a particularly important role in mobilizing the eastern electorate, as it had in past elections. It continued to favor posters with Chancellor Helmut Kohl's image over others in the East. In the final phase of the campaign, organized under the heading "Week of German Unity," campaign strategies in the new federal states emphasized the progress in unification by taking up the symbol of "flowering landscapes." The term "flowering landscapes," used by Kohl in 1990 to win the support of eastern German voters, has become synonymous with Kohl's unfulfilled promises. This is true, although the Kohl government could show remarkable progress in the build-up of infrastructure in the East.[6]

The SPD displayed posters that highlighted *Aufbau Ost* (the building up of the East), and chancellor candidate Gerhard Schröder promised to take this task in his own hands and make it a *Chefsache* (a task for the boss). Another poster featured Schröder surrounded by top SPD politicians from the eastern part of Germany.

With the passage of time, the major parties, SPD and CDU, intensified their campaigns in the new federal states, whereas parties like the FDP, whose electoral fate looked quite dismal in the East, gathered their forces in their western strongholds.[7] In those electoral districts where the PDS had a reasonable chance of gaining a direct mandate, Alliance '90/The Greens initiated campaigns to "vote intelligently," i.e., split your ballot. Alliance 90/The Greens meant to give the more important second vote to their party, but the first vote to the SPD. In their campaign speeches, the Social Democrats reinforced the idea that both votes were equally important for the party's success.[8]

Just as the CDU used Helmut Kohl to attract voters in the East, the PDS counted on the fact that Gregor Gysi was their major asset in the West. Western university towns and the intellectual milieu were the target of most campaign activity, whereas the left propensity of eastern German identity was reinforced: *Der Osten wählt rot* (The East votes for the Left). Slogans such as *Das ist immer noch mein Land* (This is still my country) and *Das ist auch unser Land* (This is our country as well) pictured a young woman as the main protagonist. This message of "power to the people" thus aimed at multiple constituencies: eastern Germans, women, and young people generally.

Although the 1998 electoral campaigns united Germans under the umbrella of national politics, the strategies to mobilize voters differed between East and West. But mobilize they did: the voter turnout in the West stood at 82.8 percent, in the East at 80.0 percent.

Electoral Encounters: Convergence and Divergence

The elections of 1994 and 1998 are often said to have been won in the East. This statement requires qualification. In the newly elected fourteenth federal parliament, 137 parliamentarians represent Berlin and the five new federal states. The most populous state in the West, North Rhine-Westphalia alone is represented by 148 members. The population in the eastern part of Germany constitutes less than one-fifth of the electorate; hence, it cannot determine national results, though it can signal important trends. Most electoral shifts that have occurred in the last two elections were visible in both parts of Germany—just more so in the eastern part. A few examples serve to illustrate this point. In 1994, the FDP lost substantially, but the loss was much heavier in the former GDR. In the 1994 and 1998 elections, the winning party's margin was enhanced by "excess seats" that were overwhelmingly gained in eastern Germany.[9]

In 1994, the CDU profited from its unexpected continued strong showing in the eastern states. Four years later, the winds of fortune changed. The share of Helmut Kohl's party fell precipitously everywhere, but most dramatically in eastern Germany (see Figure 10.1). In the western states, the CDU lost 5.1 percent as opposed to 11.2 percent in the eastern states. Particularly pronounced was the decline in the former CDU strongholds: in Saxony, it amounted to 15.3 percent; in Thuringia, to 12.1 percent. The decline in the voters' favor was accompanied by an important shift in voting behavior. One of the anomalies of the 1990 and 1994 elections had been that the CDU had gathered large numbers of working class votes, that is, votes that are traditionally seen as going to the political left. This relationship was overturned (see Figure 10.2).

The convergence in voting behavior among blue-collar workers was a step that significantly favored the SPD. However, the narrowing of the gap between East and West was seen in other categories as well; for example, in the category of white-collar workers and union members. Based on these changes, which were accentuated by a considerable narrowing of the voter turnout between the two parts of Germany, Jung and Roth, among

Figure 10.1 Federal Election 1998: West-East Comparisons

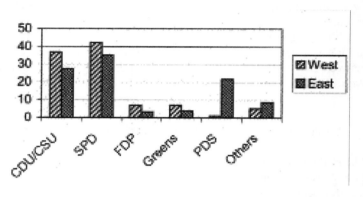

Source: Forschungsgruppe Wahlen, *Wahlergebnisse in Deutschland*: 141.

Figure 10.2 Party Support: Blue-Collar Workers in Eastern Germany

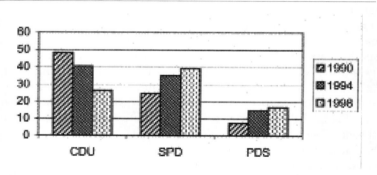

Source: Forschungsgruppe Wahlen, exit polls, 1990–98.

others, emphasize the assimilation process between East and West (Jung and Roth 1998: 18; see also Forschungsgruppe Wahlen, *Bundestagswahl 1998*). However, it is too early to tell to what extent this may be a lasting trend as opposed to a temporary adjustment. Arzheimer and Falter argue that assimilation of voting behavior is largely the result of the greater willingness of eastern Germans to change from one party to another. Due to low levels of party identification, eastern electoral volatility may well continue (Arzheimer and Falter 1998: 42–43).

Arzheimer and Falter base their caution predominantly on the issue of party identification, which remains lower in the new states.[10] Stöss and

Neugebauer, on the other hand, emphasize that party loyalties in the East have been increasing. According to their analysis, approximately half of the eastern electorate voted for the same party in 1994 and 1998, compared to 60 percent in the West (Stöss and Neugebauer 1998: 25). It might be added that while party loyalties in the East seem to be increasing, those in the West have been declining.

Due to the lack of an established party identification, the "personalization" of politics was said to be particularly strong in the former GDR. But in the 1998 election, personalization of the campaigns characterized both East and West (Jung and Roth 1998: 9–10). For example, Alliance '90/The Greens—a party that traditionally downplays the role of its political figures in favor of political issues—distributed more posters of its top candidate, Joschka Fischer, than of that featuring one of its major campaign themes, abandonment of nuclear energy. The emphasis on leadership figures was true for all parties but particularly for the CDU and SPD, who featured the two candidates for chancellor, Kohl and Schröder. Thus, eastern and western voting behavior has become more similar partly because of converging trends.

Important differences between the East and West persist. Not without irony, it has been argued that the current federal parliament represents four regional parties (Nonnenmacher 1998: 1). For the Christian Social Union (CSU), this is indisputable, since it is only represented in Bavaria and thus, by definition, is a regional party. But this verdict of regionalism is less clear when it comes to the other parties. The FDP and Alliance '90/The Greens have been thoroughly marginalized in eastern Germany. Both continued their electoral decline in 1998, although the losses were more moderate than in 1994. The vote fell from 3.5 percent to 3.3 percent for the FDP, and from 4.3 percent to 4.1 percent for Alliance '90/The Greens. Neither party is represented in state parliaments, and neither was able to garner more than 5 percent in any of the five eastern states.

Their membership base is undoubtedly anchored in the West. Of the approximately 50,000 members of Alliance '90/The Greens, less than 4,000 live in the eastern states and East Berlin. The FDP initially profited from merging with the GDR's Liberal Party (LDPD); at the end of 1990, FDP membership in the new federal states was close to 110,000. Since then, it has seen a rapid decline in membership; at the end of 1998, it stood at slightly more than 15,000 (West: 52,000; Berlin 3,256). However, it must be kept in mind that the major parties have similar problems in adding new members to their party rolls. For example, at the end of 1997 the membership of the SPD in the new federal states amounted to about 27,000, whereas the membership in the West was over 750,000. The longer this unequal distribution continues, the harder it is to maintain a proper East-West distribution in leadership. A cycle has begun that further weakens the parties in the East.[11]

To what extent the substantial changes in living standard and in employment pattern will ameliorate or even change the electoral fortunes of some of the smaller parties remains to be seen. For example, the number of self-employed, the main constituency of the FDP, has increased substantially in the last few years, although it remains below the level of the West.[12] So far, however, this has not translated into electoral success. Indeed, more voters in the self-employed category opted for the PDS (17.2 percent) than the FDP (10.1 percent).

The unequal distribution of members is even more pronounced for the PDS, the party that most clearly represents eastern interests. The PDS has seen a remarkable decline in membership, although it is still the party with the highest eastern membership. But of the roughly 98,600 members (1997), only approximately 2,500 reside in the West. Contrary to expectations, the PDS increased its vote from 19.8 percent in 1994 to 21.6 percent in 1998. The share of votes in the West grew only slightly to a marginal 1.2 percent (up from 1.0 percent in 1994). The PDS is at pains to continue its role as a regional party and, at the same time, to establish itself as a national party. The dual strategy requires a careful balancing act, since its party clientele in the former GDR is quite different from that in the "old" Federal Republic. In the West, the party attracts a very small group of intellectuals; in the East, it portrays itself as a "people's party." There, the PDS is still firmly anchored to a milieu occupied predominantly by former old regime functionaries who live in the former district capitals of the GDR and Berlin (East). Not surprisingly, this is where the PDS achieved its best voting results. White-collar workers and civil servants continue to be its main constituency. But the PDS was able to increase its share of voters among blue-collar workers from 15 percent in 1994 to 18 percent in 1998 (see Figure 10.2). The voters are evenly distributed among age groups, although the PDS did particularly well among young female voters. In all the new federal states, the PDS was able to reach the 20 percent mark; this indicates that it was able to spread its support more evenly in the territory of the former GDR, even if a more conservative south pits itself against a left-leaning north, a pattern that is found in the West as well.[13]

Just as in 1990 and 1994, five parties are represented in the federal parliament. Twenty-seven parties failed to pass the electoral hurdles, but together they received 5.9 percent of the vote. This is the highest level since 1957 (Jung and Roth 1998: 4). Important differences also exist between the eastern and western parts of Germany. Votes for "other parties" in the East jumped from 2.4 percent in 1994 to 8.6 percent in 1998; in the West they increased from 3.9 percent to 5.2 percent. At a time when political mobilization is high, smaller parties gain from dissatisfaction with the established parties, which profit right-wing extremist parties. After the surprising electoral success of the right-wing German People's Union (DVU) in Saxony-Anhalt, where it attained 12.9 percent of the vote in the April 1998 state election, fears that right-wing parties would do particularly well in the former East Germany were high.

Votes for a right-wing party are stigmatized in Germany, making electoral prediction difficult. In a survey conducted shortly before the September 1998 election, respondents in both parts of Germany agreed overwhelmingly that that "it would be very bad" (*sehr schlimm*) if the Republikaner or the German People's Union (DVU) were represented in the federal parliament.

Although the overwhelming majority in both parts of Germany condemns right-wing votes, quite a few remain at least doubtful as to just how severe their impact would be. Particularly interesting is the high percentage of respondents in the undecided category for the DVU (Table 10.1).

That the extreme right splintered into three different parties (DVU, Republikaner, and NPD) weakened its cause considerably. In addition, the success of the German People's Union in the Saxony-Anhalt election in April 1998 mobilized politicians, the media, and many civic groups. In Mecklenburg-Pomerania, concerns were particularly high that the right-wing parties might fare well in the state and federal elections that took place on the same day. As it turned out, the strategy worked well. In Mecklenburg-Pomerania, the federal vote for right-wing parties amounted to 4.3 percent; in the vote for the state parliament, they garnered 4.0 percent. It remains true that the gains for the right-wing parties were visibly higher in the eastern states as compared to the western ones (3.5 percent

Table 10.1 Representation of Right-Wing Parties in Federal Parliament (percentages)

	West	East
Republikaner represented in parliament		
Very bad	72.2	73.2
Not so bad	24.4	21.0
Don't know	3.4	5.8
DVU represented in parliament		
Very bad	68.5	71.5
Not so bad	19.1	19.0
Don't know	12.4	9.5

Source: Forschungsgruppe Wahlen, No. 1137 and No. 2018, question #43a/44a.

in the East vs. 0.9 percent in the West). That none of the extreme right-wing parties was able to pass the 5 percent threshold—or indeed, that even taken together, the three parties did not pass it—is only temporary consolation. The psychological barrier to voting for one of the right-wing parties is still high, but attitudes supporting right-wing programs are considerably higher.[14]

Not surprisingly, citizens with the highest level of dissatisfaction with democracy are found among voters for right-wing parties, the PDS, small splinter parties, and those who do not vote. But there are important differences in the social base of voters. Voters for right-wing parties tend to be male and have lower levels of education and income. Those who exhibit similarly high levels of dissatisfaction with the political system and vote for the PDS have high levels of education. Women are slightly more represented among its voters.[15]

To this day, eastern Germans overwhelmingly agree that the adoption of the West German political system in 1990 was the correct decision. Although more western Germans than eastern Germans are convinced that democracy is the best form of government (west: 88 percent; east: 73 percent), the eastern response is positive (Forschungsgruppe Wahlen, *Blitz-Umfrage* 1998). Therefore, the stark differences in the overall level of satisfaction with democracy between eastern and western Germans at first seem surprising (see Table 10.2).

While satisfaction with democracy aims at measuring dimensions of political stability, it also gauges the emotional underpinnings of system evaluation. Frustrations with the system are evident and remain an important reminder that—while often not articulated—the differences between East and West continue to be real. But the causes of the differences are less well understood than the articulations.

One important dimension of this level of dissatisfaction with democracy relates to dissatisfaction with the way unification has proceeded, while others are rooted in cultural and political differences between East and West.

Table 10.2 Satisfaction with Democracy: West and East

	1992	1993	1994	1995	1996	1997	1998
West	61	56	63	63	58	56	59
East	40	32	37	42	38	40	38
Diff.	21	24	26	21	20	16	21

Source: *Politbarometer*, cumulative responses, 1992–1998.

Explaining the Vote

While the great majority of the electorate in 1998 wanted a new government, there was much less agreement on which parties should form this government. Coalition preferences on election day and immediately after the election were almost evenly split between those who desired a red (SPD)-green coalition and those who favored a grand coalition between the SPD and CDU/CSU. Once again, the eastern and western electorates showed a remarkable symmetry. On 27 September 1998, voters in eastern Germany were almost evenly split between a grand coalition and a red (SPD)-green coalition, whereas voters in the western part gave a slight preference to a grand coalition. The number of undecided voters was, however, quite high (East: 24.1 percent; West: 19.5 percent, [Forschungsgruppe Wahlen, *Blitzumfrage*, September 1998). A few days later, the electorate remained evenly split, but more respondents had made up their minds, with less than 10 percent remaining undecided: 48.1 percent in the East vs. 46.6 percent in the West favored a red-green coalition. But 42.3 percent in the East and 44.1 in the West preferred a coalition between the major parties, CDU/CSU and SPD (IPOS, *Zur politischen Lage in Deutschland*, September 1998).

Why did eastern voters reject Kohl and the CDU with such intensity? To explain this landslide loss of the CDU in the East, greater electoral volatility, frustrated expectations, and the high rates of unemployment are often cited. At the same time, many observers, especially in the West, seem at a loss to explain why the massive transfer of funds under the Kohl government did not result in more support from eastern Germans. Members of the CDU felt a lack of gratitude; eastern German voters should feel guilty not voting for Kohl. Others cited the difficulty of conveying the complex issues of economic policy to voters; still others thought that eastern Germans blamed the economic difficulties on the CDU and did not attribute them sufficiently to the sins of the former communist government.

The economic variable undoubtedly has important explanatory power for the voting behavior in all of Germany, but it does not account for the higher rate of CDU losses in the East. Rattinger and Maier demonstrate that the perception of the economic situation has shifted toward assimilation in both parts of Germany. To the extent that differences persist, they argue, the consequences for electoral behavior in 1998 "are more gradual than categorical" (Rattinger and Maier 1998: 54).

Stöss and Neugebauer cite another factor: the conviction of many eastern Germans that the former governing coalition failed to create a socially just environment in which unification could be pursued (1998: 18). Hans Misselwitz asserts that the convergence in voting behavior between eastern and western Germans indicates an important trend away from freedom and back to equality and social justice as the most important concerns (Misselwitz 1998: 13). With its campaign slogan of social justice, the SPD was able to capture this mood much better than the CDU, which continued to rely on security and stability.

Still other explanations focus on psychological variables. One is connected to what Helmut Wiesenthal calls postunification dissatisfaction. He rejects the "rising expectation thesis," according to which unrealistically high expectations regarding the predominantly economic consequences of unification explain the frustration of eastern Germans. He asserts that the "treatment-response" and "socialist legacy" approaches are keys to explaining postunification dissatisfaction. While the socialist legacy approach explains best why older people assess unification in a more negative light, the treatment-response hypothesis combines emotional with tactical responses to perceived discrimination by western Germans. Seen from the latter perspective, eastern Germans use their dissatisfaction with current circumstances as a "vehicle for creating—or maintaining—a collective identity by exaggerating existing differentials" (Wiesenthal 1998: 17). Adding to the voices of those who emphasize attitudinal and not economic variables is Pollack: "The feeling of disdain is not only related to the objective conditions of regime change, but to the way the communication between East and West has occurred in the last few years" (1997: 9). In his view, it is not nostalgia for the past regime, but the total negation of previous life experiences of eastern German citizens that goes a long way toward explaining the feelings of eastern Germany toward unification and the political system.

East and West after the Election

In many ways, a vocal but small minority within the East has been captured by important segments of the West—in particular within the CDU/CSU—to interpret the history of the GDR solely from the perspective of anticommunism. Such a posture emphasizes the totalitarian nature of the GDR regime but ignores the everyday lives of individuals. Similarly, the work of the Gauck Agency may have deepened this division; the issue of *Vergangenheitsaufarbeitung* was primarily used to reveal and condemn. The dividing line between those who denounce the communist past in its entirety and those who seek a more balanced evaluation of the communist period is common to all postcommunist societies. But the alliance with the western German political elite elevated the former to the dominant position.

Based on this perception, the relationship between East and West continues to be shaped by clichés. Initially, all western parties shied away from admitting former members of the Socialist Unity Party (SED) to their ranks. To this day, the PDS and its role in a future Germany remain controversial. Nearly 75 percent of eastern respondents think that the PDS should be treated as a normal party with which the others should cooperate, while western opinion is almost evenly split between those who favor cooperation with the PDS and those who do not (Forschungs-gruppe Wahlen Nr. 1137; question 37). In 1998, for the first time, the PDS was able to garner the status of a Fraktion in the parliament. This has important monetary advantages, and entitles PDS members to equal partnership in the work of parliamentary committees.[16]

In addition, the PDS is now junior partner in the government of Mecklenburg-Pomerania and has played an important supporting role in Saxony-Anhalt. In other words, due to its electoral fortunes the PDS has become not only more visible, but slowly and surely more accepted. The recognition and incorporation of a postcommunist party, which has become common in the rest of eastern Europe, is making progress in Germany as well. The more accepted, and thus normal, the PDS becomes in the East, the more it becomes a lightning rod for some western politicians. What is normal in the East is not necessarily normal in the West. What, then, is normal in the relations between the eastern and western parts of Germany?

In Lieu of a Conclusion

To this day, it is thought normal that the Federal Republic is "predominantly West German in character" (Kister 1999: 4). It continues to be normal that nearly all national elite positions are occupied by western Germans. Only two of the nineteen members of the federal cabinet are eastern German. One, Rolf Schwanitz, was appointed state minister in the office of the federal chancellor; he is responsible for matters dealing with the new federal states. The other, Christine Bergmann, heads the Ministry for Family, Senior Citizens, Women, and Youth. Partly to compensate, the presidency of the federal parliament was allotted to an eastern German, Wolfgang Thierse. In his inaugural address, he was quick to point out that his election was also "an act of democratic normality in the relationship between East and West that is still not completely free of conflict or biases" (*Das Parlament*, 30 October 1998: 1). Not to be short-changed, in his own inaugural address Chancellor Gerhard Schröder reminded western Germans that many could and should learn from the personal courage, creativity, and inventiveness of the citizens in the new states. He asked for a willingness to achieve more "normality" in their relationship. "Know-all manners and whininess, contempt for the other, his preferences, his habits, all that has no place in a modern democracy."

The political landscape between East and West has changed substantially between 1990 and 1998. The 1998 election and its outcome are another indication that normality in inner-German relations demands the recognition of western dominance and eastern assertion. This is not surprising: the project of German unification contains a built-in tension. It requires attention to the differences between East and West, while at the same time, it intends to eliminate them. Eastern Germans insist on being different. Thus, it requires the recognition of different biographies, special needs, and special milieus and cultures, and, at the same time, easterners' desire to share the same economic, political, and social status as their western compatriots. Western Germans, on the other hand, would prefer political attitudes, behavior, and identity that mirror their own, but they can live with continued inequality in social, political, and economic relations. Thus, expectations are quite different. In addition, the population distribution has always favored, and will continue to favor, the West's majority position.[17]

What remains to be done to normalize the relations between eastern and western Germans is to build on the commonalities and reconcile the differences.[18] Most cleavages in Germany are, after all, cross-cutting and not coinciding. It is correct that "inner unity can not be ordered by the state; it has to grow in minds and hearts" (*Jahresbericht* 1998: 15), yet the political elite has an important role in facilitating this process. In recent months, the "recognition of biographies" has become a code phrase for the effort to foster better understanding between East and West. From Wolfgang Thierse to Gerhard Schröder, the need "to respect the difference between eastern and western biographies and to pay respect to the life-long achievements of eastern Germans" has become officially recognized (*Regierungserklärung*: 10 November 1998). But it remains to be seen to what extent this appeal will be more than lip service. After all, a successful reckoning would require "that in an emerging common German political culture the historic fact of 40 years of institutional competition between democratic capitalism and authoritarian socialism could be analyzed soberly and thought of with "cool" interests in the facts. Unfortunately, this is, in the short run, not a realistic prospect" (Wiesenthal 1998: 27). The building of a unified political community was and is based on a western interpretation of German history. Coming to terms with unification—and with electoral convergence and divergence—will require efforts to adjust established patterns of belief and conduct.

Notes

1. The generous support of the Bundespresse- und Informationsamt (BPA) not only allowed me to observe the 1998 election in Bonn but also gave me access to many decision-makers. In particular, I want to thank Wolfgang Gibowski, then Deputy Head of the BPA. Special thanks go to Dieter Roth for providing access to the data of Forschungsgruppe Wahlen. Andre Brie (PDS) and Axel Schmidt-Gödelitz (Friedrich-Ebent-Stiftung, Berlin) answered many questions and helped clarify issues. Over the past few years, my understanding of the process of unification profited from many discussions with Ulrich Albrecht, Michael Fichter, Gero Neugebauer (all Free University of Berlin), and Ruth and Hans Misselwitz (Berlin). Unless otherwise noted, data referring to eastern Germany include Berlin in its entirety.

2. *Jahresbericht der Bundesregierung 1998*: Appendix, 30.

3. Between 1990 and 1995 alone, more than 3,000 German-language studies have been published analyzing political and social change in the new federal states (Reißig 1997: 189).

4. In 1997, only 13.8 percent of the western population claims no religious affiliation. In the East the figure stood at 65.7 percent. Only 5.5 percent of eastern Germans (as compared to 41.5 percent in the West) are associated with the Roman Catholic Church (Forschungsgruppe Wahlen, *Bundestagswahl* 1998: A 13).

5. See, among others, Heribert Prantl, "Der traurige Advent der CDU," *Süddeutsche Zeitung*, 17 December 1998: 4.

6. See, for example, *Jahresberichte der Bundesregierung zum Stand der Deutschen Einheit* 1997 and 1998.

7. This section is partly based on interviews conducted in Bonn in September 1998. See also H.-J. Heims and Ch. Schwennicke. "Im Osten wird es eng," *Süddeutsche Zeitung*, 16 October 1998.

8. The so-called second vote determines the number of seats in parliament and thus is considered the more important vote. However, due to the electoral rule that a party that gains three direct mandates on the basis of the first ballot is represented in parliament, the first vote can have particular significance in voting districts with strong PDS support. In 1994, four direct mandates provided continued representation for the PDS in the federal parliament.

9. In 1994, thirteen of the sixteen excess seats were gained in the five new states. Since twelve were in the hands of the CDU, they significantly boosted its majority in the Federal Parliament from two to ten. In 1998, all thirteen excess seats, of which twelve were achieved in the former GDR, were won by the SPD.

10. According to data provided by IPOS (*Zur politischen Lage in Deutschland*, 1998), approximately one-third of the western electorate and 41 percent of the eastern electorate profess no party identification.

11. See, for example, "Wachsender Unmut unter den Ost-Grünen," *Süddeutsche Zeitung*, 29 October 1998, and the remarks by Harald Händel (representative for Alliance '90/The Greens), who acknowledged that the East-West quota has lost its importance, in particular in allotting leadership positions.

12. In 1997 on the territory of the former Federal Republic, 11.5 percent of the working population was self-employed or was a family member that helped in the business (1991: 10.8 percent). In the new federal states, including east Berlin, the figure stood at 8 percent (1991: 4.6 percent). Information provided by the Statistical Federal Office.

13. Stöss and Neugebauer (1998: 50–52) question whether the PDS might be able to fill the vacuum on the left created by the pragmatism of Alliance '90/The Greens and the SPD's move to the center.

14. Stöss and Neugebauer (1998: 58–65) distinguish between right-wing potential, willingness to vote for a right-wing party, and actual voting behavior.
15. For a detailed analysis of the influence of different levels of *Politikverdrossenheit* on electoral behavior, see Deinert 1998.
16. A summary of the changes is provided in "Abschied der PDS vom ungeliebten Gruppendasein." *Frankfurter Allgemeine Zeitung*, 29 September 1998: 6.
17. Of the 82 million people living in Germany, only 15.3 million live in the eastern part. This constitutes a decline from the more than 16 million in 1990.
18. For similar arguments, see Steinbach 1998 and Misselwitz 1998.

Bibliography

"Abschied der PDS vom ungeliebten Gruppendasein." *Frankfurter Allgemeine Zeitung*. 20 September 1998: 6.

Arzheimer, Kai and Jürgen W. Falter. "'Annäherung durch Wandel'? Das Wahlverhalten bei der Bundestagswahl 1998 in Ost-West-Perspektive." *Aus Politik und Zeitgeschichte*. B 52/98. 18 December 1998: 33–43.

Bauer-Kaase, Petra and Max Kaase. "Five Years of Unification: The Germans on the Path to Inner Unity?" *German Politics* 5, no. 1 (1996): 1–25.

Birsl, Ursula and Peter Lösche. "Parteien in West- und Ostdeutschland: Der gar nicht so feine Unterschied." *Zeitschrift für Parlamentsfragen* 29. no. 1. 1998: 7–24.

Bulmahn, Thomas. "Die deutsche Einheit im Spiegel der Sozialwissenschaften." *Aus Politik und Zeitgeschichte*. B 40-41/97. 26 September 1997: 29–37.

Dalton, Russell J. and Wilhelm Bürklin. "The Two German Electorates: The Social Bases of the Vote in 1990 and 1994." *German Politics and Society* 13, no. 1, 1995: 79–99.

Deinert, Rudolf Günter. "Die PDS, die rechten Parteien und das Alibi der 'Politikverdrossenheit'. Die Beweggründe westdeutscher Rechts- und ostdeutscher PDS-Wähler auf dem empirischen Prüfstand." *Zeitschrift für Parlamentsfragen* 29, no. 3: 422–41.

Forschungsgruppe Wahlen. *Wahlergebnisse in Deutschland 1946–1998*. 4th ed. December 1998.

Forschungsgruppe Wahlen. *Blitz-Umfrage zur Bundestagswahl 1998. West. Ergebnisse einer repräsentativen Bevölkerungsumfrage*. Mannheim. No. 1137. September 1998.

Forschungsgruppe Wahlen. *Blitz-Umfrage zur Bundestagswahl 1998. Ost. Ergebnisse einer repräsentativen Bevölkerungsumfrage*. Mannheim. No. 2018. September 1998.

Forschungsgruppe Wahlen. *Bundestagswahl 1998*. Mannheim, No. 91, 30 September 1998.

Forschungsgruppe Wahlen. *Wahltag-Befragung Bundestagswahl*. Mannheim. No. 1138. 27 September 1998.

Fuhr, Eckhard. "Wo bleibt der Schwung?" *Frankfurter Allgemeine Zeitung*, 28 October 1998.

Heims, H.-J. and Ch. Schwennicke. "Im Osten wird es eng." *Süddeutsche Zeitung*. 16 September 1998.

IPOS. *Zur politischen Lage in Deutschland*. West/East. No. 1140. September 1998.

Jahresbericht der Bundesregierung zum Stand der Deutschen Einheit 1998. Mimeograph.

Jahresbericht der Bundesregierung zum Stand der Deutschen Einheit 1997. Mimeograph.

Jung, Matthias and Dieter Roth. "Wer zu spät geht, den bestraft der Wähler. Eine analyse der Bundestagswahl 1998." *Aus Politik und Zeitgeschichte*. B 52/98. 18 December 1998: 3–18.

Kaase, Max. "Innere Einheit." *Handbuch zur Deutschen Einheit.* Eds. Werner Weidenfeld and Karl-Rudolf Korte. Frankfurt am Main: Campus: 372–383.

Kister, Kurt. "Schröders ganz normale Regierung." *Süddeutsche Zeitung.* 2/3 January 1999: 4.

Markovits, Andrei S. and Simon Reich. *The German Predicament. Memory and Power in the New Europe.* Ithaca and London: Cornell University Press. 1997.

Misselwitz, Hans. "Annäherung durch Wandel." *Freitag,* 23 October 1998: 13.

Nonnenmacher, Günther. "Von Bonn nach Berlin." *Frankfurter Allgemeine Zeitung.* 31 December 1998: 1.

Pollack, Detlef. "Das Bedürfnis nach sozialer Anerkennung. Der Wandel der Akzeptanz von Demokratie und Marktwirtschaft in Ostdeutschland." *Aus Politik und Zeitgeschichte.* B 13/1997. 21 March 1997: 3–14.

Prantl, Heribert. "Der traurige Advent der CDU." *Süddeutsche Zeitung.* 17 December 1998: 4.

Prantl, Heribert. "Der Zauber des Anfangs." *Süddeutsche Zeitung.* 28 October 1998.

Pulzer, Peter. "Unified Germany: A Normal State?" *German Politics* 3, no. 1 (1994): 1–17.

Rattinger, Hans and Jürgen Maier. "Der Einfluß der Wirtschaftslage auf die Wahlentscheidung bei den Bundestagswahlen 1994 und 1998." *Aus Politik und Zeitgeschichte.* B 52/98. 18 December 1998: 45–54.

Reißig, Rolf. "Transformationsforschung: Gewinne, Defizite, Perspektiven." In *Einheit und Differenz. Die Transformation Ostdeutschlands in vergleichender Perspektive.* Eds. Jan Wielgohs and Helmut Wiesenthal. Berlin: Berliner Debatte Wissenschaftsverlag, 1997: 188–213.

Steinbach, Peter. "Deutschland vor und seit der Wende. Von der Kenntnis der Anerkennung der Verschiedenheiten." *Aus Politik und Zeitgeschichte.* B 51/98. 11 December 1998: 24–30.

Stöss, Richard and Gero Neugebauer. *Die SPD und die Bundestagswahl 1998.* Ms. Berlin, October 1998.

Veen, Hans-Joachim. "Innere Einheit—aber wo liegt sie? Eine Bestandsaufnahme im siebten Jahr nach der Wiedervereinigung Deutschlands." *Aus Politik und Zeitgeschichte.* B 40-41/97. 26 September 1997: 19–28.

"Wachsender Unmut unter Ost-Grünen." *Süddeutsche Zeitung.* 29 October 1998.

Welsh, Helga A. "Von der Transition zur Konsolidierung: eine Bestandaufnahme." Arndt Hopfmann and Michael Wolf. Eds. *Transformation und Interdependenz.* Münster: Lit Verlag, 1998: 113–34.

Wiesenthal, Helmut. "Post-Unification Dissatisfaction, or Why Are So Many East Germans Unhappy with the New Political System?" *German Politics* 7, no. 2 (1998): 1–30.

Chapter 11

THE GERMAN POLITICAL ECONOMY
AND THE 1998 ELECTION

Herbert Kitschelt

The critical political issue throughout the final electoral term of the CDU/CSU-FDP coalition government that terminated with the September 1998 federal parliamentary election was the controversy about the continuing competitiveness of the German economy and of Germany as a place for foreign investors to conduct business. Germans refer to this topic by the notion of *Standortdebatte*. Politicians, interest groups, citizens, and academics are seeking a diagnosis, and ultimately a policy remedy, for high unemployment and a low capacity of the German economy to create new employment. Germany is in the unenviable position of having a substantial unemployment rate hovering between 9 and 11 percent among that segment of the adult population which seeks labor. Moreover, and maybe even more importantly, Germany also draws a rather low share of the adult population into labor markets in the first place. By comparison, both Anglo-Saxon and Scandinavian countries have lower unemployment rates, in spite of a much greater share of their 15- to 64-year-old citizens seeking jobs (Scharpf 1997).

The weak employment picture is accompanied by a sharp decline in direct foreign investment in Germany since the early 1990s and a large capital outflow initiated by German firms that shift production primarily into other advanced industrial economies. These shifts in investment are highlighted by a change in the current-account balance, which dropped from a net surplus of +$52.4 billion in the twelve months preceding January 1990 to a deficit of between $20 and $32 billion (annualized) between 1992 and 1997. What is more surprising, the current account balance has not staged a major comeback since 1993, although Germany's export surplus skyrocketed from a low of $12 billion (2/91–1/92) in the immediate aftermath of unification, when Germany was sucking in a lot of goods and services, to a high of $65 billion (2/96–1/97). In the election month of September 1998, the annualized export surplus reached $75 billion, while the current account balance remained slightly negative.[1] Whereas the net outflow of capital and consumer expenses abroad (particularly tourism) offset $21 billion of Germany's export surplus in 1991, since 1995 the net outflow of capital and foreign consumer spending has oscillated between $75 and $85 billion a year, and has more than offset all German export surpluses.

While there is considerable agreement on the symptoms of the German economic problem that require the attention of politicians, business, and labor, the economic actors and associated electoral constituencies advance very different diagnoses and proposals for policy therapy. In the first section of this chapter, I will sketch three alternative explanations for the predicament of the German political economy and argue that the final account is the most plausible. In the second section, I briefly describe the electoral constituencies likely to lean toward each of these scenarios. In the final section, I will turn to the dilemmas of electoral competition and economic policy-making politicians must confront in the current situation. I submit that the competitive alignments in German party politics are quite inhospitable to social and economic reforms that would address the structural problems of the German economy, unless Social Democratic leaders, headed by the new chancellor Gerhard Schröder and his Green coalition partners, can liberate themselves from the grip of those of their own core constituencies that supported their bid to displace the liberal-conservative Kohl government.

Challenges to the German Political Economy

The German economic policy debate takes place within the bounds marked by two opposite extreme alternatives. One of these extreme views argues for a more or less intransigent defense of the status quo and asserts the basic soundness of German economic institutions. The other extreme finds nothing admirable at all in Germany's current economic management and calls for a wholesale embrace of the liberal competitive model of Anglo-Saxon market capitalism, necessitating a far-reaching dismantling of political-economic institutions that characterize the German cooperative social market economy. A third and final approach proposes to reform these institutions by endeavoring to pursue a trajectory of new and untried policy innovations. This third position thus is not simply a bland peace formula between the warring alternatives at the polar opposite extremes, but attempts to step outside the conventional definition of feasible policy choices and identify new ways to work around the growing disadvantages of the conventional *Modell Deutschland* cooperative market economy.

Nothing New under the Sun: Preserving the German Model

The school of thought that defends the existing German political economy highlights the virtues of Germany's institutional arrangements throughout much of the postwar period. The specific cooperative relations between business and labor, facilitated by co-determination on company supervisor councils and works council representation in factories and offices, as well as the system of on-the-job vocational training (*betriebliche Berufsbildung*) interfaced with formal training in schools and colleges, are said to contribute to productivity improvements and human capital investments that keep the German economy abreast of international developments. More specifically, many conditions under which this model worked well remain in place and explain why it still manages to bring about respectable economic results. For example, supporters of the institutional status quo emphasize that after a temporary weakness in the early 1990s, Germany had restored its international leadership in the global economy by 1997/98, producing the second largest volume of exports globally and the world's largest export surplus measured as a percentage of GDP. All this has been accomplished in spite of one of the world's highest wage levels in industry. Wage increases have been mostly offset by productivity increases, although from the 1970s through the early 1990s Germany's productivity growth lagged slightly behind the average in industrialized countries, leading to a slow upward creep of unit labor costs (Carlin and Soskice 1997: 59). Germany is strong in a rather wide range of manufacturing industries, even though it has lost some ground in "high technology" fields.

Defenders of the status quo also point to the indisputable fact, confirmed by quantitative analysis (Alber 1998), that the German welfare state has not become an increasing burden on the domestic economy over the past twenty years. Compared to other advanced industrial democracies, the German welfare state in the late 1990s is only average in size, measured as a percentage of GDP devoted to public social expenditures. Neither the German pension levels, nor unemployment benefits, nor health care costs are particularly high or rapidly growing vis-à-vis the comparison group of countries. West Germany is one of only three advanced industrial democracies where social expenditures, as a percentage of GDP, fell from 1980 to 1994. Looking toward the future, Germany's growth prospects will enable the country to cope with the unfavorable demographics of an increasing burden of pensioners relative to the working population and the associated pension obligations and health care costs for elderly patients. If current social insurance pay-as-you-go schemes cannot accommodate all of these expenses, pensions and health care expenditures should be increasingly paid out of general tax revenue. Early retirement at age 60 should become a policy in order to relieve labor markets from demand pressures and enable young citizens to obtain lasting jobs.

What, then, in the view of status quo advocates, explains the weakness of the German economy in the 1990s, compared to Britain or the United States? The answer is straightforward: the culprits are one-time shocks and structural adjustment processes, such as the more massive entry of women into labor markets, but above all the unprecedented economic burdens of German unification. The sudden absorption of a state-planned economy that turned out to be uncompetitive in almost every sector and enterprise into western Germany and the European Union imposed punishing costs on western German business and labor. For example, the pension system has been compelled to pay out a net trans-fer of DM 12–15 billion to eastern Germans every year. And the German Labor Institute, funded by rising unemployment insurance contributions from primarily western German employers and employees, in the 1990s has engineered a net transfer of annually thirty to DM 45 billion to east-ern Germany for unemployment benefits and retraining expenses.

Additional debt financing of the eastern German economic restruc-turing in the early 1990s created another difficulty for all German em-ployment creation. The government's fiscal strategy, risking the rise of inflation, prompted the Bundesbank to raise real interest rates to punish-ing levels, thus creating an upward pressure on the German currency, destabilizing the European Monetary System, discouraging investments and private consumption, and ultimately making Germany a very costly place for business activity.

Furthermore, the rapid adjustment of eastern wage levels to those in the West and a withdrawal of many subsidies to ailing eastern firms destroyed the East German manufacturing sector and led to a shrinking of the eastern German labor market from well over eight to only about five million jobs in a span of three years after 1989. As a consequence, throughout the 1990s West Germans have transferred about 4 to 5 per-cent of their GDP to eastern Germany in order to fund public and private consumption, as well as investments to modernize the economy. Advo-cates of western German status quo institutions argue that the eastern economy creates a temporary drag on unified Germany, but this is likely to be overcome in the not too distant future. Given the external shock character of these problems, they certainly do not warrant abandonment of otherwise successful political-economic institutions.

Critics of the status quo perspective on German economic arrange-ments, however, point out that the slow but steady erosion of German competitiveness has cumulative effects not offset by new comparative advantages in innovative industries. Germany's cooperative market economy, with peaceful labor relations and a disciplined labor force trained to a considerable extent at the workplace, but with high wages and long-term labor contracts, favors industrial sectors involved in incremental innovation and gradual change of market conditions (cf. Kitschelt 1991; Carlin and Soskice 1997; Soskice 1998). The German finance system, with its reliance on bank credit more than the issue of stock market equity or venture capital, further reinforces the propensity toward structural conservatism and incrementalism. However, new industrial and service sectors, from electronics, software, or biotechnology to fashion, entertainment, business consulting, travel, or personal home care, call for more flexible labor and capital arrangements that cannot thrive in the existing institutional framework. These critics insist that it is insufficient to preserve the viability of existing industries because a competitive economy requires job creation in new industries and services, something the German political economy is evidently unable to deliver.

The problems of the *Modell Deutschland* are highlighted by the quotation from a Motorola executive, Norbert Quinkert, reproduced in an advertisement paid for by the state of Hesse and run repeatedly in *The Economist* in early 1998, evidently in order to encourage foreign companies to invest in the state of Hesse. Responding to the question why Motorola invests in Germany, Quinkert is quoted as saying:

> At first glance, the high wages, long vacations and inflexible labor laws prevailing in Germany would seem to speak against such a move. But these factors are more than offset by the German workers' high productivity and reliability. These traits make Germany very attractive to high-tech companies seeking to optimize product quality, instead of merely maximizing quantity of output. Another point should be made: Germany is also cost-competitive for those products for which labor represents a small portion of total manufacturing outlays.

The quote argues that Germany keeps a competitive edge when incremental quality upgrading of products and reliability is a key target, and when the capital costs of production far outweigh labor expenses. But these advantages do not qualify Germany as a site for producing manufacturing items or services that require frequent and fundamental innovation or that involve a large component of human capital. Because sectors in which Germany remains competitive have a modest labor input, the areas with competitive advantage are unable to generate a large number of new jobs for the twenty-first century, and thus put *Modell Deutschland* at a distinctive international competitive disadvantage, regardless of whether the country does or does not ultimately master the challenges of the German unification process.

The Market-Liberal Alternative

Without denying the burdens inflicted on Germany by the process of uni-fication, market liberals reject the explanation of Germany's economic performance problems solely in terms of the exogenous unification shock. Focusing on unification diverts attention from the main problems of German economic efficiency. Liberals primarily define Germany's competitive weakness in terms of economic production costs and market flexibility. Relative to the rest of the world, where the quality and efficiency of production has more rapidly improved over the past twenty years, Germany's wage levels and social policy entitlements look increasingly out of line. In other words, the premium German employees and the public sector can charge to business for enjoying the institutional advantages of the *Modell Deutschland* are declining. This, market liberals claim, explains why firms at the margin reduce new investment activity in Germany and accelerate investments in lower-cost production sites that by now exhibit almost the same institutional advantages, whether in other established or newly industrialized countries. In this view, a renaissance of the German political economy requires learning from Britain and the United States, especially by rewarding the marginal productivity of capital and labor more appropriately. Such reforms would lead to greater income inequalities between the winners of the current economic transformation—business owners, highly skilled professionals and technicians—and the losers of this process, less skilled workers and employees with routine task structures facing falling demand for their services.

In institutional terms, market liberals call for an end to centralized wage bargaining for all employees in an economic sector within a German region (the *übertarifliche Flächenvertrag*). This change is expected to lead to greater flexibility within enterprises in setting wages, work hours, and work conditions, and thus to greater inequality and less wage compression within the German economy.[2] Whereas tendencies toward wage differentiation have been powerful in many advanced Western economies, western Germany, and then united Germany, have been among the outliers fighting this trend and producing a gradual convergence of wages across industries and levels of qualification.[3] Liberal market advocates also call for the weakening or outright abolition of the German system of co-determination and works councils participation in managerial functions. Furthermore, market liberals demand a retrenchment of German social policy expenditures, particularly a reduction in the sick leave benefit amounting to 100 percent of the wage and to be paid by the employer for the first six weeks of illness. The liberal economic program also recommends a reduction in pension benefits in order to fight the coming demographic crisis of the German pension system, and a gradual change of the insurance scheme from a pay-as-you-go, defined-benefits system to a funded insurance with defined contributions but variable benefits, with some employee control over the investment of retirement savings. Furthermore, liberals call for a reduction of income and corporate taxation to encourage savings and investment. The ultimate objective of these reforms in the system of labor relations, collective bargaining, and social insurance is to boost labor productivity and to lower unit labor costs in order to increase the international competitiveness and profitability of German business.

Late in the game in 1996 and 1997, the CDU/CSU-FDP government responded to some of the liberals' demands with reforms of the German sick leave benefit that would have made it possible for employers to reduce the sickness wage replacement to 80 percent of the normal wage. But a massive strike, led by the metal workers' union, together with dissension among employers (to which I return below), resulted in a union victory codifying the 100 percent replacement rate in a collective bargaining framework agreement. The liberal-conservative government also enacted a reform of the pension system against fierce resistance from the Social Democratic opposition and, though less so, from the Greens. The reform provided, among other cost savings, for the gradual reduction of the standard wage replacement rate of pensions for workers retiring in future decades from 70 percent of their wage in their final work years to 64 percent, as well as for a new adjustment formula of pension levels, taking increases in the life expectancy of retirees into account.

For a number of reasons, however, it is unlikely that the liberal market reform program will do much to aid Germany's job creation and international competitiveness. For one thing, the stellar performance of German export-oriented industries and the growing trade surplus in the late 1990s show that the problem is not the trade sector of the economy. Where industries are exposed to foreign competition, they have managed to increase labor productivity and contain unit labor costs. These efficiency gains so far have even compensated for Germany's inability to gain competitive advantage in new industries, as the overall positive trade balance shows. Moreover, export-oriented and import-competing industries are much more vulnerable to exchange rate volatility than to high labor costs. The value of the German mark fell from about DM 1.40 per dollar in 1993–95 to about DM 1.70 to 1.85 in 1996–98, equivalent to a unit production cost reduction of 20 to 30 percent. By comparison, Audi car engines manufactured in Hungary at hourly wages of less than one quarter of the equivalent German wages, are only 5 to 10 percent cheaper than the same engines manufactured in Germany.

Small movements in exchange rates can thus overwhelm giant cost advantages in wage rates. For much of the trade-exposed German manufacturing sector, therefore, wage rates are quite immaterial as the main cause of competitive disadvantages. The already quoted interview with the Motorola executive indicates why Germany's export economy is not profoundly undermined by high wage costs. While more labor flexibility in the trade-exposed industries may benefit their competitiveness, it is often precisely the institutions of German business and labor relations, such as co-determination and works councils, that create managerially efficient production units. Defenders of the German institutional status quo are therefore more or less correct to claim that the real employment problem is not the declining competitiveness of the export or import competing industries, although liberals may be right that German institutional rigidities prevent investments in new industries and services that could give Germany novel competitive advantages.

Neither status quo nor liberal market advocates, however, focus on what is in fact problematic in the Germany economy, and that is its inability to create jobs in new domestically sheltered service industries, both in its high-skill and low-skill facets. Nevertheless, the liberal reform program may have some merit even in this regard, albeit at a political and social price. Germany's high wage equality, instilled by the institutions of collective bargaining, may indeed be an inhibitor of job creation, but unrelated to shallow talk about "global competition." Controlling for the effect of international trade and capital flow openness, Iversen and Wren (1998) have convincingly shown that Western political economies face a domestic policy trilemma that forces governments to sacrifice one of three objectives: sound government fiscal policy, full employment or job creation (particularly expansion of the personal service sector), and wage equality. The Anglo-Saxon liberal model sacrifices wage equality in order to maintain the public sector fiscal balance and high employment. The Scandinavian model has traditionally opted for wage equality and full employment at the expense of fiscal rectitude, a policy that has been increasingly challenged in recent years. And continental European democracies, Germany chief among them, have emphasized wage equality and an austere fiscal policy. This has yielded high unemployment and little job creation, because wage compression discourages private demand for (service) labor, while fiscal austerity prevents the public sector from expanding the payroll to compensate for private sector employment deficits.[4]

The liberal market program may be wrong-headed in terms of its choice of instruments to encourage more demand for labor, particularly in its call for lower direct income taxation. It may make sense to expect higher investment, if retained corporate earnings are not taxed or are taxed at a lower rate than distributed earnings. But the expectation that lower personal income taxes yield more investment and job growth is on a much less firm economic footing. The political-economic literature offers no solid evidence that lower personal income tax rates account for higher investment rates, economic growth, and ultimately job creation, regardless of whether one compares income tax rates cross-nationally or within the same countries over time. Lower and less progressive income taxes primarily shift the income distribution and patterns of consumption in favor of the better-off, and increase the probability of creating a permanent, economically and politically disenfranchised poverty sector in society, such as in the United States and, increasingly, Britain, where 10 to 20 percent of citizens are not functionally incorporated in the countries' capitalist economy and democratic polity.

Renovating the German Cooperative Market Economy

My selective critique and approval of the status quo and the market-liberal evaluations of the German political economy already indicate policies I would identify with a "Third Way" political-economic program that avoids the pitfalls of the polar opposite economic programs. On the one hand, this third alternative may embrace the objective of the German social market economy to maintain and improve solidarity and cooperation between business and labor and a modicum of income equality that protects society from the appearance of a large economically and politically disenfranchised underclass. On the other hand, "third way" programs select policy instruments that create a competitive environment and provide new performance incentives to enable market actors to excel in business sectors not favored by the traditional German institutional model, whether it is "high end" human capital intensive new science-based production or service industries, or "low end" personal service employment. This "third way" program agrees with the liberal market critique of German capitalism as too rigid and inflexible to generate the jobs and life chances many citizens desire. Moreover, the political regulation of German capitalism has created fixed patterns of social and labor market inclusion and exclusion that protect certain groups and sectors from market-based performance evaluations, thus allowing them to extract economic rents at the expense of other groups who suffer high permanent unemployment or are altogether excluded from labor markets.

In short, the "third way" program calls for capitalist competition "with a human face." Its guiding principle is the insertion of competition and performance incentives into the German cooperative market economy without denying citizens basic rights to a respectable minimum of entitlements to income, health care, and education that enable them to become and to remain competent participants in the marketplace and the democratic polity. The adjustment of the German political economy institutions is necessary not so much because of the "globalization" of trade and finance, but because of the technological, organizational and cultural change of occupational profiles and opportunities in the post-industrial economy. Associated with it are demographic changes that ultimately reduce the proportion of citizens actively involved in labor markets by lengthening the acquisition process of human capital through more professional training, and by extending retirement through longer life expectancy.

These objectives and guidelines have several operational consequences for a "third way" economic program in Germany. For one thing, German sectoral collective bargaining agreements must offer more firm-level flex-ibilities, a process that may already be underway, even though regional and sectoral framework agreements (*Flächentarifvertrag*) between busi-ness and labor have stayed in place (*The Economist*, December 5, 1998: 69–70).[5] Reforms must also set stronger incentives for innovative fixed and human capital investments. This requires not only a tax reform, but also a reform of the education system to create a more competitive envi-ronment for educators and students, particularly in tertiary education and professional training. Furthermore, the public sector requires stream-lining and exposure to more performance incentives. Finally, in order to create more capital and spread the participation in the higher returns of capital to average citizens, while simultaneously beginning to address the long-term problems of the German pension system, a further pension reform could build a small, but gradually growing, funded component of individual retirement accounts into the traditional pay-as-you-go sys-tem, while simultaneously cutting back on the entitlements to pensions retirees obtain from the existing system.

None of these measures, however, will address the weaknesses of Germany's economy in generating jobs in the short and medium run. In order to achieve job growth, particularly in the domestic service sec-tor, it may be necessary, as a number of analysts have suggested (Riester and Streeck 1996: 21–22; Scharpf 1997), to permit wage contracts with wages lower than agreed in conventional collective bargaining agree-ments, to supplement low-income jobs with public subsidies, or to introduce a negative income tax, implying some kind of basic "citizen-ship income" to expand demand for labor. Finally, the experiment of the Volkswagen Corporation with work time reductions and work shar-ing, as well as the trajectory of Dutch labor markets toward a prolifer-ation of part-time employment for both men and women since the late 1980s (Visser and Hemerijk 1998), illustrate how a new centralized business-labor alliance might begin to redistribute scarce jobs so as to minimize the share of citizens permanently excluded from access to jobs in the economy.

The Social Constituencies behind Alternative
Economic Programs

Each of these scenarios—the status quo defense, liberal market reform, and "third way" reforms of the cooperative market economy—would result in a major distributive fallout. Thus, the winners and losers of alternative programs constitute political camps for whose support politicians compete in the electoral arena. After identifying the winners and losers of different economic pathways in this section, I argue in the final section that German politics before and after the 1998 election can be interpreted in terms of politicians' efforts to attract and combine a multiplicity of political-economic constituencies in a winning coalition.

The advocates of the status quo institutions encompass all those who are "inside" the current system of labor relations and corporate governance and thus "own" jobs or social policy entitlements that flow from a lifetime of full-time entitlements. Pensioners, in particular, are likely to insist on the preservation of the existing system of benefits, particularly given that the current pay-as-you-go retirement scheme constitutes a direct redistribution of benefits from the now working generations to that already in retirement. Employees in public or quasi-public employment (such as most health- and welfare-related, formally non-state services) will also fight against more exposure to competition, as has been demonstrated by struggles over the privatization of the German railroads and telecommunications sector. Finally, many (predominantly male) full-time unskilled and semi-skilled workers in industry and services are likely to object to changes in labor relations that introduce greater inequality and labor market risks. Their political representatives in the union movement are particularly likely to fight against the decentralization of collective bargaining and a greater differentiation of wages. What weakens this phalanx of status quo supporters may be inter-sectoral divisions.

Advocates of market liberalization can be found primarily among private business owners, management, and professionals in the domestic economic sectors protected from international competition. These forces see a golden opportunity to employ the rhetoric of "globalization" in order to redistribute incomes from little and moderately skilled labor to capital, and to business and human capital-intensive labor. At the same time, the existing internationally exposed manufacturing and financial corporations, all businesses operating in market niches well adapted to German political-economic institutions, may be ambivalent about far-reaching neoliberal reforms because they benefit from Germany's cooperative market economy (Soskice 1998). The breakup of employer unity in support of a reduction of wage compensation during sickness at the time of the unions' strike against the government reform bill signals these divisions in the business camp.

Business and labor in the export-oriented industries may be much more sympathetic to a "third way" economic policy that seeks efficiency gains through competition, reins in the public sector, infuses the economy with flexibility in the allocation of capital and labor through firm-level bargaining, and creates employment without worsening the burdens of payroll taxation imposed on business. Supporters of the "third way" are also numerous among the younger generation, whose members are worried about obtaining decent entry level jobs in order to gain a foothold in the formal economy, and about seeing their educational investments in human capital formation paying off. "Third way" economic programs appeal to a technical and professional intelligentsia that tends to benefit from the growth of the post-industrial service economy.

This schematic reconstruction of citizens' conflicting political-economic interests ignores, of course, the existence of non-economic interests that partially crosscut and partially reinforce the alignments detected on economic policy issues. In Germany, as in most other postindustrial service economies, a divide between libertarian cultural individualists, who tend to be overrepresented among the younger, more educated, more female personal and symbol-producing service sector employees, and authoritarian cultural collectivists, who are more prominent among older, less educated, more male citizens employed in material production and clerical-administrative professions, is particularly important (Kitschelt 1994). These divisions contribute to the complexities of party competition that German politicians must grasp when they reach out to voters in electoral campaigns.

Partisan Alignments in German Politics and the Potential for Economic Reform

The German alignment of party competition is particularly unconducive to programs that diverge from the status quo cooperative social market economy. Ironically, the greatest potential to achieve a reform of *Modell Deutschland* would present itself if the two major parties, the Christian Democrats and the Social Democrats, felt compelled to work together in a grand coalition. But neither before nor after the 1998 election have the incentives for such an alliance been particularly strong.

Efforts to enact liberal market reform typically require an electorally strong party that has no ties to the labor movement and strictly appeals to voters at or beyond the level of the median income. The German Free Democrats (FDP) approximate the profile of voters who opt for the liberal market reform programs, but in contrast to their counterparts in Scandinavia or the Low Countries, the German party has remained excessively weak. Among other reasons, the party's limited appeal is due to its transparent defense of the income and status concerns of special interest groups, such as doctors and lawyers, which drowns its potential programmatic focus on overall economic efficiency improvements flowing from liberal market reforms. Moreover, the party was in government office with Social Democrats and Christian Democrats for too long to present itself as a credible challenger of the status quo of the social market economy.

In some Western democracies, such as Austria and Italy, right-wing populist, anti-statist parties have made strong bids to deregulate and liberalize social market economies, and have compelled mainstream political parties to respond to such demands (Kitschelt 1995: chapter 5). In Germany, however, the extreme right is still steeped in national-socialist programmatic visions that include a corporatist anti-liberalism in economic and social policy. This makes it an unlikely carrier of market-liberal ideas (Kitschelt 1995: chapter 6). The Republicans, the German People's Union, and the National Democrats, all of which constitute variants of the common theme of a post-fascist German extreme right, entered the 1998 electoral campaign with social protectionist appeals calling for social redistribution in favor of the economic losers of technological and industrial change. Thus, if such parties made economic appeals at all, they certainly were not likely to advance market-liberal programs.

The near-hegemonic German party for much of the duration of the Federal Republic, the Christian Democrats, constitutes a complex cross-class and cross-sector coalition of political-economic interests that makes it excessively difficult for its politicians to endorse market-liberalizing redistributive economic reform programs. As a cross-class party, the CDU/CSU attracts considerable support among unionized workers committed to the existing social market economy. What is equally important, the party overproportionally relies on pensioners whose representatives block any profound cuts in the social security system. In a similar vein, the churches who are close to the CDU and administer a large share of Germany's means-tested welfare programs with public funds channelled through their nominally private charity organizations according to the principal of subsidiarity, protect those who would be hardest hit by a drying up of public welfare funds (Alber 1996). It is for all these reasons that it took the CDU/CSU-led government so long to agree to a program of cuts in sickness wage compensation and retirement benefits under pressure from the FDP and the intensifying debate about *Wirtschaftsstandort Deutschland*. Precisely because the CDU/CSU is a cross-class alliance with heterogeneous economic and social policy interests, there is little doubt that these redistributive policy decisions worked to the party's detriment in the 1998 electoral campaign, costing it voters who opted for the Social Democrats in September 1998 because of the latter's firm commitment to the established welfare state during the election campaign.

Never before in the history of the Federal Republic has an existing government been directly voted out of office. Also, never before in a German election has such a substantial share of voters crossed over directly from previously supporting one of the major parties, the CDU/CSU, to the other, the SPD, at a subsequent election.[6] Without doubt, the Christian-liberal government's social and economic policies were a major cause of the fall of the party in the election. The overwhelming majority of the German electorate supports the *status quo* in economic and social policy, even though voters realize that some policies have to change in order to make Germany's economy more competitive.

Ironically, the magnitude and the origins of the Social Democrats' electoral success in 1998 have created particular difficulties for the party under Chancellor Schröder to engineer social and economic policy change. The party that historically has identified itself with policy reform has been elected into government with the conservative, defensive mandate to preserve the welfare state and associated political institutions. The SPD campaigned vigorously for the reversal of the pension cuts introduced by the Kohl government, and for legislation guaranteeing workers and employees 100 percent wage compensation beginning with the first day of sickness.

But it is not only campaign promises that restrict the freedom of strategic maneuvering for the new SPD government and make it exceptionally difficult for its leading politicians to devise "third way" reforms, let alone elements of a program of market liberalization. At least three obstacles stand in the way of innovation in the areas of social and economic policy for the Schröder government.

First, the very magnitude of the SPD's electoral victory in September 1998 strengthened the hands of the SPD's traditionalists and left wing, represented in the cabinet until March 1999 by Oskar Lafontaine, who headed a finance super-ministry that includes competencies previously located in the Ministry for Economic Affairs. SPD traditionalists press for a high wage and egalitarian wage economic strategy that relies on an uncompromising defense of the status quo of *Modell Deutschland*. They call for a quick redemption of campaign promises to undo the CDU/FDP government's social policy cuts and accept only minor changes in German tax legislation. They count on jump-starting the German economy and creating jobs with concerted Europe-wide declines of interest rates and boosts to consumer spending, employing monetarist policy instruments for an essentially Keynesian strategy of demand-led growth.

Moreover, they wish to reduce the standard retirement age to sixty, a demand even Green economic experts find fiscally infeasible without heroic assumptions about economic growth and employment in coming years. Traditionalists also fight low-wage contracts with public subsidies and the expansion of part-time work and job-sharing as measures to increase employment.

Based on his record as prime minister of Lower Saxony and his success in cutting social programs by DM 30 billion in November, 1999, Schröder is the most powerful counterweight to the SPD's traditionalist wing. He is seen as leaning more toward a "third way" supply-side reform of *Modell Deutschland,* with the vision to assemble a productivity coalition of business and labor that is also open to unconventional ways for creating new employment in areas cut off by traditional German labor relations and collective bargaining institutions (negative income taxation, public wage subsidization, etc.). In order to strengthen his hand against the traditionalists, Schröder relies on the backing of Hans Eichel, the successor to Lafontaine as Finance Minister, Social Affairs Minister Walter Riester, who was a vice president of the metal workers union but has always preferred unorthodox policy views controversial in his own organization, and the chancellor's economics advisor, Klaus Gretschmann. This phalanx of non-traditionalists has relatively little clout inside the Social Democratic party organization. But what may help Schröder is firm support from the powerful SPD prime ministers in the states, particularly such outspoken technocratic politicians who support "third way" economic and social policy ideas as Wolfgang Clement (North Rhine-Westphalia) and Heide Simonis (Schleswig Holstein). It is clear that Schröder's wing in the SPD must brace itself for fierce battles with its traditionalist antagonists at all levels of the party organization, and in the union movement. The current condition of the opposition Christian Democrats, heavily damaged by the Kohl finance scandal, also strengthens Schröder's hand.

A second reason why the SPD-led government faces difficulties in embracing a "third way" inspired economic and social policy reform of *Modell Deutschland* involves the nature of the red-green coalition alliance. Before the election, SPD chancellor candidate Schröder promised a red-green coalition, if the electoral success of both parties justified it, but left the door open to a grand coalition with the CDU/CSU, if the SPD and Greens failed to win a viable majority of seats in the new legislature. Secretly, many "third way" oriented Social Democrats hoped for a coalition with the CDU because that would have bound the SPD traditionalists' hands in economic and social policy affairs and favored efficiency-oriented social and economic policy reforms. The unexpectedly solid red-green electoral victory compelled Schröder to stand by his campaign promises to ally the SPD with the Greens. It also made the

CDU/CSU unavailable for a coalition in which the SPD would have clearly been in the driver's seat.

Since the party's inception in the late 1970s, by virtue of the Greens' ideology and an electoral constituency overproportionally employed in the domestically sheltered public or non-profit sector, the new coalition partner of the SPD has been even keener on the preservation and expansion of the existing German welfare state and even more opposed to "third way," let alone market-liberalizing economic and social policy reforms, than the traditional wing of the Social Democratic party. Because the Greens still draw their support more from younger than older voters, an exception to this general policy principle is the Greens' willingness to consider alternatives to the current pay-as-you-go, earnings-related pension system, and to endorse cutbacks in pension benefits.

In the longer run, the Greens' highly educated and intellectually sophisticated voters may be amenable to considering more far-reaching economic and social policy reforms, particularly if the balance of Green voters shifts to those employed in private sector postindustrial jobs. In the short run, however, the party is committed to an economic and social policy that, on balance, strengthens the bargaining power of traditionalists inside its coalition partner, the SPD, against the chancellor and his supporters. Schröder and his backers thus have to fight on two fronts against their coalition partner and their intra-party antagonists, if they wish to push toward "third way" economic and social policy reforms.

The third obstacle to such reform policies is the current condition of the CDU/CSU, as opposition party. In the short run, the voters' memory of the Kohl government's attempted cuts in sickness income compensation and retirement pensions has made it impossible for the Christian Democrats to present themselves as the standard-bearers of the German welfare state. In the longer run, however, the public memory of these policy episodes may fade and be displaced by a renaissance of the party's long-term record and reputation as builder of the welfare state in the postwar decades. Particularly if the CDU/CSU wishes to win back "centrist" voters, it cannot antagonize them by pushing a strictly market-liberal reform program. Were the SPD's Schröder wing to prevail over its antagonists inside the party and the Greens, it might have to reckon with a Christian Democratic party that will again successfully present itself as public tribune defending the German social market economy and its welfare state, particularly the public retirement scheme, against expenditure cuts and an institutional reorganization of benefits schemes promoted by an SPD-led government in pursuit of economic efficiency and international competitiveness.

As long as the SPD and CDU are on different sides of the fence separating government and opposition, they play a prisoner's dilemma game:

optimal solutions will not come about because cooperative strategies cannot be enforced, and the iterations of the game are too few and the stakes too high for any party to risk making cooperative moves and becoming the "sucker" when the other side defects. For both parties collectively, it would be best to support at least those "third way" reforms of German economic and social policy that enhance the adaptive capabilities of the German economy and social policy regime. In the long run, such reforms might also improve both parties' chances to continue to dominate German politics jointly and keep other contenders at bay. Individually, however, each of the two parties faces temptation: were one of the parties, when controlling the government, to embrace "third way" or market-liberal reforms that inflict pain on some significant electoral constituency, the other, as opposition party, would engage in populist rhetoric and bring its reputation as builder/defender of the German welfare state and *Modell Deutschland* into play in order to attract disaffected voters away from the governing party. A grand coalition, in which both SPD and CDU participate, could enforce their mutual commitment to political-economic reform and police defections from the jointly made bargain, even in the face of temporary electoral gains by more radical fringe opposition parties on the left or the right of the government alliance. Of course, the current (February 2000) crisis of the Christian Democrats also offers the Schröder government a unique window of opportunity to enact unpopular policies with little fear of effective opposition.

Overall, intra- and inter-party alignments in German politics thus currently create strong forces that explain why the Schröder government might tread lightly in the arena of efficiency-enhancing economic and social policy reforms. Additional developments strengthen the governing party's tendency toward policy immobility. The continued weakness of the eastern German economy may motivate reform initiatives, but also makes it risky in the short run to inflict more pain on a population that is already experiencing high unemployment. In the international arena, the presence of a French socialist government that is also wedded more to conventional status quo oriented social and economic policies creates an atmosphere in which German Social Democrats have an excuse not to push for European Union wide social policy reform.

What are the chances, then, that German politics will embark on social and economic policy reforms that lead beyond marginal adjustments of the social market economy status quo in the next several years? A string of SPD defeats in state elections over the next several years would certainly create an atmosphere in which SPD politicians would frantically search for new policy avenues to shore up their fading fortunes. A changing balance of inter-party electoral relations may thus hasten a shift in intra-party power relations and alliances. But at this time, it is uncertain which side in the SPD would gain from a string of electoral defeats in important state level elections. In the face of economic and social policy immobilism, the Schröder faction could make the case that only bold initiatives can save the new government in the next federal election of 2002. Conversely, traditionalists might argue that the SPD government (and its policy) must prove and communicate its firm commitment to a social market economy more credibly than in its initial year in federal government.

A further important unknown in the equation is the future conduct of Germany's labor unions under the red-green government. Were the unions in the core export sectors to push for substantial wage hikes in the face of rising profits in 1999–2000 and thereafter, they might endanger even the maintenance of employment in economically less robust sectors and enterprises, for example by prompting an increase of real interest rates by the new European Central Bank with a dampening effect on investment and employment. Such developments would intensify conflict between the different wings of the SPD, but with an uncertain outcome for government policy.

Where the balance of power in the red-green coalition may be heading in the coming years will also depend on the future policy appeals of the CDU/CSU. After the September 1998 election, the party entered a process of renewal in terms of program and personnel. As of this writing, this process has hastened an intra-party conflict within the CDU and between the CDU and CSU. It is as yet unclear what the contours of the party's new economic and social policy program will be in the future. The internal quarrels of the new opposition party certainly have helped the Schröder government to catch its breath after a bad start and to save face in spite of bruising conflicts between SPD traditionalists and reformers in the cabinet. If the CDU/CSU eventually were to commit itself to a policy program of liberal market reforms, Schröder could be emboldened to push "third way" social and economic policy reforms inside the red-green coalition. Under such circumstances, the CDU/CSU could no longer claim to be the standard-bearer of the German welfare state, and the SPD's Schröder wing could credibly present itself to the broad spectrum of voters who wish to maintain Germany's social market economy as the "lesser evil," leaving more social protectionist provisions intact than would a potential government headed by the Christian Democratic opposition. In other words, Germany's inter-party political alignment would have to approximate that of Britain or Scandinavia, pitting rather unambiguously conservative, market-liberal parties against a centrist social democracy, before it might be electorally profitable for the SPD to pursue painful economic and social policy reforms. All of this assumes that the Christian Democrats survive and quickly recover from the current finance scandal.

Finally, supra-national policy coordination at the level of the European Union or the newly constituted "Euroland" might give Schröder opportunities to press for social and economic policy reforms, should other socialist parties in Europe gravitate toward such an option. Lacking a more reform-oriented coalition partner that would tie the SPD's hands in domestic politics, the government then might claim that Europe-wide imperatives force Germany to make compromises and revise aspects of *Modell Deutschland* for the sake of European policy harmonization. While the presence of social democratic governments in almost all European Union countries currently makes SPD traditionalists hopeful they will gain from Europe-wide concertation, these governments face challenges sufficiently diverse to make possible European policy agreements that disappoint such expectations.

Conclusion

I have argued in this chapter that neither the defense of the status quo nor a strictly market-liberal program is likely to remedy the weaknesses in the German economic performance record that began to build in the 1980s and intensified after the end of the initial unification boom in 1992/93. "Third way" and market-liberal social and economic reform policies address these weaknesses in different ways, but are likely to redistribute scarce resources in such fashion as to hurt the interests of significant electoral constituencies and powerful interest groups. What is more important, none of the major German parties faces an electoral incentives structure that would permit it unambiguously to embrace a reform program making *Modell Deutschland* profoundly more flexible and adaptable in an economic world of new challenges and opportunities.

Built into the German political economy and the German system of electoral party alignments is thus a powerful bias toward preserving the status quo. This bias is reinforced by other institutional conditions I have not even touched upon in this essay, such as the federalist system of "negative coordination" among state and federal governments, which often reduces policy reforms to the smallest common denominator approved in a multi-stage decision-making process under super-majoritarian decision rules.

All this does not preclude the emergence of major reforms under the red-green government. As always, the two midwives of policy innovation could be crisis and leadership. A prolonged economic crisis would tell politicians that they cannot go on in their established ways. In some respects, Germany's unemployment rate in the late 1990s already created a sense of crisis that is reflected in the electoral shift of the 1998 federal election. What it might take now is leadership to push through initially unpopular reforms, a personal capability of politicians that usually eludes social scientific or political processes and organizational management (Miller 1992). The jury is still out on whether Schröder and his cabinet will display the capacity for leadership that would allow Germany to embark on new avenues of political-economic reform.

Notes

1. All the figures are from *The Economist's* economic statistics pages, in the issues of 3 March 1990 (p. 98), 28 March 1992 (p. 120), 9 April 1995 (p. 127), 12 April 1997 (p. 109) and 12 December 1998 (p. 105).
2. A discussion of the market-liberal demands of the German Employer's Association can be found in Collier (1995).
3. For data on these developments, see Iversen (1998a and 1998b) and a discussion of Germany in comparative context, Streeck (1997: 35–36).
4. For data demonstrating the comparatively small size of the German service sector, particularly that of unskilled services, see Esping-Andersen (1998: 301).
5. For a broader discussion of changing German labor relations due to the structural dynamic of innovation and the German unification, see Turner (1997–1998).
6. This claim is substantiated by all of the demographic institutes' post-election analyses in 1998. The results of these investigations can be easily accessed through the institutes' web sites.

Bibliography

Alber, Jens. "Wohlfahrtsstaatliche Entwicklungen in Deutschland und den USA. Zum Modellcharakter residualer Sozialpolitik in der Kürzungsphase des Sozialstaates." University of Konstanz. Manuscript. May 1996.

———."Der deutsche Sozialstaat im Licht international vergleichender Daten." To appear in *Leviathan (1998)*.

Carlin, Wendy and David Soskice. "Shocks to the System: The German Political Economy Under Stress." *National Institute Economic Review*, 1/1997, no. 159: 57–76.

Collier, Irwin L. Jr. "Rebuilding the German Welfare State," pp. 273–94. In David P. Conradt, Gerald R. Kleinfeld, George K. Romoser, Christian Søe, eds. *Germany's New Politics: Parties and Issues in the 1990s.* Providence and London: Berghahn Publishers, 1995.

Esping-Andersen, Goesta. "Politics without Class: Postindustrial Cleavages in Europe and America," pp. 293–316. In Herbert Kitschelt, Peter Lange, Gary Marks, and John Stephens, eds. *The Politics and Political Economy of Advanced Industrial Societies.* Cambridge: Cambridge University Press, 1998.

Iversen, Torben. "Wage Bargaining, Hard Money and Economic Performance. Theory and Evidence for Organized Market Economies." *British Journal of Political Science*, 28, 1 (1998): 31–61.

————. "Wage Bargaining, Central Bank Independence, and the Real Effects of Money." *International Organization*, 52, 3 (1998): 460–504.

Iversen, Torben, and Anne Wren. "Equality, Employment, and Budgetary Restraint: The Trilemma of the Service Economy." *World Politics* 50, 4 (1998).

Kitschelt, Herbert. "Industrial Governance, Innovation Strategies, and the Case of Japan: Sectoral or Cross-National Analysis?" *International Organization* 45, 4 (1991):453–94.

————. *The Transformation of European Social Democracy*. New York: Cambridge University Press, 1994.

————. "European Social Democracy between Political Economy and Electoral Competition," pp. 317–45. In Herbert Kitschelt, Peter Lange, Gary Marks, and John Stephens, eds. *The Politics and Political Economy of Advanced Industrial Societies*. Cambridge: Cambridge University Press, 1998.

Kitschelt, Herbert (in collaboration with Anthony J. McGann). *The Radical Right in Western Europe. A Comparative Analysis*. Ann Arbor: Michigan University Press, 1995.

Miller, Gary. *Managerial Dilemmas*. Cambridge: Cambridge University Press, 1992.

Riester, Walter, and Wolfgang Streeck. *Solidarität, Arbeit, Beschäftigung*. SPD-Parteivorstand. Bonn, September 1996.

Scharpf, Fritz. *Employment and the Welfare State: A Continental Dilemma*. Cologne: Working Paper of the Max Planck Institute for Social Research 6/97.

Soskice, David. "Divergent Production Regimes: Coordinated and Uncoordinated Market Economies in the 1980s and 1990s," pp. 101–34. In Herbert Kitschelt, Peter Lange, Gary Marks, and John Stephens, eds. *The Politics and Political Economy of Advanced Industrial Societies*. Cambridge: Cambridge University Press, 1998.

Streeck, Wolfgang. "German Capitalism: Does It Exist? Can It Survive?" pp. 55–70. In Colin Crouch and Wolfgang Streeck, eds. *Political Economy of Modern Capitalism*. London: Sage Publications, 1997.

Turner, Lowell, ed. *Negotiating the New Germany: Can Social Partnership Survive?* Ithaca, New York: Cornell University Press, 1997.

————. *Fighting for Partnership: Labor and Politics in Unified Germany*. Ithaca, NY: Cornell University Press, 1998.

Visser, Jelle, and Anton Hemerijk. *Ein Holländisches Wunder? Reform des Sozialstaates und Beschäftigung in den Niederlanden*. Frankfurt, Main: Campus, 1998.

Chapter 12

CONTINUITY?

German Foreign Policy at the Turn of the Century

Wolfgang-Uwe Friedrich

Continuity or discontinuity? That was the question when the red-green coalition won the German federal elections in September of 1998. Could NATO and the partner nations within the European Union trust the new German government? Would red-green follow the successful concept of integration into the various institutions that bind Germany so closely to the West?

This chapter will describe the foreign policy positions of the two government parties when they were in the opposition, specifically what positions they took with respect to NATO and to the EU, what programs they then developed, and what pragmatic policies they represent today.

Chancellor Gerhard Schröder, Foreign Minister Joschka Fischer, and Defense Minister Rudolf Scharping are the most prominent representatives of the pragmatic policies of the new government. In the first half of 1999, this new government not only held the Presidency of the European Union and of the West European Union, but also chaired the G-8 Conference. Above all, this new government led Germany's first military engagement since 1945, in Kosovo.

Old Institutions and Changing Roles

Germans do not want major changes, but the world underwent fundamental changes in the last decade of the twentieth century: war in the Balkans and in Africa, instability in the Near East and in the Caucasus, Russia's ongoing crises, tensions among the new nuclear powers India and Pakistan, China's uncertainties, North Korean aggressiveness, severe financial problems in most Third World countries, environmental problems, migration, terrorism, fundamentalism, and international crime. Europe is affected by all of these problems, sometimes more, sometimes less than the United States. But, after the end of the Cold War, Western Europe and the United States are increasingly taking different positions on international questions. The bipolar world with two superpowers, the United States and the Soviet Union, has been replaced. Now there is only one superpower, not powerful enough to establish a new world order by itself. The United States needs strategic partners, and Germany and Japan have the power to play this role.

While Germany has a special relationship with the United States, its closest partners are its neighbors in Western Europe. Among the various multipolar regional systems, Europe is the most important one. The European Union (EU) integrates fifteen states with about 370 million inhabitants and an economic and financial strength similar to that of the United States. Among the ten countries with the highest GDP in the world, there are five in Europe, led by Germany with $2.4 trillion ($28,870 per capita in comparison to $28,020 per capita in the U.S. in 1996). In 1997 the EU countries together exported goods and services worth 718 billion ECU, while imports amounted to 668 billion ECU, the intra-union trade not included. The EU contributed 20 percent of the world export and 17 percent of imports (again without intra-union trade, and in comparison with U.S. shares of 17 percent and 20 percent respectively). The U.S. is by far the EU's biggest trading partner with a total turnover of about 278 billion ECU (1997) and an almost balanced exchange. And the EU is the world's biggest exporter of capital. Britain, Germany, France, and the Netherlands in 1994/95 had a foreign investment of $770 billion, in comparison with $456 billion for the U.S. and $455 billion for Japan.

While economic questions dominate the domestic agenda and have so far led to very different answers in Britain, France, and Germany, all of these governments agree that the EU should play a more important role in international relations. The EU, however, is still no single political actor. Although there is no hegemony in Europe, Germany is by far the leading nation, while France and Britain still have their special status as nuclear powers and members of the UN Security Council. Many foreign leaders perceive German power as a potentially dominating force. However, the constitutional and other legal norms, the institutional structure of the Western Alliance, and the nation's goals clearly indicate a continuation of its policy of integration and cooperation.

The 1997 Treaty of Amsterdam went into effect in 1999. In a series of agreements and treaties culminating in the establishment of the EU, the Amsterdam accord represented a further development of the three-pillar concept of the EU structure: (1) an internal market with an economic and currency union; (2) a common foreign and security policy; (3) close cooperation in domestic and legal policies. The Treaty assumes that many areas of policy will be ever more coordinated, and that there will be a common social policy. Most importantly, a common currency was introduced on 1 January 1999. This new currency, the Euro, should take its place in international trade, and any mistakes or false signals during its introduction would, it is assumed, be gradually overcome. The economic and financial sector would also be a test of German power within the EU. The power of France was expected to be demonstrated in the common foreign and security policy. In both cases, the actual exercise of power would follow the requirement of partnership. The EU has been "damned to be successful." It is simply too important and too crucial a project for all of the countries involved to be allowed to fail. The alternative would be to fall back into a system of individual power struggles among all of the national states. This frightful prospect propels Europe to a successful EU.

For all of its shortcomings, the integration of these European countries into the EU creates something entirely new and different. Through the European Union, Germany could be incorporated into a supranational power system. In the security area, Germany was already tied within NATO. The success of this international alliance is not disputed, but after the end of a bipolar world, questions have arisen about its future. The Western powers have decided to continue with it. However, the world has not become more secure in recent years: witness the Russian crises, the war in the former Yugoslavia, the instability in the Mediterranean, international threats caused by an arms race among many countries, and the proliferation of nuclear armaments. The question arises as to whether NATO is in any position to contribute to a solution of these problems, or whether new institutions should be created to deal with them. There are lively and controversial discussions about the future of the UN, the OSCE (the Organization for Security and Cooperation in Europe), the WEU (Western European Union), and also NATO. While NATO is still the most important military alliance in the world, it clearly will have new European institutions created alongside it.

In all these discussions, the assumption has been that the European Union will continue to prosper. But there is no guarantee that this will happen at all. While more and more power is to be transferred from national governments to EU institutions, there is so far a considerable lack of democratic legitimacy on the EU level. The freely elected European Parliament plays no important role, although it is gaining somewhat more power than before. The European Commission, on the other hand, is powerful in terms of economic decisions. But the governments still play the key role, and their agenda is so far primarily formulated by national interest. The European public is still largely composed of different national audiences, as witnessed by the European Parliament elections in June 1999. Geography, culture, language, institutions, and history have created a differentiated European landscape. There is no European government that formulates a European policy, but rather fifteen governments that seek reelection by their national voters, who care most about national politics. What nonetheless binds these fifteen nations together is the shared experience of centuries of wars and destruction and the last five decades of peace and prosperity, and the knowledge, at least of their elites, that no national state is capable of solving major problems by itself.

New Leaders and Changing Parties

Between the federal election of 1998 and the Kosovo war of 1999, Germans witnessed one of the most dramatic changes in a governing coalition's foreign policy since the founding of the Federal Republic. A traditionally military-skeptical, NATO-critical, and UN-loving SPD became an advocate of intervention in the Balkans, and a more or less pacifist Alliance '90/The Greens finally agreed to support the ongoing NATO bombing of Serbia. Any political scientist who is intrigued by quantitative analysis should carefully study the events of spring 1999 and then reevaluate his or her opinion about the importance of leaders. Clearly, interests played a vital role, and institutions channeled the decisions. But what did Schröder and Fischer say in the past about NATO, military force, and the United Nations, and what did they actually decide after becoming chancellor and foreign minister? Here is the change: Once in power, Schröder and Fischer did what Kohl and Kinkel would have done, and the SPD and the Greens supported what the CDU/CSU and FDP in the past had always proclaimed as correct.

Until late 1998, Gerhard Schröder had—like his predecessors Helmut Kohl and the first federal chancellor, Konrad Adenauer—no foreign policy experience. Having visited Fidel Castro long before the election campaign began, and suffered some criticism while he sought to promote trade through a regional arrangement with the Belarussian dictator Lukashenko, he was not insensitive to the risky side of international politics. During the election campaign, Schröder visited Israel and decided to avoid any foreign policy pronouncements. In a news magazine interview, he frankly admitted his belief that while foreign policy issues could not contribute to an election victory, spontaneously made remarks could effect the outcome negatively. In other words, simple and even banal comments could create great controversies and damage a candidate's profile. Therefore, it was not clear exactly what kind of foreign policy he had in mind. His designation of Madame Sauzay, the former French president's chief interpreter, as his adviser for Franco-German relations, was described by advisors as a lark, with no significance for the alliance between the two countries.

In fact, Schröder's record on foreign policy was somewhat disturbing to those who supported *Westbindung* (Germany's attachment to the West) as *raison d'état* of the Federal Republic. As a leader in the Young Socialists, he took a radical anti-NATO and anti-American position early in his career. Many of these foreign policy perspectives were not abandoned when he became minister-president of Lower Saxony; he remained a critic especially of NATO policy. A provincial governor, however, had no need to take foreign policy positions that affected the destiny of the country. American governors running for the presidency similarly lack foreign policy experience, and often have perspectives that need to be revised once they are elected and have the responsibilities of power. Eugen Gerstenmaier, speaker of the Bundestag under Adenauer, was once asked about apparently radical positions of the then SPD opposition. He shrugged and responded that these would change once they came to power.

In the early 1980s Schröder demonstrated against NATO's dual track decision, and as minister-president of Lower Saxony he publicly opposed the Gulf War. Before becoming the SPD's chancellor candidate, he exploited popular resentments about European integration for election purposes. He seemed to be a man without principles who believed in a mere Machiavellian approach to politics: power, not principles, as the politician's only desire.

His critics were surprised once he took office. They overlooked Schröder's realism. His emphasis on the *neue Mitte* (new middle) clearly indicated that, as chancellor, he would never risk Germany's mature and trusted alliance within the Western community of nations. As minister-president, he had shown that he was above all a pragmatist. His economic credo—that there is no leftist or rightist economic policy, but only a successful or an unsuccessful one—did not endear him to the SPD faithful. Schröder is in fact an SPD leader in the tradition of Helmut Schmidt, not Willy Brandt.

Schröder's running mate in 1998, the then SPD chairman and first finance minister of the new government, Oskar Lafontaine, is far more ideological and committed to classic socialist ideals of equality and social justice to be achieved through the power of the state. Lafontaine was also a provincial governor (of the Saarland), and he had also taken critical positions on German foreign policy. But Lafontaine is closer to Brandt than Schmidt. Lafontaine has close contacts to the French left, but no real partners in the U.S. or Britain, nor any deep understanding of Anglo-American cultures. He had a long history of criticizing Helmut Schmidt. He once published a book entitled *Angst vor den Freunden* (Being afraid of our friends), in which he essentially rejected NATO's defense policy. Although he and Schröder proclaimed their agreement during the campaign, many observers expected that they would eventually fall out. His short-lived activities on the international stage after becoming finance minister, including meetings with the then U.S. Treasury Secretary Robert Rubin, showed his unwillingness to come to terms with realities. Lafontaine was a leader of the old left, and his March 1999 departure from the government was not a surprise. His policy preferences, however, have more supporters within the SPD than do Schröder's, as seen by Schröder's contested election as the new party chairman in April 1999. When Lafontaine resigned after six months in office, Schröder had won the power game for the time being. Lafontaine's successor as finance minister, Hans Eichel, is as pragmatic as the chancellor. Eichel will closely cooperate with his Western counterparts and respect the independence of the Bundesbank and the European Central Bank.

The foreign policy positions of Schröder, Scharping, and Lafontaine reflect the broad spectrum of SPD views. From the end of the 1970s until the spring of 1999, the pacifist wing of the SPD, supported by détente politicians such as Egon Bahr, was very influential in the party. More precisely, this was a nuclear-pacifist wing that was not against a land defense in principle, but rejected atomic weapons. They directed their main criticism against Cruise and Pershing-II missiles and the strategy of flexible response, and therefore against NATO, the security policy of Helmut Schmidt, and the United States. Bahr, Lafontaine, and Schröder all represented these positions. For people in this wing of the party, NATO was more a provocation and a millstone than a guarantor of peace and freedom. The détente and peace politicians controlled the programmatic direction of the SPD, which found its result in the Basic Program of 1989. This program conceived of a world of peace and détente, based upon a dissolution of military alliances, including NATO. The slogan was "common security." Atomic and chemical weapon free zones for Europe were proposed. The Bundeswehr was only to be used for defense of the territorial integrity of the country. Further, it should be transformed through disarmament into a military force that was "structurally incapable" of aggression—a difficult goal, given the tanks, rockets, and jet fighters the federal armed forces possessed.

This wing of the SPD underestimated the destructive potential of aggressive dictatorships. Leading SPD politicians demonstrated against the Gulf War, opposed the intervention in Somalia, and generally distanced themselves from the country's military. For the SPD Left, NATO and WEU were dismal examples of the "militarization" of foreign policy.[1]

The SPD's 1994 election program marked a change from this leftist direction. It credited NATO with a stabilizing role in international relations.

At the same time, however, the party voted in the Bundestag against the use of the German military forces out of the NATO region. At that time, Rudolf Scharping concentrated his energies on changing this position. Scharping discreetly encouraged a decision from the Federal Constitutional Court (Germany's version of the Supreme Court) on the constitutionality of deploying German forces out of the NATO area. The Court finally decided that such use was in fact in conformity with the Constitution, providing that the Bundestag voted in favor of any specific deployment. At that point, with the court decision providing sufficient political cover, the SPD began to change its defense policy. In December 1996 the SPD voted for German participation in the NATO peace-keeping force (SFOR) in Bosnia-Herzegovina, a clear reversal of its 1994 position. Scharping was leading the party step by step toward a mainstream defense policy. The nuclear pacifists and détente politicians of the SPD began to lose their prominence in the party. Later in 1996, Scharping was able to kill one of their projects, a planned statement calling for a reduction of NATO's role in favor of a more European security system that would have included a major role for Russia.

In 1997 the realists were successful in securing party approval for a new foreign and defense policy program, "Social Democratic Foreign Policy for the Twenty-First Century."[2] This new policy included such statements as "it is necessary to have the power and to be prepared to use military means in order to hinder the use of force" in international relations. The program carefully outlined plans to rebuild the Western European Union (WEU) into a European defense component, which would lead to a strengthening of European identity. A careful discussion of the role of NATO was included, and the Alliance was given prominent mention.

The basic elements of this policy were adopted by the SPD Party Congress on 3 December 1997. It was given a pacifist preamble, which declared that "Germany must take a point position in international politics as a civilian power (*Zivilmacht*). Its foreign and security policy should be fundamentally ecological, and part of a globally oriented economic and social policy, which would provide a far better contribution to security, peace and responsible development." What is important about this program is that the SPD did not give up on its idealist political vision, which included the strengthening of the UN and the Organization for Security and Cooperation in Europe (OSCE), but at the same time accepted the fundamentals of the Western Alliance.

The 1998 SPD election program contained the clearest statements thus far of a realistic course in foreign policy: "NATO is indispensable for the security and stability of Europe … the Bundeswehr provides an indispensable service for our society." Of course, this program also contains old confessions of loyalty to peace and détente, strengthening the UN and creating a European peace order. But most striking is the commitment to realism. The Bosnian mission of the Bundeswehr is mentioned with praise. Blue-helmet service for the UN is supported. The SPD declares its intention to offer the UN a Bundeswehr contingent for peacekeeping missions.

The Mainstreaming of the Greens

The new realism of the SPD in foreign policy owes much to the work of Rudolf Scharping and his chief deputy in the parliamentary party, Günter Verheugen. In the case of Alliance '90/The Greens, this move to the mainstream was the work of Joschka Fischer. Just as Schröder's realism could have been foreseen before he became chancellor, so Fischer, once the hero of the Greens on the barricades, had already made his transition from radicalism to pragmatism.

Fischer managed his route to the Foreign Office with some remarkable changes in his previous political positions. He began his course correction in 1979, when he spoke out against fundamentalist Green pacifism in the face of the mass graves in Pol Pot's Cambodia. This was at a time when the Greens were agitating against the NATO dual-track decision on the deployment of the Pershing missiles, and it had an impact within his party. Fifteen years later, Fischer's close party comrade, Daniel Cohn-Bendit, demanded aerial bombardment of Serbia in order to interdict the policy of ethnic cleansing in Bosnia. Fischer spoke—like Helmut Kohl—of the role of history, which prevented Germany itself from getting actively involved in the Balkans. During the Kosovo conflict, he finally completed his change of course: out of a sense of responsibility for human rights, in order to prevent the mass murder of an entire population, Fischer voted for German military deployment. This took him further than his party was then ready to go, and he needed to convince his colleagues.

Far more than the SPD, the Greens had problems in their transition to a new foreign policy. In particular, their attitudes to NATO, the European Union, and the WEU were all rooted in the past.[3] The Green movement was traditionally radical-pacifist and radical-ecological, and thereby either explicitly or implicitly anti-Western and anti-capitalistic. The Greens rejected the foreign and defense policies of the Schmidt and Kohl governments in Germany and those of Carter, Reagan, Bush, and Clinton in the United States. When Manon Maren-Grisebach, then a member of the Greens' Party Executive, characterized the peaceful intentions of the Soviet Union in 1983 as "more credible" than those of the United States, she was expressing the majority opinion in the party.

The first federal political program of the Greens proclaimed a politics "free from power," thus an absence of power politics in the foreign policy sphere and a commitment to active peace politics. They advocated the abolition of A (atomic), B (biological), and C (chemical) weapons. They took a position of equidistance between East and West, demanding the withdrawal of foreign troops from all European countries, and the dissolution of the Warsaw Pact as well as of NATO. In 1981, the party Executive publicly accused Chancellor Schmidt, Foreign Minister Genscher, and other leading members of the government and the CDU opposition of "preparing a war of aggression." This kind of total departure from reality, combined with a desperate need for publicity, was characteristic of the Greens in that period. They thought and acted as they felt, never thinking or realizing that, if they had succeeded, they would have shoved the Federal Republic of Germany into complete international isolation. Of course, there were many wings in the party/movement, and there were critical voices. But the majority that wrote the party's programs were fundamentalists (*Fundis*). The Green programs in 1987 and 1990 were also far out of the mainstream.

Two developments which had a profound impact on Green foreign policy were the crisis in the Balkans, which began in 1991 with the secession of Croatia and Slovenia from the Yugoslav federation, and the accelerated process of European integration. In 1991 several influential "realist" Greens (*Realos*) called for the recognition of the independence of Slovenia and Croatia. A year later some Greens even advocated the use of military force to liberate those held in camps in the former Yugoslavia. In December 1994 a special party conference approved German participation in blue-helmet operations. Bosnia became a turning point. Fischer openly declared after the massacre at Srebrenica that doing nothing was to be just as guilty. He and the *Realos* spoke out for military intervention. The Bundestag caucus was, however, still divided when it came to the Dayton Accords. In December 1995, twenty-two Greens voted for the government's decision on German participation, and twenty-two against with five abstentions.

European integration became the second issue that challenged the Greens' idealism. Green members of the European Parliament called for a fundamentally new and realistic approach to Europe. The party was critical of the limited democracy of the European political machinery. Under the influence of Joschka Fischer, in early 1998 the party voted for the European Economic and Currency Union. In the Bundestag debates, Fischer took pains to speak respectfully of Chancellor Helmut Kohl for his significant achievements on behalf of Europe.

The Greens' 1998 election program focused on several foreign policy issues: human rights, disarmament, strong ties to international organizations, an "ecological-solidarity world order," and a "civilianization and demilitarization of international politics." This spectrum included a strengthening of the United Nations and the OSCE, and a rejection of military force for the purpose of bringing about peace. Although the progressive integration of Germany into the European Union was approved, the program rejected the WEU, which it proposed to dissolve. NATO was to be dissolved as well, gradually being replaced by a "total European peace and security order." The Magdeburg Party Conference of 1998 also rejected NATO's eastward expansion, but Fischer and the *Realos* voted for it in the Bundestag. The *Realos* were successful on one point: "Germany must not withdraw alone from NATO: This would disturb the international dialogue and have the effect of reviving a German *Sonderweg*."[4] Still, the program called for Germany to make its own suggestions for this kind of peace and security initiative, to eliminate universal military service and conscription, to shrink the Bundeswehr to less than 200,000 men, to dissolve crisis reaction forces, and to refuse to participate in major weapons systems. NATO policies, said the program, provoke "armed adventurism, into which Germany could also be drawn."

Generally, this program was a step along the route to a new foreign policy for the Alliance '90/The Greens, as they move toward acceptance of the realistic security needs of the country while attempting to preserve the fundamental propositions of their peace positions.

Governing

These programmatic disputes meant little after the September election victory. The Greens, and above all Joschka Fischer, were now in power and had to show that they could govern. The foreign policy agenda of Schröder and Fischer includes a reform of the European Union according to the terms of the Treaty of Amsterdam, the negotiation of a new NATO doctrine designed to embrace new members from Eastern Europe, and dealing with the Kosovo crisis, which shortly was to escalate into a war.

In its first official pronouncement, the new government promised continuity in foreign policy. The new foreign minister told his staff on his first day in office "We have quite properly struck a tone of continuity in our foreign policy agenda. Why is continuity so important? It is so important not only because Germany depends so much on Europe, but because one of the most important foreign policy factors for us is the collective memory of our neighbors about German history." He then called attention to the broad spectrum of public support for the main lines of German foreign policy, and repeated the three constants that he had mentioned in a lecture in the previous June: a Germany characterized by self-restraint, permanently bound within Europe, and part of a transatlantic community.[5]

Nevertheless, the coalition agreement of October 20 does contain some new foreign policy accents that represent the political goals of the two parties. Under the rubric "German foreign policy is peace policy," the paper places as the first priority cooperation with Germany's neighbors. International law and human rights received special emphasis. In the following section on European unity, while political union was mentioned as the final goal, unity in social and ecological policy was also given status as a necessary and contingent part of overall union. The coalition agreement went on to commit the government to conflict prevention and peaceful resolution of conflicts through the OSCE and the UN. NATO was described as "an indispensable instrument for the stability and security of Europe." NATO operations that are not related to the defense of Federal territory should be tied to the norms and standards of the UN and the OSCE. Both parties affirmed that the United States "is the most important non-European partner of Germany."

The SPD and the Greens agreed on initiatives for disarmament and arms control. The government should engage itself toward a "renunciation of the first use of atomic weapons." The United Nations, as the most important institution for the resolution of global problems, should be offered stand-by forces for peacekeeping missions. The "monopoly of force" possessed by the United Nations should be supported. Germany should be prepared to become a permanent member of the Security Council. A Defense Structure Commission should have the responsibility, on the basis of a broader definition of security, to analyze the security needs of Germany and to make proposals. German-French friendship should be maintained and, in the framework of the Weimar Triangle, relations with Poland and the Czech Republic should be raised to a new level. The security of Israel should be supported, and the good relations with Russia and Ukraine should be further developed.

This foreign policy program contains potential trouble spots in only a few areas. For example, regimes that trample on human rights can scarcely be expected to be pleased with German warnings about their policies. In June 1999, Joschka Fischer received the Dalai Lama in the Foreign Ministry, as had his predecessor, Klaus Kinkel. Another point is the declaration on non-first use of atomic weapons, a fundamental element of Green identity. When Joschka Fischer brought this up on 8 December 1998 in a NATO meeting in Brussels, the three nuclear powers in the Alliance rejected it at once. The comment in the *Washington Post* that Fischer's demand had "shocked and angered" the Clinton administration might have been exaggerated, as well as the editorial's reminder that Germany is, after all, a non-nuclear power.[6] Federal Defense Minister Rudolf Scharping had already learned the United States' position about this in his conversations with U.S. Secretary of Defense William Cohen, if indeed he ever needed to ask. The German defense minister promptly tried to play down the matter, but an unsavory aftertaste of unreliability remained. It had long been the policy of the Americans, British, and French to leave potential opponents guessing about military policy and reactions as a means to deter aggression. The nuclear powers firmly believe that aggression is best deterred not by explaining what one would do in the event it occurs, but by failing to explain it. It was not that the nuclear powers intended to act first with nuclear powers, but that they thought it unrealistic to declare it. In fact, much of official Washington expected that Fischer was merely giving voice to an idealistic part of the Coalition Treaty and his own party's program, something that he knew would be turned down. At the same time, Scharping and Fischer worked toward leveraging the WEU to become the European pillar of NATO. The foreign minister attempted at Brussels to carry through the coalition agreement against his own party's preference by suggesting that WEU operations could be carried out utilizing NATO resources. Here, one can see the principle of interlocking institutions operating.

The foreign and security policies of the new federal government are generally compatible with those of NATO. On the occasion of the fiftieth anniversary of the Alliance in April 1999, the member states signed "The Washington Declaration."[7] "Collective security" remains the core of the military compact. Even though there is no foreseeable threat, this is a legitimization for NATO. There are obviously "new challenges," but there is no unanimity on how one should respond to them. Attempts by the United States to utilize NATO for global questions would be beyond its capacity. The decision that NATO made to act on humanitarian grounds with respect to the catastrophe in Kosovo is no precedent for a global policy of interventionism. It seems appropriate from the standpoint of security issues to construct Combined Joint Task Forces, but this is problematical from the standpoint of foreign policy as long as the United States holds to the view that "As we build the arch to the twenty-first century, the CJTF concept will be the keystone."[8]

The German government is under pressure from both political parties and the public not to support the use of force without a mandate from the United Nations. This self-limitation of German military power is a lesson from history, and it would serve Germany's partners well not to call this central element of democratic political culture into question. Joschka Fischer and Rudolf Scharping will unquestionably carry out a policy which takes this self-limitation seriously, and that policy will be based upon a broader political consensus than merely red-green. Respect for this aspect of German foreign policy is a precondition for the appropriate care of transatlantic relations, and it is of paramount meaning not only for Germans, but also for Norwegians, Danes, Netherlanders, Italians, and many others who think alike.

The Washington Declaration proclaims NATO to be open for further new members. While the Americans see this aspect from the perspective of a global power, the Germans see it from the perspective of a regional, European power. Unquestionably, the NATO expansion that brought in Poland, Hungary, and the Czech Republic has benefited Germany's security position. Now that the eastern borders of NATO have been extended to the Bug River and the Carpathian Mountains, the Federal Republic is factually Europe's central power. On the other hand, though a continuation of this expansion will bring Germany no further security, it would bring a risk if Russia feels threatened. Therefore, the federal government will lay increasing stress on consideration for Russia's interests and on bringing Russia and also Ukraine into the European security architecture, as was evident in Paris in 1997, with the signing of the Founding Act on Mutual Relations, Cooperation, and Security between NATO and the Russian Federation. The same is the case for the Charter on a Distinctive Partnership between NATO and Ukraine, signed the same year in Madrid. The cooperation between German and Russian troops in KFOR (Kosovo Administration Force) can be a further confidence-building measure, but it can also prove once again how difficult it is to calculate what Russian policy will be. The weaknesses of this east European great power, and its ongoing crisis, remain a major problem in international politics for the foreseeable future.

In March 1999 in Berlin, and in June in Cologne, Germany held the presidency of the European Union and succeeded in keeping the momentum going. Usually, there is some sort of breakthrough in these six-month terms of a country's presidency, but at least it was possible this time to prevent a stalemate or a retreat. The plan, which resulted, known as Agenda 2000, would regulate the financial structure of the EU through the year 2006, and it contains complicated reforms of the agricultural policies of the EU as well as structural reforms. The Germans wanted a reduction in their contributions. However, France, Spain, and Britain were able to retain their special privileges, and Germany had to accept that there would at least be no increase in its net payments. These remained at the level of about a net annual German payment to the Union of DM 20 billion. At the same time, the EU agreed to continue negotiations with potential future members and partners.

In the United Nations as well, the new government marched to a different drummer from its predecessor on nuclear questions. When the General Assembly took up the routine question of abolishing all nuclear weapons, all NATO countries traditionally voted no. This time, Germany did not vote no, but abstained. Britain, France, and the United States promptly criticized the German position.[9] These positions are not likely to change German foreign policy significantly because Germany's partners do not find themselves in a position that makes it necessary for them to agree, or to give in. Germany merely takes a minority position in the Alliance. On the other hand, they can be something of a potential risk to transatlantic relations and to German-French relations because of the changed international situation of the past several years. For example, Germany and the United States judge rogue states differently, and therefore follow a different agenda with reference to them. This harbors risks. Similarly, the expansion of NATO is differently considered. In Berlin, one is more inclined to be sympathetic to Russian sensitivities. The German Foreign Office does not welcome American involvement in the Caucasus and in the Trans-Caspian region. At the same time, Russia and other states who are looking for more independence from the U.S. look to Germany to assist them in developing this. Among states who see this as a possibility are those in Latin America and the Arab world. The German government generally follows a different policy from that of the United States in the Third World. For example, Germany is more likely to support forgiveness of debt. Thus, there are problems adrift with the World Bank, the International Monetary Fund, and the World Trade Organization.

War in the Balkans

Transatlantic relations in the first half of 1999 were totally dominated by the Kosovo conflict. As Schröder and Fischer met with Clinton on 8 October 1988, this region was already seething with trouble. On the same day, the NATO Council in Brussels voted in favor of the bombing of Serbia. However, the president refrained from making concrete demands on his German guests. The Germans felt that their commitment to the Alliance was being tested. On October 12, in Bonn, they were presented with Clinton's query whether they would support a NATO engagement without prior UN approval. After a short consultation with the caretaker Chancellor Kohl, still in office for a few more days, they agreed. The German Federal Republic stood loyally with NATO and followed the foreign policy of the superpower across the Atlantic—in other words, continuity. On October 16 the Bundestag agreed, with 500 votes in favor, 62 opposed, and 18 abstentions. The way was free for participation in air operations to avoid a humanitarian disaster. The Alliance '90/The Greens remained divided, but the SPD voted with an overwhelming majority in favor, as they had for the SFOR mission in April.

The following months led to the most serious test of the solidarity of the new government. First of all, Schröder and Fischer had to understand that the real power situation was such that, once the U.S. had reached a decision of this kind, whatever it was, all of the Alliance members had to agree. Fischer expressed it thusly: "In this Alliance, there is one melon, two apples, and a few peas." The three nuclear powers had more weight than any others, but Fischer was clearly exaggerating when he implied that Germany had no more weight than Denmark or Belgium. And the chancellor and the foreign minister found out that there are dictators who remain totally unmoved by rational arguments and who do not care about the fate of their own people. Fischer was non-plussed by reports of the massacre of Racak, by his fruitless efforts at negotiation with Milosevic and Miliutinovic, and by the incredible stream of refugees from Kosovo. Schröder and Fischer were astounded that France and Britain agreed to chair the Rambouillet negotiations jointly, without Germany, which was allowed little more than attendance. On the other hand, Germany again took the lion's share of the refugees from the beleaguered province. The new government resolved that this would not happen again.[10]

In May–June 1999, Bonn became the center of negotiations that finally led to a successful conclusion of the Kosovo conflict. In contrast to Rambouillet, Fischer, his new state secretary Wolfgang Ischinger, and the new political director of the Foreign Office Günter Pleuger played key roles. They were supported by a special Kosovo Crisis Staff under Ambassador Pauls, who assisted in creating a Russian-American dialogue. Ischinger stressed how important it would be to bring "Russia into the boat." The Americans realized this, and ultimately sent Strobe Talbott into the effort. Schröder, though Germany was not a permanent member of the Security Council, introduced discussions with UN Secretary-General Kofi Annan, then encouraged Chinese-American talks, and finally buried the unfortunate Italian plan of Massimo d'Alema. He played a significant role in bringing in the Finnish president Martti Ahtisaari as a "neutral" mediator. Among the most important results of this series of negotiations must be counted the G-8 Declaration of 6 May 1999, in which Russia gave its approval for the withdrawal of Serbian units from Kosovo and in which it was not only established that the UN would be the guarantor for the presence of international forces, but also that China would be a part of the process.[11] The Fischer Plan of April 4 included this overall concept, and also contained other vital elements of the final agreements.[12] Southeastern European countries were to be encouraged to support the process by means of German material aid.[13] The stability pact for the Balkans was called "Total Concept" (*Gesamtkonzept*) while Kinkel was foreign minister. It was nothing really new, but it was now resurrected and made a part of the general agenda. Nevertheless, it remains to be seen what will come out of it—what amounts of aid, credits, investments, and trade concessions will be offered to countries in the region. The Federal Republic had achieved within the Alliance what it had wanted from the beginning, namely, a political solution to the conflict.

On 11 June 1999, the Bundestag voted 505 to 24, with 11 abstentions, to send 8,500 Bundeswehr troops as the German contingent in the NATO peace-keeping force (KFOR). In his speech before the parliament, Fischer concluded that European security could thusly be cemented through cooperation within the triangle formed by the United States, Russia, and the EU. One of the consequences of the Kosovo conflict is the European consensus that, without a common effort to create a common foreign and security policy, they are too weak a player on the international scene.

The consensus between the government and opposition in the Kosovo issue was not shared by public opinion. According to an Allensbach survey of May 1999, only 47 percent of the population supported a military engagement of NATO forces in the case of a threat to the existence of an ethnic minority. Fully 36 percent were opposed and wanted to see NATO exclusively as a defensive alliance. In that poll, 50 percent in western Germany were in favor, but in the former area of the German Democratic Republic, only 26 percent approved.[14] Weekly polls by the EMNID organization gave a somewhat different picture, but their questions were not identical to those of Allensbach. Aside from situations in which there were civilian casualties, EMNID found that an average of 60 percent of the German public supported the air assaults and about one-third opposed them. At the same time, two-thirds of the public were opposed to sending in ground troops to fight the Serbs.[15]

At the special SPD party congress, the leadership succeeded in getting a large majority of the delegates to back the government's policies, even though the lively debate brought out many on the left who wanted to bring in the UN even more substantially than had been done. In fact, the former SPD lord mayor of Hamburg, Henning Voscherau, even got loud applause for his remark that Germany was falling back "into the old arguments in favor of a just war." There was also applause when some delegates called for a bombing pause. But Schröder's course held true.

There were even more fireworks at the Greens' special conference on Kosovo, held a few days later. The lines were clearly drawn. There was Joschka Fischer, foreign minister and realist, who left no doubt that he would not follow any pacifist course. ("If you decide for it, then I won't carry it out.") Then there were the radical pacifists like Ulrich Cremer and Bärbel Höhn, ecology minister in North Rhine-Westphalia, supported by Christian Ströbele of the old left. Fischer's old comrade in arms and former '68 rebel Daniel Cohn-Bendit passionately criticized the logic of the radical pacifists. Ludger Vollmer also supported Fischer's position. In the end, 444 delegates, a clear majority, supported the leadership's position that there ought to be a bombing pause with a time limit in order to permit a Serbian withdrawal. For the first time at a national conference, the *Realos* had triumphed.

Conclusion

After barely a year in office, the Schröder-Fischer government can speak of continuity in the basic elements of its foreign policy. This is not surprising, because foreign policy is founded upon the experiences and the interests of the nation. What is surprising is the speed with which the Greens—above all—have adapted their programmatic ideals to a realistic agenda under the pressure of events. The changes in the foreign policy vision of the SPD and Alliance '90/The Greens and the foreign policy of the new government itself show clearly the chasm between idealism and reality. People drew differing conclusions about this. In the view of Green *Fundis*, this was all a betrayal of the party's ideals. Leftist Social Democrats complained about the tendency to adapt too easily to power relationships and power politics. The Christian Democrats and Liberals, defeated in the election, saw with satisfaction that their foreign policy was largely continued.

Germany's agenda coincides with that of the West. It is characterized by continuity and calculability. Differences with the United States and other countries (export markets) are as obvious as they are soluble. Multilateral engagement is part of the recipe of Bonn's foreign policy, which will be pursued into the new millennium from Berlin. If this all appears more or less indisputable, then that is partly due to the legacy of Helmut Kohl. Germany and Europe must now build a peaceful system that goes beyond traditional power politics and the quest for hegemony.

Notes

1. Harmut von Soell, "Die SPD und die Außen- und Sicherheitspolitik," *Frankfurter Allgemeine Zeitung*, 6 November 1992.
2. *SPD Aktuell*, 18 June 1997, www.spd.de/aktuell.aussen.htm.
3. Very important for an understanding of this is Ludger Vollmer, *Die Grünen und die Außenpolitik – ein schwieriges Verhältnis* (Münster: Westfälisches Dampfboot, 1998).
4. *Sonderweg* is a term meaning a German isolationist international policy, and has special meaning to Germans. It connotes today the historical failures of integration into the West, which led to world wars, destruction, and disaster.
5. See www.auswaertiges-amt.de/6_archiv/2/r/R981028b.htm.
6. *Washington Post*, 23 November 1998.
7. NATO Press Release NAC-S (99) 63.
8. Remarks to the NATO Defense Planning Committee by Secretary of Defense William Cohen, Brussels, 11 June 1998. (See www.nato.int/usa/dod/s980611a.htm.)
9. *Der Spiegel*, no. 48 (23 November 1998), 86.

10. In 1996, the Federal Republic gave shelter to some 300,000 refugees from Bosnia-Herzegovina, while France accepted 15,000, Britain 13,000, Italy 6,200 and Spain 2,500. Sweden and Austria took the next highest after Germany, with 122,000 and 80,000 respectively.
11. *Frankfurter Allgemeine Zeitung*, 5 July 1999, 2.
12. *Deutsche Initiative für den Kosovo*, 4 April 1999. (See www.auswaertiges-amt.de/6_archiv/Int-kos/hintergr/initia.htm).
13. *Ein Stabilitätspakt für Südosteuropa*, 9 April 1999. (See www.auswaertiges-amt.de/6_archiv/Int-kos/hintergr/stabdt.htm)
14. *Frankfurter Allgemeine Zeitung*, 16 June 1999, 5.
15. I am grateful to the press and information staff of the Federal Ministry of Defense for this information, particularly Naval Captain Liedtke.

Chapter 13

A COMPARATIVE PERSPECTIVE ON THE BUNDESTAG ELECTIONS

David F. Patton

Versed in the danger of a *Sonderweg*, or a special path of German development, Germans cannot but help be comparativists. The very notion of a *Sonderweg* can only make sense in relationship to what has come before and what is taking place elsewhere. Developments in the West are the measuring stick for "normalcy" in the Federal Republic. The Social Democrats (SPD) therefore cheered when center-left parties won recent election victories in the U.S., Great Britain, Italy, and France. Hoping to ride on the coattails of Clinton, Blair, Prodi, and Jospin, they presented themselves as the "modern" alternative that would keep the Federal Republic in step with its Western neighbors.

Given the aversion to a German special path, this chapter asks whether the federal elections of 1998 indicate a normalization of Germany's electoral politics in comparative perspective. It concludes that, on balance, the German elections of 1998 reveal a convergence between the Federal Republic and other Western industrial democracies.

Patterns of Convergence

In at least five ways, the German elections resulted in political patterns that are in keeping with those of other Western democracies: (1) they brought to power yet another center-left government in Europe; (2) they showed that anti-communism was no longer an effective campaign strategy; (3) they established within the German party system a party to the left of social democracy; (4) they also revealed a regionalized party system not dissimilar to that of many other advanced industrial democracies;

and, finally, (5) they resulted in a generational change that has already taken place elsewhere.

Center-Left Governance: A Third Way?

With the triumph of the red-green coalition (SPD-Greens) in the 1998 election, Germany, like most of Western Europe, was now ruled by a center-left government. As of January 1999, a left-of-center party was the main governing party in 13 of the 15 member-states of the European Union.[1] Only in Spain and in Ireland did center-left parties not govern.

Why did voters in Germany and Western Europe elect center-left governments? The reasons naturally varied from country to country. In certain cases, voters punished center-right governments for unpopular cuts to the welfare state. This happened in Sweden in 1994, and more recently in France after the Juppé government attempted to reduce benefits for public service workers in 1995. Massive strikes followed, shutting down Paris and forcing the beleaguered government to withdraw many of its proposed changes. In 1997, French President Jacques Chirac called new National Assembly elections in an effort to retain a conservative majority prior to imposing further austerity measures. Chirac's calculation badly misfired when the French electorate dumped the conservative government in favor of the socialists, communists, and Greens.

In Germany, the parties on the left were also the beneficiaries of a center-right government's unpopular cost-cutting measures. Although the Kohl government did not carry out draconian reductions in the welfare state (certainly not by American standards), its cuts to health care, dental care, pensions and sick leave pay were controversial, and exposed the government to charges of "neoliberalism" and "Manchester capitalism." The SPD, Greens, and PDS promised to overturn many of Kohl's welfare cuts in an effort to ensure more social justice in the Federal Republic. With the exception of the Greens, these parties all picked up seats in the Bundestag; the governing parties all declined.

The problem of high unemployment contributed to center-left governance in Europe. In some cases, conservative parties had been unable or unwilling to deal with this pressing issue. For instance, although the Major government boasted of generally low unemployment figures in Britain, it suffered devastating losses in those regions (Scotland, Wales, and northern England) where unemployment had remained high. Likewise, in the mid-1990s the conservatives in France had few answers to the problem of unemployment, especially for the youth.

While center-right parties in power appeared to struggle with this issue,[2] some governing center-left parties were earning recognition for their success in combating unemployment. In the United States, Bill Clinton presided over the lowest rates of joblessness in over twenty years. In

Denmark, the Netherlands and France, center-left governments also took credit for reducing unemployment. In Denmark, where the Social Democrats governed with the Radicals, unemployment fell from 10.1 percent in 1995 to 6.3 percent in 1998. In the Netherlands, after industry groups and the labor unions had agreed in the 1980s to shorten the work week and to limit wage increases, unemployment gradually fell from 15 percent in the early 1980s to less than 5 percent in 1998.[3] In France, the government of Lionel Jospin proposed cutting the work week to 35 hours and funded public job creation for unemployed youths. Unemployment declined in France from 12.6 percent in 1997 to 11.5 percent by early 1999.[4]

In Germany, both the inability of the ruling center-right parties to reduce unemployment and the promise of a more effective center-left approach were crucial in the election of the SPD-Green government. Despite his pledge to halve unemployment, Chancellor Kohl had trouble dealing with the double-digit rates of joblessness, particularly in the East, where the share of unemployed was nearly twice that in the West. His rival, Gerhard Schröder (SPD), pointed to the positive example of the Netherlands under center-left government. In fact, Schröder's promise of an Alliance for Jobs drew explicitly upon the example of the Dutch consultations between labor and business that had proved effective against unemployment. Rather than copy the neoliberal example of the Clinton and Blair governments or the more Keynesian approach of Jospin, he focused on the corporatist example of the Dutch.

Another reason for the return of left governments is that the left was no longer as threatening to the middle classes. In the era after the Cold War debates over missile placement and the future of capitalism, the middle classes had little to fear of a political left fiscally constrained by globalization and the stringent requirements of European monetary union. Moreover, they were voting for parties that had scrapped many of their earlier policy positions. On the foreign policy side, the parties no longer opposed NATO or American military engagements. On the economic side, they no longer favored nationalization of private industry, or, in some cases, even Keynesian pump priming. In the United States, Clinton proclaimed the emergence of New Democrats who eschewed the supposed "tax and spend" and "soft-on-crime" approach of their liberal predecessors, and focused instead on balancing the budget, cutting taxes, and improving education. In Britain, Tony Blair rejected the traditional ideological divide between left and right. Instead, he promised that New Labour had discovered a "third way" to ensure more effective government, better education, and public safety. In Italy, Prime Minister Romano Prodi (Popular Party) cut welfare programs and encouraged privatization; he was joined by the postcommunist Party of the Democratic Left (PDS).

Under the leadership of Gerhard Schröder, the new red-green coalition fit this centrist mold. Schröder sounded a lot like Blair when he pledged to serve a "new middle" in Germany. Like Blair and Clinton, Schröder was friendly toward industry, tough on law-and-order issues, and concerned about education. He too presented politics as an exercise in pragmatic problem-solving rather than ideological conviction. Like Blair, he talked about social responsibilities, such as the duty to look for a job and the duty to get an education, rather than just the social right to a job and an education.[5] He was joined by Joschka Fischer, now Germany's foreign minister, who steered the Greens away from pacifism and ecological fundamentalism.

However, unlike Blair and New Labour, Schröder did not overhaul the SPD in his own image, and preferred instead to court constituents outside of traditional SPD circles. Oskar Lafontaine, the chairman of the SPD and the former finance minister, remained the darling of the party's rank-and-file by voicing traditional SPD concerns about redistribution and social justice, while arguing that governments can and must regulate the impact of globalization.[6] As a Keynesian, Lafontaine more closely resembled the left-leaning Lionel Jospin of France than Tony Blair. This, at least, is what critics on the right said when they pointed to the powerful Lafontaine as evidence that the new government would not transcend old ideological trenches.

While the constraints of globalization may have accounted for the appeal of the "third way" in the late 1990s, the movement seemed part of a broader cyclical pattern. Roughly speaking, beginning in the late 1940s the first six to seven years of the Cold War were a time of bitter ideological conflict in much of Western Europe. This was during the height of East-West tensions, when security and economic debates aroused intense emotions in West Germany, France, and Italy.

Beginning in the mid-1950s, the next ten to twelve years witnessed a broad domestic consensus that indicated to some observers an "end of ideology." During this time, the Cold War gradually thawed and most major European parties saw the merits of Keynesian economic management, an expanded welfare state, and peaceful coexistence between the blocs. Leading parties on the left either excised or tabled their Marxist doctrines and became catch-all parties.

As economic growth declined in the 1970s, a so-called "crisis of governability" arose, characterized by interest groups and regions demanding ever more from an overloaded central government. By the late 1970s, as the second Cold War began and the Keynesian consensus eroded, leading Western industrial democracies experienced a "re-ideologicalization" as the right and the left clashed over monetarism and missile deployment. Right-of-center governments in the U.S. and in Britain privatized, deregulated, and implemented a "supply-side economics" despite intense domestic opposition. In France, François Mitterrand began reforms but soon had to reverse his controversial program of nationalization and increased welfare.

By the late 1980s, the Cold War had ended and voters grew tired of the political confrontation and ideological conflict of the preceding decade. Just as political pragmatism, a Keynesian consensus, and the promise of the "end of ideology" followed the conflictual early 1950s, political pragmatism, a monetarist consensus, and the promise of a "third way" followed the confrontation of the 1980s. Once more, parties on the left and right moved toward the political center, promising pragmatism and reconciliation.[7]

If there is a long cycle, as appears to be the case, today's centrist governments, when restricted by global constraints, entrenched domestic interests, and regional pressures, will likely experience their own "crisis of governability." If this occurs, a reideologicalization of the political debate seems probable.

This may in fact already be starting. When in September 1998, Bill Clinton, Tony Blair, and Romano Prodi of Italy convened a New York University symposium on the third way; their movement was less than secure. Lionel Jospin, who headed a coalition of socialists, communists, and Greens in France, had chosen a traditional social democratic program of public job creation and work week reductions. Göran Persson, whose government had trimmed the Swedish welfare state, paid a heavy price at the polls in September 1998 when his Social Democratic Party suffered through its worst showing since 1928. The postcommunist Left Party almost doubled its share of the vote from 6.2 percent in 1994 to 12 percent. Hardly in the spirit of the third way, the Left Party demanded higher taxes on the rich, an increase in the state sector, and an end to privatization. It and the leftist Greens now tolerated a chastised Persson government.

Italy's Romano Prodi attended the third way symposium in New York, but was forced out of office a few weeks later when the communists in parliament refused to support his government's budget. The next Italian government then promised the communists a reduced work week, at odds with the third way philosophy. Tony Blair, the poster boy of the third way movement, also faced difficulties when a leading third way strategist, Peter Mandelson, resigned from the cabinet in early 1999 due to infighting and intrigue between Old Labour and New Labour factions. In Germany, Gerhard Schröder (the "German Tony Blair") came to power, but Lafontaine, as finance minister and SPD chair, seemed poised to lead the government in a leftist direction. While Lafontaine has subsequently left the government, so has Bodo Hombach, one of the leading architects of Schröder's new middle strategy.

Anti-Communism as a Failed Campaign Strategy

As Cold War tensions mounted in the late 1940s, the center-right parties of Italy, Japan, and Germany allied themselves and their nations closely with the United States and its security policies. They presented themselves to the electorate as more reliable than their opponents on the left who opposed their security policies. The governing center-right parties thrived in the polarized climate of the early Cold War, articulating an anti-communism that appealed to industry, the middle classes, the religious, and the rural voters who together formed the core of their electoral support. They attracted middle-class support by warning of the Soviet threat abroad and of Marxism and pacifism at home.

The thaw of the Cold War in the 1960s presented the governing center-right parties with a new challenge. As détente developed, voters were less concerned about the Soviet Union and more willing to support reformist parties on the left. They also expected the governing center-right parties to adjust their foreign and domestic policies to fit the détente era. This was difficult for the West German Christian Democrats who struggled with the issue of *Ostpolitik* during the 1960s and 1970s.

When the "second Cold War" broke out in the early 1980s, anti-communist center-right parties governed in Italy, Japan, Britain, and West Germany, while the left languished in the opposition. In part because of their anti-communism and their close association with the Western Alliance, the Christian Democrats in Italy and West Germany, the liberal democrats in Japan, and the British conservatives again struck many middle-class voters as being more reliable than an opposition that contained either pro-Soviet elements (PCI in Italy) or a strong pacifist wing (West Germany's SPD and Greens, Japan's socialists, and Britain's Labour party). Once more, anti-Marxism was an effective vote-getter.

The end of the Cold War reduced the appeal of anti-communism within the advanced industrial democracies. Not only did the Soviet Union no longer pose a threat, but parties of the left in Italy, Japan, Great Britain, and Germany quickly distanced themselves from the ideologies and policy positions of the Cold War era. As a result, the center-right parties of Italy, Great Britain, and Japan could no longer win elections on the basis of their anti-communism and their commitment to the Western Alliance.

One would have also expected a similar problem for the West German Christian Democrats, a party that had prospered when Cold War tensions rose yet struggled during détente. However, as seen during the election campaigns of 1990 and 1994, the CDU/CSU continued to effectively use anti-communism as an electoral strategy. This suggested that an anomaly had developed as a result of German unification. In 1990, anti-communist appeals returned, especially in the East, where an alliance of three conservative parties, sponsored by Kohl, won the critical GDR elections of March 1990 under the banner of "Freedom rather than Socialism" and a "Future rather than Socialism."

While the end of the Cold War brought about the fall of the East German communist dictatorship, it ironically re-introduced into the German party system a party that included communists. As the successor party of the ruling Socialist Unity Party, the Party of Democratic Socialism (PDS) managed an electoral comeback in the East. In the 1994 elections, its resurgence helped the CDU/CSU-FDP government by dividing the German left into three parts.[8] It also enabled the Christian Democrats to campaign against communism in the 1994 elections. In its "red socks campaign," the CDU/CSU sought to scare voters in the West away from the SPD by warning of a sinister pact between the SPD and the PDS. To summarize, several years after the Cold War, at a time when anti-communist parties elsewhere were falling from power, the CDU/CSU was running campaigns and winning elections under the banner of anti-communism. This appeared quite exceptional.

Four years later, the Christian Democrats and Free Democrats once more ran a tough anti-communist campaign. Even though the PDS had risen, and even as the PDS prepared to govern at the state level with the SPD, the governing parties could not generate much interest in their anti-communist message. Led by its strategist Peter Hintze, the CDU harped on the dangers of red-red (SPD-PDS) alliances, but few seemed concerned. The CDU/CSU and FDP learned, as the center-right parties of Italy and Japan had already discovered, that anti-communism could no longer mobilize much support nine years after the Berlin Wall had fallen. In this regard, politics in Germany had normalized by 1998.

Left of the SPD Established

In 1998, the PDS improved its share of the national vote from 4.4 percent in 1994 to 5.1 percent; its share in the East rose to over 20 percent. Whereas the PDS had previously entered the Bundestag thanks to electoral exceptions, it now returned by crossing the 5 percent threshold like all the other main parties. As the heir to the ruling communists of the GDR, the PDS's success may have appeared anomalous to western Germans unaccustomed to a viable party left of the SPD.[9] However, a look at the political landscape of Western Europe revealed that Germany became more like its neighbors in 1998. Gregor Gysi, the head of the PDS grouping in the Bundestag, was quick to point this out: "Everywhere in Europe there is within parliaments an accepted political force to the left of social democracy."[10]

While in his election-night excitement Gysi apparently forgot Britain and Austria, he nonetheless correctly identified a common feature of most European party systems. Throughout Western Europe, communists and ex-communists regularly receive between 5 and 10 percent of the vote. In this regard, Germany is now no exception.

In France, communists sit in the government; in Italy they tolerate a minority government; also in Italy, a former communist is prime minister, while in Sweden former communists tolerate a left-of-center minority government. Moreover, throughout Eastern Europe, communist successor parties revived in the 1990s, and in most cases came to power.

In Germany the PDS does not yet have an important role in policymaking at the national level. Nonetheless, its strong showing in 1998 will make the PDS more attractive to politicians in search of majorities in the eastern state parliaments. For instance, what had previously been a taboo in German politics occurred in October 1998 when the SPD agreed to govern with the PDS in the Mecklenburg-Pomerania. This red-red coalition may become commonplace in eastern Germany. Even some prominent Christian Democrats have spoken of the possibility of normalizing relations with the PDS.[11] This has already taken place at the communal level, where the SPD, the CDU, and Alliance '90/The Greens all cooperate with the PDS. However, given the strong aversion of most western Germans to the PDS, it is still improbable that the mainstream German parties will form a coalition at the national level with communists or ex-communists (as in Italy and France) or form a government that relied on communists and ex-communists for its survival (as in Italy and Sweden).

Generational Change

Helmut Kohl was the last of a cohort of national leaders that came to power in the late 1970s and early 1980s. These leaders were part of a generation that had been shaped by fascism, World War II, the hardship of the early postwar years, and the early Cold War.[12] In Great Britain, Margaret Thatcher, who governed from 1979 to 1990, had memories of appeasement and the bombing of Britain. François Mitterrand (1981– 95) had ties to Vichy France; Ronald Reagan (1981–89) made films for the army and held the rank of captain; George Bush (1989–93) had fought in the Pacific during World War II; in Germany, Helmut Schmidt (1974–82), had served as a German officer in World War II; and Helmut Kohl (1982–98) had teenage memories of National Socialism and the war, and adult memories of postwar reconstruction. As the longest serving postwar prime minister of a major Western European country, Kohl was something of an anomaly in the late 1990s, bringing his personal experience of the first half of the twentieth century to a political landscape where an entirely new generation of leaders had begun to dominate.

This generation came of age during the economic boom of the 1950s and the turbulent 1960s. As part of the "1968 generation," many were active in protest during the 1960s and 1970s. Bill Clinton, born in 1946, demonstrated against the Vietnam War; Tony Blair, born in 1953, played lead guitar for the rock group the Ugly Rumours; Gerhard Schröder, born in 1944, headed the Marxist youth organization of the SPD (although not part of its most orthodox wing) during the late 1970s, and was the first male deputy ever to address the Bundestag without wearing a tie; and Joschka Fischer, the new German foreign minister, dabbled in revolutionary politics during the early 1970s. Rudolf Scharping, the new defense minister, and Jürgen Trittin, the new minister of the environment, are also "68ers," whereas Otto Schily, the new interior minister, although of an earlier generation, served as the lawyer for members of the Baader-Meinhof gang in the 1970s.

As in the United States (where Clinton edged out Bush and Dole) and in Israel (where the youthful Binyamin Nehtanyahu defeated Shimon Peres), Gerhard Schröder in Germany benefited from his relative young age when facing a much older opponent. He appeared more energetic than Kohl and more in tune with the current problems of the day. Like Clinton, Nehtanyahu, and Blair, Schröder was comfortable on television and adept with the new technologies. The emergence of this new generation of leaders may change the dynamics of European integration. Older leaders such as Kohl and Mitterrand viewed European integration as a matter of war and peace. Will the younger generation take the process as seriously as those with memories of the war? Perhaps not. Yet it is important to keep in mind that the older generation also included policymakers, such as Margaret Thatcher and the trade and industry minister Nicholas Ridley, who were deeply attached to the nation-state model. Their successors in Britain should get along better with "post-national" leaders on the continent.

Regionalism

The elections of 1998 exposed a growing regional divide in Germany that may seem anomalous in a unifying country. In fact, it corresponds to a common trend among the advanced industrial democracies of the 1990s.[13] Regionalism is on the rise not only in Germany, but also in Great Britain, Italy, and Canada; and it has long shaped politics in Belgium and Spain.

In several regards, the German elections pointed to a more regionalized party landscape in 1998 than 1990. In 1998, the CDU won over 37 percent of the western vote, while averaging just 28 percent in the five new states and eastern Berlin, a decline of its eastern share by a third since 1990. Emerging as a de facto western party, the FDP won only 3.3 percent of the eastern vote, down from 12.9 percent in 1990. Likewise, Alliance '90/The Greens performed much better in the West than the East, where it received less than 3 percent in three of the five states. In contrast, in 1990 the eastern Greens had crossed the 5 percent threshold, while the western Greens were the ones that had fallen short. In 1998, the PDS remained a de facto regional party, winning 21.6 percent of the eastern vote, but just over 1 percent in the West. The only party that bucked the general pattern was the SPD, which nonetheless still did much better in the western states. In addition to these regionalized elections results, membership trends show a further regionalization of the party system.[14] Finally, in 1990 the parties made openly regional appeals in the lead-up to the election. The FDP campaigned for a reduction in transfer payments to the East; the CDU/CSU ran a campaign against the PDS that struck many easterners as insensitive to the Eastern experience; the PDS in turn asserted a systematic western bias against the East.

The regionalism in Germany paralleled the regionalism of other Western countries. In the 1997 British general elections, the Conservative Party did not win one seat outside of England, while in Scotland the separatist Scottish National Party increased its share of the vote from under 15 percent in the 1980s to over 21 percent (and a second place finish) in 1997. In Canada, the western Reform Party won the second most seats in the parliamentary elections of 1997, but none of its 60 seats were won east of Manitoba; the Bloc Quebecois dominated only in Quebec; and the Liberal Party won 101 of the 103 districts in Ontario. In Italy, the Northern League became the largest party in northern Italy, while the postfascist National Alliance established its base in southern Italy. As these cases indicate, regionalism is not just a product of peripheral ethnicity but a rather common feature of many nation-states in the 1990s.

As globalization and supranationalism chip away at national sovereignty, constitutional debates arising within established democracies unleash intense regional demands: in Canada, the Quebec question and the indigenous population question provoked a constitutional crisis and a western Canadian backlash. In Italy, the corruption of the postwar Italian republic in the early 1990s led to constitutional gridlock and fertile ground for the Northern League. In Germany, the transfer of western institutions and western elites eastward during unification sparked eastern resentment over a "representation gap" (*Vertretungslücke*) and "second-class citizenship." In Britain, heated debates over Europe and constitutional reform exacerbated regionalism in the Celtic fringe. Regional demands in turn were fueled by uneven economic development: the northern Italians felt burdened by the southern Italians; the poorer (yet oil rich) Scots resented the richer (yet oil poor) English; the western Germans grew weary of subsidizing the much poorer eastern Germans.

Patterns of Divergence

In at least one regard, the German elections of 1998 set Germany apart from its advanced industrial neighbors: the German parties on the far right remained relatively weak and divided.

In regard to the strength of its environmentalist party, Germany used to be quite remarkable in the mid-1980s, but other countries have since then caught up. Sweden, Switzerland, France, Finland, and Austria all have environmental parties winning between 4.5 and 7 percent of the national vote; in the Netherlands and in Luxembourg, the leading environmentalist parties recently won 7.3 percent and 9.9 respectively, both surpassing the mark of 6.7 percent recorded by the German Greens in 1998. Nor are the German Greens the first environmentalist party to be in the national government; they are joining Greens in France and Finland already in power. However, in one regard the Green achievement is noteworthy: Joschka Fischer is the first Green to head a foreign ministry.

Relative Weakness of the Far Right

Apart from the Iberian peninsula and the British Isles, most Western European countries have seen right-wing parties entering national parliaments by appealing to xenophobia and anti-government populism.[15] In Scandinavia, the Norwegian Freedom Party finished second to the Labour Party after winning over 15 percent of the vote in the last national elections. In Belgium, far-right parties received over 10 percent of the national vote in 1995: the xenophobic Flemish Bloc (Flaams Bloc) won 7.8 percent; the anti-immigrant Front National, based in Wallonia, won 2.3 percent. Jörg Haider's Freedom Party of Austria (FPÖ) became the third-largest party in Austria, winning nearly 22 percent of the vote in the December 1995 national elections and capturing 27.6 percent in the European Parliament elections of 1996. Despite its winner-take-all electoral system, France also has an established force on the far right. In recent national elections, LePen's Front National has captured 15 percent of the vote. In the Swiss parliamentary elections of 1995, the anti-foreigner Freedom Party (formerly the Auto Party) won 4 percent of the vote and seven seats in the lower house, while the xenophobic Swiss Party (in alliance with the Ticino League) won 3.1 percent and three seats.

With established far-right parties in neighboring Belgium, France, Switzerland, and Austria, one would expect the far right to have some success on the national level in the Federal Republic. As is the case for its neighbors, multiculturalism, political asylum, and the perception of "foreigner crime" stir up resentment among Germans, while double-digit unemployment provides fertile ground for protest and scapegoating. Such conditions led to far-right success elsewhere, but they did not produce the feared breakthrough of the racist right in the German elections of 1998.

Whereas Jean-Marie LePen and Jörg Haider mobilized and successfully integrated right-wing protest in France and Austria, the German right has not yet found its unifying party and its unchallenged leader. Throughout the 1990s, aspirants such as the former SS soldier Franz Schönhuber, the millionaire publisher Gerhard Frey, and Holocaust-denier Günter Deckert tried and failed to unite the German far right. Instead, it remained electorally divided among the Republikaner (1.8 percent in 1998), the German People's Union (1.2 percent in 1998), and the NPD (0.3 percent in 1998). This fragmentation and infighting explains in part the low overall numbers in Germany. Totaling just 3.3 percent nationally, the combined results of the three rightist parties in 1998 did not approach the results of the far right in France, Belgium or Austria. Nonetheless, they still put the level of German far right support above that of the Netherlands, Britain, Portugal, and Spain.

In certain regions, the German far right performed quite well in 1998. Just as the FN did well in the industrial suburbs of Paris, the FPÖ in the working class districts of Vienna, and the Flaams Bloc in industrial Antwerp, the German far right garnered 7.7 percent of the vote in the decaying outer districts of East Berlin (Hellersdorf/Marzahn).[16] And, like the right wing Freedom Party of Austria, which did well in the border regions of Tyrol and Carinthia facing Italy and Slovenia, the far right secured what were among its best results in the remote eastern Saxon districts abutting the Czech Republic.[17] Like their colleagues abroad, the German anti-foreigner parties did disproportionately well among younger working class men who vote for the far right in part to protest their often difficult economic situation.[18]

Conclusion

On balance, the German elections pointed to a convergence of electoral trends in the Federal Republic and other Western industrial democracies. Had the Kohl government been reelected, then it would have bucked the West European tendency toward center-left rule, the failure of anti-communist campaigns, and generational change. If the German voters had elected an SPD-led grand coalition with the CDU/CSU, then this too would have appeared more "normal" than a reaffirmation of center-right rule. Within the EU, Austria, Belgium, Luxembourg, and the Netherlands all have coalitions between the two largest parties in parliament.[19] Germany's East-West partisan divide, if perhaps not a sign of "normalcy," can in no way be viewed as abnormal among advanced industrialized democracies at the end of the century. Overall there can be little talk of a "special German path" in 1998, and if at all, then only in regard to the relative poor showing of the far-right parties.

Notes

1. In Belgium, the Christian Democrats head the government, but the Socialists place 53 percent of the parliamentary seats in this center-left alliance. In Luxembourg, the prime minister is a Christian Democrat, but the Social Democrats hold one-half of the posts in cabinet. See "A Continental Drift to the Left," *The Economist*, 3 October 1998, 59–60.
2. When the center-left governments in power failed to address unemployment, they too were punished. In addition to the numerous corruption scandals, high unemployment hastened the return of the right in France (1993) and in Spain (1996).
3. Beatta Willms, "Das Vorbild ist schwer zu kopieren," *tageszeitung*, 4 December 1998. See also Beatta Willms, "Mit dem Konsensmodell auf du und du," *tageszeitung*, 4 December 1998.
4. "Schielen aufs Château," *Der Spiegel*, 11 January 1998, 132.
5. Markus Franz, "Einverstanden, sagt Tony Blair und nickt," *tageszeitung*, 4 November 1998, 11.
6. Oskar Lafontaine and Christa Müller, *Keine Angst vor der Globalisierung: Wohlstand und Arbeit für alle* (Bonn: Dietz, 1998).
7. Oddbjørn Knutsen has tracked the shift to the center in his study of thirteen Western European countries from 1982 to 1993. See Oddbjørn Knutsen, "Expert Judgements of the Left-Right Location of Political Parties: A Comparative Longitudinal Study," *West European Politics* 21, no. 2 (April 1998): 63–94.
8. Whereas many Social Democrats had expected to become the dominant party in the five new states of eastern Germany, they now had to share votes with the PDS. As a result, the CDU managed to win the majority of the eastern electoral districts in 1994, thereby acquiring enough overhang mandates to assure its narrow victory over the SPD.
9. The Federal Constitutional Court banned the Communist Party of Germany in 1956.
10. "Wir sind die linke Opposition," *Der Spiegel*, special election issue, 29 September 1998, 29.
11. These included the former federal president von Weizsäcker, the former CDU general secretary Heiner Geißler and the GDR's last prime minister Lothar de Maizière.
12. Felipe Gonzalez, although of a later generation, had lived through a repressive regime in Spain and was part of the first generation of post-fascist democrats.
13. See David F. Patton, "Germany's Party of Democratic Socialism in Comparative Perspective," *East European Politics and Societies* 12, no. 3 (Fall 1998): 500–526. See also David F. Patton, "The Rise of Germany's Party of Democratic Socialism: 'Regionalised Pluralism' in the Federal Republic?" *West European Politics* 23:1 (January 2000).
14. Both the FDP and CDU sustained a large relative drop in eastern membership in their parties; the SPD (96.7 percent western) and Alliance '90/The Greens (94 percent western) continue to have a disproportionately far greater share of western members within the party, whereas all but 2 percent of the PDS members in 1995 were eastern Germans. The membership numbers for the FDP, CDU, SPD, and Greens are all drawn from Oscar W. Gabriel and Oskar Niedermayer, "Entwicklung und Sozialstruktur der

252 | *David F. Patton*

Parteimitgliedschaften," in *Parteiendemokratie in Deutschland* (Bonn: Bundeszentrale für politische Bildung, 1997), 281. The PDS membership number comes from Patrick Moreau, *Die PDS: Profil einer antidemokratischen Partei* (Munich: Hanns-Seidel-Stiftung, 1998), 97.

15. Hans-Georg Betz, *Radical Right-wing Populism in Western Europe* (New York: St. Martin's Press, 1994).

16. In April, the German People's Union won nearly 13 percent of the vote in state elections in the depressed eastern state Saxony-Anhalt, doing particularly well among young, unemployed men.

17. For instance, in Bautzen-Löbau the DVU won 4.8 percent of the vote; the Republikaner 1.4 percent; and the NPD 1.4. The Republikaner did well in Baden-Württemberg.

18. See Betz, *Radical Right-wing Populism in Western Europe*.

19. One might add France to this list in view of the cohabitation between Chirac (RPR) and Jospin.

APPENDIX

Table A.1 Bundestag Elections since 1949—Party Percentage of the
          Second Vote

Year	Percent Voting	CDU/ CSU	SPD	FDP	Greens- All. '90/Gr.	PDS[1]	Other Parties[2]
1949[3]	78.5	31.0	29.2	11.9	–	–	27.8
1953	86.0	45.2	28.8	9.5	–	–	16.5
1957	87.8	50.2	31.8	7.7	–	–	10.3
1961	87.7	45.3	36.2	12.8	–	–	5.7
1965	86.8	47.6	39.3	9.5	–	–	3.6
1969	86.7	46.1	42.7	5.8	–	–	5.5
1972	91.1	44.9	45.8	8.4	–	–	0.9
1976	90.7	48.6	42.6	7.9	–	–	0.9
1980	88.6	44.5	42.9	10.6	1.5	–	0.5
1983	89.1	48.8	38.2	7.0	5.6	–	0.5
1987	84.3	44.3	37.0	9.1	8.3	–	1.4
1990	77.8	43.8	33.5	11.0	3.8[4]	2.4[5]	5.4
1994	79.0	41.4	36.4	6.9	7.3	4.4[6]	3.6
1998	82.2	35.1	40.9	6.2	6.7	5.1	5.9

The data in this and the following tables come from the election reports published by the Federal and State Statistical Offices in Germany as well as the Forschungsgruppe Wahlen e.V.

[1] In 1990, the Greens in the West and the Alliance '90/The Greens in the East had not yet united. The Greens won 4.8 percent in the West, amounting to 3.8 percent in the enlarged Federal Republic, as listed here. The separate Alliance '90/The Greens, included under "other parties" for 1990 only, won 6.2 percent in the East, which amounted to 1.2 percent in the entire Federal Republic. Under the special electoral arrangement for 1990, which divided the Federal Republic into two electoral areas (East and West), the eastern Alliance '90/The Greens won parliamentary representation by passing the 5 percent minimum, but the western Greens did not. By 1994, a merger had created the all-German party which took over the name Alliance '90/ The Greens.

[2] In 1949, including BP (Bavarian Party) 4.2 percent, Center Party 3.1 percent, DP (German Party) 4.0 percent, KPD (Communists) 5.7 percent, and independents 4.8 percent.

In 1953, including BP 1.7 percent, DP 3.3 percent, GB/BHE (a new refugee party) 5.9 percent, and KPD 2.2 percent.

In 1957, including DP 3.4 percent and GB/BHE 4.6 percent.

In 1961, including GDP (a merger of DP and BHE) 2.8 percent, and DFU (German Peace Union) 1.9 percent.

In 1965, including DFU 1.3 percent, and right-wing NPD (National Democratic Party) 2.0 percent.

In 1969, including NPD 4.3 percent.

In 1990, including Alliance '90/Greens 1.2 percent (based on 6.2 percent in the East), and the Republikaner 2.1 percent.

In 1994, including the Republikaner 1.9 percent.

In 1998, including DVU (German People's Union) 1.2 percent, and the Republikaner 1.8 percent.

[3] In 1949, a one-vote ballot only.

[4] Based on 4.8 percent for the Greens in the electoral region of the West. See footnote 1.

[5] In 1990, the PDS won parliamentary representation by netting 11.1 percent of the vote in the electoral area of the East. In the West, the PDS received only 0.3 percent, producing a total of 2.4 percent in the entire Federal Republic.

[6] In 1994, the PDS won parliamentary representation by scoring plurality victories in four single-member districts on the first ballot (all in eastern Berlin). That was one more first ballot victory than necessary to set aside the 5 percent minimum requirement on the second ballot for gaining proportional representation in the Bundestag. As a result, the PDS ended up with a total of 30 Bundestag seats, based proportionately on its second ballot result of 4.4 percent. The PDS won only 1.0 percent of the second vote in the West, but 19.8 percent in the East.

Table A.2 Distribution of Bundestag Seats since 1949

Year	Total	CDU/CSU	SPD	FDP	Greens-All. '90/Gr.[1]	PDS	Other Parties[2]
1949	402	139	131	52	–	–	80
1953	487	243	151	48	–	–	45
1957	497	270	169	41	–	–	17
1961	499	242	190	67	–	–	–
1965	496	245	202	49	–	–	–
1969	496	242	224	30	–	–	–
1972	496	225	230	41	–	–	–
1976	496	243	214	39	–	–	–
1980	497	226	218	53	–	–	–
1983	498	244	193	34	27	–	–
1987	497	223	186	46	42	–	–
1990	662	319	239	79	8[3]	17[4]	–
1994	672[5]	294	252	47	49	30[6]	–
1998	669[7]	245	298	43	47	36	–

[1] In 1990, under the special one-time arrangement that divided the Federal Republic into two electoral areas (East and West), Alliance '90/The Greens won parliamentary representation by passing the 5 percent minimum in the East. The western Greens fell below 5 percent that year. By 1994, the two parties had merged and taken over the name Alliance '90/The Greens, which competed throughout the Federal Republic.

[2] In 1949, BP (the Bavarian Party) 17, the Center Party 10, DP (the German Party) 17, DRP (the German Reich Party) 5, KPD (the Communist Party) 15, SSW (a Danish minority party) 1, WAV (the Economic Reconstruction Union) 12, and independents 3.

[3] In 1990, the eastern Alliance '90/The Greens only. The western Greens failed to win representation in that year.

[4] In 1990, the PDS won parliamentary representation by netting 11.1 percent of the vote in the electoral area of the East. It received only 0.3 percent in the West, resulting in a total of 2.4 percent of the vote in the entire Federal Republic.

[5] In 1994, the CDU/CSU won 12 and the SPD won 4 "additional seats" or *Überhangsmandate*, an unprecedented high number. As a result, the CDU/CSU-FDP government coalition's majority margin was raised from 2 to 10 seats in a Bundestag of 672 rather than 656 seats.

[6] In 1994, the PDS won 30 Bundestag seats, based on its 4.4 percent of the second ballot vote. The 5 percent minimum was set aside for the PDS, because it had won four single-member districts on the first ballot (all in eastern Berlin). The regional concentration of the PDS was reflected in the contrast between its eastern result of 19.8 percent of the second ballot vote and its western result of only 0.9 percent.

[7] In 1998, the CDU won no "additional seats," but the SPD won 13. That raised the red-green coalition's majority margin from eight to 21 seats in a Bundestag of 669 rather than 656 seats.

Table A.3 East-West Differences in the Bundestag Elections, 1990 to 1998 Voter Turnout, and Party Percentage of the Second Vote

	Percent Voting	CDU/ CSU	SPD	FDP	Greens- All. '90/Gr.	PDS	Other Parties
1990							
Total	77.8	43.8	33.5	11.0	3.8[1]	2.4	5.4[2]
West	78.6	44.3	35.7	10.6	4.8	0.3	4.4
East	74.5	41.8	24.3	12.9	6.2	11.1	3.8
1994							
Total	79.0	41.4	36.4	6.9	7.3	4.4	3.6[3]
West	80.5	42.1	37.5	7.7	7.9	1.0	3.9
East	72.6	38.5	31.5	3.5	4.3	19.8	2.4
1998							
Total	82.2	35.1	40.9	6.2	6.7	5.1	5.9[4]
West	82.8	37.0	42.3	7.0	7.3	1.2	5.2
East	80.0	27.3	35.1	3.3	4.1	21.6	8.6

[1] In 1990, the Greens in the West and the Alliance '90/The Greens in the East had not yet united, and it is important to keep their results separate for that year. The Greens won only 4.8 percent in the West, amounting to 3.8 percent in the enlarged Federal Republic, as listed here. The separate Alliance '90/The Greens won 6.2 percent in the East, as also listed in this column. The eastern party's result translated into 1.2 percent in all-German terms, and this total has been included here under the column "other parties" in order to keep it separate from the western Greens' all-German total of 3.8 percent. Under the special electoral provision for 1990, which for this election only divided the Federal Republic into two electoral areas (East and West), the eastern Alliance '90/The Greens were able to win a marginal parliamentary representation of 8 seats by passing the 5 percent minimum within their region. Having failed to meet the 5 percent minimum in *their* own region, the western Greens were excluded from the Bundestag during the next four years. Well in advance of the 1994 election, a merger had created the all-German party, which took over the name Alliance '90/The Greens. If such a united party had existed in 1990, it would presumably have attracted a total of 6 percent of the popular vote within the enlarged Federal Republic and won a corresponding number of approximately 40 seats.

[2] In 1990, including Alliance '90/The Greens 1.2 percent (based on 6.2 percent in the East), and the Republikaner 2.1 percent.

[3] In 1994, including the Republikaner 1.9 percent.

[4] In 1998, including DVU (German People's Union) 1.2 percent, and the Republikaner 1.8 percent.

**Table A.4 The Bundestag Election of 1998 in the Western and Eastern Länder
Percentage of the Second Vote by Party (1994 results in brackets)**

Land	Percent Voting	CDU/ CSU	SPD	FDP	Greens- All. '90/Gr.	PDS	REP[1]	Other Parties
Baden-	83.1	37.8	35.6	8.8	9.2	1.0	4.0	3.5
Württembg.	(79.7)	(43.3)	(30.7)	(9.9)	(9.6)	(0.8)	(3.1)	(2.6)
Bavaria	79.2	47.7	34.4	5.1	5.9	0.7	2.6	3.6
	(76.9)	(51.2)	(29.6)	(6.4)	(6.3)	(0.6)	(2.8)	(3.1)
Berlin (West	81.7	29.5	39.6	6.7	13.5	2.7	2.2	5.8
only)	(79.5)	(38.7)	(34.6)	(7.2)	(12.3)	(2.6)	(2.8)	(1.8)
Bremen	82.1	25.5	50.2	5.9	11.2	2.4	0.7	4.0
	(78.5)	(30.2)	(45.5)	(7.2)	(11.1)	(2.7)	(1.7)	(1.6)
Hamburg	81.1	30.0	45.7	6.5	10.8	2.3	0.6	4.0
	(79.7)	(34.9)	(39.7)	(7.2)	(12.6)	(2.2)	(1.7)	(1.7)
Hesse	84.2	34.7	41.6	7.9	8.2	1.5	2.3	3.8
	(82.3)	(40.7)	(37.2)	(8.1)	(9.3)	(1.1)	(2.4)	(1.3)
Lower Saxony	83.9	34.1	49.4	6.4	5.9	1.0	0.9	2.3
	(81.8)	(41.3)	(40.6)	(7.7)	(7.1)	(1.0)	(1.2)	(1.1)
North Rhine-	83.9	33.8	46.9	7.3	6.9	1.2	1.0	3.0
Westphalia	(81.8)	(38.0)	(43.1)	(7.6)	(7.4)	(1.0)	(1.3)	(1.5)
Rhineland-	83.9	39.1	41.3	7.1	6.1	1.0	2.2	3.1
Palatinate	(82.3)	(43.8)	(39.4)	(6.9)	(6.2)	(0.6)	(1.9)	(1.2)
The Saar	84.8	31.8	52.4	4.7	5.5	1.0	1.2	3.3
	(83.5)	(37.2)	(48.8)	(4.3)	(5.8)	(0.7)	(1.6)	(1.6)
Schleswig-	82.4	35.7	45.4	7.6	6.5	1.5	0.4	2.9
Holstein	(80.9)	(41.5)	(39.6)	(7.4)	(8.3)	(1.1)	(1.1)	(1.1)
Berlin (West	81.1	23.7	37.8	4.9	11.3	13.4	2.4	6.4
and East)	(78.6)	(31.4)	(34.0)	(5.2)	(10.2)	(14.8)	(1.9)	(2.5)
Berlin (East	80.1	14.7	35.1	2.1	7.9	30.0	2.6	7.6
only)	(77.2)	(19.5)	(33.1)	(1.9)	(6.9)	(34.7)	(1.9)	(2.0)
Brandenburg	78.1	20.8	43.5	2.8	3.6	20.3	1.7	7.2
	(71.5)	(28.1)	(45.1)	(2.6)	(2.9)	(19.3)	(1.1)	(0.9)
Mecklenburg-	79.4	29.3	35.3	2.2	2.9	23.6	0.6	6.1
West Pomer.	(72.8)	(38.5)	(28.8)	(3.4)	(3.6)	(23.6)	(1.2)	(0.9)
Saxony	81.6	32.7	29.1	3.6	4.4	20.0	1.9	8.3
	(72.0)	(48.0)	(24.3)	(3.8)	(4.8)	(17.7)	(1.4)	(1.0)
Saxony-Anhalt	77.1	27.2	38.1	4.1	3.3	20.7	0.6	6.0
	(70.4)	(38.8)	(33.4)	(4.1)	(3.6)	(18.0)	(1.0)	(1.1)
Thuringia	82.3	28.9	34.5	3.4	3.9	21.2	1.6	6.5
	(74.9)	(41.0)	(30.2)	(4.1)	(4.9)	(17.2)	(1.4)	(1.1)

[1] The right-wing Republikaner Party.

Table A.5 Landtag Elections 1995 to 1998—Party Percentage of the Second Vote (percentage gains or losses since last Landtag election in parentheses)

Land	Percent Voting	CDU/[1] CSU	SPD	FDP	Greens-All. '90/Gr.	PDS	REP[2]	Other Parties
Hesse	66.3	39.2	38.0	7.4	11.2	–	2.0	2.2
19/2/95	(-4.5)	(-1.0)	(-2.8)	(0.0)	(+2.4)	–	(+0.3)	(+1.1)
North Rhine-	64.0	37.7	46.0	4.0	10.0	–	0.8	1.5
Westphalia	(-7.8)	(+1.0)	(-4.0)	(-1.8)	(+5.0)	–	(-1.0)	(+0.8)
14/5/95								
Bremen	68.6	32.6	33.4	3.4	13.1	2.4	0.3	14.9[3]
14/5/95	(-3.6)	(+1.9)	(-5.4)	(-6.1)	(+1.7)	(+2.4)	(-1.2)	(+6.7)
Berlin	68.4	37.4	23.6	2.5	13.2	14.6	2.7	5.9
22/10/95	(-12.4)	(-3.0)	(-6.8)	(-4.6)	(+3.9)	(+5.4)	(-0.4)	(+5.4)
West	71.2	45.4	25.5	3.4	15.0	2.1	2.6	6.0
	(-12.5)	(-3.6)	(-5.4)	(-4.5)	(+6.8)	(+1.0)	(-1.1)	(+5.4)
East	64.0	23.6	20.2	1.1	10.0	36.3	2.9	5.8
	(-12.2)	(-1.4)	(-11.9)	(-4.5)	(-1.4)	(+12.7)	(+1.0)	(+5.4)
Baden-	67.6	41.3	25.1	9.6	12.1	–	9.1	2.8
Württembg.	(-2.5)	(+1.7)	(-4.3)	(+3.7)	(+2.6)	–	(-1.8)	(-2.0)
24/3/96								
Rhineland-	70.8	38.7	39.8	8.9	6.9	–	3.5	2.2
Palatinate	(-3.1)	(0.0)	(-5.0)	(+2.0)	(+0.4)	–	(+1.5)	(+1.0)
24/3/96								
Schleswig-	71.8	37.2	39.8	5.7	8.1	–	–	9.1[4]
Holstein	(+0.1)	(+3.4)	(-6.4)	(+0.1)	(+3.2)	–	(-1.2)	(+0.9)
24/3/96								
Hamburg	68.7	30.7	36.2	3.5	13.9	0.7	1.8	13.2[5]
21/9/97	(-1.2)	(+5.6)	(-4.2)	(-0.7)	(+0.4)	(+0.7)	(-3.0)	(+1.2)
Lower Saxony	73.8	35.9	47.9	4.9	7.0	–	2.8	1.5
1/3/98	(0.0)	(-0.5)	(+3.6)	(+0.5)	(-0.4)	–	(-0.9)	(-2.3)
Saxony-Anhalt	71.5	22.0	35.9	4.2	3.2	19.6	0.7	14.4[6]
26/4/98	(+16.7)	(-12.4)	(+1.9)	(+0.6)	(-1.9)	(-0.3)	(-0.7)	(+12.7)
Bavaria	69.8	52.9	28.7	1.7	5.7	–	3.6	7.4
13/9/98	(+2.0)	(+0.1)	(-1.3)	(-1.1)	(-0.4)	–	(-0.3)	(+3.1)
Mecklenburg-	79.4	30.2	34.3	1.6	2.7	24.4	0.5	6.4
West Pomer.	(+6.5)	(-7.5)	(+4.8)	(-2.2)	(-1.0)	(+1.7)	(-0.5)	(+4.8)
27/9/98								

[1] CSU in Bavaria.

[2] The right-wing Republikaner Party.

[3] Includes 2.5 percent for the right-wing DVU (German People's Union) and 10.7 percent for the voter initiative AFB (Work for Bremen and Bremerhaven).

[4] Includes 4.3 percent for the DVU, which in 1993 had won 6.3 percent. Also 2.5 percent for the SSW (Danish minority party).

[5] Includes 4.9 percent for the DVU and 3.8 percent for the populist Statt-Partei, which in 1993 had received 5.6 percent.

[6] Includes 12.9 percent for the DVU.

NOTES ON CONTRIBUTORS

Gerard Braunthal is Professor Emeritus of Political Science at the University of Massachusetts/Amherst. His most recent books are *Parties and Politics in Modern Germany* (Boulder, Colo.: Westview Press, 1996) and *The German Social Democrats Since 1969: A Party in Power and Opposition* (2nd rev. ed. Boulder, Colo.: Westview Press, 1994). He is also the author of numerous studies on German domestic politics. His current research focuses on right-wing extremism in Germany.

Clay Clemens teaches Government at the College of William and Mary. His most recent publications include *The Kohl Chancellorship* (London: Frank Cass, 1998), co-edited with William Paterson, and *NATO and the Quest for Post-Cold War Security* (New York: St. Martin's, 1997). His articles have appeared in *West European Politics, German Politics, International Affairs,* and *Armed Forces and Society.*

David P. Conradt is Professor of Political Science at East Carolina University. He is the author and editor of numerous books on German and European politics, including *The German Polity* (New York: Longman, 7th edition, 2000); *Germany's New Politics* (Providence and London: Berghahn, 1995); and *Politics in Western Europe* (New York: Chatham House, 2nd Edition, 1998). He has also contributed frequently to professional journals. He has been a guest professor at universities in Cologne, Konstanz, and Dresden.

E. Gene Frankland is Professor of Political Science at Ball State University. His primary research and teaching interests are comparative politics and environmental policy. He has written scholarly articles on parliamentary recruitment, political socialization, and the green parties of Germany, Britain, and Austria. He co-authored with Don Schoonmaker *Between Protest and Power: The Green Party in Germany* (Boulder Co: Westview, 1992). He is currently co-editing with John Barry *The International Encyclopedia of Environmental Politics* (forthcoming 2001).

Wolfgang-Uwe Friedrich is Professor of Political Science at the University of Hildesheim and Director of the Deutsch-Amerikanischer Arbeitskreis

(German-American Research Group). He is the author of numerous publications on German foreign policy and German-American relations.

Wolfgang G. Gibowski has long been identified with polling and election research in Germany. One of the founders of the Forschungsgruppe Wahlen, he became Deputy Director of the Press and Information Office of the Federal Government in 1990. Since 1999 he is the spokesperson for the consortium of German corporations negotiating a settlement of the claims of World War II foreign laborers. He is the author of numerous studies of German electoral and voting behavior and has also conducted extensive surveys of American attitudes toward Germany.

Mary N. Hampton is Associate Professor of Political Science at the University of Utah. Her research interests are in international relations, international security, American foreign policy, German politics, and German security and foreign policy. Her book, *The Wilsonian Impulse*, was published in 1996. She has written many articles on German foreign policy. The most recent, "The U.S., Germany, and NATO: Creating Positive Identity in Trans-Atlantia," appeared in the journal, *Security Studies*. She also co-edited with Christian Søe the 1999 book *Between Bonn and Berlin: German Politics Adrift?* (New York: Rowman and Littlefield, 1999).

Herbert Kitschelt is Professor of Political Science at Duke University. From 1993 to 1996 he held a joint appointment with Humboldt University, Berlin. Among his recent publications are *The Transformation of European Social Democracy* (New York and Cambridge: Cambridge University Press, 1994), *The Radical Right in Western Europe* (Ann Arbor, MI: University of Michigan Press) 1995, and, co-authored with Zdenka Mansfeldova, Radoslaw Markowski, and Gabor Toka, *Post-Communist Party Systems* (New York and Cambridge: Cambridge University Press, 1999). He is also co-editor and contributor to *Continuity and Change in Contemporary Capitalism* (New York and Cambridge: University Press, 1999). He has recently participated in several projects on welfare state retrenchment in advanced postindustrial democracies, resulting in volumes edited by Paul Pierson and by Kozo Yamamura and Wolfgang Streeck, both now in preparation for publication.

Gerald R. Kleinfeld is Professor of History at Arizona State University and Executive Director of the German Studies Association. He is co-editor of *Germany's New Politics*, and the author of numerous book chapters on the PDS, German-American relations, and Germany in Europe.

David F. Patton is Associate Professor of Government at Connecticut College. He is currently a Visiting Scholar at the Center for European

Studies at Harvard University. He is the author of *Cold War Politics in Germany* (New York: St. Martin's Press, 1999). His articles have appeared in journals such as *East European Politics, German Politics and Society*, and *West European Politics*.

Klaus Schoenbach is Professor of General Communication Science at the University of Amsterdam, where he also teaches in the international Ph.D. program in the Amsterdam School of Communications Research. Schoenbach's research interests include political communication and media audience research, and he has published dozens of articles and book chapters on these topics. His English books include *Germany's Unity Election: Voters and the Media* (Cresskill, NJ: Hampton, 1994) with Holli A Semetko, and *Audience Responses to Media Diversification: Coping with Plenty* (New York: Lawrence Erlbaum, 1989) with Lee B. Becker, as well as books in German on radio news, success factors of newspapers, and political communication in local elections.

Holli A. Semetko is Professor of Audience and Public Opinion Research and also the Chair of the Department of Communication Science at the University of Amsterdam, where she also teaches in the international Ph.D. program of the Amsterdam School of Communications Research. Semetko's research interests include cross-national comparative research on media content and effects and political communication. Her recent books are *On Message: Communicating the Campaign* (Beverly Hills and London: Sage, 1999) with Pippa Norris, John Curtice, David Sanders, and Margaret Scammell, and *Germany's Unity Election: Voters and the Media* (Cresskill, NJ: Hampton, 1994) with Klaus Schoenbach.

Christian Søe is professor of political science at California State University at Long Beach. He is editor of the annually revised anthology, *Comparative Politics* (seventeen editions) and writes on German party politics, with special attention to the FDP. He is one of the editors and authors of *The Germans and Their Neighbors* (1993), *Germany's New Politics* (1995), and *Between Bonn and Berlin: German Politics Adrift?* (1999).

Helga A. Welsh is Associate Professor in the Department of Politics at Wake Forest University. Her publications have focused on East German history and politics, the unification of Germany, and democratization processes in Central and Eastern Europe. Several of her most recent publications have addressed the role of communist elites in system maintenance and system collapse. Her current research deals with issues of regime change in twentieth-century Europe.

INDEX